Former deputy editor of the *I[...]*
Hanning is co-biographer of D[...]
exclusive collaboration of *News [...]*
Mulcaire for an exposé of the ph[...]
new evidence from key figures, *Love & Deception: Philby in Beirut* is the result of twenty years of research into one of the Cold War's most mysterious episodes.

'In a masterly narrative, James Hanning has plotted through the intrigue to explain the murky and controversial climax of Britain's biggest spy scandal'

Tom Bower, author of *The Perfect English Spy*

'James Hanning has identified a real gap in our understanding of Philby, giving life to figures such as Eleanor, the woman he fell for in Beirut, who have hitherto been ignored. His fresh and illuminating book fills in the often missed human dimension, and is full of new information and insights, bringing home the human cost of treachery'

Andrew Lownie, author of *Stalin's Englishman*

'James Hanning's deeply researched and fluently written book brings into focus for the first time the story of an intelligent and talented woman who tried and failed to lead a private life with the man she loved in the wilderness of mirrors that was Beirut at the height of the Cold War'

Michael Holzman, author of *Kim and Jim*

'I am always gripped by the Philby story, and James Hanning succeeds in putting new flesh on this fascinating period in his double life. Maximum betrayal, maximum stress, maximum misbehaviour, maximum booze – I thoroughly recommend losing yourself in lives which I trust are far more terrifying than your own'

Marina Hyde

'James Hanning's *Love & Deception: Philby in Beirut* is the first book in many years to disclose new information on the traitor-spy Kim Philby. Hanning has dug deeper than anyone since Phillip Knightley and E. H. Cookridge to expose the cover-ups, lies and propaganda surrounding Philby's final days in Beirut. A gripping tale of romance, intrigue and disloyalty'

Charles Glass, author of *They Fought Alone*

'Meticulously researched and elegantly written, James Hanning's study of Philby in Beirut interweaves the personal and public life of the spy to create a fascinating read. It reveals a complex man who beneath a charming, vulnerable veneer was ultimately as duplicitous in his relationships with the women who loved him as he was to his country. Hanning evokes the cosmopolitan atmosphere of post-war Beirut with verve. His exploration of the Cambridge spy ring draws on extensive research including many interviews with people close to the characters involved'

Rachel Trethewey

'You may think the Philby saga has been mined to exhaustion but that is clearly not true. One of the most intriguing aspects is the final period in Beirut where he was still working as an MI6 "stringer". Displaying his formidable skills as an assiduous researcher, James Hanning has continued digging and has discovered new gems that illuminate the tortured but living relationship between Kim and his wife, Eleanor, and the mystifying intrigues that surround Philby's last days in Beirut. Definitely a recommended read'

Stephen Dorril, historian of MI6

'A fascinating and brilliant story of the complex relationship between the master spy Kim Philby and his third wife, the American Eleanor Brewer. The author weaves a compelling narrative from their first meeting to the final denouement some years later. James Hanning has unearthed much new information and has written a book of real power'

Richard Frost, editor of
Tim Milne, Philby's oldest friend

LOVE & DECEPTION

PHILBY IN BEIRUT

JAMES HANNING

corsair

CORSAIR

First published in Great Britain in 2021 by Corsair
This paperback edition published in 2022

1 3 5 7 9 10 8 6 4 2

Map by Barking Dog Art

A CIP catalogue record for this book
is available from the British Library.

ISBN: 978-1-4721-5594-8

Typeset in Garamond by M Rules
Printed and bound in Great Britain by Clays Ltd, Elcograf S.p.A.

Papers used by Corsair are from well-managed forests
and other responsible sources.

MIX
Paper from
responsible sources
FSC® C104740
FSC
www.fsc.org

Corsair
An imprint of
Little, Brown Book Group
Carmelite House
50 Victoria Embankment
London EC4Y 0DZ

An Hachette UK Company
www.hachette.co.uk

www.littlebrown.co.uk

To the people who live in Lebanon, and to my parents

Contents

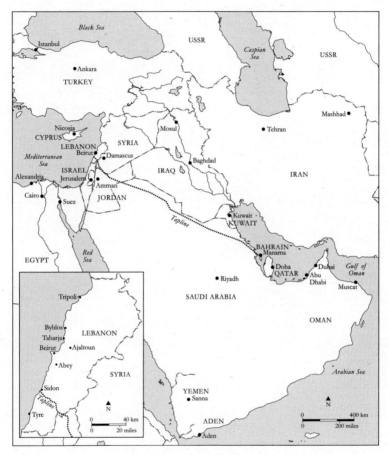

The Middle East in the late 1950s

The scale of Philby's betrayal is barely calculable to anyone who has not been in the business. In Eastern Europe alone, dozens and perhaps hundreds of British agents were imprisoned, tortured and shot.

David Cornwell,
aka John le Carré, *The Pigeon Tunnel*

Kim Philby is perhaps the most famous name in twentieth-century espionage. Accounts of his life have concentrated, with good reason, on upbringing, his formative student experiences in the 1930s, his exploits during the war and the culmination of his career.

But his years in Beirut in the 1950s and 1960s call for a telling of their own. Following accusations of treachery against him in Britain, that period encompasses his curious return to his original career as a journalist, in the Middle East. Those years take in his mysterious contribution to the geopolitics of one of the world's most unstable regions. But they also include elements in his personal life remarkably at odds with the man many think they know.

Hearing from those with whom he mixed socially in Beirut, another side of the hardened spy emerges – sentimental, kind and emotionally vulnerable. What follows is based on existing histories and many new interviews, with and by those who knew him and his associates in Beirut and London. The intention is not to join in his denigration, though there is plenty to deplore, nor is it an attempt to excuse him, though his good points are not hidden. It is an attempt to offer a picture of the whole man.

This account is not designed exclusively for spy buffs, though they will find some fresh material, nor is it intended for those interested solely in the human and emotional aspects of the story, intriguing though those are. Philby, after all, was not just a spy. He wasn't just anything. But he was one person, not two or more, and he remains an enigma to most and is certainly far more easily condemned than understood. But surely there can be no beginning of understanding without reference to his whole personality, and what happened in Beirut sheds as much light as any other period.

Timeline

August 1962	Flora Solomon complains to Victor Rothschild about Philby's journalism
October 1962	Cuban missile crisis
December 1962	Anthony Blunt arrives in Beirut
December 1962/ January 1963	Nicholas Elliott arrives in Beirut
January 1963	Philby disappears
May 1963	Eleanor goes to London
July 1963	Philby is confirmed by Edward Heath as the 'Third Man'
September 1963	Eleanor flies to Moscow
November 1963	John F. Kennedy assassinated
23 April 1964	Anthony Blunt signs secret immunity deal with British government
June 1964	Eleanor flies to US
November 1964	Eleanor, with new passport, returns from US to Moscow
May 1965	Eleanor leaves Moscow
14 November 1968	Eleanor dies in the USA
1971	Philby marries Rufina Ivanovna Pukhova
8 November 1979	*Private Eye* names 'Maurice' as Blunt
15 November 1979	Thatcher confirms Blunt was working for the USSR
26 March 1983	Anthony Blunt dies
11 May 1988	Philby dies
9 November 1989	Berlin Wall comes down

'You do realise your husband was not an ordinary man?'
Nicholas Elliott of MI6, early 1963

Beirut beckons

On the morning of 30 May 1963, a secret meeting of Britain's top public servants was called at Admiralty House, central London. It was attended by the Prime Minister Harold Macmillan, his Foreign Secretary the Earl of Home (later Sir Alec Douglas-Home), Sir Dick White, head of the Secret Intelligence Service, SIS, more commonly known as MI6, Sir Bernard Burrows, chairman of the Joint Intelligence Committee, the cabinet secretary Sir Burke Trend and one other official. The purpose of the meeting was to inform the Prime Minister of the arrival from Lebanon the following day not of a head of state or other dignitary or even of a wanted criminal, but a forty-eight-year-old housewife, born Eleanor Kerns, from Spokane in Washington State, USA. She would be bringing two children with her, and the media would be doing all they could to make public as much as possible about her. The interests of the British state were precisely the reverse. The purpose of the meeting was to discuss how the government would handle her potentially embarrassing arrival and how little the government could get away with saying. The mood of the meeting was that as long as the new arrival, Eleanor Philby, was not indiscreet, the government should continue to give little away. Any slips might be enormously damaging to Britain and the West's interests.

At the same time in Lebanon, where she had been living, the final touches were being put to a major logistical operation to get Eleanor and the children out of the country in secrecy. Glen Balfour-Paul, Dick Parker of the US embassy, former CIA operative Miles Copeland and Mr Ingham, the local BOAC manager, contrived to keep their names off the passenger list. On 31 May, three cars took Eleanor and two excited children to Beirut airport. After four months of anguish and uncertainty, here at last was some security and a chance to catch her breath. The glass of champagne she was offered as she collapsed into her first-class seat can rarely have been more welcome.

The party arrived in London, on the hottest day of the year, to an airport full of expectant journalists. But a long wait on a sweltering plane until long after the other passengers had disembarked helped persuade the journalists that their tip about her arrival must have been wrong. The threesome made their furtive way to waiting cars and away to obscurity.

Eleanor was to describe her arrival in the remarkable book she wrote four years later. It tells an extraordinary human story of passion, secrecy and deception, seen through the eyes of a thoughtful, capable, artistic woman who happened to fall in love with a man who became one of twentieth-century espionage's most notorious figures. What follows draws unashamedly from Eleanor's own testimony, a book which in recent years has justly received more attention among students of post-war history than the cursory and partisan treatment it received when it was published in 1968. At that time, Eleanor was treated merely as collateral damage in a bigger story about the Cold War, and although she was certainly that, there was not a lot of human concern in evidence. There was an ideological war to be fought, and the book was denounced as 'sad' and 'pathetic', with little empathy or attempt to understand the notably unpolitical Eleanor or appreciate the revealing detail about her husband that the book provided. She was not a saint, and in some respects was little more than ordinary, but someone who in modern terms might be called 'relatable' whose extraordinary story merits retelling, using both her own memory and building on it, remarking on some of its omissions and complementing it with evidence from others who were close to her and her friends at the time.

The extraordinary drama that characterised the later life of Eleanor Kerns was in no way anticipated by her upbringing. She was born in Washington State, only child of Blaine and Caroline Kerns (née Callard), a blameless middle-class Irish-American couple whose forebears had helped open up the American west. Blaine, a keen fisherman and American football player, had been brought up in Lewiston in neighbouring Idaho and studied electrical engineering in Pittsburgh before joining the Westinghouse Electric company as a salesman. On 31 August 1910, at the age of twenty-nine, he married Caroline Grace Callard, of Spokane, 300 miles east of Seattle, Washington State, at her parents' home. They set up house in Howard Street, Spokane.

In September 1913 Eleanor Caroline was born. As a child, she attended the local school. Theirs was a Republican-voting household of middle-class respectability, occasionally the subject of polite interest from the local newspaper, which was inclined to report deferentially on the unexceptional activities of the well-to-do. One summer, for example, it reported simply that 'Mrs Blaine L. Kerns will be spending a month with her mother, Mrs T. H. Callard, in Seattle'. It was also remarked that she had arranged a 'pretty little dinner' at her home for a visiting notable from Seattle. This was a time of women as homemakers above all, and the base from which her daughter launched herself was firm enough to see her travel first across the United States and then across to Europe.

For all the attractions of domestic life, there was an acknowledgement that the world could be improved, that social progress could be made. One of the causes for which Mrs Kerns organised a fundraising 'smart bridge tea' at the house of a friend was the women's building at the University of Oregon campus at Eugene. In fact, the hall, now known as the Gerlinger Hall after the woman who helped raise the bulk of the funds, was something of a trailblazing enterprise, celebrating the sufficient increase in the number of women undergraduates for them to have their own quad.

At eighteen, Eleanor enrolled at the University of Washington in Seattle, and majored in liberal arts, English, history, economics, Romantic languages and fine arts, graduating with a BA four years later. But she had also shown a capacity for arts administration, handling the Spring Art Shows for two years, and one year her parents paid for her to attend a summer school studying fresco techniques with the celebrated exponent of Mexican muralism, the politically provocative Diego Rivera, then just coming to prominence in the USA. She showed further precocity chipping in to help the university staff with assessing and grading the younger students' work for three years. On completion of her degree she enrolled for further study during the summer, specialising at the California School of Fine Arts in philology, architecture and Asian art and history.

This was not a promising pursuit for someone who needed to earn a living, though, so she enrolled in a nine-month series of courses in business management at Seattle's celebrated Metropolitan Business College, working part-time as assistant to the college's head of personnel to help pay the fees.

Her first full-time job was hardly in keeping with her artistic leanings either. Far from it. At the age of twenty-three she was taken on as the secretary to the manager of the well-established American Brake Shoe & Foundry Company, where she became an expert in the brake shoe business, acting as receptionist, a touch typist, a switchboard operator, the compiler of weekly reports and the minutes of board meetings, the keeper of payroll and billing records and of the company's scrap inventories. While not what she wanted to do for ever, it was emphatically a position of responsibility, and doubtless an impressive addition to her curriculum vitae at a young age.

Little more than a year later she struck out, fearlessly, on her own. Her first job away from home was in San Francisco, in the office of a buyer for Woolworths, at the time one of the largest and most flourishing chain stores in the US, which had complete responsibility for relations with all the company's stores in the western part of the country. But within a year she had the opportunity to move on once more, again with a further increase in salary to a job of yet more responsibility. It demanded great attention to detail but it also offered more scope for her creative leanings. She joined J. Walter Thompson, one of the world's largest and most creative advertising agencies, initially as a secretary, and she was to show her abilities quickly. After a few months she was promoted to take administrative charge of the work of the company's five chief copywriters. This was a real 'the buck stops here' job, requiring her to see advertising copy through from an initial idea to its final form, taking on board trade and legal niceties. As she said later, 'carelessness could cause the loss of a million-dollar-a-year client'. In her two years at JWT, she worked dovetailing words with artwork, and later moving into research and media work, which included writing radio commercials.

Each time she switched jobs, she received a pay rise of around 15 per cent. By the age of twenty-nine, she was earning a very healthy $1800 a year. Had she been a man, she would doubtless have been earning more, and with yet more responsibility. By any standards she was doing well.

Following the Japanese attack on Pearl Harbor in December 1941, the United States needed its ablest for the war effort. Eleanor joined the Office of Civilian Defense as a Junior Information Specialist on $2000 a year, working directly with Ralph Block, a former journalist who had just been appointed Assistant Regional Director and who was to become a major player in US wartime public information policy. There she was responsible for producing reports, posters and broadcasts for public consumption, occasionally standing in for her boss in representing the local division. One task was producing a weekly fifteen-minute broadcast explaining the fine detail of Civil Defense policy, seeking to comply with rigid government guidelines while not sending the listener to sleep. Eleanor excelled at this. The Office of War Information (OWI), which oversaw her department's work, considered her reports the best any government agency had produced.

Public service suited her. She was conscientious, had a good eye for detail, was a team player and had sufficient imagination to lift humdrum public information alerts from the important but dull into something that rewarded attention. Still, though, she was not catering for her creative side. She was also pining to see Europe, even with the Second World War at its height. In 1943 she made a formal application for an enhanced role with OWI, explaining that she was interested in the artistic 'promotion of ideas', suggesting that her 'instruction and actual experience in lithography, lettering, poster design, industrial design and oil and watercolour techniques' might be usefully deployed for propaganda purposes. Whatever she may have expected this to lead to, it brought a huge change to her life. While still not thirty, she was accepted for employment in the Office of War Information as a Junior Regional Supervisor.

The OWI had been set up because US policymakers needed to explain why defeating fascism was so important. 'The principal battleground of this war,' said Archibald MacLeish, a poet, administrator and noted anti-fascist who was a moving spirit behind OWI, 'is not the South Pacific, it is not the Middle East. It is not England, or Norway, or the Russian Steppes. It is American opinion.' Not long before the Pearl Harbor attack, 80 per cent of the American public opposed the US going to war. Isolationism remained the conventional wisdom. The OWI's job was made harder still by the public's scepticism towards highly targeted and professional advertising techniques, seen by many as spivvy. As Allan M. Winkler notes, the hard sell wasn't popular. 'The truth sometimes seemed lost ... audiences were being encouraged, even pressured, to buy products they neither wanted nor needed as advertisers sold their own conception of the Good Life in an effort to make consumer demand match America's ever-increasing production.'

But the threat of fascism – or merely US self-interest and domestic politics, if you prefer – meant this message had to be conveyed, and those behind the new-fangled messaging were driven largely by idealistic aims of promoting President Roosevelt's 'four essential human freedoms' and his Atlantic Charter's assertion of self-determination of nations, equal trading rights and security for all. 'Most were passionate interventionists who had sought American entrance into the war long before the attack at Pearl Harbor,' wrote Allan Winkler. 'For them it was a battle between the forces of fascism and the forces of democracy ... Through propaganda, they wanted to communicate what they considered the basic American values of freedom and democracy to friends and foe alike in all corners of the earth.'

It was an engaging message, and though Eleanor was not political by disposition, her previous work in advertising made her the right person in the right place at the right time. And people liked her. A colleague from the time called her 'A lovely girl, really, and very capable.'

She took up lodgings at New York's Hotel Wellington in the summer of 1942, and, with the title of Regional Supervisor, began her preparation for setting foot in wartime Europe. She was to be based in New York, at 224 West 57th Street, and, having been selected for the Overseas Operations, she could expect to go abroad fairly promptly. In the months following March 1943 she held a variety of positions, initially as an assistant to the supervisor of Swedish, Swiss, Icelandic, Trinidadian and Russian outposts, before herself being assigned as regional supervisor for Turkey and the Balkans.

Within three months she was told she would be off to Istanbul, where she would undergo yet further training, and it took some months before her move took effect. Turkey had worked hard to maintain its neutrality during the war. Nonetheless, Germany and the Allies worked equally hard to persuade the country to take sides, making it the target of an extensive propaganda onslaught from both.

Egemen Bezci, an academic who has specialised in the battle to win Turkey's wartime support, has written extensively on OWI's work sabotaging news outlets and applying psychological pressure in the newspapers.

'They wrote material and submitted it to the newspapers, which would simply publish it, unchallenged,' he says. US archives confirm that officials would talk about how this month, say, 'with the money you sent us, they bought this journalist who wrote this piece of pro-American news'. In her book, published in 1968, Eleanor scarcely elaborates on her work in Turkey, tantalisingly saying only that she had been taught how to get rid of someone who was following her and how to kill a man in thirty seconds. Bezci says: 'It is very unlikely that someone working for the OWI in her role would not be doing some sort of espionage. Psychological warfare, propaganda, something.'

She was, though, working in the library and information services, for nearly two years. How much undercover work she did is unknown. It may have been very little, and that her training was a mere precaution. Certainly her later life suggests little aptitude for guileful skulduggery. She was far better suited to her ostensible work, which included organising the first American exhibition in Ankara. She also worked in Istanbul and Izmir.

In truth the propaganda war had been all but won by the time Eleanor arrived. Sensing which way the wind was blowing, Turkey had broken off its contentious sales of chromite to Germany in February 1944, and severed relations entirely in August. By February 1945, Turkey had sided formally with the Allies, having been told that was a condition of it attending the inaugural meeting of the United Nations.

A month before the end of the war, a senior colleague praised the presentability of Eleanor's work, the accuracy of her judgements and decisions, her effectiveness in presenting ideas, in planning, laying out work, instructing and training, maintaining team morale and making and sticking to deadlines. Overall her work was judged to be good, and four months after the war finished she won a further promotion and salary increase, putting her up to $3400 a year. Given how strategically important Turkey was and how conventional rules of contact with journalists were flouted in the cause of winning the war, it is tantalising how vague Eleanor's State Department file is in alluding to her propaganda work.

It was to prove a short stay. The war won, the Office of War Information's work was done. The OWI and its functions were terminated and Eleanor was told to return to the United States. But she wanted more, and had not completed her particular brand of danger tourism. She took a boat to Greece and then flew to Rome and on to Paris. There she presented herself at the

American Information Offices for consultation and reassign-
ment. From France, with much of Central Europe in ruins,
she moved on to Czechoslovakia, where she spent a year as
an Information Specialist, and was largely responsible for the
setting up of the American Library in Prague, working for the
OIC (part of the State Department). She worked extremely
hard, six days a week, and met Czechoslovakia's leading politicians Edvard Beneš and Jan Masaryk in the process, but she left
Prague, unable to find affordable accommodation other than in
expensive hotels. She returned to Washington.

Scott Anderson, whose book *The Quiet Americans* examines
the CIA's disastrous ill-preparedness for the Cold War in the
early post-war years, cites the setting up of such institutions – a
CIA programme run through the State Department – as one of
the very few successes. 'People coming in off the street to check
out books – those libraries were more effective than bombs in
spreading American cultural, going into political, influence.'

Notwithstanding the continent-wide trauma of a world war,
Eleanor had enjoyed Europe and wanted more. She did return
briefly to San Francisco, working in an architect's office, but
hankered for a return to the fray. In February 1947, she was
posted to Germany and Austria, as a consultant in Arts and
Crafts for the American Red Cross, which was running a network of clubs aimed at helping German civil society back on
its feet. The work, initially for the Red Cross and later for the
US army at its Bad Nauheim base, was seemingly ideal, involving working in training schools, setting up craft shops, photo
labs, decorating, designing and building stage sets for a revue
in Berlin. She stayed for ten months, overcoming a disdain
for widespread black marketeering. She told her prospective
employer that she would be happy to be posted abroad for the
next year, and was willing to travel frequently. Being a home
bird could wait.

But her mind was not entirely on her work. Despite her peripatetic life in tumultuous post-war Europe, as a new, East–West conflict brewed, she had become friendly with a similarly suitcase-happy figure, a journalist she had met in Istanbul. Sam Pope Brewer was a six-foot-three, good-looking graduate of Phillips Exeter Academy and Yale (1931). He dressed in a three-piece grey suit, and his sartorial tastes did not mislead. He was serious, courtly, correct and sober and was destined for an impressive career.

His mother, Bessie Marsh Brewer, was a celebrated etcher, lithographer, painter and holder of left-wing views who moved in the circles of New York 'Ashcan' artists who sought to depict life as it was lived by the majority, sometimes on the street, rather than that seen in the more genteel depictions of the early twentieth century. She studied at the New York School of Allied Design for Women and at the Art Students League with Robert Henri and John Sloan, and often brought a caustic, satirical and political eye to images of womanhood. Sam's father sold insurance.

Sam Brewer was a man of the world. He had crossed the Atlantic a couple of times before graduating, and was earning acceptable money as a journalist in Europe. He was bright, very ambitious and an assiduous developer of useful contacts, inside and outside government.

While covering the Spanish Civil War for the *Chicago Tribune*, he had met an English journalist, Hilde Marchant, four years younger than him, described at the time as 'tiny, pert, pretty', who was also covering events in Spain. They had married in London in 1937, and she became a star feature writer for the *Daily Express*, writing extensively on the effects of wartime evacuation in Britain, and established an impressive reputation as a war reporter. She stood on the cliffs of Dover to report on the Battle of Britain, and wrote a book called *Women and Children Last: A Woman Reporter's Account of the Battle of Britain.* She had an element of self-destructiveness, or so it seemed at the time. A colleague described her as being 'not unlike an earthbound Spitfire'. Sam, meanwhile, had thrived, often being a useful conduit for stories from intelligence sources that helped the Allied cause, yet retaining an enviable reputation for independence. He narrowly escaped execution in the Balkans during the war, having been arrested on suspicion of being a German spy, possibly because of his wife having been born there.

Notwithstanding the constraints of wartime reporting and the reliance on official sources, Sam's wartime exploits with the *Chicago Tribune* in the Middle East caught the eye of Cy Sulzberger, then covering the same beat and a foreign affairs columnist of the *New York Times*. Happily, Sulzberger's family owned the paper and Cy saw in Sam the sort of drive he wanted to develop as he rebuilt the *Times*'s foreign reporting after the years of the war. But for the high-minded Sulzberger there was a problem. During the war a number of journalists had 'double-hatted', also picking up information for their intelligence services. In a time of war against anti-democratic forces, this was understandable, even admirable. In peacetime, journalists were meant to be more detached, and Sulzberger insisted on Brewer severing his intelligence connections. 'I made him swear he had broken all his ties . . . That was a must,' Sulzberger recalled.

In early 1945 Sam had signed up to a full-time job, which meant a whole new round of travel. Nevada was woven into the schedule. The war had not been kind to Hilde and Sam's relationship. Both were dedicated to journalism, at the expense of one another. They spent the latter stages of the war apart, and in late October 1946 he travelled to take advantage of Reno's quickie divorce laws, on the grounds of Hilde's desertion, said on the official papers to have been for 'upwards of three years'.

Sam reported from Germany, Turkey, Yugoslavia and Palestine in the two years after the war ended, but he and Eleanor kept in touch enough for their friendship to grow and, indeed, for romance to bloom. They travelled to Italy together and got engaged. Remarkably for one so devoted to his trade, when in Rome Sam wrote not a word of journalism. If separating a journalist from his typewriter is a sign of something, this was love. The wedding took place in Paris, where Sam was based covering the UN General Assembly, on 8 October 1948.

In the unlikely event that Eleanor thought married life would mean, in the strictest sense, settling down, she was in for a shock. With the contentious partition of Palestine and the establishing of the State of Israel, Sam continued to be in demand, and they spent several months living in the St Georges Hotel in Beirut, including a month at the Arab–Israeli peace talks on Rhodes. But a small degree of domesticity, at least, was beckoning, when Sam was posted briefly to New York. A year or so after their wedding, on 16 September 1949, the *New York Times* carried a happy announcement: 'A daughter was born to Mr and Mrs Sam Pope Brewer of 61 West Ninth Street on Sept 3 at the Woman's Hospital. Mrs Brewer is the former Miss Eleanor Kerns, daughter of Mr and Mrs Blaine L. Kerns of Seattle ...'

There was to be plenty of transatlantic travel for the happy trio. They sailed on the *Île de France* on 1 November 1949, from New York to Le Havre, when little Annie was barely two. They were heading for Madrid for two years, seemingly a happy chance. Eleanor had acquired the rudiments of Spanish at college. But Sam, living up to his vigorous youthful promise, or at least causing a good deal of trouble, created waves in Franco's regime by writing articles exposing its corruption. At one point he had his journalist's credentials withdrawn, and was afraid that Franco's thugs might do him or his family real harm by arresting or even kidnapping him. For safety's sake Eleanor and Annie moved across the French border to Saint-Jean-de-Luz while Sam went to stay with a US embassy friend. The *New York Times* stood by its reporter and the regime backed down, or so it seemed. Six months later, as part of a face-saving deal, yet another spell of extensive travelling began. The Brewers returned to New York in November 1951 and in early January boarded the SS *Uruguay* in New York, bound for Rio de Janeiro, Sam having been made bureau chief for the whole of South America.

The stint there started badly with bad news from home: Sam's much-loved and entertaining mother died soon after they arrived. Thereafter, things stabilised somewhat and the couple were promised a more enduring base than either had had for years. They enjoyed occasional visits from relations, including Sam's adoring sister Ann. But after a few months, Rio was struck by an outbreak of cholera, and for Annie's safety the family moved to Peru. The South America job required an enormous amount of travel for Sam, which Eleanor felt was no bad thing. They were not getting on well – he was unable to switch off from work, and she found him frustratingly inert when housework needed doing.

After nearly four years in Brazil and Peru, Sam was bored, and in November 1955 they took the steamer out of Rio de Janeiro for the last time, returning once more to New York. There they were able to enjoy to the full the city they both knew well, staying (with the family dachshund) at a small hotel near Washington Square. It was a brief pause. Sam had managed to secure what he wanted, a return to Beirut, but things were not good between them. Eleanor told a friend she had the impression Sam would not have minded if she and Annie had not followed. In the end, Eleanor and Annie did follow Sam to Beirut, where he would find fulfilment in work, at least.

The arrival of the Brewers in Beirut might have been designed as a compromise between Sam's professional career, the demands of home building and his wife's interest in the arts. Certainly, on Sam's side, there would be no shortage of stories to keep the New York desk happy.

Lebanon was a melting pot of religious and ethnic groups where democracy was always going to be a work in progress. France had an interest in the region going back centuries, including as protector of the Maronite Christians in the 1860s, and had ruled the country directly following the First World War. Independence from France was established over a few years during the Second World War, and in its aftermath a parliamentary system of government was established.

A 'confessional' regime came into being, to reflect the hetero-geneity of the country and keep all factions happy. Compromise was written into a 'National Covenant'. The president would be a Maronite Christian, the Speaker of the parliament would be a Shiite Muslim, the prime minister a Sunni Muslim and the deputy Speaker and deputy PM should be Greek Orthodox.

Lebanon opposed the establishing of the Israeli state on its borders, and offered a mildly supportive role to the Arab countries which went to war against Israel in 1948. In the years shortly after Israel came into being, around 120,000 refugees made their home in Lebanon, many of them in temporary camps around Beirut. Many more were to follow.

The growing influence of nationalism in the region, inspired in part by Egypt's Gamal Abdel Nasser, installed as president in 1954, suggested the old colonial powers would face con-tinuing challenges to their dominance, with the country's long-established factions anxious to ensure at very least a defence of their influence. But the country was changing. A higher population growth rate among Muslims, the emigration of many Christians and the influx of refugees was tilting the country towards Islam. Such stability as there had been was under further threat.

Westerners often found Lebanon not just charmingly mysterious but downright confusing. According to the British writer Sacheverell Sitwell, 'The individual you feel certain is a Moslem turns out to be a Christian; but is he, then, Greek Orthodox or Maronite? Or Armenian? What language does one expect them to speak? One does not know.'

To add to the occasional sense of menace, as Philip Mansel, a historian of the region, notes, Beirut had long been a city of guns. 'Many Lebanese kept a gun in the house; taxi drivers kept a gun under the driving seat, although it was rarely fired. Fathers had sons photographed holding a gun, even when they were babies.'

Looking outwards, for Sam, Lebanon was a gateway to a part of the globe becoming more interesting and influential by the week. The closure of the Palestinian ports after the creation of Israel in 1948 meant Beirut became the main West-facing port of entry to the Arab world, and increasingly the city was favoured over Cairo as a base for journalists and intelligence services. The West's financial big hitters saw Beirut as the safe place to tap into the new Arab oil wealth, and the wealthy themselves used it as a place of fun in which to fritter their small change, away from the disapproving eyes of their compatriots. The prostitution business did a roaring trade (as did most other businesses), policed, or at least overseen, by the elite which ran the country.

That elite, the Maronite Christians, were sufficiently numerous and wealthy to sit on top of the pile – to the frustration of several voluble Muslim groups – resulting in a highly diverse country with enough stability for its visitors to indulge themselves in some style.

But the politics of the region were very different from what we see today. The old colonial powers, Britain and France, were still in evidence, but their influence was dwindling. Heading the queue to replace the waning bosses was the United States, sensing after 1945 that turning its back on the wider world often meant small fires developing into big ones. Vast new discoveries of oil in the Middle East and a perception that communism was on the march meshed with an American optimism about improving the world's lot. If to some that looked like colonialism in a new guise, the USA as a whole was confident it could do a better job of it than the French and the British had. American governments were now more inclined to protect US interests while making the world a better, freer place.

The devil, of course, was in the detail, and some US governments tried harder than others to reconcile these aims. But the cynic who looks at the late twentieth century and sees only US politicians manipulating power, chasing oil and bowing to the Israeli lobby regardless of Israel's behaviour should be conscious that for many in Washington, intentions were nobler than that. While the marketplace exercised its customary irresistible force in global affairs, a handful of American diplomats believed that a degree of man-made good could be done in the region. With a benign hand, the countries of the Middle East could thrive once freed from the French or British colonial yoke. That hand, not altogether surprisingly, was to be an American hand.

These well-meaning diplomats 'were convinced beyond all doubt that the United States could succeed in the Middle East where Europe had not, to the benefit of U.S. business, commercial, and political interests as well as the Middle Eastern peoples themselves, who would be uplifted through U.S.-style democratization and development'.

Those advocates helped set up an organisation called the American Friends of the Middle East, which was accused of being anti-Zionist and of having no Jews on its governing body. It was, we now know, part-funded by the CIA and Aramco, and in addition to serving their political goals, provided a useful vehicle for US intelligence gathering. Two of its moving spirits, cousins, showed a patrician concern redolent of their grandfather Theodore Roosevelt, believing that democracy and development could pave the way to competent and independent nationhood for many Arab states. Kermit ('Kim') and Archie Roosevelt saw no reason why the USA's endorsement of Israel's existence should jeopardise the autonomy of the newly independent Arab states. Both were admirers of the more defensible aspects of British imperialism, and, educated, like eleven other recent Roosevelts, at Groton, a religiously inclined school designed to produce boys who would promote the public good, understood something of the ethos that produced so many British diplomats. As historian Nigel Ashton puts it, they 'brought a dash of New World idealism to their version of the traditional British imperial "Great Game"'. Unfortunately for the British, though, they also saw themselves as defenders of indigenous nationalists, including Egypt's Gamal Abdel Nasser, a bête noire of the British.

This was the era when Britain's old-school practitioners of the arts of espionage were beginning to look anachronistic, even unworldly. The Yanks were coming, as Malcolm Muggeridge recalled: 'From those Elysian days I remember so well in London when the first arrivals came among us, straight from their innocent nests in Princeton or Yale or Harvard, in Wall Street or Madison Avenue or Washington, DC. How short a honeymoon period lasted! How soon our British setup was overtaken in personnel, zest and scale of operations, above all, expendable cash! . . . The OSS-CIA network, with ramifications all over the world, came to outclass our once legendary Secret Service as a sleek Cadillac does an ancient hansom cab.'

The US's confident aspiration to combine a can-do, idealistic promotion of local autonomy with a casual assertion of US interests had its adherents, but it did little to persuade British spooks that their time was up in the Middle East, so the politest of uneasy partnerships persisted. The paradox in the US position was made all the more obvious by the US- and UK-inspired coup against Mohammad Mossadegh's democratically elected government of Iran in 1953 and constant attempts to dictate terms to the Syrian government. Where some in the States saw a 'moral alliance' between Christianity and Islam against communism, many in the street saw a naked demand for oil.

Further US incursions in the region, often in support of Israel, over the coming decades were to add to the low regard in which the country was held in some Arab countries. And at the start of that period, mounting civilian unhappiness at British colonial complacency in Egypt was coming to the boil.

Wherever he looked, Sam Pope Brewer was not going to be short of things to write about, and cosmopolitan Beirut, with the US-backed President Camille Chamoun in power, was as good a place to watch from as any. This being the 1950s, it was assumed in middle-class circles that most women, particularly recently married ones, would be the homemakers, at home with the children and presiding over the cooking, or at least over those doing it. And, despite the political upheavals, it was a good place to bring up children. Domestic staff were cheap and plentiful, the schools (both for foreigners and Lebanese) were good and children were essentially safe to go where they pleased.

Eleanor had had a worthwhile, interesting and impressive career working for her private-sector employers and latterly serving her country. She was now at the stage of her life where convention expected her to subordinate her own career and the need to earn money to the demands of being a wife and mother. She was never going to compete with Doris Day as the cake-baking homemaker so emblematic of the 1950s, but she was by nature loyal, dutiful and a devoted mother. The affordability of home help was particularly welcome, because Lebanon offered a thousand opportunities for what used to be called 'hobbies', like painting and archaeology. For the latter, Beirut was an ideal base. There was evidence of human life from over seven thousand years ago. Here the Phoenicians – credited with being the first people to use an alphabet – lived profitably for nearly three thousand years. One of its main centres, Byblos, is believed to be one of the longest inhabited cities in the world. In 64 BC, the region was overcome by Rome and Christianity established itself there. Arab Muslims conquered the region in the early seventh century, though the Maronite (Christian) church managed to retain a degree of autonomy around its base at Mount Lebanon, north of Beirut. The Druze emerged around the eleventh century, an offshoot of Shia Islam, also basing themselves near Mount Lebanon. During the years of the Crusades, the Maronites allied themselves again with Rome, a connection which served them well during the years of the French mandate during the early twentieth century. The second half of the last millennium was dominated by Ottoman rule, which came to an end a hundred years ago.

Socially, there was plenty going on. The British and American embassies were well established, and the legacy of French rule ensured that French culture – from high fashion to upmarket restaurants and hotels to agreeable cafés on the city's palm-lined pavements – was well represented in the most accommodating of climates.

And the nightlife was a magnet for those with money to spend in the region. Venues like Les Caves du Roy, where the well-heeled could enjoy dinner and dancing, would attract the likes of Sidney Poitier and, later, Shirley Bassey. Other venues, like the Kit Kat Club, offered opportunities for those in search of even more time-honoured entertainment.

As a city that offered a sense both of discovery and of the exotic, while also providing stimulating company and the comfort and safety in which to bring up a family, Beirut could hardly have suited the Brewers better. They had a beautiful, spacious apartment in the Durafour building overlooking Beirut's spectacular seafront, where Sam's sleuthing instincts could be indulged to the full. 'He was a dedicated journalist,' remembers a colleague. 'He didn't care where the story was coming from. If a minister was in town he would call everybody who could possibly help in order to get the story. And he got a good few scoops as a result.'

Abu Said Aburish was a distinguished and well-connected Beirut-based Palestinian journalist for *Time* magazine. His son Afif, then in his teens, would do work experience for Sam at their apartment on the Corniche during his summer holidays, generally 'clippings', cutting out stories from the newspapers to be filed for reference. Eleanor was often there, too, he recalls: 'She was always helping with Sam's paperwork, doing whatever he needed for his work, playing the supportive wife, providing whatever the husband wanted.

'I always remember that in the summer, when it was really hot, I would go to the kitchen and help myself to water, and Eleanor was always kind and would say "Go on, have a Pepsi from the fridge", or "Can I get you anything to eat?", or "Take whatever you want." She was very kind like that.'

Often, though, Sam was away. Not for nothing was Beirut considered the best-placed city for access to the rest of the Middle East. Eleanor did not begrudge the fact that one week New York wanted an eyewitness piece from Egypt on Nasser's rabble-rousing nationalism, the next week something on the latest spasm among the Saudi princes, the next on the prospects of Syria merging with Egypt. These were all on Brewer's patch. He was safe, knew the right people, had a way with a pen and above all was trusted by the New York desk.

But the life Eleanor was ending up with – comfortable if slightly exotic domesticity and motherhood – was not the one she had sought. She had married at thirty-five, at the time comparatively late, as if marriage was double-edged – both an achievement and a surrender. Being attached to one of America's most trusted journalists was doubtless an enviable role, but the lustre of the serious-minded, conscientious, deep-voiced, good-looking Sam and his compulsive professionalism had worn thin. On bad days, he seemed to her work-obsessed, ponderous and unappreciative. Even so, an affair was the last thing on her mind.

2

When Kim – 'nothing like a former spy' – met Eleanor

If Beirut was the Middle Eastern crossroads through which every politician, diplomat and businessman in the region passed sooner or later, the St Georges Hotel was the top Beirutis' mini-Beirut. For the city's illustrious expats wanting to know what was going on, the St Georges was a reassuring earth mother. If you were part of its charmed circle, you only needed to enter its orbit every few days to be topped up with the latest high-grade gossip, only some of which reached the newspapers.

Today, once more, Sam was away, which would normally have allowed Eleanor time for herself. But she had a duty to perform for her husband. On this particular day, Wednesday 12 September 1956, Sam had arranged to welcome to Beirut someone he had known on and off for twenty years. Kim Philby and Sam had become friends as journalists covering the fascist side during Spain's civil war, and later, in the late 1940s, when they both happened to be posted to Istanbul. Sam had always enjoyed the droll Englishman's company and was delighted when, at the beginning of the 1950s, his gossipy and well-placed chum arrived in the States. The British still saw themselves as the senior partner where espionage was concerned, the US having only recently felt the need to establish a large and well-organised intelligence network overseas. The appointment to Washington of one of the rising stars of the British Foreign Office was an affirmation of solidarity. There they had enjoyed lunching when Sam's work in New York allowed. Kim was undoubtedly a top contact, and Sam's berth at the *New York Times* ensured that Britain, or Philby at least, had a hearing with one of the country's most powerful newspapers. There was a degree of trust between the pair, of a sort not uncommon at the time. 'This was an age before Vietnam, so American journalists and diplomats and intelligence officers treated each other with a great deal more personal friendship and candour than was the case later,' says Frank Wisner, son of the CIA's Frank G. Wisner, who played a central role in covert operations encouraging East European resistance to Stalin. Now, in Beirut, Philby reverted to being a correspondent, this time for the *Observer* and *The Economist*. Their news organisations not being competitors, he and Sam could help one another.

To Eleanor, it was clear that Kim was a useful acquaintance for Sam. Other friends couldn't help admiring the loyalty Kim had shown to an incurably drunken and difficult friend. Guy Burgess – his Foreign Office house guest in Washington DC five years earlier – had embarrassed the British government in a number of ways in Washington, and Kim had always been on hand to explain away his friend's usually drunken excesses. But then came more than a simple breach of diplomatic etiquette on Burgess's part, resulting – astonishingly – in Burgess ending up in Moscow, accused of being a Russian spy, and it had cost Kim his career. It was not the sort of story that particularly interested Eleanor, but she gathered that the more red-blooded elements in the US administration had become convinced Philby was also a communist sympathiser, if not a downright agent, and wanted him removed. The British had had to acquiesce and Kim resigned.

To the industrious Brewer, the clever, accomplished and urbane Philby – even though now no longer on the inside – was the sort of contact no decent hack would sneeze at. In the way of such friendships, before the misfortune over Burgess, in Washington Sam and Kim had drunk a great deal of bourbon together and traded top-grade diplomatic tittle tattle, the better for them both to keep one step ahead of their bosses. Philby had also had extensive contact with James Angleton, who soon afterwards became the CIA's head of counterintelligence, and the pair had talked shop over weekly boozy lunches, usually at Harvey's restaurant in Washington. (Angleton, like Philby, liked a drink, but was not at that stage drinking the 150–200 units a week that he reached later in life.) Another contact was Frank G. Wisner, later a Philby sceptic, but for the most part the appointment of a man of Philby's quality was seen as a plus, both for the Americans and the British. In any case, in Brewer's eyes, for professional and personal reasons this was a likeable guy with whom he was well advised to keep in. He knew Philby as a family man who had had to leave his wife and five school-age children behind in England and wanted him to feel welcome in Beirut. Philby had been down on his luck but had been rescued by a return to journalism covering much of the Middle East. There could be no better moment to resume the friendship.

It was Sam's custom to visit the St Georges most mornings. Always smartly dressed, usually with a bow tie, he would stop at the concierge's desk to collect his mail and cables, fold them tidily into an armful of newspapers and stride purposefully towards the bar for his usual, a Gibson – a dry martini garnished with a small onion.

Twice in recent weeks, Sam had made an appointment to

meet Kim and twice he had had to cancel when he was called away on a story. He swore he wouldn't postpone again. But once more, something had come up, and yet again he was going to have to bale out. Affable old Kim, he knew, would understand and certainly wouldn't take it personally, but he decided the least he could do was to arrange for Eleanor to buy the new arrival a drink and introduce him to 'our friends' at the St Georges bar, of whom there were many.

One such friend was Bill Eveland whose true role was not well understood in these circles. Though not formally acknowledged as an employee of the CIA, he reported directly to its director Allen Dulles, and spent much of his time in neighbouring Syria combating an allegedly increasing Soviet threat. Eveland came from a modest background and was as far from being an Ivy Leaguer as can be imagined. He, like Eleanor also from Washington State, had acquired an excellent level of Arabic while serving in Iraq and had a notable sympathy for the Palestinian cause. He had arrived in Beirut some months earlier, having been told that Sam was a journalist who could be trusted, and a good ally to have in Lebanon. These two gangling men became good friends and regular partners at the bar of the St Georges.

There was no disapproval in the fact that they were co-chairmen of the hotel bar's renowned Ten a.m. Club. This was an age when a steady, steadying intake of alcohol during the day was unremarkable, and among journalists its absence would have been considered positively eccentric. Eleanor and Annie, then seven, also liked Eveland, and he would often drop round to the Brewers' flat on the Corniche for a bite to eat, sometimes helping Annie with her homework. So when Sam was called away, Bill and Eleanor were the obvious people to do the introductions. Eveland, of course, had heard the claims about Philby and was curious to meet him. But he was also a keen student of Middle Eastern history, and in that world, the name Philby meant a lot.

Kim's father St John Philby was a brilliant man who nearly fifty years earlier had gained a First in modern languages, later acquiring a decent level of Arabic, Baluch, Hindi, Persian, Punjabi and Urdu. He was to prove far too disputatious for his first posting, claiming to have been 'the first Socialist to join the Indian Civil Service', and later his impetuosity led him to compromise his loyalty to the Crown. He married Dora Johnston in 1910 in Ambala, in the Punjab, with his cousin Bernard Montgomery (later of Alamein fame) as best man, and they called their first child Harold Adrian Russell, nicknamed 'Kim' after the hero of the Rudyard Kipling novel.

St John and Kim had first been in Beirut over three decades earlier, in 1923 (when Kim was eleven and St John was a senior official in Jordan), and the proud father was delighted to be welcoming his slandered son back to the world he longed for him to appreciate. In 1930 St John converted to Islam, aiding his access to both King Abdul Aziz Ibn Saud, the creator and first king of Saudi Arabia, and to the holy city of Mecca. Cecil Hope Gill, British chargé d'affaires at Jeddah, said of St John Philby at the time: 'He made no pretence whatever that his conversion was spiritual', but that it was a long-deliberated decision arising in response to his 'disassociation from British ideals'.

St John Philby had – like his son – attended Westminster School before going to Trinity College, Cambridge, and had fallen out with powerful figures in Whitehall, to the extent of making injudiciously open-minded remarks about Nazism and the wisdom of going to war, resulting in him being briefly interned. Nonetheless, he had established a titan's reputation as an expert on the Middle East, having been an adviser to the king, and being one of very few Westerners to cross the Rub' al-Khali, Arabia's Empty Quarter, the largest area of sand in the world, from east to west. Crucially, he also represented Saudi interests in the deal that began the end of British dominance of the local oil market. The scheme allowed Aramco, rather than Anglo-Persian (of which he was also a consultant), to export Saudi oil round the world. One of the reasons he gave for favouring a deal with the Americans was that, unlike the other offers, there seemed to be no imperialist strings attached. Nonetheless, a State Department official called the deal a 'stupendous source of strategic power and one of the greatest material prizes in world history'. Most of that oil was being transported through the 750-mile Trans-Arabian Pipeline ('Tapline'), which ran across Saudi Arabia, through Jordan and Syria, reaching the Mediterranean at Sidon in Lebanon. American interests were closely tied to the security of Tapline: governments would fall if it was interrupted, and preventing such an occurrence was one of the givens in conversation at the St Georges.

After Ibn Saud's death in 1953, St John showed a characteristic lack of tact, criticising the extravagance and corruption of the Saudi royal family, then led by the late king's eldest son King Saud, causing him to go into exile in Beirut. His seventy-one years had done nothing to mellow a considerable conceit. In Beirut, he was a celebrity, and nowhere more so than among the St Georges powermongers.

Kim's arrival in Beirut in 1956 was an opportunity for the pair to bond once more, and for father to offer son a hand – and some top-of-the-range local contacts – to aid his rehabilitation. This he sought to do during Kim's first days in Beirut. Their relationship had not always been a smooth one, Kim having been critical of his father early in life, but he still found plenty to look up to. Besides that, he was aware that his father's connections had helped his posting to Beirut.

The encounter between Eleanor and Kim at the St Georges on 12 September 1956 went better than Sam Brewer could have hoped. Both were on best behaviour, and both were more than capable of making themselves liked. Eveland had heard tales of St John Philby from his boss Allen Dulles, a friend of St John, but he found the son less imposing than he had imagined. He was, he later wrote, 'quiet, polite and physically unprepossessing ... nothing like a former spy'. Philby, indeed, was not a big man. He was five foot nine inches tall, blue-eyed, pale-skinned and lean. His voice was deep and melodious, and his manners exceptional.*

To Eleanor, Kim looked not so much like a regular lunching partner of Washington's most powerful people as simply a nice guy with an endearing stutter, pitched into an unfamiliar place, and in a state of uncertainty. He was sharing the house that his father preferred to use up in the hills. It was a small but beautiful house – indeed, that was its name, Mahalla Jamil, address: near Café Florida, Ajaltoun. The fact that he wasn't in the middle of town must have seemed singular – a mark, perhaps, of that same family loyalty, which might be to the detriment of a journalist whose ear was supposed to be close to the ground, although the cheapness and coolness of living out of town was clearly a bonus.

Now Kim needed to surmount his indifference to the Middle East. For all his father's introductions to the highest in the land, Kim was the new boy. Eleanor later wrote that she had initially been touched by 'his loneliness ... He knew no one in Beirut ... a certain old-fashioned reserve set him apart from the easy familiarity of the other journalists'. She thought him

---

* In Eleanor's own account of her first meeting, she says she was at the St Georges that day by chance and someone pointed out Philby with his father. She says Sam had asked Eleanor to make Philby feel welcome, should she bump into him. She alludes only briefly to St John having been there and she makes no mention at all of Eveland, whose own version makes no mention of St John having been present, curious given how keen he had been to meet him.

'a man who had seen a lot of the world, who was experienced, yet seemed to have suffered'. She was not the first woman to be taken by his vulnerability. Not only was he living out of town, but he came across as a good family man pained at having to leave his wife and five children back in England. Kim struck Eleanor as kind, unassuming and unusually sensitive. He was clearly something of a hit that day, but one who needed a bit of looking after, notwithstanding the presence of his eminent father. A friend who knew him during his time in Beirut said, many years later, 'Kim had a way of making women fall for him'. Another friend recalls St John's remark on seeing an attractive American woman hovering expectantly around his son: 'Poor Kim, he's in trouble again.' A young Californian visiting Beirut could not take her eyes off him, describing him as a 'manly teddy bear'. Another woman said he had 'a touch of animal roughness'. Said Aburish, chronicler of goings-on at the St Georges, said 'his very being carried a sexual suggestiveness'.

Professionally, too, Kim needed a hand. He was extremely adept at assimilating information, and he would need to be. The reason for Sam's absence that day was that he had had to go to Cairo at short notice. Egypt had been gradually sliding into international prominence for some years, and things were coming to a head. To many British eyes, the worst suspicions about the country's leader, the charismatic Gamal Abdel Nasser, were coming true, and British readers of the two prestigious journals Kim was representing would expect authoritative reporting.

It would be easy to caricature Britain's Prime Minister Anthony Eden at that time as a colonialist overlord wanting to put the upstart Nasser in his place. It would also not be far wrong, and it was an image Nasser was adept at exploiting. Eden was alarmed by Arab nationalism and the aspiration to create an effective Arab state across the whole of North Africa, a prospect which also appalled the French. As Foreign Secretary,

Eden had considered trying to organise a counter-coup following the toppling of King Farouk in 1952 but had been talked out of it. He was also concerned that Nasser's open flirtation with Moscow was more than a political tease. In 1955, Eden had been a key mover behind the Baghdad Pact, a pro-Western defence partnership of Iraq – a British favourite at the time – Iran, Pakistan, Turkey and the UK, and was miffed at Nasser's refusal to join. Nasser, too, was annoyed, both by Iraq lining up alongside the colonialist British and by Eden's lofty manner, and approached the Russians, proposing an arms deal.

Earlier in 1956, the Western-inspired Alpha plan, which had sought to provide financial aid for the resettlement of Arab refugees and provide security guarantees for Israel, had collapsed.

Not only had Eden failed to take on board the realities of the post-war world, but he was grievously misreading the signals from Egypt and riling Britain's American allies in the process. For all the personal warmth and amicable rivalry between the wartime allies, the US was unimpressed by the management of the British empire.*

This divergence was most evident over Egypt. Soon after the coup of 1952, the US had identified Nasser as the man to groom. 'We wanted in Egypt a leader whose views were more or less consistent with ours while, at the same time, being consistent enough with his own people's to sustain him as a popular leader. If he had to be "anti" anything [. . .], we preferred it to be "imperialism" rather than Israel,' said one diplomat.

Nasser's commitment to Egyptian autonomy was a worldly one. He needed to appeal to his supporters, but he understood the constraints on both himself and the US, whose commitment to

---

* For a full discussion of the competition between the US and the UK, see James Barr's *Lords of the Desert*.

Israel required that on occasions its support for Nasser would have to be covert. Such subtleties would be sufficient to see off any Soviet blandishments. As British dreams for the Middle East became more and more outlandish, so US deference towards British diplomacy declined. The Americans agreed to encourage the British to give up their Suez Canal base, and the British army agreed to leave Egypt in 1954.

When the British ambassador arrived at Nasser's residence to protest at the Egyptian arms deal with the Russians, two of the most senior US officials were hiding upstairs, having enjoyed a drink and advised Nasser on how to handle the announcement without alarming the Jewish vote back in the States. The British had had the chance to be on the inside track with Nasser and missed it. The hieroglyphics were on the wall.

But Britain wasn't looking. When, in March 1956, Bill Eveland and two other senior American diplomats arrived in London, they met an impassioned Scot named George Kennedy Young, deputy director of MI6, who was to play a notorious role in official below-the-radar activities. The Americans expected a congenial chat, but Young's blood was up. His abundant references to 'gyppos', 'wogs' and 'snipcocks' shocked the well-mannered Americans, but not as much as his plans. He denounced the CIA's Kim Roosevelt for creating 'a monster in Nasser' and supplying 'pure rubbish' as intelligence on Egypt. Further, the British had a three-part plan. First, whether the Americans liked it or not, they would imminently engineer a change of government in dangerously pro-Nasser Syria, presumably via Iraq, Britain's ally. Second, with the help of the CIA if possible, they would go after 'Nasserite' elements in Saudi Arabia. Third, his allies weakened, Nasser would find his own government 'tumbled', if necessary by force.

The British were talking wildly of killing Nasser, the leader the Americans had promoted. The signals the British and Americans were sending were chaotically different. In any case, subsequent events were to coalesce into a foreign policy disaster unmatched by Britain for nearly fifty years.

Nonetheless, in part because of shifts in personnel, American attitudes were also shifting. Nasser was exceeding what the US regarded as his brief, and threats to withdraw aid for the building of the Aswan Dam merely antagonised him. But the British and Americans could not agree on how to deal with him. The British deny claims they wanted him murdered, but certainly the feasibility was examined, and a number of outlandish schemes were examined. (These reached the Americans, who shared them with Nasser himself, who enjoyed musing on the hilarious impracticality of the possible methods.) Nonetheless the Americans thought he was getting above himself and wanted him manoeuvred into pliability.

On 26 July 1956 Nasser nationalised the company which ran the Suez Canal. It was in anyone's language a provocative move, but as Sam Pope Brewer reported at the time, Nasser seriously underestimated the anger of London's reaction. Britain imported a third of all the oil that came through the Canal, and, as Eden put it, Nasser could not be allowed to have his hand on Britain's windpipe. Britain was bound to react and, militarily, who knew what might happen? Sam Brewer told *New York Times* readers that weekend how: 'Bank clerks and schoolteachers and Moslem Holy men are taking time off to learn to handle fire arms . . . Truckloads of recruits roll through Cairo daily.'

To a man such as Kim Philby, with few illusions about imperialism, subjugation of local peoples, public-school clottishness and the march of history, this must all have been reassuringly predictable. He had arrived in the Middle East at the highwater mark of British colonialist wrong-headedness, so there was plenty to talk about when Sam got back to Beirut. For one thing, the *New York Times* man would have been intrigued to know more about one of the architects of British policy, the arch-imperialist G. K. Young of MI6, who was one of Kim's greatest admirers.

Philby's aura of previous accomplishment had impressed Eleanor, and the Brewers were more than happy for him to drop round, if only to distract them from any marital discord. Sam, with his journalist's inability to switch off and his delight in Philby's company, always enjoyed gossiping with a man he first suspected might be working for his country's intelligence service when Kim was with *The Times* in Spain and who he believed might still be on its payroll. Philby may well have suspected the same of Brewer, so familiar was his host with official thinking. All the more reason to enjoy his bourbon. They knew how to rub along together, though rarely going below the superficial. On one occasion Sam asked Kim over a drink if he was a Soviet spy. Kim's laugh was typically insouciant. He replied, 'Everybody knows that, don't they?'

Beyond a natural concern for human suffering and an essentially liberal, slightly left-of-centre outlook, Eleanor had little interest in the minutiae of politics. In her book some years later, she made no mention of the mayhem over Suez that had called Sam away that day. She was variously described as mild, unpresuming, neither warm nor hostile . . . didn't make a strong impression, trusting, simple . . . tall, attractive, good looking, elegant in an uncomplicated way, artistically inclined and intelligent, but quite uninterested in political developments. A friend said she had 'integrity, courage and humour . . . she could not be described as intellectual but she was certainly intelligent'. Journalist Dick Beeston said she was a 'rangy, steady-drinking American, who looked tough and sophisticated. Underneath she was a romantic and politically naïve.' Another said: 'She wasn't particularly glamorous but she had a certain kind of presence.' Susan Griggs, who knew her better than most, remembers her great smile and sense of humour. 'She was very wry, funny and slightly sarcastic – smartass kind of funny. She was very smart, well informed and sensible.'

An acquaintance at the time, Celia Adams (who never liked Philby), recalls sitting with Eleanor and telling her she had just got engaged to Michael Adams, the *Guardian*'s Middle East correspondent. Eleanor offered congratulations, adding with mock-weariness: 'So you're joining the happy band, are you?' The irony did not seem entirely frivolous.

She may not have been instantly memorable to some, but Kim looked beyond first impressions.

As the days and weeks went by, the more Kim seemed to Eleanor to have had a raw deal. She learned how his impressive public-service career had come to an end in 1951. How much she learned from either Philby or her husband at that point cannot be known, but what sophisticated folk on Beirut's diplomatic circuit would have known is this.

In 1951, suspicion had been growing that a British diplomat had been leaking information to the Soviet Union. The evidence from intercepts of Soviet signals suggested that a man working at the British embassy in Washington, codenamed HOMER, had been in close touch with the Russians in 1944–5, a key moment in the development of nuclear weapons. Thanks to technological advances, the evidence was becoming more and more suggestive that HOMER was Donald Maclean, another brilliant Cambridge graduate. Plans were in train to question Maclean, by this time back in London, yet he was never questioned. He – and even more surprisingly his Foreign Office colleague Guy Burgess – vanished from London one Friday evening, boarding a France-bound steamer at Southampton. They were next heard of, astonishingly, in Moscow, having defected to the Soviet Union.

Philby, who like Burgess had been at university with Maclean, was one of very few people in a position to get word to Maclean that he was about to be arrested, but, as the British pointed out, that was purely circumstantial, and certainly insufficient to convict him in court. Philby's accusers said his friendship with Burgess alone suggested an appalling lack of judgement and a danger to security. But Kim was a good egg, his friends in London insisted. And the Americans, upstarts in the espionage game, had misinterpreted the signals. What the Americans saw as obvious, the British saw as obviously misleading. 'The fact that Burgess who is now known to have been a Soviet agent was permitted by his Masters to share a house so long with Philby makes it highly improbable that Philby was himself a Soviet agent.' But the Americans were insistent. If their confidence in MI6 was to be preserved, he had to go.

As far as his friends were concerned, Philby had been treated disgracefully, and he was to be put through the mill again in 1955 when, following a 'revelation' in the *New York Sunday News*, Marcus Lipton MP, under parliamentary privilege, repeated the claim that Philby had worked for the Russians. Now the messy uncertainty needed to be cleared up. The British state could no longer shrug its shoulders. Whether it knew or not, now that he had been named there needed to be an official line as to whether he was or wasn't a traitor. As might be expected, given their famed rivalry, much of MI5, the 'Security Service' charged with domestic security, believed he was. Most of MI6, or the Secret Intelligence Service, many of whose operatives work abroad, believed he wasn't.

The Foreign Secretary's statement in parliament that November was clear. Harold Macmillan told the House of Commons: 'While in government service he [Philby] carried out his duties ably and conscientiously, and I have no reason to conclude that Mr Philby has at any time betrayed the interests of his country, or to identify him with the so-called "Third Man", if indeed there was one.'

'He really could not have done me a better turn if he had wanted to,' said Philby later of his accuser Marcus Lipton. The injustice had been confirmed, said his friends. All the more reason why he, his wife and five children should be helped. He had been guilty only of excessive loyalty to a rather wild friend, and he should be shown a little in return. A possible candidate for a knighthood was now on the scrap heap. It was an appalling waste. At forty-three, he was clever, popular and still had an enormous amount to offer. But the accusation had taken a toll, and he was grateful to accept the offer from W. E. D. Allen, the former press counsellor at the British embassy in Ankara, who invited him to the family home in County Waterford, Ireland, to help compile a history of his family's business. He wrote copious loving postcards to his children, spent his weekends walking and was relieved to have a settled income for a six-month spell, while lamenting that it would not be sufficient to send his sons to Westminster.

He returned to London, where his wife Aileen, from whom he was effectively estranged, was in hospital. His friends were well aware that he needed a job. An injustice had been done, and through some judicious string-pulling by Nicholas Elliott (a former MI6 colleague whose father had known St John at Cambridge) and David Astor, co-owner and editor of the *Observer*, it was arranged for him to return to his original career, journalism. Calls were made, following which he would now be covering Lebanon for the London-based weeklies the *Observer* and *The Economist*. He would be paid £3000 a year (worth around £75,000 today), plus travelling expenses, which in Philby's case turned out to be substantial.

The Brewers smiled upon his presence in Beirut, to the extent that they could when he came into town only twice a week to file his copy and pick up his post. Increasingly his trips included dropping in on the Brewers' flat. There his rehabilitation would progress. He would find homely comforts, both in the kitchen and in helping with the shopping, and he was invited to spend his first Beirut Christmas with them. He, like Bill Eveland, was welcome any time, and it is not hard to imagine generous American hospitality being offered all the more willingly for Kim's immaculate, low-key British manners.

The old charmer played the grateful visitor role to a tee, and Eleanor's daughter Annie adored him. He had always been good with children, and used to love going upstairs at parties and saying good night to them. Children are more straightforward, he felt. Their bad moods pass quickly.

Kim's appearances at the Brewers' flat that autumn would have been both convivial and mutually beneficial. Kim rarely failed to be amusing, and he still had a lot to offer an eager journalist like Sam. Six weeks after Kim and Eleanor had first met at the St Georges, on 29 October, after extensive planning with the British and French, Israeli troops had crossed the Egyptian border, invading Sinai. A few days later, British and French troops followed them in, achieving some military gains, but the Suez Canal itself was effectively inaccessible. The whole event was a humiliation for Britain, reaching its nadir as British troops withdrew following pressure from the US and others.

Kim's old-world solicitousness struck a chord with Eleanor. She particularly admired his skill in writing letters, of which there were many. 'He was for her a master of those mysterious, civilised European ways she found so attractive,' remembered Patrick Seale. She also enjoyed his willing recourse to humour. Sam, by contrast, was a more serious presence. 'Once in a while Sam would jump up and down with a great guffaw of laughter, but chiefly he was serious,' remembers Afif Aburish. Eleanor told a friend that her husband 'thought of nothing but work and that she no longer felt herself a part of his life'. Philby's approach to work – or at least to journalism – was more ruminant, essentially to stay on top of the gossip, keep in with his handlers in London by affecting willingness and flexibility but generally presenting something sound but unchallenging at the end of each week. For him the news was not so much for chasing, or even breaking, more for digesting. In any case, tireless sleuthing left no time for frivolity and fun, on which Sam was less keen. If Eleanor had not exactly had a wandering eye, Kim's extraordinarily flattering attentions struck all the right notes. And Kim's manners were concealing something. Eleanor had helped him settle in, and he had come to admire her more than Sam realised. Before long Kim was beginning to suggest an affair. That Christmas the Brewers held a big party, inviting many of Beirut's big hitters, including government ministers. Initially she had resisted his advances, but by Christmas a page had been turned. He left on a work trip to Syria in the early new year filled with protective thoughts towards Eleanor, whose unhappy state her husband was doing little to mitigate. Philby's attentions added to her confusion. She and her husband had a seven-year-old daughter, and now she was falling for someone else. This, emphatically, was not in the script.

The spring of 1957 was barely less politically charged than the previous autumn, and Sam continued to be away a lot. Increasingly Kim would meet Eleanor to do the shopping or simply for coffee. Both enjoyed the integrity of the local establishments not frequented by Westerners. Their rendez-vous extended far and wide, first to the Lebanese army's 'Bain Militaire' swimming club or the YMCA beach, and later for picnics further afield. Sometimes Sam's driver Nehad would take Sam's work car, a fancy, air-conditioned Packard, and drive them out of town, away from prying eyes, to the mountains or up the coast a few miles to historic Byblos.

It is a mark of Kim's singularity that he continued to function well as both a journalist and a secret lover, even when living at Ajaltoun. He had an office of sorts at the Normandy Hotel, where the post arrived more promptly than up in the hills, and he could use the excellent bookshop nearby, the Levant Library, to buy the Lebanese, British, French and German newspapers, which he would read for an hour every morning before a routine tour of the British and then American embassies and their press officers.

Sometimes Kim's father would drop by at the Normandy, even though he had only seen him earlier that morning. Kim was trusted by local journalists, who had little interest in who he was beyond being the son of St John and therefore, it didn't need saying, pro-Arab rather than pro-Israeli. The house became something of an institution, and on Sundays he would invite fellow journalists to escape the heat of the city and have lunch, which he excelled in preparing. Sam Brewer, perhaps with 'Sunday for Monday' deadlines in mind, or more likely using that as an excuse, generally declined the invitation, but Eleanor went with alacrity, often with Annie and one or two of her friends. The children revelled in Kim's company, the adults in his food and copious amounts of drink.

In any event, her infatuation had grown rapidly. In her book, she talks of her spring outings with Kim, six months after they met, as 'not just sightseeing', although in truth they had got beyond the 'just sightseeing' stage sooner than that. 'This was the beginning of a deep friendship. It seemed to me that I had never met a kinder, more interesting person in my entire life.' They continued to see one another *à deux*, with Eleanor in a state of mounting confusion and indecision.

Kim and Eleanor continued to conduct their relationship in secret, and only three or four people knew about it. In such circles, secrets leak, but there was sympathy among Eleanor's friends for the fact that her husband was so immersed in work and lacking in grace at home. The Brewers' next-door neighbours in the flat on the Corniche were the Mecklins. John was with *Time* magazine and his wife Shirley was a good friend of Eleanor. Some evenings Shirley and a friend would pick her up from her flat, drop her off with Kim, go to a film, pick her up again afterwards and take her home. Sam, entirely unaware, was always happy to see her going out with friends.

Being the new boy who had been through a tough spell in England, Kim came into his own in Beirut. While some correspondents would scurry about the region, sweatily clocking up contacts of varying reliability, Kim rarely seemed to move very far. The journalistic scufflers would report on who said what, and who was visiting where, but the bigger picture was one of interpretation, in knowing what mattered and what could be ignored. Based in Ajaltoun, he was often seen at the Normandy Hotel's bar, or Harry's Bar near the British embassy, or less often the smarter and pricier St Georges, where a couple of glasses of something fortifying would help him judiciously identify the region's geopolitical shifts. The less he moved, the more he seemed to know. Besides, his forty-a-day smoking habit endorsed his general aversion to physical exercise without an identified goal.

In this and other respects, Kim was a man apart from the run of international hackery. Of all the international flotsam and jetsam that came through Beirut, he was a figure of some substance, a man who seemed to know and understand what was going on, and one people encountered with pleasure. He had the gift of likeability in abundance.

Kim and Eleanor's besottedness with one another, still known only to a handful, defied convention, not that expectations of that were high in Beirut. One husband discovered that his wife was allowing Kim and Eleanor to have secret trysts in their home and stepped in to stop them, but this was the exception. Those who wanted to play away found plenty of opportunity. 'I was disgusted by the behaviour of some of the husbands I met at the embassy,' said one young visitor at the time. And those who were mere spectators had plenty to gossip about. The Kit Kat Club was always available for diplomats to let off steam, and not always in ways that flattered them, but louche behaviour could crop up anywhere. One male official in the British embassy was asked by an MI6 colleague if, in the line of duty, he wouldn't mind sleeping with a female counterpart in the Egyptian embassy (he declined). The head of public affairs of a large international company flirted a little too keenly and publicly with the wife of a comparable big hitter. The husband arranged for a bullet to be put in his leg. A sheikh from an avowedly Muslim country lowered the tone at the St Georges bar by swigging Rémy Martin cognac from a bottle. And a Saudi general offered a Lebanese businessman and his wife, sitting next to him, $16,000 for a night alone with the wife. In such company and in that era, Kim's occasional roguish bottom-pinching seemed like mere horseplay, usually forgiven with the help of one of his deftly deployed apologies.

Eleanor's marriage had been tolerable, at best, and the buffeting it had taken over years of travelling between cities had taken a toll. Sam could be demanding – she used to joke that in his eyes her soufflés were never quite right – and was disapproving of how she ran the home. But they had carried on together, the marriage cemented by the presence of Annie, although Kim's ease with children would have made Sam look remote and uncaring by comparison.

The first sign of things coming to a head with Sam occurred one evening when Eleanor, accompanied by Kim, was given a lift back into town after one of his bibulous Sundays up in the hills. Sam came out and told Kim that he was no longer welcome at his house. He was a bad influence. Whatever was going on – and it was whispered that Sam's driver Nehad had told Sam of his wife and Philby's countryside trysts – he didn't like it. He was putting down a marker, but of what was not quite clear. Maybe Sam doubted Kim and Eleanor could be having an affair, but felt he should say something just in case. Sam's warning shot, if that is how it was intended, was never going to derail Kim and Eleanor's passion. Certainly for Eleanor the appeal of being with this kind, lovely, clever, popular Englishman was immense. The fact that they were both married didn't bother them; if anything, it made them enjoy the moment all the more. Aileen, Kim's wife, was in England and off the scene. Kim had explained how she was attention-seeking and difficult to live with. And, curiously, Sam might just as well have been in England, too, for all the difference his presence made. He was away so much, and either blind or indifferent when he was in Beirut, that much of Eleanor's social life was carried on with Kim regardless.

In some ways the situation was uncomfortably unsustainable, but that didn't seem to matter. Kim and Eleanor spoke of resolving things, but to no constructive end. Eleanor said later that Kim had always been amused by the idea of having a mistress, and hoped Eleanor might agree to some sort of arrangement along those lines. But with Annie there, she found that inconceivable.

Beirut's expat community was a friendly one, and six decades later its occupants speak of their time there as a golden age. New arrivals would be encouraged to join the party, sized up and invited to the next social engagement, of which there was always one coming along any day. Kim's affability meant he would always make friends, and Eleanor was also a popular figure. To anyone who asked, he would explain his misfortune over Burgess and Maclean as follows: he had not known Burgess very well, and never imagined he was a communist. Burgess's job in Washington had been a 'last-chance appointment', and by offering to put him up, Philby was making 'the sort of gesture anyone would make to an old undergraduate acquaintance'. A man down on his luck who had been loyal to a friend was thought to deserve a bit of carefree happiness.

The Americans and the British were particularly close, their children often attending either the American Community School, the International College or the Collège Protestant Français, and families meeting at weekends to venture into the countryside. The person Eleanor became closest to was a Scot named Lorraine Copeland (born 1921); the two had met when their husbands' paths had crossed in neighbouring Syria some years earlier. Lorraine and her husband Miles, a businessman and former diplomat, arrived in Beirut from Egypt in mid-1957, having spent much of the previous fifteen years posted in Egypt, Syria and continental Europe. Lorraine was clever, decent and gently humorous.

Lorraine's son Stewart – who became famous as the drummer with rock band the Police – describes her as 'an unsocial animal who did what the diplomat's wife was supposed to do – she was a quiet, bookish, retiring mother'. Soon, though in charge of the couple's four spirited children, she enrolled at the American University of Beirut, founded by American missionaries nearly a hundred years earlier, to study archaeology. Sometimes she and Eleanor, or Isobel Fistere, would go off on a dig into Syria or Jordan, often run by James Pritchard, head archaeologist at the University of Pennsylvania, or Francis Hours, a witty, omniscient Jesuit lecturer and – her husband aside – Lorraine's best male friend. 'Like all the other women she knew and hung out with in Beirut, Eleanor had interesting things to do during the day. These were clever, thoughtful women. They did not stay home and bake brownies,' says Susan Griggs (née Fistere).

These trips were the start of an impressive career for Lorraine Copeland that was to provide many new insights into early prehistory in the near Middle East.

Her University of London colleague Andrew Garrard described her as 'intellectually curious and absolutely tireless in her pursuit of her interest in early prehistory, both in field studies, where she worked and lived in difficult conditions, and when analysing archaeological materials at her home. She was very hospitable with a good sense of humour and enjoyed engaging with students as well as more senior people in her field.'

The Copelands were a popular couple, and were frequent party-givers at their home, the Tarazi Villa, an Arabesque mansion in the hills above Beirut. Their daughter Lennie, who was eleven when the family arrived in Beirut, remembers Kim well, and was often tasked, and kept busy, with ensuring his glass was never empty: 'Everybody loved Kim. He was just an affable guy, always cheerful, and seemed almost innocent, kind of childish really. My bedroom was by the bar, and he was generally close by. He didn't talk to me like a child, he seemed to treat me like an adult. He just seemed ingenuous.' The tall, slender Eleanor would be elsewhere at the party, just enjoying things. 'She struck me as serious, a mild person, solid, not flighty, which may have been one of the things Kim saw in her. I don't have a strong impression, but she was a decent, straight person.'

Younger brother Stewart recalls the very apt choice of film that the Copelands would screen in the latter years of their Beirut party-throwing. 'I remember the tinkling of glasses,' he says, 'and how they used to play the movie *La Dolce Vita*, I must have seen the beginning of that movie ten times. My big brother told me there was a nude scene at the end so we had to stay up. We used to sneak in and watch from underneath the grand piano. I don't think we ever made it to see the end of the movie. The whole city was very *dolce vita*. It was a party town, where the newly rich Saudis would spend their money on some fun. With the Christians running the place, it was a fleshpot. You could drink, you could gamble, you could have loose ways and hedonistic pursuits.'

Though less outgoing and seven years younger than Eleanor, Lorraine and she got on well. 'Archaeology was a bond and they had similar interests,' remembers Lorraine's son Miles Copeland III. 'They were best friends. They hung around together. Eleanor was normal. She was neither Miss High Class or Miss Low Class. Just a good, solid person.'

But Eleanor could see that Kim's relations with Aileen back in England were not good and getting worse. Her mental state was poor and Kim's attempts to appease the effectively single mother of five from afar with what she saw as none too generous cheques and fag-ends of the charm being deployed in Beirut were never likely to be successful. From her end of the telescope, at the very least he was swanning about in the sun, enjoying only the easy, school-holiday parts of family life and enduring none of the drudgery. Things were so bad that the doctor had advised Kim to stay away, or so Eleanor was told. They had married just over a decade earlier, and the demands of expensive schools and Kim's foreign posting were taking their toll on her life in the very ordinary Sussex town of Crowborough. Further, following the 'Third Man' allegations, the newspapers were showing interest in the family, and reporters outside the house added to the sense of being besieged.

The everyday grumbles of her marriage to Sam were one thing, but Eleanor's infatuation had blinded her to the likely cost of the path she had put herself on. Her head had been so comprehensively turned by Kim that she was on course for breaking up the sort of steady marriage that nice, middle-class Irish-American girls were supposed to aspire to. When confronted by the prospect of separating from the father of her daughter, she was not at all sure it was the right thing to do. Kim told her often that if she was unhappy she should take charge and do something about it, but she was not able to countenance divorce.

Kim went on a work trip to Saudi Arabia. In a letter she quotes in her book, Eleanor recalls Philby saying that 'it must be nearly 900 weeks since I was anything like so happy as I am now'. He expresses the hope that they might be together by the spring of the following year.

Both felt the strain of the situation, and Eleanor decided the time had come to act. Any fears she might have had that her dreamlike relationship was merely a reckless English roué's fling were banished. Kim was in it for the long haul. He was there for her, wanting her. There could be no doubt where his heart lay.

But his own marriage was unresolved. Eleanor could be forgiven for thinking that Aileen was deserving of little sympathy. This most solicitous of men could never be inattentive, surely, without good reason. But the view from the Home Counties could scarcely have been more different.

Kim and Aileen Furse had met in 1937. She was two years older than him, but much less worldly.

She had once set her much-admired hair on fire after her mother refused to allow her to cut it in the fashion of the time, and would give herself bruises to avoid having to play games. Any sympathy her siblings might have had evaporated at the senselessness of the attention-seeking injuries she inflicted upon herself. When she moved away from home to live alone in her early twenties, it was on medical advice. She and Philby met while he was on leave from a spell covering the Spanish Civil War for *The Times*. One of his biographers writes that at that time 'she was not at all a wise or well-balanced woman ... it was astonishing that Kim took up with her, and their decision to live together [. . .] illustrated the almost reckless way in which this careful man contracted permanent relationships'.

They had been introduced by Flora Solomon, who was to play a decisive role in Philby's later life. She was a tireless promoter of Jewish causes and held a senior position at Marks & Spencer in central London. Aileen's cousin Neil Furse, who worked at the same store, felt that Aileen, having lost her father in the First World War, was in need of guidance. He asked the kindly Mrs Solomon, a family friend, if she could help. The twenty-four-year-old was bemused by the world of commerce, so Mrs Solomon invited her to be her assistant.

M&S was a Jewish company. For someone with Aileen's horsey, Home Counties background, where Jewishness mattered (and not for the better), such a job was not an obvious berth. But it offered stability away from home to a young woman whose privately educated teenage years had been marked by tantrums and rebellion.

When Mrs Solomon introduced the poised, well-travelled young reporter, Aileen was eager to admire, and vice versa. He liked her spirit and engaging laugh, her slim, attractive figure, and applauded the edge of rebelliousness she had shown. In the language of her time and milieu, she was a spirited filly, and there was no need for Philby to know of the self-harm that had marked her teenage years. It seemed to be genuinely in the past. They began living together – with rather more haste than Mrs Solomon approved of – in a flat in Drayton Gardens, South Kensington, that they shared with Kim's adoring and all-forgiving mother Dora. She was not the world's first prospective mother-in-law to let slip that she thought her son could have done better, a feeling Aileen herself shared. '[She] never really conquered a slight fear of him due to the fact that he was on a different plane from herself,' wrote one biographer.

Aileen was captivated, and it was not long before the couple pushed the boundaries yet further, children arriving before they married, their first daughter Josephine being born in 1941. Aileen's mother Mrs Alleyne (she had twice remarried), a model of respectability who lived in a vast house in Queensgate Place, Kensington, cannot have approved. Nor, according to one report, did she like the fact that she understood Kim to have been a communist in his past. But then so had Aileen, in a fleeting act of rebellion, and their friend Flora Solomon, though from a banking family and a political refugee from Soviet Russia, was also vigorously left wing. No harm in that, surely, when there was antisemitism and fascism to fight, and with her company keen to ensure its staff were well-looked-after. Whatever the strength of Mrs Alleyne's misgivings, they didn't stand in the way of young love. Kim and the arrival of the couple's first children brought new steadiness to Miss Marks & Spencer, as Kim sometimes called her, and to Kim himself, who adored young children. John and Tommy were born before the end of the war, and Miranda just afterwards. The Philbys moved to Turkey, in 1947, when Kim was made MI6's head of station.

Aileen seemed to blossom. She had escaped her family and made her own way, marrying a personable and gifted husband. On the face of it, Turkey was an idyllic posting. But Aileen's travails were aggravated. At one point she was overcome by an undiagnosed and serious illness. With the help of Kim's MI6 friend Nicholas Elliott, then posted in Bern, she and Philby visited a specialist in Switzerland who diagnosed acute septicaemia. But the doctor angered Philby by saying that he believed the injury that had led to Aileen's illness had been self-inflicted, which Kim thought absurd. Subsequent enquiries revealed this was quite likely to have been the case. He had been deceived.

Some progress was made, but her problems had not

been properly resolved when Kim and his family moved to Washington for his big new job liaising between British and US intelligence.

The family's stay in Washington was curtailed by Burgess and Maclean's disappearance and Philby's subsequent resignation. By this time, there were seven mouths to feed, their fifth child Harry having been born in 1950. They returned to England and settled in Hertfordshire. Kim's stellar career had come to a shuddering halt. With a wife and family to support, he needed to find a new job. He tried several, but he was well suited to none. How relieved he had been, therefore, to be offered a return to journalism in 1956. But it did not come without worries. He was having to leave his beloved children at home in England in the care of an unhappy and unstable wife. He told his father that he suffered a series of nightmares, some of which he told Eleanor about. These featured 'Aileen committing suicide and all the children in tears and shrieking the house down'. But a job was a job.

3

Beneath Kim's surface

Kim and Eleanor's relationship was an exquisitely happy one. Within days of meeting they were falling for one another. If love was blind, who cared? The Kim Philby with whom Eleanor fell so comprehensively in love was the one most people saw – the amiable, stuttering, clever, kind, amusing former diplomat who was down on his luck. But that was no longer the Kim Philby that his wife Aileen saw. Others, too, had reservations. They were a small minority, but their number was growing.

Sustained periods of stability and happiness had been rare in Aileen's life. The accommodating variant of Kim's personality had helped provide versions of them, but for Aileen those days were long gone. If many of her difficulties stemmed from childhood, they were compounded by her concerns about her husband, whom she had encountered almost as far back. And far from slipping away imperceptibly, they were mounting. Nobody apart from Kim himself knew the entire truth about his past. Certainly Eleanor didn't.

What follows takes in aspects of his life that his partial account to Eleanor may well have omitted. With Kim Philby, there was always a lot beneath the surface that he chose not to reveal. Eleanor had come up against some disagreeable people during the war and enjoyed a sense of herself as being at least moderately wise to the ways of the world. But for all the adopted cynicism and comedy knowingness – and the undoubted intelligence – she was an innocent. She had heard the whispers about Kim, but saw no reason to doubt the word of someone so self-evidently sweet-natured and sensitive. Everyone else loved him, so she was the luckiest of all. Aileen, too, had been won over by that superficial impression of him nearly twenty years earlier, but how much had Kim failed to tell Eleanor?

In 1929, the year of the Wall Street Crash, the seventeen-year-old Philby had been riled by the failure of the British government to confront the devastation the economic downturn was causing. This came to a head when, in 1931, rather than seizing the moment and taking on the forces of capitalism with a dose of Labourite regeneration, at the very least, the Prime Minister, Labour leader Ramsay MacDonald (one of the Labour Party's founders), took a decision that continues to hang over a party forever exploring the acceptable limits of compromise. He formed a coalition with the Conservatives and Liberals, setting up a National Government. For those who had joined Labour expecting a crunch moment such as this to be grasped with alacrity, there could hardly have been a better advertisement for the shortcomings of social democracy. When it came to it, moderate, incremental, accommodating Labour ducked it, and the student politicians of Cambridge were appalled. A much harder line, advocated by some of Philby's colleagues in the Cambridge University Socialist Society, of which he was treasurer, was becoming de rigueur. The Society's membership jumped from two hundred members in 1933 to over six hundred in 1936. By 1938 it had reached nearly a thousand, almost one in five of all undergraduates. Those like Philby who had been wavering on the border between social democracy and something more regimented found the liberal democratic path harder to defend than ever.

All of these impassioned young souls were finding their own way. Kim's friend the brilliant and flamboyant Guy Burgess (Eton and Trinity College) was shameless in all things, not least his politics. He was an early convert to communism, and he was joined by his slightly older, infatuated Marlburian friend Anthony Blunt (a fellow of Trinity). Another was Donald Maclean, who decided to go to Moscow as a teacher to see for himself.*

'I had already decided, after a good look around me,' Philby said much later, 'that the rich had had it too damned good for too damned long and that the poor had had it too damned bad and that it was time to change. In England at that time the poor really were a different people ... With many of the poor it was a question of getting enough to eat.'

'The question I kept asking myself was what I could do to change matters. All the Ramsay MacDonald business left me very disillusioned, but while others moved quickly to communism, I had to consider the possibility that what had happened represented perhaps a peculiarly British failure of the Left, rather than a wider one, so I made up my mind to see how it was in other countries.' It was in his quest to be 'absolutely certain' that he decided to go travelling.

As a boy Philby had been accustomed to amusing himself during the holidays. His friend Jim Lees said the solitary, serious Philby was used to being 'farmed out' during holidays until he was sixteen, after which he usually spent the summer travelling alone in Europe. In the summer of 1932, the twenty-year-old Kim, studying economics at Trinity, Cambridge, and his Westminster school friend Tim Milne, then reading classics at Christ Church, Oxford, teamed up in Paris, intending

---

* Philby, who recommended Maclean to the Russians, claimed late in life that he didn't meet Maclean until the mid-1930s, but they were only a year apart at Cambridge and were both members of the university's Socialist Society.

to go on a walking holiday in the Balkans. Kim's interest in the impending German election caused the pair to delay their walking for a fortnight and pause in Germany. On the evening of Saturday 30 July, Philby and Milne went to an eve-of-poll rally in Munich addressed by the charismatic young leader of the National Socialist party, Adolf Hitler. 'What impressed and alarmed us was the totally uncritical attitude of so many perfectly ordinary German men and women. Our predominant feeling was contempt for the whole circus – the showmanship, the schoolchildren prancing around in gymnastic displays, the stupid petit-bourgeois citizens swallowing it all.' The elections the next day saw the Nazi Party vote double from two years earlier to over 37 per cent of the total (rocketing up from just 2.6 per cent four years earlier), making the party the largest in parliament. Though it lacked an overall majority, it was meeting a longing for strength and stability. 'The Nazis were not yet in power, there were no concentration camps, Germany was still a free country; but we felt we had seen into the future.'

During the Easter break in his last year at Cambridge, two months after Hitler had become Chancellor (January 1933), the two ascetic undergraduates headed for Berlin, Milne with Plato and Aristotle in his rucksack, Philby with Marx in his. The day of their arrival, 21 March, was the anniversary of Bismarck's 1871 convening of the Second Reich's Reichstag, a strikingly progressive foray towards democracy. Philby made amiable conversation with his fellow guests in their cheap lodgings, suggesting earnestly that the rise of Nazism was not a revolutionary movement at all, despite the scenes of celebration on the streets, but 'merely a reactionary means of preserving capitalism against the advance of socialism; and that the form it was taking in Germany was likely to lead to war'.

That evening the pair stood on a balcony to watch the celebrations surrounding the latest cynical gesture towards democracy, the opening of a version of the Reichstag (the original building having been mysteriously burned down four weeks earlier, a month after Hitler had come to power). Kim Philby was on the spot at the dawn of the Third Reich. To someone inclined to see fascism as an ill-disguised variant of essentially exploitative capitalism, these events fitted the analysis perfectly. This was vindication taking place before his very eyes.

For Milne, his friend was 'the most independent-minded person I had ever met'. Yet, says Milne, Philby must also have seen in Marx 'a golden key to the interpretation of history and of political and economic struggle', while admiring Lenin – of whose works he added a twelve-volume German edition to his luggage – as both a theorist and a practitioner. For a clever, idealistic and socially concerned young man, his eyes already opened by anti-capitalist writers and undergraduate friends, the sweeping, sometimes violent tide of reactionary and racist politics in Germany left a deep impression.

The lesson of his time abroad was emphatically that this was not just a British glitch. The problem was capitalism. Many years later, he said: 'In Germany, unemployment was rife, fascism was on the rise, and the working class fared equally badly. The democratic socialists were unimpressive. They seemed to fold at critical moments. But all the time there was this solid base of the Left, the Soviet Union. I felt that it should be kept there at all costs.' The subsequent success of fascist parties across Europe can only have hardened those convictions.

Having completed his final year at Cambridge, in June 1934 Philby headed once more to the maelstrom of Central Europe, this time, at the prompting of a Parisian communist associate of his tutor, to Austria. Here he first discovered sex (including in the snow), courtesy of his Jewish, part-Hungarian hosts' left-wing daughter, and he went on to experience the thrill of comradely fighting for a cause. Having witnessed the brutal crushing of

Viennese socialism by Chancellor Dollfuss, he expended his energies helping left-wingers and other refugees from Nazi Germany. This was idealism at work, much of it undercover. He helped socialists, in hiding and at risk of being shot by the Austrian police, to escape to Czechoslovakia, persuading a friend to donate four of his old suits to his 'sewer rat' friends to give them respectability at passport control. Within months of devoting himself to the anti-fascist cause, he had what he called a 'passport marriage' to Lizi (pronounced 'Litzi'; the girl with whom he had had the fling), and helped her escape Nazism. He later told a friend that Lizi had been sentenced to death, so, if true, he had saved her life. While there is no evidence of this, he may have made the claim in order to ward off criticism from the likes of Hugh Gaitskell, then an academic in Vienna and later leader of Britain's Labour Party, who felt that by helping activists to escape, Philby and his like were abandoning their friends and weakening the forces of the Austrian opposition. 'He behaved like a gentleman,' Lizi was later to tell her daughter, the writer Barbara Honigmann. 'And he was a Marxist, a rare combination ... He stammered, sometimes more, sometimes less. Like many people with a handicap he was very charming. We fell in love immediately.'

In 1930 in Birmingham, a brilliant young businessman of Czech/Jewish extraction called Oscar Deutsch opened a cinema, one of many, corrupting an old name for his own benefit and calling it ODEON, the acronym from Oscar Deutsch Entertains Our Nation. Oscar had a similarly brilliant cousin, Arnold Deutsch, by training a chemist who had also studied philosophy and psychology, being awarded a PhD just five years after first arriving at university. Arnold had been a follower of Wilhelm Reich, the Freudian Marxist psychoanalyst and sexologist who advocated greater sexual freedom to achieve personal fulfilment and was glibly dubbed 'the prophet of the better orgasm'. Arnold was also a Soviet intelligence officer.

In London, Lizi kept in touch with a close friend from Vienna, Edith Suschitzky, a Bauhaus-trained photographer and avid reader of Wilhelm Reich. The precocious Suschitzky had been deported from Britain when – using a false name – she was seen taking part in a communist rally in 1931. She returned to Vienna and met Alexander Tudor-Hart, an English doctor who was studying orthopaedics. They married and fled Vienna for London. Both Tudor-Harts were committed communists, and Edith resumed her friendship with her first lover, Arnold Deutsch, when he was posted to London in 1934. Checks having been made on Kim's politics and background, before long he had been recommended to Deutsch for possible recruitment.

It is commonly believed that Philby's overbearing father had predisposed him to subvert the established order in Britain. One of his closest associates, however, believes that it was St John's frequent *absences* from his son's life, rather than the attitudes he passed on, that laid the ground. That gap was filled by Arnold Deutsch, not the stone-faced apparatchik with snow on his boots of caricature, but a man of enormous charisma for whom the young Kim quickly showed the same unquestioning admiration that Edith Tudor-Hart, at seventeen, had shown. Philby and Deutsch might have been made for one another. Talking years later, Philby evinced a form of devotion for Deutsch, speaking of the first time they met as 'an amazing conversation' with a 'simply marvellous man' who, plainly, 'loved people'. 'The first thing you noticed about him were his eyes. He looked at you as if nothing more important in life and more interesting than you and talking to you existed at that moment.' He was 'a kindly alien', had a marvellous education, humanity and a fidelity to building a new society with new human relations. He was well brought up, composed and had a marvellous sense of humour. The rebel in him had found a mentor of his own, one obviously moved by the poverty on his doorstep in a way his headstrong father didn't seem to be.

Deutsch, too, was delighted to find in Philby a willing recruit to Moscow's cause, and reported to his bosses as follows: '[Philby] comes from a peculiar family. His father is considered at present to be the most distinguished expert on the Arab world ... He is an ambitious tyrant and wanted to make a great man out of his son. He repressed all his son's desires. That is why [Kim] is a very timid and irresolute person. He has a bit of a stammer and this increases his diffidence ... He enjoys great love and respect for his seriousness and honesty. He was ready, without questioning, to do anything for us and has shown all his seriousness and diligence in working for us.'

Deutsch said Philby referred to his parents and his entire social milieu 'with unfeigned contempt and hatred'. This was music to the ears of the NKVD, the state security agency of the Soviet Union, the predecessor of the KGB. They believed, probably wrongly, that St John Philby was working for British intelligence, and wanted Kim to spy on him. Remarkably, he agreed to do so.

Theodore Maly, another key figure in recruiting from Cambridge, said in April 1936 that Philby was his favourite: 'I like [Philby] the most ... I only wonder where such a young man acquires such extensive and deep knowledge. At the same time, he is very modest, even too modest. When discussing work plans, he does not have any doubts about his personal life. He is so serious that you forget that he is only 26 years old.'*

It was not just anger that Philby had to offer. He was articulate (despite the stammer), had charm, a talent for languages, drive, a sense of adventure, a calculating mind, a talent for dissimulation and he was ripe for the plucking. Though he

---

* In fact he was only twenty-four at the time.

disdained many of his father's opinions, he shared a talent for troublemaking and a contempt for facile opinion. He also had the 'strain of irresponsibility' that he regarded as an essential part of the rounded human being.

Whereas in the late 1930s many on the left in Britain went to fight on the side of the communists in the Spanish Civil War, or joined the Communist Party of Great Britain, or both, Philby chose to go undercover. He had become convinced that support for the Soviet Union as the bulwark against fascism was the only effective course, and he was encouraged to offer that support covertly. It is this choice that angers his British critics. Couldn't he, like the others who signed up to work for the USSR, have been honest enough to wear his politics on his sleeve, by joining the Communist Party? No, because he could be more effective this way, rather than being – as he might have seen it – a lost oddball among the millions of naïve souls playing the democratic game. As Deutsch put it: 'An avowed communist can never get near the real truth, but somebody moving as real bourgeois among bourgeois could.'

Cecil Day-Lewis once said: 'No one who did not go through [the 1930s] can quite realise how much hope there was in the air then, how radiant for some of us was the illusion that man could, under Communism, put the world to rights.' For some, this ideal, this end, justified any means. The young man who had been chastising himself for submitting to the likelihood of a 'bourgeois career' now had a sense of mission. Philby's suitability for this sort of work distinguishes him, even in the double-dealing world of spies. With an overbearing father, he had been used to keeping his thoughts to himself and, in the words of his friend Tim Milne, 'shutting off the world from the inner keep'. Plus, secrecy brought its own thrill, and maybe he already knew that he excelled at it. Anthony Blunt, for whom art history was always going to be the most powerful calling, contrasted himself with Philby, whose chief ambition had long been to be a spy. He had an astonishing facility for deceit. Having also the convictions, he was ready to play his role.

And it was indeed playing a role. He converted himself, for public consumption, into a supporter of fascism, usually – there were a small number of exceptions – brushing off his leftist undergraduate leanings, to those insolent enough to ask, as youthful folly. He edited the English-language publication of The Link, an organisation that sought to foster Anglo-German friendship, meeting Joachim von Ribbentrop, appointed as Hitler's ambassador to London in 1936, and on occasion flying to Berlin. He shunned old friends which, much later in life, colleagues said upset him, but this was all grist to his mill. Not only would his development of a bogus new political persona help him in the future, it was also useful at the time, Moscow wanting to be apprised of Anglo-German relations. After a bad start – she thought him 'the rather stuffy sort' – he started a relationship with Frances Lindsay-Hogg (née Doble), a noted right-wing actress with Francoist sympathies, barely mentioning his true politics and allowing her to assume he shared hers. Notwithstanding alarming reports from Russia of Stalin's murderous regime, and the paranoia-driven purges that saw some of his contacts in London simply vanish (often murdered), his course was set. As far as his associates were aware, his wife Lizi simply ceased to be part of his life.

An unshakeable amiability saw him breeze into journalism, some of it covering the Spanish Civil War. This was a largely Moscow-inspired move, and while he was there he was tasked with assisting – or possibly perpetrating – the assassination of General Franco. He made his first move into the underbelly of the British state by following his friend Guy Burgess into Section D of what is now widely known as MI6 in July 1940. This was at Brickendonbury Manor, Hertfordshire, the gimcrack 'school for spies' and forerunner of the Beaulieu-based training centre, which he later joined, for the Special Operations Executive (SOE). There Kim's intelligence and talent for deception, in the noblest of causes, earned him much credit as a teacher, but joining SOE had meant no longer being close to the 'friends', as SIS's employees used to refer to themselves, which took him further from power than the aspiring subversive wanted.

Kim, though, was making his own friends along the way. One of these, who he had met at Brickendonbury, was Tomás Harris, and the pair were to become extremely close. The half-Spanish Harris had been a painter in his youth but had turned, very profitably, to art dealing. He and his wife Hilda were accomplished social entertainers, offering hospitality, chiefly to MI5 and MI6 employees, at their magnificent house, Garden Lodge, in Kensington. Philby recalled gatherings with his set: 'Tommy was an amazingly generous fellow ... We had a little drinking circle at his place. You'd drop in to see who was around. Tommy, as the host, was there most of the time. The others came and went. The regulars were me, Burgess, Blunt and perhaps Aneurin Bevan. Victor Rothschild dropped in from time to time but he wasn't one of the regulars.' Also on the roster were Tim Milne and Peter Wilson, later chairman of Sotheby's, who was to buy half of one of Harris's houses. Harris, knowing of Philby's Spanish experience, had mentioned him to another occasional visitor to the Kensington soirées, Dick Brooman-White of MI6, who was looking for someone to identify Iberian spies who MI5 would then arrest as they arrived in Britain. Philby, of course, fitted the bill perfectly.

A much earlier application to join the civil service – as his Soviet masters wished – had been withdrawn after his true politics risked becoming apparent, but when this new opportunity, in 1941, appeared, his charm and connections were sufficient to see him in. Besides, by this time recruiters were more worried by applicants with a fascist rather than a communist past, and his name was given by Brooman-White to Dick White of MI5, thence to Section V's head, Felix Cowgill, whose deputy, Colonel Valentine Vivian, took Kim and his father St John – a friend of Vivian for over three decades – to a doubtless agreeable lunch. While Kim was in the lavatory, St John was able to assure Vivian that his son's communism was 'schoolboy nonsense'. He was now a 'reformed character'. And that was that. He was in.

Such nepotism is easily mocked and the shortcomings in due diligence remain breathtaking, even allowing for the urgent needs of the time and a degree of informality. But the notion that young Philby, so English, so decent, so likeable, might be a traitor would have been just as far-fetched to the hundreds of people who knew him later in his career. It would not, did not, occur to them, and even many of those who had been alerted to specific suspicions about him found it scarcely imaginable. The comparable progress of his Foreign Office colleagues Guy Burgess and Donald Maclean seems to have been similarly problem-free. Maclean had been posted to Paris before the war and married Melinda Marling, the left-leaning daughter of a Chicago oil executive, before being called back and spending most of the war in London before a spell in Washington.

For some of Philby's Cambridge contemporaries, the decision to sign up to serve the Soviet Union was to be the source of life-defining anxiety. Philby never admitted to any such concerns, only to minor quibbles. He was ideological, truly committed, and he needed to be. His loyalty to the cause must have been tested countless times, yet he stayed true to Stalin and communism. The alternative view is that he only stayed loyal to Moscow because not to do so would have meant risking a death sentence, the Russians feeling he knew too much.

Yet his commitment seems to have been sincere. He was an unflinching believer in a way that Anthony Blunt, who did what he could to distance himself from the USSR after the war, was not.

Philby's deception, in contrast to Blunt's, was a pretence of astonishing proportions and durability, and the first few months of the war provided the sternest test of that loyalty. Many of the Soviet Union's intelligence officers including Deutsch had been withdrawn and/or purged by Stalin in the late 1930s, leaving just one in London, who knew next to nothing about Philby.*

In late August 1939 Germany and Russia signed a non-aggression pact, and a week later Germany invaded Poland, which Britain had pledged to defend. By not meekly acquiescing to Nazi aggression – the prospect of which had radicalised so many – Britain was bringing to reality the war that Philby had predicted six years earlier. What he had not predicted was that he, with his secret support for Stalin, would be lining up alongside the Nazis. The pact came as a huge shock to the left and meant Philby's support for Stalin could well be hastening the fall of Britain to fascism. He let his bemusement show, asking his handlers why the pact was necessary and what had happened to the single-front struggle against fascism, but he knuckled down nonetheless. Philby's co-conspirator Anthony Blunt said later that the pact was 'a tactical necessity for Russia to gain time, as indeed turned out to be the case, to give them time to rearm and so to get stronger to resist what was clearly going to happen'.

Maybe sensing Philby's discomfort at the pact, Moscow

---

* Theodore Maly, who had been involved in Philby's recruitment, for example, had been recalled to Moscow. Before returning to Moscow, Maly, who seemingly anticipated his fate, told Philby to 'continue on the true path'. Maly was shot for purported disloyalty. His name was cleared in 1956.

reciprocated, manifesting great distrust of Philby, and in February 1940 all contact with him was ended. It is unclear if he had passed information to the Russians that ended up in Nazi hands, but his evasiveness on this much later in life suggests he may well have done.

Yet his commitment endured. He displayed what his biographer Genrikh Borovik calls a 'submissiveness coefficient' and wanted to stay the course. Christopher Andrew reports that his subsequent career as a Soviet agent 'was due only to his persistence in trying to renew contact with Soviet intelligence, which had lost interest in him'. When relations resumed early in 1941, he retained the conviction, or conceit, of a believer. And with the Soviet Union back as an ally, having made its strategic decisions first to defer and now to renew its fight with Hitler, the British and the Russians were on the same side again. For the time being at least, there was no contradiction between immediate British and Soviet aims. Philby's work, at the time mostly Spain-related, was unambiguously in the service of defeating fascism, his original motivator. Or that, at least, was what he could tell himself.

The twists and turns of Philby's war are beyond the scope of this book. Much remains the subject of speculation in a field where there is both a public appetite for novelty and a desire among some authors to paint Philby even blacker than the facts can bear, so caution is needed. Inside MI6, he was open – and not alone – in pressing for the sharing of more intelligence with the West's Russian allies. But historians are divided as to how much influence he had.

Some believe Philby helped scupper wartime US/UK/ German talks, fearing that, had Britain done a deal with Hitler – which would have saved thousands of British lives – many German troops would have been freed for the assault on Moscow. It has also been claimed that Philby under-represented the strength of German opposition to Hitler, which meant it was given little support by the Allies.

Those looking for a stick with which to beat Philby will enjoy the idea that he helped prolong the war in order to help achieve total defeat of Germany – which would have suited long-term Soviet goals – but the evidence remains thin. As Nigel West points out, 'Philby was never in a position to generate reporting on the German opposition'.

But Philby did have an interest in stoking Soviet fears that London and Washington were plotting against Stalin. A striking example of this concerned the flight of Rudolf Hess, a close associate of Hitler, who flew solo to Scotland in May 1941, hoping to arrange peace talks with the Duke of Hamilton. Whether Hess was 'expected' is still unclear, but some believe that the trip was part of a fiendish British plan to make peace with Germany (rather than vice versa), which would markedly improve Hitler's chances of then seeing off the communist menace from the east. Philby told the Russians he had attended an evening in Germany before the war, at which he had witnessed Hess dining with Hamilton. This was the precursor to Hess's extraordinary visit, he said, confident that evidence of it would be bound to play on Stalin's sense that the West was double-dealing.

Philby's claim lay unchallenged for nearly seventy years, until the papers were made public. It turned out the dinner was an invention. 'My father never met Hess,' says Lord Selkirk, the peer's son and an authority on Hess's mysterious mission. In short, Philby had exaggerated his own knowledge and contacts, and had invented a dinner to support his belief, a belief that could only have sown suspicion. As Christopher Andrew and Oleg Gordievsky put it: 'contributing to Moscow's distrust of British intentions was to be one of Philby's main achievements as a wartime Soviet agent.' He is not the first or last spy – or journalist – to gild the lily, but it does invite speculation as to what else he told Stalin and why.*

There has been comparable uncertainty over two long-standing Catholic critics of Nazism, the Vermehrens. Erich Vermehren was a military intelligence officer living at the Abwehr's foreign headquarters in Istanbul. In 1944 he and his wife decided they could no longer work under the Nazi regime. After a huge process of reassurance and persuasion, Nicholas and Elizabeth Elliott were able to help them escape Turkey via Egypt, ending up, hugely relieved, staying in London at the Drayton Gardens home of Kim Philby's mother Dora. Elliott's smooth landing of these two big fish from under the noses of the Nazis was praised to the skies, and further defections followed.

The allegation against Philby is that the religious Vermehrens revealed to London the names of the anti-Hitler, anti-communist individuals (many of them Catholic) who might work towards the setting up of a liberal democratic Germany after the war. This was not something the Russians wanted. The claim from Phillip Knightley, on the evidence of an unnamed MI5 officer, was that when Allied officers went to find them after the war to help with the necessary political reconstruction, most of them had been shot. Historian Richard Bassett, who spoke extensively to Erich Vermehren late in life, believed at least a dozen of the names were eliminated in one way or

---

* There is some evidence that he suppressed information that might have encouraged London to speak to dissenting factions in Germany – including Admiral Wilhelm Canaris, who was eventually hanged for treason a few weeks before the end of the war. See Richard Bassett, *Hitler's Spy Chief: The Wilhelm Canaris Mystery*. Towards the end of the war Moscow was less keen than ever on Germany reaching an early peace – with anybody. By that point, it envisaged an all-out military defeat of Nazism and the imposition of an essentially puppet, pro-communist government in Berlin. In the event that occurred only in what became 'East Germany'. Philby was not merely following orders. He wrote: 'One of the reasons I acted as I did was because the total defeat of Germany was almost a personal matter for me. I had strong feelings about the war and I was directly responsible for the death of a considerable number of Germans.'

another, often taken to Soviet prison camps, and some returned after 1955.

But spy writer Nigel West reports that in Vermehren's MI5 Personal File there was indeed a list, but it contained only six names. Three of those were executed for their part in the 20 July plot to kill Hitler, and two more lived on decades after the war was over. The fate of only one remains unknown. There is no sign of there having been any further list.

Russian leaders could not believe the insistence of Philby and others that the British had so little interest in spying on Russia – MI6 had not had a base in Moscow since 1936. London had been anxious to demonstrate loyalty to 'our Soviet allies', and Churchill, in principle, wanted the Russians to be 'told everything', but such openness was discouraged by an essentially mistrustful Moscow. Donald McLachlan, author of a book on naval intelligence, said the Russians simply did not want to collaborate. Yet on occasions the refusal of the British government to hand over to its Russian allies the raw material made perfect sense, like that from Ultra, information derived from the breaking of German codes, for example. The British feared leaks, which would have been disastrous, from Moscow to the Nazis, quite rightly, as was later acknowledged in Moscow. Instead, Moscow had to rely on material being provided covertly by the Cambridge spies.

Soviet scepticism was spreading. Not only did they mistrust their allies in the war against Hitler, they mistrusted their own agents. A report by Elena Modrzhinskaya that surfaced in late 1943 caught a mood among a faction in Moscow, and fed it yet further. She concluded that Philby and his friends had been planted by British intelligence and that the extraordinary bonanza of information – documents in their thousands – they were providing should be treated with extreme suspicion. In support of her case, she pointed out that 'not a single valuable

British agent in the USSR or in the Soviet embassy in Britain has been exposed with the help of this group, in spite of the fact that if they had been sincere in their cooperation they could easily have done so'. The reason was simpler, though not one likely to convince her plot-fixated bosses: there were none.

Philby's analysis work for the Iberian sub-section of MI6's Section V, from October 1941, was based in St Albans, Hertfordshire, where he lived with Aileen and his rapidly expanding family. But he often needed to be in London for work, and also mixing socially with both work colleagues and friends from Cambridge. Another venue for wartime conviviality, a flat owned by a friend in Bentinck Street, became a scene of almost Babylonian excess, at least in the minds of some excitable writers, possibly because when there was an air raid, eight people would have to sleep in the same room. Two of Kim's contemporaries from Cambridge, Tess Mayor, then working for MI5, and her beautiful, lionised friend Patricia Rawdon-Smith, had been offered a lease on the flat, which was owned by Tess's boss Victor Rothschild. The pair were delighted to accept, but needed an extra person to help pay the rent, and invited another friend from Cambridge and a colleague in MI5, Anthony Blunt, to join them.

Before long Blunt mentioned that his friend Guy Burgess was also in need of a flat, and it was agreed he should move in, too, on condition that 'he doesn't bring pick-ups back' (which of course he did). The goings-on at Bentinck Street were doubtless far more staid than espionage fable has claimed, as Blunt was to point out many years later. There was a war on, after all, and gregarious though these bright young things were, they had serious jobs to do where thousands of lives were at stake. But amid the fire-watching and the earnest talk, there were social gatherings at which accomplished Cambridge chums like Kim Philby were always welcome.

Kim Philby and Anthony Blunt had not been close, but they

came to appreciate one another during the Bentinck Street years. Both were friends, admirers and fellow mitigators of the various forms of damage done by Guy Burgess, who had been instrumental in the professional advance of both of them. Biographer Phillip Knightley was told by Philby that one day in 1941 Blunt had approached Philby and given him a fright, saying: 'I know what you're doing. Well, I'm doing it too.'

In 1943, when Kim's work moved, the Philbys and their daughter Josephine moved from St Albans to London. He was doing sterling work for MI6 in the battle against Germany, and that battle seemed to be going the right way.

As Allied forces advanced on Germany and with the bipolarity of post-war Europe looking inescapable, the summer of 1944 was a watershed for Philby. The various shades of wartime ambiguity that had marked relations between the liberal democratic West and the Moscow-oriented eastern part of Europe had evaporated. With Europe riven in two, Philby's desire to challenge capitalism required a far deeper commitment than that of the early years of undergraduate dilettantism or even of his experiences of brutality on the streets of Vienna. As if to confirm his commitment, according to recently released Russian papers, as the end of the war approached, Pavel Fitin, chief of Soviet foreign intelligence, secured Stalin's agreement to pay their London comrades, Philby being offered the most, 'of course'. They all rejected the money, although seemingly Philby had accepted a 'bonus' some months earlier. On 18 August 1944 he sent a note to Moscow expressing thanks for the 'gift'. He was pleased that 'more closely than ever [it] connects me with those whom I have always considered to be true companions and friends, although I have never seen them. Both the message and the gift allow me to definitely think that I have made some contribution to the greatest achievement of the Soviet people in the fight against fascism.' And in choosing that path to oppose fascism, he had levered the irksome gap – unnoticed by many of his friends – between him and his own privileged British elite into a chasm. There was no room for wavering. He was truly committed. Philby and his employers in London SW1 were on opposite sides.

By way of confirming this, he achieved a remarkable career move. Through a series of manoeuvres so deft they belong in a manual of office politics, he managed to get himself made head of Section IX, a new anti-Soviet department of MI6. As Ben Macintyre puts it, 'The fox was not merely guarding the hen house, but building it, running it, assessing its strengths and frailties, and planning its future construction.' It was a masterstroke by as natural a penetration agent, let alone spy, as can be imagined.

But there was to be a reminder of how high the stakes had become. In August, an extremely nervous Konstantin Volkov of the NKVD walked into the British consulate in Istanbul. He had sent messages saying he wanted to meet the vice-consul, Chantry Hamilton Page, but – shockingly – these had been ignored, so here he was, in person. He had a proposal. In return for asylum in Britain and a generous capital sum, Volkov would provide the British with a list of Soviet agents in the UK and more in Turkey. The danger to Philby was clear.*

This was not the first time he had had a scare. In 1937 a Soviet intelligence officer had defected and had mentioned 'a young Englishman, a journalist of good family, an idealist and fanatical anti-Nazi', who had been sent to Spain to kill General Franco. This had indeed been a task assigned to Philby, but the mission had been aborted, and he came close to losing his own life when his three fellow passengers died as their car was hit by a republican shell. Walter Krivitsky couldn't identify the

---

* Precisely what Volkov was able to offer remains the subject of some debate, but it is sufficient to assume he could do great damage to Soviet interests.

putative assassin by name and, Spain being the *cause célèbre* of the day among the socially concerned middle classes, the 'good family' description did not usefully narrow the field.

But Volkov said he could also produce documents, copied or stolen from the highest quarters in London and now held, he claimed, in an unoccupied flat in Moscow, to which he had easy access. The existence of these documents would prove the guilt of those he accused. It was an astonishing offer. Volkov was deputy head of Soviet intelligence in Turkey. His information was priceless, and he insisted that the utmost security be observed. There was to be no electronic transmission of messages, and strictly only those who needed to know should be informed. If the British didn't bite within three weeks, the deal was off, but he knew what the British badly needed to know, so surely they would. He knew, for instance, that in London one of these agents was acting as the head of a section of British counter-espionage.

The British ambassador of the time would have no truck with spookery and, besides, this was far too big a deal to be handled locally. With MI6's chief in Turkey out of the loop entirely, ten days later news of the offer reached Sir Stewart Menzies, head of MI6, by diplomatic bag, as Volkov had insisted. Menzies summoned the obvious person, the ever-reliable Kim Philby, to discuss the next step. Philby, no doubt, would know the right thing to do. He duly declared the offer 'something of the greatest importance' and, secretly terrified, asked to sleep on it overnight. 'The only course was to put a bold face on it,' he later wrote.

That evening he conferred urgently with his London handler, who conferred with Moscow, who conferred with Turkey, creating a spike in traffic between those embassies. Philby realised he needed to strangle this scheme in its cradle, and the following morning put forward a plan with that in mind.

Unhelpfully, though, Menzies had a contribution to make. The previous evening, while Philby was plotting with his Soviet masters, Menzies crossed St James's Park from his office on Broadway for a drink at his club, White's in St James's. There, perhaps unsurprisingly, he bumped into Douglas Roberts, head of one of Britain's intelligence-gathering bodies, based in Cairo, called Security Intelligence Middle East. Roberts was a Russian-speaker who happened to be on leave in London, and was surely just the chap to fly to Turkey and arrange to have Volkov and his wife spirited away to British-controlled Egypt – as the Vermehrens had been – and on to London.

Menzies was delighted with his suggestion, not least because, unusually, it hadn't depended on Philby attending to the difficult bits. What could be easier than to ask Roberts? Philby, seeing a potentially calamitous situation becoming completely unmanageable, feigned delight. But he was in luck. As it happened, Roberts was terrified of flying (which Menzies, surprisingly or not, didn't know), and ruled himself out unreservedly. Nicholas Elliott, then stationed in Switzerland and with easy access to Istanbul, was another obvious 'King and Country' candidate, so Philby didn't encourage that idea either. Finally, as if reluctant but wanting to help Menzies out, Philby said he would go – to his boss's 'obvious relief'.

Philby's supposedly hurried preparations were so thorough, his storm-delayed flight so circuitous, consular weekends so sacred (there was sailing to be done) and protocol so rigid that attempts to reach their man were not made until after Volkov's deadline had elapsed. When asked why no one had come sooner, Philby told a colleague, 'Sorry, old man, it would have interfered with leave arrangements.'

Philby and another British official tried to reach Volkov via the Soviet consulate's phone line, but were fobbed off with the hollowest of excuses. Philby did his best to look disappointed as the pair considered what to do next, but he knew his bacon had been saved. During Philby's almost comedically slow passage to Istanbul – 'I thought he was just irresponsible and incompetent,' said a colleague – Moscow had sent two 'couriers' to Istanbul. Volkov and his wife, both on stretchers and heavily sedated, were put on a plane to Moscow, where Volkov admitted planning to reveal the names of 314 Soviet agents in Turkey. Some years later, Eleanor asked Philby if he had ever killed a man. Philby said not directly, explaining that in Istanbul someone had discovered that he was a Russian agent. In that case, he said, it had been absolute necessity that the man be killed. This was presumably Volkov.

Phillip Knightley asked Philby about the episode in the late 1980s, but aside from telling him that Volkov 'was "a nasty piece of work" and deserved what he got', Philby was reluctant to discuss it. As with so many episodes in the Philby story, there was to be a sequel, as we shall see.

It had been the narrowest of squeaks and had shaken him hugely. Who was to say another defector, now disabused of any hopes for a brighter future under Stalin, might not pop up at another Western embassy? The pressure was both enormous and, as long as he stayed in the West, unending. (Had he confessed to the British, despite his extant beliefs, he risked either a long prison sentence or even execution for treason, or murder.) His old Westminster School friend, travelling companion and now deputy in MI6 Tim Milne, though unaware of the double game Philby was playing, remembers 'a perceptible change' in Philby's drinking around that time. Before 1945, he had barely seen Philby much the worse for drink. After that, particularly with non-work friends, 'he was not usually aggressive or unpleasant: just drunk'.

His co-conspirators Burgess and Maclean also found that the strains of this double life called for industrial quantities of alcohol. Anthony Blunt, also a keen drinker, was never as driven by pure politics as the others and wanted to return to his studies, as far as his previous commitments to the Soviet Union and to his friends would allow. Philby had no such qualms, and his work continued. After the war, as the Soviet Union sought to surround itself with friendly countries, Philby served his Moscow bosses by identifying to them British-backed subversives sent to foment difficulties in the region.

It was not until 1946 that he formally jettisoned his life with Lizi, although they had barely seen one another for years. He explained to Valentine Vivian that he needed to extricate himself from another element of his impetuous youth in order to do the decent thing with the mother of his children (or to remedy his 'sordid private life', as an MI5 memo put it). In September of that year he travelled to Paris to meet Lizi and arrange the divorce. Kim and Aileen, seven months pregnant with their fourth child, married a week later. The couple had moved into a large house in Carlyle Square, the twenty-year lease paid for by Mrs Alleyne.

Malcolm Muggeridge recalls visiting the Philbys there: the family 'made a most pleasant impression; [Aileen] was pretty, sensible, a good but not doting mother, intelligent but not intellectual . . . She and Philby seemed very happy together; he was quite at his best with his children and the sunshine of domesticity . . . she and Philby gave me no sense of strife or strain; all that was nicest and simplest and gayest in Philby came out, it seemed to me, when they were together with their children.'

Aileen had hoped Philby might return to journalism after the war, but he was doing too well to leave MI6, having been awarded the Order of the British Empire in January 1946. He was trusted, popular, efficient, professionally accomplished and heading for a senior position. In February 1947 came Philby's posting, purportedly as first secretary but in reality as head of station for MI6, to Istanbul, where his protégé Nicholas Elliott had recently served. This was an in-the-field position that gave him an opportunity to shine in a country of mounting strategic importance as tensions rose between East and West. The family was installed in a palatial home abutting the Asian side of the Bosphorus. Aileen's problems had receded, and, though she had domestic help, her hands were full with four lively children born barely five years apart. An Istanbul-based American colleague of Kim recalls Aileen the supportive wife complementing Kim's charm: 'Of a frightening thinness, I never saw her triste: she was always full of laughter, not a little of it attractively self-deprecatory, and she was good and easy company.' Fate was to be cruel to her indeed.

Kim's daily commute to the consulate on the European side was an agreeable ferry journey. It was the diplomatic high life indeed. 'I remember liking him definitely,' remembers Feyhan Sporel, whose parents were friends with the Philbys in Istanbul. 'He was fun to be with and he adored his children. Josephine [Sporel's contemporary] was always saying: "Daddy bought me this, Daddy did that." It was always Daddy, not Mummy. My father never bought me presents like Kim did.'

According to someone who visited him at the time, professionally he had been 'entirely corrupted' by the diplomatic life. 'All passion, it seemed, was spent. He had become a *routinier* and a voluptuary [. . .] He would ensure professional standards; but would not disturb the ancient habits of the professionals. He was both efficient and safe.'

How wrong this was, and he was excellently placed to exert an influence. Increasingly the West saw menace in the Soviet insistence on controlling parts of Eastern Europe, and welcomed any opportunity to take advantage of exiles, or prospective exiles, disenchanted with life under Moscow rule. As MI6 sought to recruit as many penetration agents as it could from the USSR's southern fringes, so Philby, via his friend Burgess, sabotaged any such plans, handing their details over to his KGB masters. 'We knew in advance about every operation that took place, by air, land or sea, even in the mountainous and inaccessible regions.'

In 1948, he interviewed Ismail Akhmedov, who had defected from Soviet military intelligence to Turkey in 1942. Here, too, was an opportunity to assist his Russian colleagues. Akhmedov told Philby about his sister-in-law back in Russia, a Stalin critic. Philby suggested he write her a letter, telling her of his freedom, which Philby said the British embassy would ensure reached her. Thus he acquired the name and address of another enemy of the regime, all grist to Stalin's mill. It was only years later that Akhmedov realised 'this dirty trick was used by Philby to victimise a poor innocent lady'. Hers was one of many names of military and political figures Akhmedov passed on, believing he was talking to a loyal servant of the Crown. Though ostensibly as professional as ever, Philby let slip a couple of questions that would be of more use to a foreign Soviet mole contemplating his long-term future – 'how [does] the Soviet intelligence treat foreigners who work for them?' – than to his bosses in London. He also failed to ask questions about Akhmedov's background, presumably because his masters in Moscow had already filled him in.

Philby's ideological drive burned as brightly as ever. In 1948 a celebrated collection of writing was being edited by a young Labour Party member, Richard Crossman. In *The God That Failed*, six eminent writers, including André Gide, Arthur Koestler and Stephen Spender, wrote of how they had moved on from their early belief in communism, or 'ratted', as Philby put it. Their eyes had been opened, they wrote, to the horrors that had been committed by Stalin, and the book became one of the most influential documents of post-war anti-communist writing. But Philby's path was set, his mind was no longer open.

Hugh Trevor-Roper later said it had 'withdrawn from the world of ideas'.

Aileen did not like Guy Burgess and felt he was a bad influence on Kim. She once said that one thing was certain: Guy was not coming to stay again. Predictably that didn't prevent his visit to Istanbul of August 1948, which, like so many others, was the occasion for considerable misbehaviour of the sort that suggested an underlying tension – shared by both men – as much as boys simply letting off steam (at which, admittedly, Burgess excelled). On one occasion Burgess jumped into the sea from a second-floor balcony of the house at Vaniköy, injuring his back. His days were spent sloping around the family home in a revealing dressing gown and his evenings spent out, while Philby fretted about the danger to their security of his libidinous double-agent friend on the loose in Istanbul. Not that Philby was always a steadying influence as a supervisor. The pair got through fifty-two brandies in one long afternoon at the Moda Yacht Club.

For his posting in Istanbul, Kim had asked his secretary Esther Whitfield to come with him. Whitfield was widely admired, knew the Philby family well and liked and admired Aileen enormously.

Philby mentioned to Aileen that Burgess, famous for his ill-concealed homosexuality, had developed a passion for Esther. To Aileen, and others, it was far more likely that the ever-attentive Whitfield and Philby himself were having an affair (and they may well have been) but, remarkably, this far-fetched story was true.* This dissonance added to Aileen's sense that there was more to the man she had married than she had realised, and he was showing signs of being preoccupied. The charm was hiding something, but what?

---

* The Whitfield-Burgess relationship is an extraordinary one, with her being one of the few people to find even a hint of heterosexuality in Burgess.

Philby's libido and his attractiveness to women would have fed the suspicions of anyone, let alone a vulnerable, exhausted partner in urgent need of human attention, affection and medical care. Aileen's old trouble re-emerged, and she immersed herself in mounting bouts of self-harm and pyromania. A visit from Dora Philby, for whom Aileen had more admiration than affection, provided brief reassurance that the adored son was not conducting an affair with Whitfield, but Aileen's problems persisted. One day she returned from a drive, evidently having been attacked in her car near the house at Vaniköy and with her head badly grazed. Kim was enormously upset and insisted they move house. Neighbours had been sceptical and she later admitted her injuries had been self-inflicted.

In the summer of 1949, Kim was appointed to be Britain's chief liaison with the CIA and FBI and was posted to Washington with his family. It was a hugely prestigious position, and brought him into contact with the most senior figures in the US administration, as well as friends like Sam Pope Brewer and Miles Copeland from earlier years. It was the start of the superpower era when American espionage was to supersede that of the British, by tradition the experts (with a high-handed way of showing it). The popular and respected Philby, who had served so impressively in Turkey, a country regarded by the US as on the front line in the confrontation with the USSR, was an admirable antidote to any such friction, an ideal appointment at the dawn of US involvement in NATO. He appeared to thrive, and in many respects he did, but Esther Whitfield said Philby hated America, and found Washington horrible and false. His work there, though, was invaluable to his Soviet masters. According to former chief of counterintelligence Oleg Kalugin, the damage Philby did at that time to the West was 'enormous'. 'Among other things,' wrote Kalugin, 'he passed along precise information about Western efforts to parachute Russian-speaking illegals into the Soviet Union. The information, along with many of his other tips, led to the capture and execution of dozens of Western agents in the Soviet Union, a by-product of his work that (on the surface at least) never seemed to bother Philby.'

By the late 1940s, most of Europe belonged to one camp or another. The Balkans didn't quite fit the pattern, with Marshal Tito in Yugoslavia establishing a brand of communism that aspired to independence from Stalin. Neighbouring Albania was regarded by some in the West as being up for grabs, and they sought to restore King Zog to the throne he had lost in 1939. The country was not only critically poor but under the iron rule of a Stalinist dictator, Enver Hoxha. Encouraged by émigrés and British mavericks who had had experience there during the war, in late 1949 MI6 and the CIA collaborated with Albanian refugees to organise an armed landing on the Albanian coast. A second one was arranged for the spring of the following year. During that time, Philby flew several times from Washington to Italy and Greece, and knew of the plans.

The appropriate forces were alerted and the arriving 'liberators' shot, some as they landed by parachute. The entire episode was a mistake, based on poor preparation and a misreading of the extent to which Albanians would welcome their 'liberators' on the ground. The émigré groups had been thoroughly penetrated by Hoxha's people, so their arrival was not the surprise they had hoped, and Kim Philby, with the help of Guy Burgess, played his part in passing on information about the plan. His role in the deaths of would-be 'liberators' of Albania came to be one of the major charges levelled at Philby after his exposure, partly because it is the most easily identified, in outline at least. Whether his role was decisive is uncertain, and an academic debate continues. Mikhail Liubimov said: 'We didn't need Kim Philby to tell us the British were coming. It was clear to us in any case.' Precisely what he did and how many men's deaths he was directly responsible for are unknown, but his ultimate loyalty is clear.

During this period, Teddy Kollek, then an official with the Israeli government but later long-standing mayor of Jerusalem, happened to see Philby in Washington. Kollek had attended Philby's wedding to Lizi in 1934 in Vienna, and knew all about the happy couple's politics. He told Angleton that Philby was a communist, but the warning had little effect.

Burgess's stay in Washington was the highwater mark both for Philby's work for the Soviet Union and for that of Guy Burgess and Donald Maclean. Countless words have been written on this episode, but the bare bones are as follows. It became clear that Donald Maclean had been identified in the US as a possible Soviet mole. Mentally he had been in a poor state, indulging in heavy drinking, recklessness and homosexual affairs, culminating in a breakdown in Cairo in 1950. Now back in London and working on the Foreign Office's American desk, if he was questioned, as seemed probable within days, he would be likely to break down and risk exposing them all. Philby knew that Maclean was now under suspicion, but the initial problem was how to get word to Maclean in London.

The conduit was to be Guy Burgess, who, in an extraordinarily incriminating breach of spy protocol, had been living in Philby's house in Washington, where he had indulged himself to his customary excess, resulting in him being sent home by the British embassy. Burgess was to return to London to alert Blunt who would pass word on to Maclean. Meanwhile, in Washington Kim did his best to look perplexed at this extraordinary turn of events.

A plan was hatched to exfiltrate Maclean from London to Moscow, but was Maclean in any state to make so crucial a trip on his own? There continues to be dispute as to what exactly happened. What is known is that a few days before Maclean was due to be questioned, Burgess and Maclean took a steamer to France from Southampton harbour on the night of Friday 18 May 1951 and travelled to Moscow. Neither was ever seen on British soil again.

Philby's final words to Burgess as they said goodbye in Washington had been 'Don't you go too'. Such a move would not only confirm Burgess's guilt but point strongly to his own. But he did go, and Philby was furious, never fully acknowledging why Burgess, the man he had rescued from countless scrapes, incriminated him by going, too. He is not alone there. In the middle of the night, Esther Whitfield took the message from London that the pair had gone, but didn't wake Philby. He was astonished when she told him the news, she said, but with even more reason than she realised. Philby had fooled her, too.

Some accounts claim Maclean wanted a 'final fling' in Paris before being deposited in Soviet hands. True or not, it was decided that Burgess, as unlikely a candidate for keeping anyone on the straight and narrow as can be imagined, should be his chaperone.

What transpired suggests that Burgess was felt to be of no further use in the West. The London *rezident* Sergei Korovin told Burgess that once he had deposited Maclean in Soviet hands (in some still unspecified location, possibly even Moscow) he would be allowed to return. Burgess was tricked into staying.

It is fair to assume that Anthony Blunt, who in playing a major part in devising the British end of the escape plan never envisaged Burgess ending up in Moscow, was appalled at how the Russians 'took him out' by refusing to let Burgess return after he had delivered Maclean. Curiously, though, he did suggest later in life that he thought Burgess had made the decision to take some sort of radical action, at least, for himself. 'I have no doubt that the suggestion was made by Guy himself. He realised that his career in the Foreign Office was ruined. ... he knew he was finished and decided to get out, not taking into account the consequences that this action might have for his friends.' On the other hand Burgess told Graham Greene that he planned to deposit Maclean in Prague and then go to visit W. H. Auden in Ischia: 'But I found in Prague it was too late, I was caught up in things.' Blunt was required to play an important part in misleading investigators in the aftermath of the pair's disappearance. Before the sleuths arrived at Burgess's flat (or possibly at the same time – accounts vary), he hurriedly removed incriminating material, and some months later had helpfully passed on to MI5 the contents of a black box belonging to Burgess containing various personal items. Blunt had 'only just remembered' he had this, he said, although of course by then he had removed anything truly revealing.

Not only had Burgess's disappearance thrown a spotlight onto Philby and Blunt. It also raised the possibility that Moscow, in luring Burgess away and thus casting suspicion on Blunt and Philby, felt these two were dispensable. Had they really wanted to see them protected, surely they would have sent someone else with Maclean, like Yuri Modin, for example, who offered to go.

The subsequent questioning of Philby would have made him feel more high and dry than ever. Moscow could not be in touch as any sign of that would have condemned Philby – still under surveillance – at a stroke.

The Americans were convinced of Philby's guilt. Philby, with hollow heroism, pre-empted the sack when he met Sir Stewart Menzies. 'I'm no good to you now and never will be again,' he said. 'I'll put in my resignation. I think you'd better let me go.' Menzies was in no position to reject the resignation, much as he would have liked to. He had received a message from the CIA's director Walter Bedell Smith, the gist of which was 'fire Philby or we break off the intelligence relationship'. The message had been drafted by Bill Harvey, whose long-standing dislike for Philby would have been enhanced by Guy Burgess having drawn an obscene caricature of his wife Elizabeth at a party.

But the British, particularly his friends in MI6, were far less sure of his guilt, and here he was, playing on that. Had McCarthyism played a foul trick? How could this embodiment of a nice, virtuous man be anything other than a loyal servant of the Crown? Nonetheless, he was out, a truly burned-out case. He was to receive £4000 (worth well over £100,000 today), half immediately and the rest in £500 payments every six months, but the payment was not an official recognition of innocence. On the contrary. An internal Security Service memo by his chief interrogator acknowledged that while it could not be proved, 'for all practical purposes it should be assumed that Philby was a Soviet spy throughout his service for SIS'. His passport was confiscated, briefly, and he was ostentatiously observed at home by visiting police. His phone was bugged. He continued to be questioned, but he had taken the precaution of befriending, and drinking with, the obliging office archivist, so he was familiar with what investigators were likely to have unearthed about him. Just as he was fearing that he was losing track of the lies he had told and was in danger of contradicting himself, for lack of hard evidence, the questioning stopped, to his delight. The words of FBI boss J. Edgar Hoover proved correct: 'For my part, I conclude that [Philby] is as guilty as hell, but I don't see how you are ever going to prove it.' Work and money, though, continued to be a problem. He was on the verge of being appointed to a job covering the Indian elections for the *Daily Telegraph*, and another on the *Observer*, but nothing came of either.

The five years from 1951 to 1956 were spent in the UK, initially in Heronsgate near Rickmansworth, north-west of London, with Aileen, from whom he was increasingly estranged (but whose wealthy mother was paying many of their bills), and, by now, their five children. Philby looked for work – and came close to getting a job with Shell in Egypt, without success – and had to make do with a handful of scarcely satisfactory positions. He was drinking more and licking his wounds at the injustice he claimed he had been done. An American former colleague, James McCargar, writing in a newspaper article in 1967, recalled trying to rekindle their association: 'He was seedy, nearly haggard, and appeared to me embarrassed by my gesture. He did not pursue the connection and eventually dropped from my sight altogether.' What McCargar did not admit is that he had been encouraged to get alongside Philby by James Angleton. According to McCargar, both believed – notwithstanding their own suspicions about him – that Kim might still resurface in the ranks of MI6, possibly even as its head. If so, having shown a degree of support in this way might prove advantageous. Another omission from his article was some personal news Kim had mentioned – that his wife Aileen had become 'insane', had tried to kill him and was now sleeping in a tent in their garden. Intentionally or otherwise, Philby had diverted McCargar from his intention of asking about MI5's investigation into his past. His spirits were low. 'Several times during this period I revived the idea of escape,' he wrote later. 'The plan, originally designed for American conditions, required only minor modifications to adapt it to European circumstances.' But each time the immediate danger passed.

Some friends slipped off the scene, but Tim Milne, a companion of over twenty-five years, remained loyal, even when Philby tested that loyalty by conducting an affair with an actor, Connie (Constance Ashley-Jones), a friend of Milne's wife Marie, which often kept him in London overnight, supposedly staying with his mother. Aileen found out about the affair, adding to the tension between the couple. Philby drank more and more, and on one occasion, when they were out to dinner, the couple had an argument which ended with him punching and shattering the car's windscreen. Aileen drove home alone.

In the early 1950s he also managed to stay in close contact with Anthony Blunt, Surveyor of the Queen's Pictures and by now director of the Courtauld Institute, to whom he could talk, sometimes in his office at the Courtauld, more freely than to almost anyone. Blunt's calling was always art history, and as a friend and distant relation of the royal family he had been asked to perform some delicate tasks in Germany on their behalf as the war ended. Blunt admitted many years later that after Burgess and Maclean fled he had had 'orders' to go to Russia and he 'refused'. He had indeed cut down his spying activities enormously, but the KGB does not let go easily. He continued to defy KGB attempts to lure him to Moscow and had done everything possible short of incriminating himself to escape the USSR's clutches, trusting that his previous allegiance could never be proved. Nonetheless he shared a huge guilty secret and, when Burgess and Maclean needed help, felt he should aid those who had chosen the same path in the 1930s, if only for reasons of self-preservation.

Philby's thoughts of escape went right out of his head, he wrote, when he received, 'through the most ingenious of routes, a message from my Soviet friends, conjuring me to be of good cheer and presaging an early resumption of relations. It changed drastically the whole complexion of the case. I was no longer alone.'

This may have been the occasion when, at considerable personal risk, Anthony Blunt played messenger between Yuri Modin and Philby after the Russians became aware of Philby's urgent need of money. In the immediate years after 1951, Philby's use to the Russians would have been, as a former colleague put it, either 'nil or vestigial', but he was in a bad way and very short of money. A colleague believes that it was the prospect of missing his children that prevented him fleeing to Moscow in that period. In a scene of cinematographic furtiveness, Blunt, at that time under only minimal surveillance, met Modin just off London's Caledonian Road to receive an envelope containing £5000.* He passed it on to his hugely relieved friend before returning to his respectable life as an art historian of global repute.

The Burgess and Maclean scandal had cost Philby his job, and there was to be no respite. Was he the 'Third Man', who had tipped them off, or not? MI5 had failed to prove it, although its boss, Dick White, assumed that he was. Most anxious to know, of course, was Aileen. She had knowledge of parts of the truth about Kim. For all the love and sensitivity he showed towards the children, there was a cold side to him. He was adept at dismissing the unwelcome and sailing on – the very skills a long-term agent would need. The tell-tale signs in his professional life were piling up. Aileen thought she had married a mild, gently dissenting, left-inclined free-thinker, but maybe a talent for cold-blooded mendacity that occasionally revealed itself had equipped him to be, simply, a traitor. It seemed increasingly likely, yet she wanted to protect their children. She knew the case against him was alarming, but someone with known mental health problems making such an assertion about so genial a figure would look unbalanced and vindictive. Even to venture such a thought would appear callous towards her own children. She was trapped.

One of Philby's allies towards the end of his life was one of his biographers, Genrikh Borovik. He says that Philby was told that Aileen could be cured if she admitted that she had invented much of what she had claimed. To get her to make such admissions, Philby had to challenge and cajole her, which he did over

---

* According to Modin, Philby observed the handing over of the money from nearby, but Modin, knowing that to meet Philby would breach protocol, chose not to do so.

about ten days. Peeved at having failed to realise that his wife's injuries were self-inflicted, Philby eventually secured an admission that this was the case. She attended an expensive clinic, but this was no help at all to Philby. Increasingly she came to see him as the cause of her illness.

If her husband was indeed guilty, notwithstanding her mental state, that made her if not exactly powerful but, to him, dangerous. She would ask friends questions like: 'To whom should a wife's allegiance belong – her country or her husband?'

Most couples will be familiar with the embarrassment of quotidian domestic grumbles being aired in front of friends. In the category of 'Do we really have to discuss this now?' issues, a remark of Aileen's is surely in a class of its own. On one occasion, at one of their dinner parties with Patsy Collins, a schoolfriend of Aileen, and her husband Douglas, founder of the Goya cosmetics firm, an exasperated Aileen shrieked across the table: 'I *know* you're the Third Man!' Philby would explain later, with saintly patience, that doctors had found she was suffering from a syndrome that made her want to hurt most the people she loved most. 'That is why she tried to set fire to your house in Turkey,' he told an old friend, who must have been wondering.

One day Aileen called Nicholas Elliott, Philby's old MI6 friend, and told him Kim had gone ... 'I think to Russia'. Elliott was horrified. Could those wild, US-led allegations be true after all? She had had a telegram, she said. 'It says: "Farewell forever, love to the children. Angel."'* Elliott rushed to the Philbys' house to see the telegram, but Aileen said it had been read out to her. He chased the original through the Post Office, but it was nowhere to be found. She made a series of mysterious observations, leaving Elliott perplexed. His mind

---

* Angel is a nickname derived from Philby's initials: H.A.R.P.

was put at rest by a telephone call later that day to their home, answered by Philby himself.

The effect was the opposite of what Aileen had intended. She had drawn attention to her unstable state, and increased sympathy for her husband. A call she made to the Foreign Office, reporting him as the 'Third Man', was similarly ineffective.

She also tried Kim's father, expressing the concern that her husband might not only vanish to Moscow but take the children with him. St John Philby wrote to his wife: 'Aileen's letter seems to me to have been pretty fair tosh, and it seems pretty clear that she is not in command of her senses.' Any hope she had of winning the care of the children would have been remote indeed.

Although Philby had left MI6 and was in serious need of work, there is reason to believe that he may have been given odd pieces of off-the-books freelance work by his former colleagues. But the British failure to prove Philby's disloyalty continued to rile many among the USA's intelligence community. Nicholas Elliott had worked for Philby during the war. He knew the British needed to take the allegation seriously. Knowing Philby as well as anyone did, he made an offer to his bosses in MI6. He and his friend would go away for a weekend together. 'They went off to Newmarket and got royally drunk,' remembers a friend of Elliott. After two days of boys' bonding, Elliott came home and told his boss: 'There is no chance Philby is a double agent. Absolutely none.'

How much influence that weekend had on official thinking cannot be known, although it seems to have brought some reassurance. In September 1955 John Sinclair, head of MI6, wrote an internal memo to Patrick Dean, chairman of the Joint Intelligence Committee, saying, presumably with some relief as he had never been a believer in Kim's guilt, that recent investigations had failed to find any disloyalty in the many cases he had handled. Nonetheless, things were coming to a head. Another attempt to bring him down was launched, even though his accusers still had no killer blow to use against him. In 1955, an official statement from the British government was needed. Thanks to a statement partly drafted by Nicholas Elliott and Dick Brooman-White, two of Philby's fiercest defenders, the Foreign Secretary Harold Macmillan cleared him, and in unnecessarily generous terms. Philby's press conference in his mother's flat was a professional's triumph, a masterclass in deceitful effrontery, demanding evidence from his accusers. Yuri Modin could only admire that 'rock' of a man. He called Philby's sangfroid and impudence in turning the tables 'truly breathtaking', 'a virtuoso demonstration' in which 'the legendary Kim ... played his cards with consummate cunning'. Actor Judi Dench reported years later that her husband Michael Williams used to tell young actors to watch Philby's performance. 'Here was a man we knew was up to no good, wiping the slate clean,' she said. 'It's a complete lesson in acting. It's wonderful. And, of course, he was totally believed.' Philby's hosting of Burgess in Washington had been 'an imprudent association', admitted Philby. 'I have never been a communist,' he assured the media. 'The last time I spoke to a communist, knowing he was one, was in 1934.'

Aileen's unhappiness was if anything aggravated by the Macmillan statement, and it catalysed matters to Philby's advantage. His friends, notably Nicholas Elliott, were spurred into action. As far as possible, he could and should be treated as an innocent man. The Americans would never agree to him returning to MI6, but he was entitled to earn a living, and one could be arranged for him that could also be of use to the country he had served with such distinction. His friends arranged for him to be sent to Beirut to cover Lebanon for the *Observer* and *The Economist*. An internal Whitehall memo later revealed the thinking, or at least part of it: 'It was thought that in view of the nature of his past employment with Her Majesty's Government, it was better that he should not be destitute ... it was wise to proceed on the belief that it was in the public interest that Philby should have some employment.'

And, by way of paying a debt to a wronged man, MI6 would allow him once again to pick up the work he had done previously for them, though with more discretion than ever. Beirut was not just any old posting, convenient though it was to have Philby out of London. It was a hub of international espionage, and was overtaking Egypt in the minds of Western security bosses as a place of safety and influence. Globally it was one of MI6's biggest stations, from where, with the help of various pliant media outlets, a number of propaganda operations across the Middle East were being run. And with Philby's father on good terms with many heads of state in the Middle East, he was ideally placed to be, at the very least, a useful pair of ears for the British government.

Whether the *Observer* was aware that Philby would be moonlighting for MI6 is uncertain. The paper later carried a piece by a staff writer saying that the Foreign Office felt it was unfair that, despite being cleared, Philby was unable to find work as a journalist. Nonetheless, the *Observer* was given a 'cast iron promise' that Philby had 'no further connection with British intelligence'.

To a man who prided himself on decency, helping his friend find work was the least Elliott could do, and Philby was delighted at the turn of events. 'What's the betting I'll be a war reporter again within six months?' he wrote to a friend. And he was.

4

Settling into the city of spies

With a back story like Philby's, it is no surprise that his arrival in 1956 caused a stir in Beirut's sophisticated circles. Even amid that city's exotica, he stood out as enigmatic, though in a low-key way. The humblest follower of a soap opera, let alone the spyhunters of the world's most powerful nations, would have wondered what his game was, and for whom he was playing it.

For one thing, the fact of his being employed in Beirut at all was down to his friends in MI6, who felt not only that he had been traduced but also that with his contacts and affability he could still be of use to them. Not everyone shared this view. The Americans still wanted his head on a plate, and even some of his former colleagues were advocating setting a trap for Philby that would tempt him to pass over to the Russians some irresistible nugget, the use of which would expose him. But with his clearance by Macmillan, those forces had retreated, for the time being at least. And, as luck would have it, this being the upper echelons of English public life, Philby had been at school with MI6's head of station in Beirut, Godfrey 'Paul' Paulson. Philby couldn't be formally taken on by 'the firm', but there were bits and pieces he could do, often for cash payment, which would keep his hand in. Philby was warned off any dealings involving the Soviet Union, and encouraged to turn his attention towards

President Nasser's activities outside Egypt and domestic matters in Saudi Arabia, where family connections would help. But it was, as far as such things can be, an arm's length relationship, initially at least, overseen by Paulson in person. A new head of MI6, Dick White, was appointed, moving across from MI5 in the hope of it raising its game, shortly after Philby's move to Beirut was arranged. White had long believed in Philby's treachery, but he agreed to the Beirut tasking continuing. When asked why, White later said: 'it was safest to leave him there because if he were brought back to London it would be impossible to convict him or to prevent him seeing his old colleagues in SIS (MI6) and picking up old threads.' In other words, in the absence of proof, he was as near to being out of harm's way as possible. In truth, it seems there was another reason for White's acquiescence. It seems he went to the Foreign Secretary, Harold Macmillan, in the hope of reversing the decision. They discussed the matter but Macmillan, though close to White and an admirer, had been influenced by the previous MI6 head that Philby should be kept out of the way. Macmillan's involvement in the decision becomes more significant in the light of later developments.

He was being used by MI6, though deniably. Genrikh Borovik reports that news of his foreign trips – particularly to Saudi Arabia, where doors opened easily for him and about which Whitehall felt poorly informed – were always welcome by MI6 in London.

The Russians had barely been in touch for five years other than, in London, to help him out financially. And for as long as he was only doing comparatively minor errands for the British, he was not considered worth reactivating. The reward – probably scant – would not have justified the risk, which would have been huge, given the surveillance the Russians assumed he was under. Not that his own trustworthiness was taken for granted in Moscow. Stalin had died, but suspicion lived on, and arguably with more reason than ever.

If an angry and frustrated Aileen back in England was tormented by her belief as to where Kim's political allegiance really lay, by the spring of 1957 Eleanor, by contrast, was too close and too much in love to see the wider picture, and this was probably their happiest time together. Nor did she realise that some of those close to her – many of whom were familiar with the world of espionage – knew more than they were letting on. Not about her affair, about which few knew, but about Kim's suspect political loyalty. During the fun in the sun, she thought she knew the big secret – the fact of their affair – but there was even more going on than she imagined.

If Kim was working in Beirut thanks to MI6, he was *not* working in London because of the CIA. They had a continuing belief in his guilt. One of those expected to keep at least half an eye on him was Bill Eveland, who had been at the St Georges the day Kim had met Eleanor. He was the same age as Eleanor and their shared Washington State upbringing provided a further bond amid the snootier east coasters who proliferated in US diplomatic circles. He was at very least an obliging source when his friend and drinking partner Sam needed a reliable steer or a 'well-placed source' for a quote. In his autobiography Eveland mentions no specific request by his superiors to keep tabs on Philby, but with the CIA convinced of Philby's guilt, it would be extraordinary if his opinion was not sought. Besides, in Beirut of that epoch, a formal tasking might have seemed otiose. Nobody was *just* a diplomat, *just* a spy or even *just* a friend. The distinction between gossip and intelligence, rarely sharp, can never have been foggier. Few relationships were pure and exclusive, as Eleanor was to discover.

The bar of the St Georges, for example, was spook central. Those who were not known to the staff were treated with great but finite courtesy, whereas those in its charmed circle were greeted like royalty (which sometimes they were). Its cast of characters invited speculation as to their true loyalties. At around this time the US State Department had grown nervous that conventional US diplomacy was being compromised by the covert and often unlawful activities of the CIA, generally performed using the cover of the embassy. While there would always be a degree of overlap, it sought to minimise the number of 'funnies'. 'Suddenly PR firms, consultants, marketing companies in Beirut mushroomed, as all the spies changed their cover stories,' remembers Afif Aburish, whose brother Said wrote the definitive description of life at the St Georges.

His book, *The St. George Hotel Bar*, was scrupulous in setting out how global politics was mirrored in the allegiances of those who drank at the hotel. Sam Brewer, encouraged by his friend Bill Eveland, took the view that, by refusing to sell arms or help with damming the Nile at Aswan, the Americans were inadvertently and unwisely pushing Nasser towards the Soviet Union, a concern Nasser cannily did not discourage.

John Mecklin, the Brewers' neighbour and the bureau chief for the Middle East of *Time* magazine, and several other correspondents did not agree, giving the Egyptians more credit for their ability to run their own affairs. They admired Nasser's aspiration to strengthen an Arab sense of nationhood by bringing its peoples together, but believed neither Nasser nor his followers would have any enthusiasm for Moscow rule. Among the Americans in Beirut, an excessive concern for a creeping communist menace was not confined to the St Georges, but it had a willing audience in Sam. Said Aburish wrote that Sam 'considered the Arabs to be decades removed from effective self-rule, and his writing betrayed a boredom with the Middle East in general'. In the 1940s Sam had been the coming man, but as the 1950s went on he was growing if not too comfortable, then certainly over-reliant on the safety of the 'official sources' with which the St Georges abounded.

The St Georges combination of alcohol and secrets was irresistible to a great many other journalists. According to one member of staff: 'It is impossible to tell the number of spies who came to the bar. There were more of them than ... anyone ever knew ... Perhaps there were more spies than journalists. After all, most of the journalists were also spies.' Ralph Izzard of the *Daily Mail* was a frequent drinking partner of Kim. John Slade-Baker of the *Sunday Times* was also an insistent presence, though not Kim's cup of tea, possibly because Kim knew or suspected Slade-Baker was also in the pay of MI6, which he was. Another regular, Colin Reid of the *Daily Telegraph*, had also been in MI6 during the war. Kim used to file his copy for *The Economist* on Wednesdays and would often come across news items that wouldn't qualify for the *Observer* news pages on Sunday, so he would trade them with their colleagues. From such deals, a degree of unsuspected solidarity arises, which Kim would have been adept at exploiting.

John Fistere was another often seen at the bar. He gave a weekly lecture on business communications at the American University, while also promoting America's White Fleet (non-combat military vehicles) and advising King Hussein of Jordan. He was assumed by many to have been on the books of the CIA. Some said he had been sent to the Middle East by the Agency specifically to prove that Kim Philby, a frequent attender of his generous parties, was the 'Third Man'. This notion gained currency when Fistere hired Philby's eldest daughter Jo to work for him. But Fistere's own daughter Susan emphatically denies this, saying the CIA 'had no need' to employ him. 'He, like a good American, was happy to tell them anything they wanted to know, although my mother always used to say "would that he was CIA – we could have done with the extra income".'

In any event, there was no shortage of American interest in Philby. London might be wishing the whole business would just go away, but powerful people back in Washington were not so complacent. Even if they were not convinced of his guilt – and many were – they wanted the issue settled, and any number of people could have been deputed to pass on any information they received about Philby. So many, indeed, that Ali Bitar, the hotel's celebrated barman, was aware of a curious aura around Philby, that people didn't behave naturally in his presence. But then, as Bitar put it, 'how do you monitor someone who never said anything even when he drank enough for a dozen people?'

Jimmy Barracks, the CIA's head of station in Beirut and a St Georges regular, tried to sign up Said Aburish to monitor Kim's behaviour, and in particular his friendship with Haig, one of the hotel's Armenian waiters who was known to have left-wing leanings. Aburish turned the offer down. He liked both Haig and Philby and found the whole thing 'distasteful'. Staff at the hotel found the idea curious, if not positively inept. Colleagues would tease Haig gently about his membership of a leftist political party, but they regarded the uncomplicated, dedicated waiter on tables as the least suitable of people for high-grade espionage.

Another spy and St Georges regular was Mary Hawthorne, who bore the misleadingly dull, tell-tale title of Political Officer at the embassy. Where Bill Eveland was deputed to cosy up to and keep tabs on the Lebanese President Camille Chamoun, which he did with considerable success, Hawthorne reported to her CIA bosses on the leader of the opposition, Raymond Edde, a charming and principled leader of the Maronite group. This being Beirut, inevitably there were rumours of an infatuation, at least, between Hawthorne and Edde.

Some of the 'stars' of the international espionage game – Maurice Oldfield (whose epicureanism led to him having a soup named after him), Anthony Cavendish, Kim and Archie Roosevelt, Muhammad Hassanain Haikal, Nasser's right-hand man – would make the occasional appearance, but few people knew why. And there were some faintly laughable attempts at trying not to look suspicious, of which the most absurd was a Yugoslav spy who claimed he was in Beirut selling bicycles. Quite why he thought the well-heeled and generally chauffeur-driven clients of the St Georges might find themselves in need of a bicycle is not known.

Neighbouring nations were also well represented at the St Georges bar. To be absent was to risk missing out. Egypt and its allies the Syrians would be there, as would the more West-leaning Jordan and Iraq, each one professionally charming and jealously eyeing the local competition. A Lebanese public affairs official with the Iraqi Petroleum Company was widely believed to be also working for MI6, but that was never more than a rumour. Most intriguing of all was the barman of the St Georges, Ali Bitar, around whom intrigue swirled but whose composure and evident discretion remained assured.

An Alawite born in north-west Syria in the days when both countries were under French rule, he was handsome, good at languages, considerate and sociable. Though a non-drinker himself, he famously made the best martini in Beirut.

Very unusually for a man of his background, he married a Druze woman, which caused considerable upset in traditional circles – the Druze discourage marrying out – but their relationship was strong and they overcame any disapproval.

As a barman, Ali Bitar was a model of accomplishment, but more than that. Just occasionally, recalls Afif Aburish, in less busy moments he would drop in a supposedly innocuous question, maybe about one of the bar's more shadowy customers, which, days later, would set Afif wondering: 'Why the hell was he asking me that?' 'If you are in Lebanese security,' says

Afif, 'where would you go to find out what was going on? The St Georges. They needed somebody, because the PM might be there, or the next candidate for PM, or the minister of defence, or leader of the opposition.' And indeed, years later, when he was living in California, which in itself may be revealing, Ali admitted that he had been working for Lebanese Security from the early 1950s. His work was unpaid, and the pride of doing that line of work seems to have been – or perhaps had to be – reward enough, sufficient even for him to have turned down offers from MI6, the CIA and KGB, he said.

This was now Philby's milieu. He was at home. After a spell on trial with the *Observer*, he had slipped smoothly back into journalism once more, and knew how to produce the requisite supply of serviceable and thoughtful articles, even if his strike rate of agenda-setting news stories was low. Bob Stephens, one-time Middle East editor of the *Observer*, looking for evidence of bias, later found only 'diligent and honest reporting'. He said: 'His writing was clear, better than competent, and where he sought to interpret political trends seemed to have a remarkable degree of accuracy in the light of subsequent political events.' The *Observer* felt it got a good deal out of the arrangement, but he seemed to be something of a part-timer, not always available to travel when the office required.

Another journalist, Fred Tomlinson, said his copy was always beautifully clean, easy to sub, always filed on time. He found Philby a man of exceptional kindness, sensitivity and popularity. David Astor, who had been responsible for the paper taking Philby on, had only one complaint: that when the paper took a position against British Foreign Office policy, Philby's position did not always chime, often giving too much weight to government thinking. How little he knew.

His biggest crime, for which the *Observer* staff ticked him off, was when he referred to an official who Philby was known to dislike as having '*graced* an occasion' (author's italics). This gently subversive use of irony was inappropriate in a paper of record, he was told.

Patrick Seale, who was Philby's deputy on the *Observer* in Beirut and was to write extensively about him, noted much later: 'The most striking thing about Philby was that he was not doing very much. He led a pretty domesticated life. His routine was to get up late ... make his way hand in hand with Eleanor to the Normandy – not the smartest hotel – to collect his mail and have a few drinks; to do a little shopping, a little cooking; take a siesta; perhaps put in an appearance at a party; return home to a bottle of vodka citronné cooling in the ice box.'

On the face of it, his outlook was clouded by the prospect of his secret affair continuing unresolved or becoming known to Eleanor's cuckolded husband, or an enraged and unstable wife back in England who suspected the truth of his twenty-year commitment to the destruction of British parliamentary democracy and the likely prison sentence that would go with that, but Philby knew what he wanted. One evening, when he was hoping Eleanor would go over to see him at the flat he had moved into in the middle of town, Eleanor said she couldn't – she was expected at a party given by the Mecklins in the flat next to her and Sam's. Philby lost his temper. He rang Eleanor at the party and told her if she didn't go round to see him he was ending the relationship. She left the party and called the furious Philby on a telephone nearby. He asked her why she put up with fools like Bill Eveland and Sam, cooking for them and so on, when he knew she hated it, and that he wasn't standing for it any longer. Eleanor went over to Philby's flat and calmed him down, but it was a turning point. Soon afterwards, she went to Sam and told him she wanted a divorce, but she didn't let on as to what had catalysed things.

As ever with Kim and Eleanor, things were not

straightforward in other respects. The backdrop had shifted once more. Eleanor's mother Caroline died in Mendocino County, California, in March 1957, at the age of sixty-eight, leaving her father Blaine, then seventy-seven, alone and in need of care. Eleanor went for a few days on her own to Istanbul and decided she needed to go home, but she and Kim now knew – notwithstanding Kim still being married – they wanted to be together, not that they were ready to tell Sam that.

He agreed that, having taken the liner across the Atlantic, she would also arrange for a 'quickie' divorce in Mexico. A shaken Sam asked Bill Eveland to come to the port to see his wife and daughter off ('for Annie's sake'). If the intention was to make Annie happy, it didn't work. Sam and Bill Eveland sat in the cabin and drank champagne with Annie. While Eleanor was off sorting out the luggage and paperwork, Annie became hysterical thinking her mother would not be coming with her. Calm was restored when Eleanor reappeared, and the boat sailed.

While she was away, Eleanor received a friendly letter from Sam expressing his sadness at the prospect of divorce. It seems he suspected Eleanor was having an affair, but he had no idea it was with Kim. Meanwhile, Kim was contemplating a future for them together. He wrote in a letter: 'We shall take a house in the mountains: she will paint; I will write; peace and stability at last.'

Kim's value to his news outlets as a reliable performer was well established, all the more welcome as the region was showing signs of unrest. While lip service was paid by the Americans to the notion of self-determination in the region, there were very obvious limits. Notwithstanding its diverse population, Lebanon's most powerful politicians meant it was the most pro-Western nation in the region, and for many reasons – including the Tapline oil terminal at Sidon – it needed to stay that way. Successive US ambassadors had spoken of the plucky Lebanese as ambassadors for the free market, and how that made them natural partners for the US. But the understanding this 'little country' had of the marketplace meant the Lebanese knew their own value, the price of which President Chamoun was adept at securing from Washington. In January 1957, the US President had unveiled the 'Eisenhower Doctrine', under which a Middle Eastern country could ask the US for economic or military assistance if it was being threatened by armed aggression. In doing so, Chamoun was showing a further willingness to be seen as 'the US's man', and would have no truck with desta-bilising elements from Syria or Egypt. In March of that year, Eisenhower won $200 million in economic aid for the region from Congress.

The writing of what was effectively a blank cheque showed the US was not planning to take any chances in the election of June of that year. Briefcases full of cash were liberally dis-tributed among key Lebanese politicians to ensure voting went the right way, with Bill Eveland and CIA colleagues generously oiling the wheels. The vote took place over several weeks across the country, with the initial results showing a swing in support of the pro-Western position. One former prime minister, Saeb Salam, was defeated, having campaigned with his head heavily bandaged after he had been clubbed by a gendarme in the street protests against the government. He, according to Sam Brewer's report at the time, had been 'one of those Moslem elements . . . that have tended to stir up hostility between Moslem and non-Moslem groups in the populace'. We may or may not accept that Sam Brewer was unaware that his friend and drinking partner Bill Eveland had orchestrated the corruption. In any event, he felt able to write that unusually for the Middle East, 'the voting and counting had been scrupulously honest'.

This was the start of a new chapter. Kim's father St John had moved to Riyadh the previous autumn, now better regarded by the new Saudi regime, which wanted to call on his contacts and use him as a high-level fixer. The move had upset his wife Dora back in England, torn between irritation with her husband and supportive admiration. She had not visited him in Saudi Arabia since 1947, and played little part in his Middle East existence, but she tried to watch from afar. She told him that 'it always makes me feel mad when I've seen for years people plucking your brains for nothing'. This being St John, by April 1957 he had blotted his copybook once again and was back in Beirut.

Arthritic and depressed, Dora was in a bad way. Only recently had she discovered that her husband had married Rozy, who she had heard about but assumed was merely the object of a passing passion. She was a famously slim and pretty 'slave girl', whose Baluchi family from Sindh had settled in the Buraimi oasis (on the border of what is now the UAE and Oman, and the subject of a dispute with the British) and had been chosen by one of Ibn Saud's countless wives as an ideal 'present' for St John in 1945, when she was about sixteen and he was sixty. By the mid-1950s, St John and Rozy were barely getting on. They had endured the death of two young children, but two more, Khalid and Faris, survived, and St John's other family was often to be found living at Ajaltoun. This brought out the best of Kim's manners, if not his greatest displays of affection. He suffered the family shouting matches in silence, while hating them. Kim did not approve of what he regarded as the slovenly way Rozy was bringing up the children, but his father didn't seem to mind. Kim, to whom his mother was completely submissive, had omitted to mention St John's other marriage to her. Though consonant with the chauvinist assumptions of the day, this must have caused much hurt. Far from feeling sheepish, St John – becoming even more self-important with age – had pretty much given up on the knighthood he believed, inexplicably, was his due from the British establishment. Notwithstanding their problems, he suggested that Dora might like to move from London to share his 'contentment' in Lebanon. That way, he suggested, 'there would be about a dozen of us to lay the foundation of a Philby colony in one of the nicest countries in the world'. The thought of living as a spare wife under the same roof as Rozy and her sons did not appeal.

Dora remained in London, punctuated by occasional stays in Crowborough, consoling herself with gin. In late June 1957, as St John prepared to visit London, Kim brought the news to his father that Dora had died in her sleep. She was sixty-eight. An archivist who read Dora's letters to her husband before they mysteriously disappeared said they were a 'sad account of neglect, illness, loneliness and despair over many years'. Her death shook both men hugely, both having taken her for granted for years. Kim Philby said later: 'My mother literally drank herself to death. Towards the end she was drinking a bottle of gin a day. The trouble was that my father was a terribly insensitive man as far as women were concerned. He had no regard at all for their feelings. It wasn't deliberate. He just didn't understand why my mother should feel the way she did.' St John, who had assumed Dora would always be there for him, was very upset by her death.

Well into the autumn of 1957, Eleanor was still in the United States. Her father required more attention than she had anticipated and the divorce took longer than the new couple had realised. In her absence, Kim wrote a number of deeply emotional letters. While she was away attending to the care of her father, her mind was only on the new love of her life. There could scarcely be a clearer signal to herself that her heart had moved on. Divorce was indeed the right step.

Philby was still not free of his own obligations and seems

to have taken no steps towards divorce himself. From Crowborough, Aileen, in an increasingly chaotic house, continued to dog his Levantine escape. Things had been bad enough before he went to Beirut. He had been continuing the affair with Connie, seemingly indifferent to the fact that Aileen was in danger of drinking herself to death. Her mother hired a private detective to keep watch on Connie and Kim, to see where such money as they had was going, but Kim carried on regardless.

The affair with Connie ended when he went abroad, but money was a continuing worry. Kim thought his wife incompetent and profligate. From Beirut he told Aileen that he would send what she needed for household expenses as long as she provided receipts. Often these failed to materialise. If she can afford 'the luxuries of risking her neck at point-to-points, she can damn well send me the receipts,' he insisted. 'No receipts, no money.' He was 'fed up with her idleness'.

In Philby's continuing absence, late that autumn Tim Milne and his wife Marie visited, taking the children to the zoo. Aileen was clearly in a bad way, and to make some extra money had taken a job as a cook in a private house off Sloane Square. The move to the large house in Crowborough, subsidised by Aileen's mother, had not been a success and Aileen felt more isolated than ever. Someone who saw her in those months said she was 'obviously a very sick woman, both mentally and physically', someone who 'talked only nonsense'. Journalist Clare Hollingworth spoke of Aileen as someone who appeared deranged. In recent times she had crashed the car and been in and out of a variety of hospitals. She too was drinking heavily.

In the run-up to Christmas of 1957, a telegram arrived from England. Aileen, at forty-seven, had died on 11 December. The coroner found she had been suffering from 'congestive heart failure, myocardial degeneration, respiratory infection and pulmonary tuberculosis'. Those most familiar with Aileen's difficulties saw other causes.

The intelligence world had had Aileen's decline on its radar for a while. An MI5 report on her psychiatrist's findings read as follows: 'He is convinced that she possesses important security information about her husband and her own communist past . . . In [Aileen's] opinion and that of her psychiatrist, Philby had by a kind of mental cruelty to her "done his best to make her commit suicide".' The psychiatrist believed Philby might even have murdered her, although he was almost certainly in Beirut when she died. MI5's Arthur Martin revealed after her death that another psychiatrist alerted MI5 to say she had told him that if she was found dead in suspicious circumstances, Kim would have been responsible. And one night in Beirut, one of Philby's children, frustrated at their father's harsh insistence on the child not staying out late, spat in frustration to a friend: 'He killed our mother, you know.' The remark was not meant literally, but it says plenty about their father's attitude to his troubled wife. The convenience of Aileen's tragic end ensured that suspicion hung around it. Nicholas Elliott went to his grave believing that the KGB had murdered her to prevent her from providing evidence of her husband's guilt. Boris Volodarsky, an LSE academic who has specialised in studying the deaths of Russian citizens outside the USSR, believes this is unlikely. For one thing, Aileen had no hard evidence of what he had done, merely a long-standing hunch.

As so often, Tim Milne was on hand to help, and pitched in immediately after Aileen's death. Philby came back to England for the funeral, taking three weeks off work. (Some claim he didn't attend the funeral, but this is denied by one who was present.) 'Characteristically,' wrote Milne many years later, 'he insisted that the youngest children [both under twelve] should not be told of her death before he arrived, as he wished to tell

them himself; he was never one to shirk an unpleasant duty.'
Philby's sister-in-law Melanie Learoyd took responsibility for the
children, settling around £700 of unpaid bills (around £16,000
today) and the clearing out of the house, sending some of Kim's
favourite pieces of furniture to Beirut and selling the rest.

Others, in varying ways, remember Philby's response in
less favourable terms. Whichever version is the correct one,
in Beirut there was no pretence at grief. One reported him as
having said: 'She can't even die in an uncomplicated way, it has
to be all crumbed up with problems', another that at an embassy
party he burst in to announce: 'Great news! Aileen has died!' In
yet another, fellow journalist Richard Beeston recalls Christmas
shopping with his wife Moyra in Bab Idriss, one of Beirut's
arcaded squares, and bumping into Philby. 'I have wonderful
news, darlings,' he said. 'I want you to come and celebrate.'
Moments later, at the Normandy Hotel, he whipped out the
telegram and explained that his wife had died. What a merci-
ful escape he had had. He was now free to marry 'a wonderful
American girl'. The Beestons were shocked at his exuberance
and said so. He explained how ill she had been and that her
dying was all for the best for everyone.

Beeston was not alone in having expectations of this 'wonderful American'. Philby was regarded, in that ghastly phrase,
as 'a ladies' man', and might be expected to have set his sights
on somebody nubile and vivacious, and certainly to have – in
the words of the time – 'played the field' before settling down
again. Eleanor, then forty-four, was married, tall, slim and not
an obvious 'catch'. Many who knew her say they remembered
little about her. They found her pleasant but not particularly
forthcoming. She was intelligent, dressed unspectacularly and
rarely made much of an impression on first acquaintance. Those
who got to know her found more to like, admiring a knowing
humour, a straightness and a fine appreciation of the arts. Her

steadiness and constancy made her an unlikely candidate to 'run off' with anyone, let alone an unknown quantity like Philby.

Philby wrote to Eleanor to tell her of Aileen's death, and despite being 'dazed by the news' he asked her to marry him. He told her he was going to England until late January, and hoped that they might get married while he was in London. In the event, things didn't move anything like as quickly as Kim had hoped. Eleanor's father still needed her attention and the divorce turned out to be anything but a 'quickie', taking months to resolve.

But journalistically, Kim had more than ever to keep him occupied. Lebanon was in turmoil, under as much pressure as any country from the emboldening influence of Nasser. Neighbouring Syria, which had been under the same French-protected mandate as Lebanon until just fourteen years earlier, was now allied with Egypt in the newly formed United Arab Republic, was making overtures to the USSR, wanted its say in developments and was supplying arms and materiel for the rebels. At the end of April, Nasser further antagonised the West, visiting Moscow and being treated with the most emphatic and friendliest of welcomes.

By signing up to the Eisenhower Doctrine, President Chamoun had put himself, in the eyes of many compatriots, on the wrong side of Nasser and the Arab nationalist cause. His government, led by the Maronite Christian elite and supported by the US, was enjoying the country's economic boom, but many in the Muslim population were missing out and were increasingly resentful, and admiring of Nasser. In Lebanon, barricades separating Christians and Muslims were erected, snipers roamed the streets and anti-government rebels took control of Tripoli, Tyre and Sidon. Violence had been mounting on the streets for months and had now reached a state of civil war. It was later estimated that around three thousand people died.

President Chamoun, himself a Maronite, aspired to be a unifying figure, but the discontent and radicalism on the streets was having none of it.

To Washington, this was at best a flexing of Muslim muscle and at worst serious mischief-making by the Soviet Union. Though many in diplomatic circles were sceptical as to how much Moscow was seeking to make trouble, that was the angle most likely to galvanise the US electorate. The elements were there for the most dangerous of international escalations. President Chamoun feared for his safety, and around this time asked Bill Eveland to drive round one evening to look after the contents of the family safe in case the worst should happen. Eveland was moved to tears.

Moderate voices in the American administration advised caution. The question now was whether, when parliament was considering its choice for the next president, Chamoun should stand for a second term, which would have been in breach of the constitution and, even if amended, would certainly be in breach of its spirit. And if he did, reluctantly, would the US continue to support him? Or should parliament postpone the vote, scheduled for late July? President Eisenhower did not want to stand idly by, fearing a ripple effect across the region if Lebanon wobbled or even fell to what he saw as a dangerous combination of Arab lawlessness and Soviet connivance. Sam Pope Brewer told the *New York Times*'s readers: 'A Middle East diplomat said today that it was important for Lebanon to have the avowed support of Middle Eastern states when her foes in the United Arab Republic [Egypt and Syria] were accusing her of being a tool of western imperialism, even if such backing went no further than moral and diplomatic support.'

Would the US's allies in the region remain loyal? Of the four countries of the Baghdad Pact, Turkey and Iraq were first to express support. Iraq, led by the Hashemite King Faisal II, had been steadfast in its support for the West, although many of its population resented its backing for the invasion of Suez and the king's backing of a union with Jordan.

Amid the mounting turmoil, on 4 July 1958, American Independence Day, Kim received a cable from Eleanor with good news. The divorce was complete. He replied in the customary punctuation-free manner of the medium: 'Clever wonderful you fly happily song in heart life is miraculous greatest love Kim.' The same morning, he ran round to Sam Brewer's apartment to tell him that his wife had confirmed that they were now divorced.

Philby told a hungover Brewer about the divorce, adding that he planned to marry Eleanor. In contrast to Kim's effusiveness, Brewer's response is a homage, self-mockingly or not, to emotional constipation, to a manly concord that allows matters of the heart to be raised only *in extremis*. Brewer, who had been expecting this, replied flatly: 'That sounds like the best possible solution. What do you make of the situation in Iraq?'

In truth, Sam was very wounded by the desertion of his second wife. Unsurprisingly Eleanor does not linger on this in her book, and the reader is invited to believe that Sam's commitment to his work overrode all other considerations. His initial reaction to his wife's intention to marry Philby had been downbeat, but he was very hurt by her taking up with another man. And, the new CIA head of station Ed Applewhite later asked him, what if the 'Third Man' stories were true? There would be serious consequences for his daughter's upbringing, Sam confided in Frank Wisner, who was to try to offer succour and help him in subsequent legal exchanges between them.

Sam was extremely upset, but Beirut was a small pond and everyone needed to rub along together. After the affair became public knowledge, few showed much disapproval, despite being friendly with Sam. An account written a few years after Philby teamed up with Eleanor went as follows: 'Although he had stolen Eleanor ... public sympathy seems to have been wholly on Kim's side.' 'Everyone liked Kim so much,' a British friend said, 'so there was no sign of two factions which might normally develop in a case like that.'

So Philby, of course, was able to continue in his own, insouciant way, but there were many others who wanted to know if there was anything in the 'Third Man' stories.

Miles Copeland, husband of Eleanor's dear friend Lorraine, had been a musician before the war and some reports record him as having played with the Glenn Miller Band. With typical opacity, Copeland both encouraged the rumour and disdained the thought that he would have played with anyone so conventional.* Now at the helm of his own firm, Copeland & Eichelberger, he was scarcely just 'an ex-diplomat'. He was the third in the 'Arabist' triumvirate, with Kim and Archie Roosevelt, which aspired to the idealistic encouragement of local democracy in the region. In person he was Mr Genial but his methods were quintessentially covert, and had been since wartime days.

He and his wife Lorraine had met during the Second World War in London, which became his favourite city and second home. He was a member of the Counter Intelligence Corps, and – setting aside the self-mythologising at which he excelled – played a considerable role in misleading the Nazis into believing that the war-ending Allied attack would be near Calais rather than in Normandy. He had a good war, living near Harrods, enjoying the kudos of being a young, on-the-same-side American abroad and eventually falling in love.

Among those he encountered in London was Kim Philby, and they later spent time together in Washington. Copeland – unwittingly in competition to Philby – saw his foreign service

---

* Dennis Spragg, an expert on Glenn Miller, believes the claim was probably an example of Copeland's occasional generosity about his own achievements.

role as helping prevent Soviet expansionism and, hand in hand, lifting countries towards economic prosperity and – sooner or later – democratic enlightenment, with the help of charismatic leadership. Looking back on his career in his book *The Game Player*, he wrote that: 'Frivolous distractions apart, every activity I have undertaken over the last thirty-five years has been in one way or another related to my hope of identifying potential leaders and guiding them to their rightful destiny, through democratic means if such were available but unhesitatingly by other means if they were not.'

In 1947 he, with Lorraine, was sent to Syria, where, after two more years and a bizarre episode when he arranged for his own house to be the subject of gunfire in a bogus 'attack' by subversives, he helped arrange the switch in leadership – ostensibly in the defence of democracy – that unseated the country's leader Shukri al-Quwatli. (There were to be two further coups before the year was out, prompting one UK official who had been disturbed one weekend to tell an agent in the field not to bother warning London of impending coups 'unless they are communist'.) Later, in an Egypt unhappy at the continued rule of King Farouk, his plan to 'find and groom a messiah who would start out in Egypt, and then spread his word to Africans and perhaps other Third World peoples' culminated in Nasser – the Muslim Billy Graham, as he called him – coming to power in 1954, two years after Egypt had had a change of regime. In 1953, he and Kim Roosevelt – dubbed the Quiet American by Philby, which Graham Greene adopted for his novel of that name – were on the scene when the British and Americans conspired with the Iranian people to oust Mohammad Mossadegh in Iran and install the Shah, a coup which undermines Western protestations of good faith in that country to this day. In short, the arrival of Miles Copeland at passport control did not bode well for incumbent governments.

Largely for financial reasons, in 1953 Copeland joined one of the world's leading management consultants, Booz Allen Hamilton, acquiring the sort of enigmatic status that characterised his career. Whether he had actually left the CIA, as Copeland himself claimed (and sources close to the CIA have recently suggested he had), or whether the new job was just cover remains unclear. In any event he remained a loyal alumnus of the CIA. In fact, so loyal an alumnus was he that he formally rejoined before resigning again in May 1957, to set up in business with his friend James Eichelberger. This didn't prevent him helping distribute the slush fund for the election in June of that year. Yet outside the circles of people whose work required them to know about Miles's work, people used to say merely 'we thought he might be CIA'. This was a rumour that gained currency following a whisper among his children's classmates, though it was one that hardly distinguished itself from many others in 1950s Beirut.

Miles was a popular figure, but his expansive, gregarious demeanour, his tendency towards self-promotion, his background in the CIA and his involvement in a variety of coups meant that nobody was ever quite sure whose interests he was serving. As Wilton Wynne, *Time*'s correspondent in Beirut, claimed, Miles was 'the only man who ever used the CIA for cover'.

From her and Sam's shared time in Syria, Eleanor knew a little of Miles's background, but to her his work was irrelevant. That period was the beginning of a friendship that flourished further in Lebanon. 'We had a lot of family outings and picnics with Kim and Eleanor. We spent a lot of time visiting sites,' remembers Stewart Copeland, 'driving into Syria to visit these amazing abandoned sites, these humungous crusader castles. The Bedouin would stop to fill up with water but that was it. There was no one else there.'

At weekends, the Copelands used to hire a beaten-up boat to putter along the coast to visit Jounieh and Tabarja, an hour or so north of Beirut, often accompanied by Kim, Eleanor, Annie and whichever of Kim's children were on holiday from England. The Philbys and Copelands of this world are rarely off duty – and who knows what secrets Miles trustingly passed on – but to their families those boat trips were emphatically down time. Lorraine and Miles, like Kim and Eleanor, were cultured companions. Miles, an autodidact, aspired to immerse himself in the culture of wherever he was living, applying his formidable brain to assimilating local mores and history. Lorraine was eager to learn more of local history, picking up Arabic in the process. Eleanor had studied Persian fine art in California and was keen to broaden her knowledge. She and Lorraine attended the same classes at the American University of Beirut.

The fellowship between Britain and the US – however illusory and ineptly handled politically in that period – was implicit. As Frank Wisner, who grew up in the 1950s, the son of a senior CIA man who had known Philby in Washington, put it: 'It was a different day. You can't exaggerate the strength and importance of that relationship. I knew my father's generation. There was a genuine affection and fondness and, even more, a sense of collaboration with the British. My father used to say: "I know the British lied to us over Suez," but the relationship was still strong. Feelings were very deep and respectful.'

The carefree partying, picnics and boat trips that Eleanor and Kim enjoyed with the Copelands were just that, with a bit of work gossip thrown in. Kim and Miles shared a sense that they were a little more worldly than many of their compatriots in intelligence. Both claimed an insight into the delusions and follies of their political masters, and it was their job to mitigate them.

Stewart Copeland's memories of trips up the coast were

formative in a way that had little to do with high politics and espionage. The boat would pull in beneath the crusader castle at Byblos, on the top of the hill overlooking the bay. 'The women would sunbathe on the deck and the guys would be chuckling at the other end of the boat,' says Stewart. 'Harry [Philby] and I climbed up right to the top, and as Eleanor wasn't actually his mum but his stepmum, we could both look down and admire her loveliness. To an eleven-year-old, Eleanor was very pretty. To put it another way, for an eleven-year-old with budding genes, she was hot.'

The Americans had insisted on Kim's departure from MI6 in 1951, and remained concerned as to what damage he might have done in the past and might continue to do. The CIA's James Angleton, Philby's weekly lunch partner in Washington, became almost mesmerised by what he thought might be his duplicity. At one point, he had broken out, asking if his friend's loyalties lay with Moscow. A laughing Philby told him: 'You'll never get anyone to believe you.' Angleton's doubts about Philby remained, as did those of Frank Wisner, whose boring job title (CIA's Deputy Director of Plans) belied his immense global power to destabilise unfriendly governments.

When Miles Copeland, now employed by the private sector, and Lorraine arrived in Beirut in 1957, the alumnus had another, moonlighting mission. Angleton had asked him to open his eyes to who Philby really was. He asked Copeland to see as much of the Philbys as he could, asking him to wine, dine and entertain them and as many of their friends as they liked, and to send the bill to him, Jim Angleton. 'We'd hold a buffet dinner for forty people on a night we were sure Philby was free to be one of them,' said Copeland senior. Copeland's own view was that Philby was loyal to London. He enjoyed Philby's company and liked him enormously, but where a vast entertainment budget was at stake, Copeland, ever the pragmatist, agreed that one couldn't be too careful and was prepared to go along with his former boss's scepticism. 'I didn't have the slightest suspicion that he was a Soviet agent,' he said later.

Copeland was a trusted figure to both London and Washington. He was also asked by MI5 and the FBI to report on any signs that Philby might be working for the Russians. He had an occasional tail put on Philby, not by the CIA but by a friendly contact in the Lebanese Sûreté, just to see what he was up to. When out alone, Philby would practise his old tradecraft, shaking off his tail in order to be unobserved. Copeland later claimed that Philby kept a secret flat in an out-of-the-way part of Beirut, but that may have been confused with the places where he secretly met Eleanor. In truth, he saw no reason to think Philby had ever worked for the Russians, or was doing so now, and he continued to doubt it.

Copeland's eldest son, Miles Copeland III, would occasionally ask why as a family they saw so much of the Philbys, a question the father would always duck.

The younger Miles remembers that the relationship with Philby suited everyone. 'Kim ended up as a journalist doing what journalists do, finding out what was going on, so it was a pretty fitting job, and my father's job was to know what was going on, and Philby would come across stuff and supply information as well, so it was a natural friendship . . . so we went on picnics and so on.'

Philby would have enjoyed Copeland's company and his limitless alcohol, while also taking advantage of Copeland's excellent connections and enthusiasm for indiscretion.

The friendship between Lorraine and Eleanor was unaffected by any mutual watchfulness between their husbands. Her son Miles doubts that Lorraine would have ever been told that her husband had been asked to keep tabs on their friend. Had she known that her husband's association with Philby was more than merely social, it would not have bothered her, says Miles III. 'My mother ... was a realist above all, like my father,' he recalls, saying she would have been indifferent to any 'phony moral issues' that might have been raised. 'We as a family never went to church, nor did we individually later. So she would not have had a problem with my father keeping an eye on Kim – what harm was there in that?'

Lorraine was and remained a good friend. Nobody's fool, she had no reason to doubt the loyalty of her friend's new partner. It is easy to imagine Philby's many admirers dismissing the dark talk as the ravings of McCarthyite obsessives. Lorraine used to tell her children to keep an eye open for evasiveness. 'You can always spot a spy by how much bullshit they talk,' Lorraine would say. She was presumably not excluding her husband Miles, always an entertaining teller of stories, tall and otherwise.

A dozen or so years earlier, it had been Philby in the driving seat. Britain's spies were supposedly the old masters of the espionage game. But that was before Suez, when the British had embarrassed themselves enormously. Over sixty years later, that adventure looks a pitiful last kick of a country desperate to reassert control, blind to the fact that the world had moved on and forelocks were being tugged in a different direction, initially across the Atlantic and later elsewhere. The USA had become the force to be reckoned with. The tide was going out on British influence.

Philby's own life, too, was unsure. He knew that at any moment he might be rumbled. But he also knew that without the killer proof against him he was untouchable. The whisperers had done their worst in 1955 and failed. He had to be prepared for the day when he might need to take rapid action, but for the time being he was to carry on in the same apparently carefree manner. Besides, he might yet be given a decent hand to play in the game at which he excelled, espionage.

5

1958 – some old friends resurface ...

By the spring of 1958 Philby had been in Beirut for nearly two very eventful years. During that time, the British government had humiliated itself over the Suez Canal and the Americans had fixed a Lebanese election. Of more immediate professional interest, he was using his father's contacts to settle back into the life of a journalist. Though he had been mistakenly cleared of being a Soviet agent, to his disappointment he was not having the chance to behave like one, the Russians having had no contact with him, but he had resumed work on the quiet for MI6. And more personally, back in England, in just the last year his mother and then his estranged wife had died, the latter enabling him to become engaged to the adored Eleanor.

But the next few months were likely to be eventful as well. As soon as Eleanor returned from the States, where her mother had died and her father needed caring for, they intended to marry, and the home from home that he wanted for himself, Eleanor and her daughter Annie and his visiting children would become a reality. And politically Beirut was taking centre stage as a weathervane of great power intentions, with many in the USA fearing Islamic- and Soviet-inspired anarchy where previously the West had exerted control. Nineteen fifty-eight was to be a turning point in Middle Eastern and global politics. There was chaos in Beirut, and neighbouring pro-Western governments were wobbling.

When Sam Brewer responded to Philby telling him he planned to marry his wife by asking him what he thought about the instability in Iraq, he was conforming entirely – comically, tragically – to type. Work came first. And his sleepless antennae were not wrong. Ten days later, on 14 July 1958, angry rebels unseated Iraq's monarchy, killing the Hashemite King Faisal II, Prince 'Abd al-Ilah and Prime Minister Nuri al-Said. The new government was casting covetous eyes on Kuwait. Chaos seemed likely, and its consequence for neighbouring countries was incalculable.

Faisal's cousin King Hussein of Jordan was alarmed by the news from Iraq and, isolated, even talked of invading to try to restore Hashemite rule. And in Saudi Arabia, King Saud, the West's favoured candidate to take over leadership of the Arab world from Nasser, had recently been removed from power by his brother.

The US, increasingly inclined to see the region as being destabilised by the Russians, decided to project its strength. Eisenhower later said in his memoirs that 'we feared the worst ... the complete elimination of Western influence in the Middle East'. He moved to deter any incursion into Kuwait, sending clearer signals than the West managed thirty-two years later. Two destroyers from the Sixth Fleet were on hand in readiness for an evacuation of all US citizens in Lebanon. Tanks and police riot gear were flown in. The US navy doubled its numbers in the area. In Washington, a sense was growing that if the US's allies in Lebanon could not be saved, the region would be in flames. Amid the violence, Bill Eveland made a nightly solo car journey to the president's palace to deliver cash for

Chamoun's slush fund to keep the government afloat. There was continuing talk of G. K. Young's dream, an Anglo-American crusade to restore order. Maybe the new government in Iraq could be overthrown. The Turks could help unseat the Syrian government. Israel might take on Nasser. In response to such talk, Moscow moved twenty-four divisions up to the Turkish border. In a region where mistrust between the major powers was intensifying, the potential for calamitous miscalculation and understandings was mounting.

In truth the political crisis in Lebanon was in the process of being overcome, or at least addressed, when 1700 US Marines waded onto the beaches of Beirut to reinforce the government's hold on power. As Bruce Riedel of the Brookings Institute put it, it was 'the beginning of decades of seemingly endless American combat missions in the Middle East. In retrospect, Beirut in 1958 was a decisive turning point.'

The good intentions of the US's Arabists, compromised by their country's thirst for oil, were producing unforeseen consequences. More retrospection comes from Bill Eveland, who wrote in his memoir *Ropes of Sand*: 'By using Lebanon as a base for the CIA's covert operations, America undermined that country's stability and precipitated attempts by its Arab neighbors to bring down the Lebanese government. Although the might of US military power saved Lebanon from possible fragmentation in 1958, the country never recovered completely and America was left with few friends in the Arab world.'

And if President Eisenhower, hero of the Normandy beaches of 1944, was expecting a glorious rerun of D-Day, he was disappointed. The Marines were met not by snipers and mortar fire but fashionable bikini-clad mothers with children enjoying a summer dip, and soon thereafter by vendors of cigarettes, drinks and sandwiches. Nonetheless, the soldiers, and the three aircraft carriers moored offshore, had made a point. Three days earlier, Kim had assured colleagues with total confidence that the invasion was about to happen, yet nobody believed the Americans took the Soviet threat seriously enough to go to those lengths. He was proved right, mystifying colleagues as to how he had been so certain. And the invaders were met with a very Lebanese response. A deal was brokered whereby the Lebanese army would 'accompany' the US troops, and the Muslims would agree not to shoot at them. They were treated as guests, not occupiers.

Explaining the American decision to send troops, US ambassador Dick Parker said thirty years later: 'We reacted because we thought there had been a "Nasserist" coup in Baghdad. In fact we were reacting to the blank check we had given President Chamoun of Lebanon earlier under the Eisenhower Doctrine, through which we were confronting Nasser. President Chamoun cashed the check on the morning of the 14th. We had given him this check because of UAR subversion coming from Syria, which people kept denying but which was factual. This subversion, however, and we had conveniently overlooked this, was in part made possible by the fact that we had been up to our ears in buying the 1957 election for Chamoun ... We did this with money, just as the French, British, and the Egyptians had done.' Philby, inclined to see any such manoeuvrings as doomed imperialist thrashing about, applied his wintriest wit, referring to Eisenhower's White House as 'the tomb of the well-known soldier'. The young John F. Kennedy warned that the US should stop demonising Nasser, who had had far less to do with the Iraqi coup than the US had believed.

Lebanon's politics continued to be rocky. In the event, President Chamoun stood down, and after two more months of killing and political horse-trading he was replaced by the head of the army, Fuad Chehab. The symbolism of a change at the top then settled matters considerably. Chehab acknowledged

This charming man ... Kim Philby emerges from obscurity to present a carefree front to photographers in 1955

Eleanor's Office of War Information personnel file

Aileen Philby, the wife Kim left behind in England, opens the door to inquisitive journalists

Sam Pope Brewer, the *New York Times*'s highly regarded Middle East correspondent

The Maclean family. Donald Maclean fled to Moscow in 1951 after he came under suspicion as a Soviet spy; his wife Melinda and their (by then three) children followed later

From top left, clockwise: Anthony Blunt, Donald Maclean, Guy Burgess and Kim Philby, four of the high-achieving Cambridge graduates who signed up with Stalin to combat fascism

The Philbys' fifth-floor flat had a distinctive balcony, which now shows none of the love that Eleanor poured into making it stylish and attractive

The St Georges Hotel, where Beirut's politicians, business people, journalists and spies congregated and exchanged secrets

The Normandy Hotel, where the Philbys would collect their mail and drink, and which they treated like a club. On the right is the Lucullus restaurant

The good times: Kim and Eleanor at the Elliotts' beach house

Eleanor (*extreme left*) and Kim talking to the thirteen-year-old Mark Elliott at the Elliotts' beach house. On the right are Elizabeth Elliott and Colonel Alexander Brodie, the UK's military attaché in Beirut

Nicholas Elliott, Philby's former MI6 protégé, his Beirut boss for two years and his most resolute defender

Miles Copeland, Philby's drinking and gossiping chum, 'the only man who ever used the CIA for cover', seen here in later life

Glen Balfour-Paul, Lorraine Copeland and Eleanor letting their hair down in party city

British ambassador Sir Ponsonby Moore Crosthwaite (*right*), seen here strengthening diplomatic ties with Lebanon's Fouad Chehab, President from 1958 to 1964

Flora Solomon, friend of Philby's family and redoubtable campaigner for refugees, who told Simon Marks 'It's firms like Marks & Spencer that give Jews a bad name'

Myrtle Winter: Linguist, acrobat, dancer, mountaineer, sailor, campaigner for refugees and spy

Two miles every day . . . round and round

that the Muslims had not benefited from Lebanon's wealth and that the country had come to be seen as too pro-Western. Essentially, though, an opportunity for change was spurned. The new president left the confessional constitutional arrangements alone. In the view of many, this left the way open for yet more intra-factional squabbling and bargaining at the expense of strengthening civil society.

Eleanor, preparing at last to leave the USA, had secured her freedom to marry Kim and found a care home for her father, but there remained the question of Annie. The Lebanon to which Eleanor was returning was not a happy place. Shortly before she flew from San Francisco, she wrote to Sam saying she felt it was no place to bring a nine-year-old girl, and that she planned to leave her at a new school in Switzerland. Landing in Geneva, Eleanor and Annie took a two-hour train journey to the school at Vilars. The letter, as Eleanor intended, reached Sam after the deed was done, so he was furious at not being consulted, a breach of trust that was to further colour their relations. Sam's resistance to engaging with such domestic issues was one of her complaints against him. Nor had they discussed custody more generally.

In the meantime, with his father now back in Riyadh, Kim had taken the opportunity of moving down from the hills and settling in the unlikeliest of areas. He had chosen the Muslim-rebel-held Basta area, as far as can be imagined from the rarefied world of diplomatic cocktail parties. As soon as she returned to Beirut Eleanor moved into this most vernacular of areas, perhaps another reason for leaving Annie in Switzerland. It was poor, lawless and in the very heart of political agitation. This may have appeased a puritanical urge in Kim to stand shoulder to shoulder with the poor and downtrodden or it may have simply been easier to slink into obscurity there. In her book Eleanor was gracious enough to describe it as 'cheap and colourful', but in truth she hated it. Kim, with the conceit of the impregnable, in this case at least, was impervious to its dangers. 'He would sit out on his terrace at night and listen to the guns going off,' she wrote, uncomprehendingly.

But security had been restored, and Eleanor was back in Beirut and could now marry Kim.

The role of stepmother, or prospective stepmother, is never an easy one, but Afif Aburish remembers admiring Eleanor's relationship with Kim's children. 'She wanted them to have what they wanted – for them to be looked after, for them to be comfortable, and properly fed and so on – but she didn't let them get their way all the time,' he says. Another family friend recalls Philby's children complaining about her – including that she was too strict. She had usurped the place of their lively, loyal and loving mother, whose death had surely been hastened by Kim's mind so clearly being elsewhere.

Kim, a devoted father, remained crazy about Eleanor, and she happily looked after Miranda and Harry, his two younger children, in Beirut during school holidays. But it was not a time of constraints. Stewart Copeland remembers hitchhiking, when still not in his teens, down to Al Burj, Martyrs' Square, in clapped-out Mercedes taxis. 'Nobody ever worried about us wandering free. For Harry, coming from a boarding school in England it must have been heaven on earth.' He recalls Eleanor taking advantage of this ambience, sometimes indulging in a little strategic bribery. If the children's presence was becoming irksome, she would wave some cash at them and suggest they go to the cinema.

Their social equilibrium returned, and they were free to enjoy one another's company and the city's watering holes unencumbered. Among the regulars who Kim and Eleanor saw, mainly at the St Georges, was a remarkable woman called Myrtle Winter. Remembered as strong, funny, clever, a prolific gossip and a tireless campaigner, Winter also had an extraordinarily accomplished career. Her CV makes exhausting reading. Born in 1916, she was the daughter of Colonel C. B. Winter, CMG, DSO, a descendant of Nicholas Winter, a Gunpowder Plot conspirator, and a distinguished linguist whose mastery of languages equipped him for extensive work for the British countering Russian influence in Persia and elsewhere. His daughter's career was even more colourful. She became a cabaret entertainer, a Bluebell dancer, acrobat and trumpeter. This was in defiance of a bout of polio, after a doctor said it was doubtful she would ever walk again. (She explained she didn't want to walk, she wanted to dance.) After her sister Hazel was born blind, the family agreed that the disability should not hold the sister back, and everything was done to ensure Hazel's life was unencumbered. But nor was it to be a bar to Myrtle, who travelled widely, her mother and Hazel as chaperones. She cycled to India, swam the Bosphorus (and was met on completion by Mustafa Kemal Atatürk), performed for Atatürk in Turkey and King Farouk in Egypt, entertaining in Syria and Iran before, in the company of mother and sister, climbing Mount Ararat by way of relaxation. Myrtle helped her sightless sister enjoy life to the full by encouraging her to dive with her off the top diving board of Beirut's swimming pools.

By 1936 Myrtle had reached Vienna and was awarded a diploma in German, and then attended the London School of Economics for three years, studying anthropology. In the early war years, MI6 was in urgent need of linguists. Myrtle already had Arabic, Urdu, Farsi, Greek, Italian, German and French under her belt, so she was a natural, and was sent to Cairo as an interpreter. There she set tongues wagging with her vivid blond hair, her skills as a horse rider and yachtswoman, her panache behind a camera and a talent for drinking a pint of beer while standing on her head.

She joined MI6's Iberian branch, which was then run by Kim Philby, and spent time in Gibraltar as one of two hundred 'special examiners', working as a censor with Imperial Censorship as head of Special Branch with a staff of sixty. Here she was responsible for a team opening mail, binning any pro-Nazi leaflets and replacing them with anti-Nazi propaganda. They would comb every piece of correspondence for, in most cases of letters to loved ones, inadvertently revealing passages, or messages with hidden meaning intended precisely to escape detection. It served not merely as a safeguard but, to the trained eye of the highly gifted people, mostly women, charged with reading them, was an invaluable source of intelligence. After Italy joined the war and the Mediterranean became too dangerous, it was decided they should move, and in June 1940 a convoy of twenty ships left Gibraltar, heading for Liverpool. With only one sloop offering protection, the convoy lost three ships to German attacks off the coast of Portugal before reaching Liverpool, the hub of British censorship.

But it had been decided that the whole operation should be moved yet further, and the Special Examiners should be moved to Bermuda, 3500 miles west, effectively a global hub for communications. Myrtle was in charge of a staff of about sixty, out of a team of 1500 'censorettes', as they were dismissively known, capable of vetting around 200,000 letters a day. Latterly she worked interrogating German submariners before heading home for home for England in June 1944. She then spent a spell on loan to the US Office of Strategic Services, for whom she prepared propaganda for enemy-occupied territories.

Subsequently, until 1949, she worked for the Foreign Office's Research and Analysis Department, as head of the department preparing political reports on Arab Affairs at the British embassy in Cairo, being awarded the MBE for her work.

The creation of the State of Israel in 1948, and the war it triggered, caused around 800,000 Palestinians to flee the threat of ethnic cleansing, forcible eviction and massacres. Of those, around 100,000 took refuge in Lebanon. Many at the British embassy, while publicly endorsing British support for the creation of the State of Israel, were horrified and felt the Palestinians had been betrayed by the West.

Myrtle, described by those who knew her as forthright, intelligent, independent, not one to suffer fools, dynamic, generous and loyal, was among those appalled at the treatment of the refugees, both for the fact of their eviction and for their treatment, as second-class citizens, in refugee camps. After a spell in journalism, in 1951 she became a public relations officer for the United Nations Relief and Works Agency for Palestine Refugees in the Near East, Lebanon & Middle East, and, using her personal skills and talent as a photographer, she became a ferocious advocate for their cause. Three years later she was invited to set up the audiovisual department of the United Nations Relief and Works Agency. Her obituary in *The Times* described her as an immensely caring individual and called her appointment to UNRWA 'brilliant'. 'The photographic archive of her department (now safely stored in Vienna) is the greatest single testimony to the plight and total devastation of the lives of the million and a half Palestinian refugees spread over Lebanon, Syria and Jordan.'

Another of the colourful birds in Beirut's diplomatic quarters who quickly understood Lebanese ways was Theo Larsson. His Swedish family had migrated in the nineteenth century to the Holy Land in expectation of the Second Coming and ended up owning the American Colony Hotel in Jerusalem, which helped his impeccable connections. Larsson had known Kim Philby since boyhood. Kim's father, as British Resident in Amman, had been responsible for introducing Larsson's father, the Swedish consul in Jerusalem, to Jordan's then ruler Emir Abdullah, and their boys hit it off, too. Theo arrived in Beirut in 1957 and set himself up with a couple of rooms at the Normandy. His first port of call when he arrived was to see President Camille Chamoun, an old business acquaintance and former Lebanese ambassador to London, who advised him that in Beirut 'nothing is forbidden except an empty pocket, in which case, nothing is forgiven'.

As if to prove the point, Larsson told the story of how he was having lunch with a Lebanese MP at the Normandy Hotel as the US Marines were coming ashore. 'The Americans are crazy,' said the individual, explaining that he and twenty-two other MPs had offered to abstain from a vote to amend the constitution and allow a second term of office, for a comparatively modest fee of $10,000 dollars each. This would have quelled much of the dissent and fended off the need for the invasion, but the Americans had refused. When Larsson expressed surprise that such a vigorous critic of Chamoun would sell out in that way, his lunch partner said that for $10,000 he would vote for the Israeli Prime Minister.

That year, 1958, also brought a changing of the guard in diplomatic circles, with the arrival of a new British ambassador, who was to become entangled in the story of Kim and Eleanor in a way he could never have imagined. Sir Ponsonby Moore Crosthwaite (thankfully, generally known simply as Moore) was an aesthete, as intelligent, buttoned-up, shy and pedantic a figure as a fifty-something public-school English bachelor can be. As a young man he was described by a friend as 'immensely tall and immensely handsome ... oddly enough he looked like a Shakespearean Moor ... dark and beautiful'. At Oxford he had met the poet Louis MacNeice, part of a brilliant triumvirate of rebellious aesthetes who had been at Marlborough together. Through MacNeice, Crosthwaite became friendly with the other two. One was John Hilton, who went on to study architecture in Stuttgart and became probably Crosthwaite's closest friend. Making up the trio was Anthony Blunt, a first-class languages student at Cambridge, who went to visit Hilton in Germany. Blunt's partner on the trip, which left England on 22 August 1929, was Crosthwaite, recently graduated from Oxford and due to join the Foreign Office and who wanted to improve his German. In Germany Crosthwaite also lodged with Stephen Spender, another homosexual, MacNeice-inspired acquaintance, which did not go entirely well. Crosthwaite had not been Spender's first choice of companion. He wrote to a friend: 'Moore is a great social success, rather to my annoyance. I alternatively feel infuriated with him and rather like him. I feel at home with him on the whole, because under his veneer of public schoolishness, and his pompous aestheticism, he is a neurotic.'

Neurotic or not, Crosthwaite's appointment to so prominent a post as the Beirut embassy might have been intended as a corrective to the sort of loose behaviour the city attracted. There was something of the bishop in the brothel about him. Responding to a sobering embassy report on the plight of the Palestinian refugees, he was chiefly exercised by the writer's syntax. He disdained the use of adverbs ('lazy'), warning one member of his staff that 'an appropriate adjective or verb will always suffice to convey your meaning'. He returned the report – heavily defaced with red-ink corrections, with an ancillary copy of *Fowler's Modern English Usage* – to a junior colleague, Alan Munro. 'Mr Munro,' he wrote, 'there are two anacoluthons and one litotes in this. Get rid of them!' Mercifully these scandalous lapses did not impede Munro's rise to the British ambassadorships to Algeria and Saudi Arabia.

Crosthwaite collected Roman glass and was an assiduous supporter of the arts. In his time in Beirut he and Lady Yvonne Sursock Cochrane teamed up and were responsible for the restoration of a derelict Druze manor house at Abey, which was then used by the British embassy as a summer house, of which he was extremely proud. His idiosyncratic tenure as ambassador was marked by an insistence that all embassy staff should wear white suits – often purchased on the cheap from local tailors – for the Queen's Birthday reception (so they looked like a 'clutch of second-rate entertainers', remembers Alan Munro). In the absence of the customary 'diplomatic wife', Crosthwaite's elderly mother would often preside at these and other events, not always to the delight of Lady Yvonne. She provided a much-needed feminine touch. On one occasion, when a male member of his staff asked for permission to get married, he replied: 'Must you?'

If a picture is emerging of a publicly stern and uncomfortable homosexual, that is precisely what he was. Homosexuality was not only illegal but made many homosexuals in public life – unless of Burgessian flamboyance and indifference – susceptible to blackmail. It was deeply suspect, and brought a Masonic sense of brotherhood. That group's time together in Germany, one of the discovery of the illicit, left deep ties. Some, like Christopher Isherwood and Stephen Spender, defied convention and refused to conceal their sexuality. Others did, and, oblivious of unkind comments about 'limp-wristedness', hoped nobody noticed.

The utmost care was necessary, and the deeply patriotic Crosthwaite was tormented. His friend Spender, whose liking for men had not prevented him marrying twice and having two children, stayed at the Beirut embassy in 1961 with his second wife, pianist Natasha Litvin. He said Crosthwaite then was 'like a man encased in a carapace'. Though only in his mid-fifties, reported Spender, he was already contemplating retirement, having become, in Spender's words, 'stuffy' and 'conventional', while remaining 'absolutely gay'. Brian Sewell described Moore as 'querulous, secretive, ashamed and terrified of being identified as homosexual', so supportive friends who were in on the secret were highly prized.

One male British academic recalls being driven deep into the Lebanese countryside for a jaunt, and being asked by Crosthwaite: 'Do you play games?' He said he didn't. They returned immediately to Beirut. The matter was never discussed, deniability being everything. Another well-bred young Englishman was invited up to stay at Abey, and spent an entire evening on the terrace, sitting rigid with politeness, watching the sun go down. In an episode both hilarious in its straitlaced Englishness and tragic in the repression it suggests, barely a word was spoken before the young man went up to his bedroom, unfurnished but for a bed, no 'impropriety' having been even mentioned, let alone taking place. He is reputed to have had happier times in his next ambassador's posting, to more liberal Sweden.

Privately Crosthwaite was a worrier, but also a much more sympathetic character than his professional persona suggested, showing huge kindness to those close to him and none of the moralising imputed to him. He was also generous with the use of his almost regal embassy car, a vast, bronze-coloured Austin Princess, complete with fold-down seats. He would frequently put this at the disposal of Eleanor and Lorraine and their friends for watercolouring or archaeological jaunts into the hills. Above all, he was extremely conscientious, which is one reason why, as we shall see, his inadvertent entanglement with the Cambridge Five was to cause him such distress.

Stephen and Natasha Spender were not Crosthwaite's only sophisticated friends. Another was Freya Stark, world-renowned writer and expert on the Middle East, who used to visit a variety of ruins in a wide-brimmed hat (always tilted to the right, following a childhood accident) accompanied by Crosthwaite and his embassy colleague Alan Munro, impressing them greatly with her encyclopaedic knowledge before ritually beating them both at Scrabble in the evening. A diplomat's work has many guises.

Remarkably, the gunshot in the streets of 1958 Beirut had done little to spoil the essential party spirit that prevailed at night-time. One writer talks of revellers being locked into night clubs until 4 a.m. when the curfew was lifted. And the hostilities barely intruded on the cocktail party circuit, which continued to welcome glamorous and celebrated visitors from the West. Beirut was something of a magnet for a certain calibre of celebrity. James Bond's creator Ian Fleming used to pass through, picking up plot ideas and seeing friends. American writer Martha Gellhorn, generally with journalism in mind, would visit what she called 'a lovely boom town, an entrancing mixture of Asia Minor and France, with scenery to lift the heart and glamour hotels all over the lot and more abuilding'. Around the same time as one of Gellhorn's visits, a jaded and incoherent Briton turned up one weekend at the British embassy. After a little too much rest and relaxation in Beirut, he had missed a flight to Jordan, where he was due back on set first thing the following morning – not in Amman but in the spectacular Wadi Rum, a further hundred miles south of the capital – if he was to avoid serious consequences. The drunk in question turned out to be Peter O'Toole, whose absence from the set of David Lean's award-winning *Lawrence of Arabia* would indeed have been noticed. No private planes were available, not that Israeli airspace would have welcomed them, and O'Toole lacked the necessary visa. Smart work by the embassy located a driver willing to take a relieved O'Toole the nearly 500 kilometres by road via Syria.

Although Beirut had a very established smart set, an ambassador's day called for a wide range of skills with an eclectic array of people. On one occasion there was a lunch party at the Palais Sursock, home of Yvonne Sursock Cochrane, patron of the arts, the grandest of the city's *grandes dames* and standard-bearer for a Greek Orthodox family, originally from Constantinople (now Istanbul) that had settled in Beirut in 1714. As food was served, several magnificent Sudanese men, 'six foot four, scars on their cheeks, in gold caftans, glided silently around the table serving the food', reported one of the lunchers. Among the guests were Sir Ponsonby Moore Crosthwaite from the British embassy, a hotel owner and his wife, a leprosy specialist who had just flown in from Africa and two American men, then appearing at the Casino du Liban, doing a camp act imitating the wholesome Andrews Sisters, famous for their 1941 song 'Boogie Woogie Bugle Boy'. Towards the end of the lunch, Crosthwaite, perhaps nettled by a tinge of loucheness among his lunching partners and keen to offer a corrective, suggested a toast be drunk to the Queen. This struck the ersatz Andrews Sisters as singularly quaint, provoking an impassioned debate as to whether 'us old queens' also deserved a tribute. 'There was nearly an international incident,' reported someone who was there. 'Moore was about to walk out.'

While Eleanor was broadening her mind, Kim would be popping into the Normandy, chatting with journalist friends and playing the role of a man with his finger on the Middle East's pulse. But he had a new string to his bow. Earlier that year, a mysterious figure had approached him at his regular berth at the Normandy, introducing himself as Mr Petukhov and, in an East European accent, complimenting him on the depth of his articles and wondering if he would have time for a conversation

about the prospects for a Common Market of the Arab countries. A furtive rendezvous was arranged at Kim's flat at a time
when Eleanor was at a sculpture lecture. The truth that Kim
had longed for materialised. Here, at last, was the opportunity
for an active return to the Soviet fold. He had been carrying
around the burden of being a traitor, without even the thrill of
behaving treacherously.

Now he was being invited back into play. 'I have been waiting so long for you,' said Philby. It was the start of a series of
secret meetings with Petukhov, generally once a week (often on
Wednesdays) or once a fortnight, usually on neutral ground, at
which he would keep his handler informed of what was being
said in the most elevated diplomatic circles – and elsewhere.
His priority was to find out the intentions of the United States
and British government in the area. Yuri Modin, who probably
handled and translated many of his despatches, reported that
'Philby sent us excellent reports that attracted much attention
at the top . . . he served us well.'

Philby was in a good position to help Moscow at that time,
specifically through his knowledge and understanding of the
Middle East, where in several countries the USSR had no diplomatic representation. Also, says his friend and former MI6
deputy Tim Milne, being British would have been a huge help.
'It is likely that some of his Arab contacts passed him information in the belief that it was destined for the British government.
He may even have recruited some of them as agents, ostensibly
on behalf of [MI6], but actually, though they did not know it,
for the KGB.'

Years later, Philby denied trying to recruit for the KGB under
the guise of doing so for MI6. That would have been making
things too complicated, he claimed, though he seemed to
handle other complicated matters without difficulty.

Those years, following the granting of her divorce, wrote

Eleanor, were the happiest of her life. She enjoyed looking after Kim's children and her own; Annie had now rejoined her in Beirut, and the family indulged an ever-growing collection of animals of varying degrees of domestication. Kim had his journalistic obligations off to a tee and Eleanor was happy to play the dutiful wife, often taking dictation from Kim (without notes) before cabling his article to the appropriate news outlet. Kim never even needed to read it through, a skill he had inherited from his father. They had a hasty marriage in Beirut, but given Eleanor's previous marriage in France and her Mexican divorce, it was not considered legally sound. A second ceremony was held in London in January 1959, but not before Philby had paid a courtesy call on Aileen's mother to inform her. Eleanor had to wait on the steps of the Albert Memorial while Kim went in to see Mrs Alleyne – of whom Eleanor was terrified – to tell her the news.

They took advantage of the time for Kim to show his new bride some of the sights, including, of course, his favourite London pubs, and made sure that Eleanor got to know those of Philby's five bereaved children she had not previously met.

For Eleanor, things could not have been better, and Kim, remarkably, appeared as carefree as a man can be when very little separates him from the opprobrium of an entire nation and a long prison sentence. To most people Philby was a cheery and charming soul with a weakness for alcohol. 'Everyone seemed to warm towards him,' says Miles Copeland III, 'he drank, he stuttered, he was a ladies' man type. He would have a couple of drinks too many, but I know my father liked him and liked Eleanor.'

Kim's father liked Eleanor, too. They got on very well, and she was proud that St John said she was his favourite of Kim's wives. When Kim and Eleanor married, he wrote to congratulate her, before filling her in on his latest travels around Saudi

Arabia. He ends up saying how pleased he was to hear of their marriage, warmly welcoming her to the family.

The marriage took place at the register office in Russell Square, London, at 11 a.m. The registrar, a woman, told Eleanor she would never regret marrying an Englishman, a kind thought, though Eleanor felt it betrayed rather too much jingoistic complacency for her liking. Afterwards they bought champagne at Harrods, went to their friends the Ivenses, lunched on oysters at Wheeler's and spent the rest of the day at Douglas Collins's flat. Annie, too, was there. A few days later, Tim Milne and Marie arrived for an early evening drink at the flat at which the Philbys were staying. Eleanor came to the door looking shattered. After an extended boozy lunch, Kim had simply carried on drinking and passed out. The drink was getting to him, as it got to at least two others who had taken the same path and, until their defection, had been under the same strain, his colleagues Guy Burgess and Donald Maclean. Philby, though, rarely let anything slip.

By the summer of 1959, domestically speaking Kim was, in a popular phrase of the day, 'under new management'. He continued to go to the Normandy and the St Georges, but now rather more to the latter. He was no longer among the gritty surroundings of Basta and had moved with Eleanor into a small, comfortable flat on rue Kantari on the edge of the Christian quarter, complete with enticing terrace looking towards the sea. Eleanor equipped it stylishly with Arab rugs and wall coverings, and it now felt truly like home. Although Beirut was a city of parties, both Kim and Eleanor were happy staying in. They were content in one another's company, and Eleanor saw the home-loving, mellow Kim who completed the *Times* crossword (always in under nineteen minutes). Otherwise they would read poetry or listen to music, often Beethoven sonatas (he remembered all the opus numbers and would often be moved to tears) or Enrique Granados's Goyescas and he would stand and wave his arms listening to Tchaikovsky. He would howl with laughter at P. G. Wodehouse, wallow in Gerald Durrell's animal stories and become engrossed in the crime stories of Rex Stout, and sometimes he would work on a long-term project, a history of Russia (not mentioned in Eleanor's book). Eleanor would often sculpt or read about high art. They both continued to enjoy alcohol, but its unquestioned consumption, heavier and more habitual than is fashionable nowadays, was a measured, routine part of their day, a move away from the undignified bingeing that had characterised the more stressful periods of Philby's career. They would sometimes be seen out, walking hand in hand, Kim often wearing a seersucker suit from the United States that, like all his clothes, Eleanor had bought for him.

At weekends there would often be a one- or two-day trip out of town. 'We all knew each other, and I remember Kim and Eleanor at picnics,' remembers Alice Brinton, whose parents were part of Beirut's Anglo-US set. 'Kim was always great fun. He was very good with kids. We were treated like little adults by him. I remember him once bringing his pet fox. He wouldn't let anyone touch the fox, who he said was very shy.' This sensitivity was much noticed. The son of a colleague spoke with particular feeling: 'I realised my parents did not have a clue how to relate to children. Kim did, very much so. One summer I spent a lot of time over at their flat. It was full of bonhomie, a family atmosphere, Kim was very kind to me in a way that my father never was. I was a very introverted, shy, fourteen-year-old … and there was a party at their flat. Kim came across the room, sat down next to me and chatted happily, and that was *totally* genuine.' Children were treated as adults in more ways than one. His son Harry was said to mix a fierce martini. Kim and Eleanor's liking for alcohol was not exceptional, at least at that stage. 'It was a drinking society in those days,' says Brinton.

'Everyone drank, they took Bloody Marys and dry martinis in Thermoses. In hindsight I wonder how all our parents got down the hill sometimes.'

One visitor to the Philbys' flat that year was young Frank Wisner, son of the senior CIA man of the same name who had been friends of the Brewers when Eleanor was with Sam. As a Princeton student attending summer school at the American University of Beirut, the young Wisner was invited to the flat one afternoon to help him settle in Beirut. He remembers Eleanor being extremely friendly and accommodating, sitting on the floor with one of Kim's daughters, playing 'struggle' songs from the 1930s on a phonograph, but on that occasion, he did not meet Philby. 'It was fun, and she was a pleasant person. She had a fabulous collection of Lead Belly, the great black American singer who sang songs of the left of the struggles of the day and we sat and listened. Meanwhile, I could see through an open door, the stockinged feet of Kim Philby as he slept. I remember, from the conversations around the music, that she had a strong left-wing bias. She would say: "You've got to listen to this, this part really captures the mood."' Eleanor had been an admirer of Eleanor Roosevelt, the public-spirited wife of former President F. D. Roosevelt, leaving behind her Republican-voting upbringing.

Philby still had his enemies, who must by 1959 have been seething more than ever at his rehabilitation. One of those who had to mediate between those convinced of his guilt and the needs of diplomacy with an ally was Ed Applewhite, who arrived as CIA station chief in Beirut in 1959. He had been asked to keep tabs on Philby, but received little help from MI6. Personally he kept an open mind for a long time, deciding that the best way to learn more was to become professionally friendly with him. His children and Philby's attended the same schools and their families socialised together, Applewhite making copious notes after each meeting. He finally concluded that Philby was 'much too sophisticated to give his allegiance to such a doctrinaire business as Marxism'.

Part of the disguise that was to take in Applewhite and so many others was Philby's occasional affecting of indignation at the continuing suspicion against him. On one occasion, Applewhite invited the young Frank Wisner to join him and Philby for lunch. Wisner's father had been one of the leading sceptics about Philby's loyalty back in 1950/51, and had made no secret of it, but Applewhite – to the extent that he can have thought about it – assumed that was water under the bridge, and Wisner was looking forward to making Philby's acquaintance after the previous false start. He remembers Applewhite greeting Philby on the street with the words: 'This young man is going to join us for lunch, I'd like to introduce you to young Frank Wisner, you perhaps remember his father.' 'Philby stopped,' recalls Wisner. 'He stared at me for a matter of seconds and said very clearly and brusquely: "I know your father well." And turned on his heel and walked away', leaving the pair dumbfounded on the pavement.

But there was yet more in store to enrage his challengers. Late that year, his friend and most implacable defender, his former MI6 chum Nicholas Elliott, was told he was to leave his posting in Vienna and return to the city in which, seventeen years earlier, he had won the heart of his then secretary Elizabeth. He was made MI6's head of station in Beirut. Nicholas and Elizabeth marked their first night back in the city with a meal at the famous Lucullus French restaurant. There they encountered – possibly not by chance – Kim, Eleanor and St John, dining at a nearby table. '[Kim] came across and gave me a hug,' remembers Elliott. There was something almost poetic that this high point of the rehabilitation of Kim – now contentedly married, no longer living his 'unconventional, secluded life of the Muslim quarter', as Eleanor put it – was reached in the company of his wife and father. 'It was a most agreeable reunion,' said Nicholas with characteristic understatement.

Now Kim, as the local 'old hand', was in a position to repay the support that Nicholas had given him during the eighteen years of their acquaintance. He understood the lie of the land, and was excellently placed to help his friend settle in. Kim, it seemed, had served his apprenticeship back in the fold, and had done nothing to step out of line. If Paulson was encouraged by some colleagues to doubt Kim's loyalty, Elliott would be freer to come to his own view. He told the embassy's press attaché that Philby was sound and could be trusted with secrets: 'He was one of us,' he confided, omitting to mention that he was *still* 'one of us', and of course ignorant of the fact that he was also still 'one of them'.

On the face of things, this was indeed a happy sign of MI6's renewed faith in Philby, although there are reasons to think the reverse. Maybe Elliott's arrival would make Philby drop his guard. An increased workload from MI6 might prompt more frequent secret contact with the Russians – which might at last throw up proof of his treachery. If that was indeed the game Elliott was being asked to play, as some have claimed, he played it with the greatest reluctance.*

Only one in six of the pieces Philby wrote for the *Observer* in the twelve months before Elliott's arrival involved travel outside Beirut, almost as if his magisterial scanning of the skyline from the bars of Beirut was sufficient. Yet after Elliott's arrival, in 1961, nearly half of his pieces had a non-Beirut dateline, generally Cairo, Tehran or Kuwait. As a journalist, he had been on cruise control, publicly assimilating and regurgitating for his readers an acceptable version of whatever he picked up, and not

---

* Phillip Knightley (*Philby: The Life and Views of the KGB Masterspy*, p. 206) believed that was Dick White's plan. Elliott strongly denied it, as did White.

necessarily even attending press conferences others regarded
as essential. Now there seemed more fire in the belly, whether
in the interests of his current or ostensibly previous employers,
or more likely both. Eleanor felt his frequent meetings with
Elliott – implicitly covert, whichever master he was serving –
always seemed to him more like proper work.

Though Kim was employed by two distinguished London-
based media outlets, he never seemed overworked. This was
the age when any newspaper worthy of the name would have
a correspondent stationed in all the major capitals of the
world. Further, their word for what was happening on the
ground was essentially unchallenged by the foreign desk,
whatever ingenious wheeze the editor might have come up
with from London, Paris or Washington. It was a licence
for all sorts of lax behaviour. 'He was neither Observing nor
Economising,' remarked one old hand as he watched Philby
order another drink.

Also living in Beirut was Edith Hall, born in 1906, the daughter
of British parents in Chantilly in France, where they worked at
the celebrated Boussac horseracing stable. As a result she spoke
excellent French. Her first job had been as a typist in the Foreign
Office. Later she went travelling, ending up in India during the
war, spending nine months in the naval office in Bombay and
then six years in Colombo, in what is now Sri Lanka, the last
four of which were in the Naval Office. Returning to Europe,
she joined SOE as a clerk for the last year of the war, and in
June 1945 moved to OSS (forerunner to the CIA), with offices
next to MI6's in Ryder Street in central London.

In the early 1950s, seemingly, at least, she put all that behind
her, and, having answered an advertisement in *The Lady* magazine, accepted a job as a nanny, looking after the children of

the influential Sursock family, with whom she worked for nearly twenty years.

Her employers got wind of several occasions when she was seen lunching with Philby at the St Georges Club, a much more low-key and understated venue than its hotel namesake. Looking back, the family believes she had been tasked by either British or American intelligence services to be a fly on the wall. 'There are good reasons to be a spook in a Sursock household,' says Alfred Sursock Cochrane. His aunt Linda Sursock 'held a very high-powered political salon and had long been at the centre of power since the 1920s, then, as a Francophile, was on very good terms with the French High Commission and during the independence days up to the seventies had her finger firmly on the political pulse of the country which at the time played a far greater social and financial role in the Middle East than it does now.'

Kim was supremely good at living a double life, and when under pressure was able to raise his game. But inevitably there were moments when even he was guilty of inattention. Theo Larsson recalled one Saturday when Kim, who had just filed for the *Observer*, and he were having a drink in Joe's Bar. 'I've just had a pat on the back from my masters,' said Philby.

'What, both of them?' asked Larsson.

Larsson recalled: 'Philby swung round with a wild look on his face. "What do you mean both of them?" he demanded, with no trace of his stammer. Rather surprised, I explained that I was referring to the two journals he wrote for and he relapsed into his normal friendly self.'

Another time, Charles Dowsett, then a lecturer in Armenian at the School of Oriental and African Studies, was visiting from London, and was invited to a party for St John Philby. It was decided that the two men, plus his friend John Carswell, Kim, Eleanor and others, should go out for a meal afterwards.

Dowsett mentioned he would like to eat a really good kebab, and wondered if anyone could recommend somewhere. Kim piped up confidently, 'Oh, you should go to Vrej.' Eleanor, overhearing this, was mystified. She had never heard of Vrej. They took a taxi to the end of a tramline, to a tiny hole-in-the-wall establishment with only six tables in the Armenian district, by the Beirut river. 'The kebabs were great,' said one who was there. One Beirut resident said later: 'It was clear to me this was where Kim met his contacts.' Either way, it was a part of Kim's life Eleanor knew nothing about. If she did ever query what he was doing, he would say that as he was working for MI6 (which was as much as he had permission to tell her), so he could not elaborate.

There was always time for relaxed family gatherings, including with the Elliotts. Nicholas was almost a caricature of a public-school chap. He was tall, well-turned-out (favouring double-breasted suits) and unfailingly courteous, as his father Claude, a highly regarded former Eton Head Master, would have hoped. He was '5ft 9ins tall. Brown hair, prominent lips, black glasses, ugly and rather pig-like to look at. Good brain, good sense of humour', according to Philby's description of him for an internal MI6 report. Nicholas and Kim shared an enthusiasm for ribald jokes and, when back in England, a devotion to watching cricket. Frequently their wives were left chatting as these senior spies transformed one another into giggling schoolboys. One such occasion was a lunch given by the Elliotts attended by Humphrey Trevelyan, Britain's ambassador to Iraq, who was then staying with him. Trevelyan expressed a desire to meet the sage of Saudi, pushing diplomacy to remarkable levels, given St John Philby's reputation for cantankerousness. At that point he was rounding off an agreeable summer of Athenaeum lunches and cricket at Lords by spending a few days enjoying Beirut to the full.

Following plenty of wine at the Trevelyan lunch, St John and Kim left the Elliotts' mid-afternoon, well refreshed, continuing a pattern set a few days earlier when Eleanor had had to put both father and son to bed, so drunk were they. Undaunted by this precedent, the pair, outrageously, planned to go to have a drink with Theo Larsson, who, though they had forgotten, had invited them to his beachside house for lunch (crevettes vols au vent followed by roast lamb with asparagus and then a chocolate soufflé, a menu chosen by Kim and his putative host), and had been waiting three hours for them. Even the Philby charm didn't appease the fuming Swede, who had put out copies of St John's books for the author to sign. He turned them down.

Undaunted, the effusive pair emerged later at a party given by John Fistere. There St John was taken ill, looking 'cardiacky'. Kim, himself the worse for wear, took his father back to his hotel, the Normandy. Only in the morning – by which time he had had a beer and a second heart attack – did St John agree to a doctor being called. Arriving at the hospital on 30 September 1960, he was awake only briefly, pronouncing in the afternoon: 'God I'm bored', and dying soon afterwards. Kim the insistent atheist omitted the word 'God' in his version of the story.

After his death at around 5 p.m., the body was taken to the American University hospital. The following morning Kim arranged for it to be bound in a shroud, according to Muslim custom, and it was carried up the hill to the Bashura cemetery. As the journey would take a while, the unhappy couple decided to drop in at the Normandy Hotel. There they bumped into two journalists Kim didn't like, who defied hints about the funeral being very private and insisted on coming along.

The poorly attended burial was paid for by the proprietor of the Hotel Normandy where St John had spent a lot of time while out of favour in Saudi Arabia. Anwar Lamel, the barman, was one of the pallbearers. St John's body was lowered into his grave and heavy stones placed on top. The diary of John Slade-Baker, of the *Sunday Times* and MI6, who was present at the ceremony, recorded: 'The whole ceremony was simple and very quick almost as though they were burying a peasant instead of one of the leading Orientalists in the world.'

Kim found time to file a story that was unusual even by an unusual journalist's standards. The *Observer*'s headline the next day read: 'St.J. Philby dies, aged 75.' Below it were the words: 'From H.A.R. Philby, Beirut, October 1', and a brief and factual news story.

His father's death took a terrible toll, prompting many to believe that his father was in some deep-seated way the key to the double life of which St John was ignorant. Tim Milne's view is that it was St John's absences, rather than his presence, that shaped Kim. St John was in the Middle East for much of Kim's childhood, leaving the boy to be doted on by his mother, grandmother and three sisters. Kim had followed his father from Westminster to Trinity, Cambridge, and emulated his father's non-conformism and contempt for comfortable assumptions, but he wanted to be his own person, a man of reason above all.

'I was perhaps the only member of his wide acquaintance to whom he was never rude, and to whose opinions he invariably listened with respect,' he wrote. Kim chose to fight fascism, whereas St John stood for the fascist British People's Party and was briefly sent to prison for expressing anti-British remarks.

Nor had Kim felt, he wrote, 'the slightest temptation to follow his example' of converting to Islam or spending long periods in Saudi Arabia. 'The limitless space, the clear night skies and the rest of the gobbledygook are all right in small doses. But I would find a lifetime in a landscape with majesty but no charm, among a people with neither majesty nor charm, quite unacceptable. Ignorance and arrogance make a bad combination, and the Saudi Arabians have both in generous measure.'

But Kim owed his adoring, admiring father a lot, including the support and contacts that got him into journalism, *The*

Times, the civil service, the Athenaeum and latterly into the highest of circles in the Middle East. He also inherited his conceit – fashionably called exceptionalism – and a seditious sense of determination, as is evident in St John's edict: 'If you feel strongly enough about something you must have the guts to go through with it no matter what anyone might think.'

And latterly, the two had bonded in Lebanon. The author and journalist Anthony Cave Brown recalled waking up in a Beirut hotel one day in 1959 as a magnificent ochre dawn was breaking, hearing a noise in the street. He looked out of his window to see Philby father and son, arm in arm, singing 'Bang Bang Lulu', the sort of popular British song – generally about sexually obliging young women – that, at the moment of an anticipated expletive, would revert to the chorus, providing hours of simple schoolboy hilarity.

Bang, bang, Lulu; Lulu's gone away
Who's gonna bang bang, now Lulu's gone away

Lulu had a boyfriend who drove a garbage truck.
Never collected garbage, 'cause all he did was ...

Bang, bang, Lulu; Lulu's gone away
Who's gonna bang bang, now Lulu's gone away

Now, Lulu had a baby, it came as quite a shock.
She couldn't name it 'Lulu', because it had a ...

Bang, bang, Lulu ... etc.

Notwithstanding his own revelry and the late nights at Beirut's infamous Kit Kat Club, St John worried that Kim was not doing anything serious with his life. He told him he had gone from being someone with convictions at university to being a playboy journalist. It was a mark of the still unbridged gap between the pair. Eleanor's feeling, expressed much later, was that it was a good thing St John didn't live to learn what his son had been doing. But, she speculates, maybe he would have admired the tenacity his son showed. It was perhaps with this in mind that Philby *fils* wrote that, had his father lived to know of his work for the Soviet Union, he 'would have been thunderstruck but by no means disapproving'. Signing up with Stalin, after all, was nothing if not serious.

The death of his father and the loss of his unconditional love provoked a breakdown. Anthony Cave Brown, the authority on the Philbys' relationship, believed that Kim turning more than ever to alcohol in the following weeks was down in part to the ever-present strain of playing double or treble games, but also a knowledge that had he been less drunk himself that night, he might have saved his father had he taken him to hospital more promptly. In a letter to a friend he wrote that 'morale is pretty low around these parts' on account of Eleanor's father having died on the following Thursday, 6 October.*

In Beirut, everybody had a tale of Philby's alcoholic excess, often with Eleanor matching him drink for drink. He was drinking large quantities, but generally harmlessly. If he embarrassed himself or his friends, a morning-after phone call and buckets of charm would ensure all would be forgotten. Susan Griggs remembers Kim and Eleanor leaving a party arm in arm, both very drunk. They stumbled, but hung onto one another as they fell, ensuring that both badly damaged their outer elbows. Both were in plaster for weeks.

---

* In some accounts Philby reported that it was Eleanor's uncle, not father, who had died, suggesting maybe Philby himself, in his own grief, had made a mistake. In another message Kim sent to his friend Molly Izzard on 10 October, he did not make the mistake.

On another occasion, at a cocktail party given by Nicholas Elliott and his wife Elizabeth for his visiting parents, Philby turned to Sir Moore Crosthwaite and said of the woman (the wife of an embassy staffer) standing next to them: 'Don't you think Anne has the finest breasts in Beirut?' Elliott, with whom Philby enjoyed countless schoolboy jokes, loved telling the story, more amused by the number of people the remark annoyed than annoyed himself.

There was also an evening when he and Eleanor invited an elderly ex-army officer to dinner, seating him next to a young woman to whom he was attracted but with whom he was making no progress. Kim knew the woman was unlikely to reciprocate, but told the man that the woman was extremely shy, and that all that was needed was the liberal use of hands under the table. In fact, the story goes, she tried to 'pound the officer's head into his soup', much to the drunken Philby's amusement.

When being collected to go on picnics, the Philbys would often claim they needed to drop by at the Normandy to collect their post, which invariably turned into one for the road (or more) before the day had even started. And once the site had been seen and the meal and picnic wine finished, there would be an excursion nearby to buy miniatures, to complement the supplies they hoarded from aeroplane trips. One account has them drinking over forty between them.

Much of the time they seemed happy drunks, 'bruised and scarred by a hundred falls against the furniture,' wrote Patrick Seale. Drinking was something they had enjoyed earlier in their lives, but both had had it more or less under control. Kim's drinking had deteriorated as the pressure on him grew, but equally there were spells of comparative sobriety when it was an agreeable aid rather than – for Kim at least – an indispensable refuge.

Susan Griggs remembers lunches hosted by her parents, the Fisteres, in the later stages of the Philbys' time in Beirut. 'Kim and Eleanor were falling down drunk by the time they went home for their afternoon nap. And they'd rise up again at six and go out and drink some more. I don't know how they made it. For months and months I refused to believe that Kim Philby was a great master spy. I used to say he was incapable after midday. "He can't possibly be a double agent." Wrong. He totally could be. They would arrive at my parents at one and by three they were falling around the street and breaking their elbows. They drank Chateau Musar, or white Ksara, from the Bekaa Valley, and by the evening they got onto the brown stuff.' And yet, even in a more disapproving age (but perhaps a less disapproving place), people went on inviting the Philbys. They were popular and fun.

How could he hold so much drink and never give anything away? Philby later told Phillip Knightley: 'It wasn't a trick or anything like that. It was just that something within me seemed to be aware that there was a limit to what I could say, a limit beyond which I could not go. No matter how much I drank it was always there.'

Drink, it seems, had become not a threat to his big secret but an accessory to it. But the drinking, always part of an inner search for balm in his tormented double life, was rarely larky by this point. The death of St John was one of those episodes that brought about a deep dive into the alcoholic abyss. He was to come out of this one, but there were to be more. Some things were immune even to Kim Philby's charm.

6

What's wrong, darling?

The death of St John Philby, unsurprisingly, was a watershed in his son's life. Kim spent much of the autumn of 1960 tidying up his father's estate in Saudi Arabia – no easy matter, and he didn't relish the task of making his young half-brothers financially comfortable while he and Eleanor struggled to pay the school fees. His own worries about money continued, although after the intestate Aileen's death he had set up trusts to ensure his children had help on their way in life. Shuttling backwards and forwards to Jiddah on family business, he had little time for journalism, and wrote just three short pieces for the *Observer* in the last three months of the year.

Christmas was spent – expensively – in London, enjoying a fond reunion with all five of the Philby children. They stayed in England for a month, much of it at the White Hart pub in Nettlebed, Oxfordshire, where Kim looked forward to some traditional English roasts. Things were getting back on an even keel, and life after St John was coming to take shape.

There were still children to be educated and bills to be paid, but Kim's own self-esteem was boosted by a renewed sense of being useful, both to MI6 and to the KGB. And with that came extra cash, or being 'in the chips,' as he would call it. One day, shortly before they left Beirut for London, Kim came home to

Eleanor in rue Kantari and scattered ten $100 bills around the sitting room. Eleanor naturally assumed it had come from MI6.

In the New Year, the Philbys' lives returned to an agreeable routine. As far as Eleanor was concerned, a sort of normality had been restored. Kim seemed to have few worries in his work for MI6, with Nicholas Elliott, one of his oldest friends, now by his side as a trusted and grateful boss. Eleanor's daughter Annie attended the francophone Collège Protestant Français and for a long time struggled with her French. But she thought Kim a delight, and night after night he would help her overcome her concerns and generally cheer her up. Eleanor got on as well as stepmothers can hope with Kim's children and she was enjoying her continuing trips into the countryside around Beirut with her friends.

Beneath the surface, though, trouble was brewing for her husband. Alone, Philby would need to shoulder alarming news from abroad, as we shall see. In London, a fellow Soviet mole was caught and imprisoned for several decades, a sentence that shocked even the most patriotic of his foes. In Helsinki a well-placed Russian who had defected to the West was talking authoritatively about a group of five British traitors that sounded very much like Kim and his associates. And in Israel, an old friend who knew of his politics in the 1930s turned, crucially, against him. Each of these events might have rebounded disastrously for him, or maybe each could fizzle out into nothing, as so many scares had done before. He couldn't be sure, but in any event each was beyond his control. No wonder he was feeling the pressure, and even making the odd mistake. Eleanor, on the other hand, recalled that period, anticipating 'years of happiness in store'. The inadequacy of the phrase 'blissfully unaware' can hardly be expressed.

Nonetheless, following a deep trough after his father's death, Philby was trying to get his drinking back into some sort of orderly pattern. There were spells when Eleanor chastised him for his excess – and she, too, was susceptible – but the drier periods saw a return to a degree of conviviality and good cheer.

Around this time John Midgley, another Cambridge contemporary, came to stay, but as Kim's boss, as foreign editor at *The Economist*, rather than a friend, as part of a tour of his Middle East correspondents. Midgley had been unimpressed with the quantity and quality of Philby's work, and his father's death had called for several weeks off. Midgley's man on the spot was keen to remedy the matter and present himself as committed, wise to the surroundings and hardworking. Unusually, Kim made a point of going to the airport to meet the important visitor. He and Eleanor left a friend's early evening drinks party to take a cab to the airport. This was a moment to show off his local command to his boss. He pushed himself to the front, seizing Midgley's passport and peremptorily waving it at the relevant person in uniform. The official was not amused, and made the distinguished new arrival wait until everyone else had gone through. On boarding a cab, Philby, who tended not to deploy his skills as a linguist needlessly, felt this was a special occasion and barked out instructions in Arabic – a language for which he had no fondness – for them to be taken home. They were taken back to the party they had just left.

The Philbys' social life in Beirut resumed its customary course. Kim always told Eleanor that he didn't enjoy big parties, and preferred a quiet night in, preparing *boeuf en daube*, but he was always expected and always a success, if you include the frequent need for an apology the following day. Besides, if he was to keep a finger on the pulse for his various bosses, he could not afford not to go. Among Beirut's eminent visitors was George Brown, a rising star in the Labour Party, who was to be made Foreign Secretary after Britain's next election. His evident Zionist sympathies had to be given a more acceptable gloss by embassy officials. At another event at the embassy at the end of March 1961, he was surprised to bump into an old Cambridge acquaintance, Sir Anthony Blunt, Surveyor of the Queen's Pictures, who was on a lecture tour with the British Council. He was a friend of the ambassador, Moore Crosthwaite. Kim seemed to know everyone.

In late 1961 he went to Tehran to write a reflective report on the challenges facing the leader, Dr Ali Amini, followed by a newsier account of how a Western military presence had deterred Iraq from invading Kuwait, a lesson forgotten by Western diplomats and politicians nearly thirty years later, and then to Cairo at the height of the summer for a meeting of the Arab League.

The presence of Nicholas Elliott allowed him an expanded role, which included keeping an ear to the ground and suggesting the recruitment of assets for MI6. Around this time, senior MI6 officer Maurice Oldfield, an occasional visitor to Beirut and someone who took a great interest in journalists as sources, was developing the idea of 'unconscious' agents or assets. They were not aware that they had been recruited as sources or contacts but were helped in their careers and would develop 'friends' who would meet occasionally and converse about suitable topics or suggest certain actions. They might or might not be told at a later stage that they, effectively, had been recruited. Some officers questioned such behaviour, which they regarded as unethical, but Oldfield – often mistaken for a liberal figure – was very successful in using it.

That said, whether these would have been paid informers, investigators or merely useful patriots willing to exchange gossip – rather as journalists cultivate such people – matters little in this context. It cannot be known for sure if Philby was encouraged to recruit for MI6, and little evidence has emerged until now, although spy writer Chapman Pincher claimed that he was helping 'to recruit and run agents'. The MI6 files are, of course, closed, and its sources are protected to the grave and beyond, but Elliott, a newcomer to the Middle East, would have welcomed a man as well connected as Philby being alive to all possibilities. That, surely, was what he was there for.

It seems one such intended source was Dick Dyerson, now in his nineties. He had done his national service in the Intelligence Corps during the war and learned good French working as a waiter in Switzerland. He moved into magazines and later joined *The Economist*. He was invited to meet two ex-servicemen at a private house in clubland in London's St James's. They explained that there was a job going seeking to extend the reach of *The Economist*, then selling a modest five thousand copies a week, in Europe, the Middle East and Africa. Dyerson, who had some knowledge of sales promotion, was struck by the implausibility of extensive amounts of expenses-paid travel when any increase in sales would be slight and 'would be evaporated with the cost of this Phileas Fogg adventure'. He was unconvinced by the two men's claim that the magazine appearing in far-off lands 'would encourage the advertisers'.

Nonetheless, he was intrigued and when he arrived in Beirut in early February 1962 he called upon the *Economist*'s correspondent, Kim Philby, as arranged. Though it seems now that Dyerson was never likely to fit the MI6 mould, Philby arranged for them to meet twice, once at home for a meal with Eleanor and once at a hotel. Dyerson's strong suspicion was that he was being sized up.

Stephen Dorril, author of *MI6: Fifty Years of Special Operations*, says: 'Dyerson's tale is fascinating and cannot be totally dismissed because it fits in with what was happening in that period. *The Economist* had a very close relationship with MI6 and had direct links through other journalists such as Brian Crozier. His experience is not unusual. As a former

Intelligence Corps member who travels to many places and meets people in whom MI6 might have an interest, he is an obvious target for recruitment. The strangeness of elements of his story – of not really knowing what is going on – is also not unusual.'

In the event, the Philby story moved on again. In the spring of 1961, George Blake, a Dutch-born employee of MI6, had been sent to MECAS, the Middle East Centre for Arab Studies, effectively the language school, in the hills at Shemlan near Abey, to the south of Beirut. Philby did not know Blake, nor did he know that Blake had been recruited by the Russians during the Korean War, reporting himself shocked at the damage being inflicted on innocent civilians. Prompted largely by idealism, though other factors must have played a role, he had worked silently for the Soviet cause in ever-higher positions. One night at the theatre in Beirut, he bumped into Nicholas Elliott, a man he had never liked or trusted and regarded as an antisemite. How fortunate that they should meet, beamed the station chief, because he had been planning to come up to let Blake know that the office in London had been in touch. They had said Blake was in line for another promotion and would he please come to England to discuss the matter in the next few days. Blake, still in his thirties and full of promise, was suspicious. He imagined this was a trick to lure him onto British soil where he could be arrested, and to avoid that he would need to confess to his activities to his wife and flee, but first he contacted his Russian controllers. They disagreed, seeing no reason to think this was a trap, and that he should go to London as suggested, so he went.

His instinct was correct. The chance meeting at the theatre had been no such thing. It was the first part of a trap. In London he was questioned, reacting angrily to the suggestion that it was torture and blackmail rather than conviction that had driven him, and he confessed. The maximum penalty for breaching the Official Secrets Act was fourteen years, but the case was separated into five time periods, and the judge ordered three of his penalties to be served consecutively – making a total of forty-two years. Blake's crime, which had caused the deaths of many people and the exposure of hundreds of British agents to the Russians, was, said Lord Chief Justice Parker, one of the worst that can be imagined 'other than in a time of war'. The weight of the sentence was stunning, attracting huge public and media attention.

Blake's fate astonished Philby. If he needed reminding of the treacherous nature of the commitment he had made in the 1930s, this was it. Dick Beeston, ever on the lookout for a story for the *News Chronicle*, dropped round to see Philby the following day. There had been a party the night before. 'Kim was looking terrible, nursing a hangover which made him even more incoherent ... Kim's appearance had strikingly deteriorated since I had last seen him. And there is little doubt that Blake's arrest and his savage forty-two-year sentence precipitated Kim's further decline.'

But his torment was of a peculiarly painful type. He had known nothing of Blake's activities, and vice versa, so there was every chance of Blake's fate having no bearing on his own prospects of remaining undetected. It merely emphasised the trouble he would be in if the old whispers turned out to be true. He had to carry on, with the same outward insouciance as before. But the drinking was getting worse.

Phillip Knightley says Philby was so saturated with alcohol that often two martinis would send him rolling into the gutter. Frequently he would have to be carried to a taxi.

Accounts of the time suggest a kind of alcoholic descent, and in a sense Kim's entire life was just that, but for all the pressure life was continuing as before. Kim and Eleanor and Nicholas and Elizabeth Elliott would potter on, observing Britain's gradually declining influence in the region, telling silly stories and generally having fun in the sun. Though worried about Kim's drinking, Eleanor found him the same loving, solicitous and caring husband she had always wanted him to be. If he had other worries in his life, as far as she could tell, they were for his children, back in England.

Notwithstanding the difficulties, she had found her soulmate, and a most articulate one. Previously he had written her a letter analysing her character, evidently in response to something she had written. Eleanor described it as being 'as loving and attentive as any woman could wish'.

Kim wrote that she was among 'the easiest, most soothing presences I have ever met', and praised her for accepting him for what he was, rather than trying to change him. He soothed her fears of being awkward and discontented, and assured her of his love: 'That is solid fact.'

Eleanor mentions that it was only in 1962 that she came to be aware of the unresolved tensions in Kim's life. Some of them are apparent in a letter he wrote her from a part of Arabia where he had no access to alcohol, and as a result had very lucid dreams, often involving 'violent desires', invariably frustrated.

This 'violent desires' is curious. She claimed in her book that Kim was never violent, and generally he was the least physically imposing – or even active – of men. He was on the whole equable rather than moody, but moments of crisis would occasionally bring out an aggressive side.

An Indian journalist, Willy Lazarus, often Philby's host in Cairo, told of how he would sometimes have to grapple with the drunken Philby late at night as he deliriously demanded 'Where's Eleanor? You've hidden her somewhere!' The next morning, all would be forgotten, the sweet-natured Kim restored.

And, like so many stories about Philby, Moyra Beeston's

tale of his 'Chinese burn' is both revealing and unsatisfyingly inconclusive. One night, having a last, post-party drink with the Beestons at Joe's Bar, round the corner from the British embassy, Moyra asked Kim if he was the 'Third Man'. He grabbed her by the wrist and replied: 'You know Moyra, I always believe that loyalty to your friends is more important than anything else ... What would you do if you knew something awful was going to happen to a friend and only you could do something about it?' This, remarkably for a supposedly ice-cool super-spy, was effectively an admission that he had indeed tipped off Maclean in 1951. By the standards Philby was espousing, his behaviour, chiming with the writings of G. E. Moore and E. M. Forster, was admirable. Institutions and '-isms' take second place to real human relationships. And whereas in a comfortable world loyalty to friends is an easily ticked and generally unchallenged part of the modern creed, to that generation of 1930s Soviet-leaning Utopians, whose political ideals were yearly being tested by reality and failing, this one achieved a particular, bonding, defining status. Without that, they were merely a handful of clever, unpatriotic drunks.

But in 'looking after his friends' in 1951, he had also done something more self-serving. Maclean had been on the verge of a breakdown, and under interrogation might well not only have confessed but incriminated Philby and others. Better, then, to hasten his departure by both tipping off Maclean, and also – knowing the inevitable had arrived – seeking to get on the right side of it. It was not the first time that a spy's true motives were hard to discern even after the event, and there would be another example along soon.

The joshing with Nicholas Elliott was entirely on the surface, and there was a limit to what work Philby could do for MI6 in Beirut. He could not break through 'the wall of Anglo-American caution'. Elliott may have continued to trust his friend, but protocols set in London had to be observed. He had to be professional. Kim made several trips with Eleanor elsewhere in the Middle East in 1961 and 1962 – to Tehran in early 1962 and Egypt and Jordan later that year, for example – which resulted in no immediate output for either the *Observer* or *The Economist*. Presumably they served Elliott rather better.

He saw his Soviet contact Petukhov once every ten days or so, but was not able to tell the Russian anything that couldn't be inferred from others in the area. He remained well connected, of course, but his reports were like his journalism: soundly analytical but lacking an arresting 'top line'. On one occasion he was asked by his Soviet bosses to recruit a signals official from the Pakistani embassy. He thought this a risky proposal, given the unlikelihood of a man who mingled with ambassadors being friends with a Pakistani cipher clerk, and he refused. Seemingly it was not the only time he was asked to do something outside his comfort – or safety – zone. Despite being 'upset and surprised' by the request, he remained meek and uncritical in dealings with his bosses. 'Sometimes it was hard for the Centre to take into account the circumstances on the ground,' he told Genrikh Borovik mildly.

MI6 never asked Philby to find out about Russian operations in Beirut or cultivate Russian contacts, a sure sign that they did not wholly trust him. 'I did not understand right away that it would be very difficult for me to be truly useful to Moscow,' said Philby later of his time in Beirut. 'The British and Americans were cautious with me. And I had to be cautious with them, so as not to arouse any new suspicions ... My work in the Middle East did not give me great satisfaction. Nor to the Centre, I imagine.' Kim would have been a useful analyser of shifting sands and as an absorber of party chat, but Moscow was also mistrustful, perhaps knowing how close Kim had been to Elliott.

Christmas 1961 was spent with the family in England, and Kim and Eleanor took the opportunity to see some London entertainment, particularly enjoying a West End performance of *Beyond the Fringe* in its pomp, starring four satirists destined for international acclaim – Alan Bennett, Peter Cook, Jonathan Miller and Dudley Moore. A couple of months earlier, Prime Minister Harold Macmillan had also seen the show, and had to endure seeing his lofty, public-school self savagely lampooned on stage.

The break in London must have been welcome respite from a life that to Kim was becoming increasingly unsustainable. To Eleanor, though, it was an agreeable switch of scene from an exceedingly pleasant existence in an exotic location to one of the cultural capitals of the world. In the late spring of 1962, Nicholas Elliott's stint in Beirut was coming to an end. Philby's friend had been very much 'the devil you know', and his replacement, Peter Lunn, might make different demands. Journalistically he was not setting the world on fire, and the Russians were evidently unable to make the best use of his talents. Theo Larsson reported that Kim seemed to be going through some sort of personal crisis. 'Eleanor came to ask if I could help,' he wrote, 'but I was just as much in the dark as she was.' Kim's drinking got harder to cope with. 'At a party at our house he fell all the way down the outside step, and had to be manhandled into a car to take him home.'

In April 1962, Aristotle Onassis's yacht *Christina* arrived off Beirut. One passenger was Sir Winston Churchill, then a venerable eighty-seven-year-old, who was to be the recipient of a priceless Phoenician glass jar from the Lebanese government. He was too unwell to go ashore, so an official delivered it. Also on board was Bill Deakin, the first warden of St Antony's College, Oxford, who made time to see Philby, a contemporary from Westminster School. The pair spent a long evening together, Deakin concluding that Philby, reluctant to end the evening, was in a bad way.

A few months earlier, at the end of 1961, unknown to Philby until later, Anatoly Golitsin, a senior man on the KGB's NATO desk, turned himself over to the CIA head of station in Finland. This was the sort of thing that Philby had long feared. Golitsin had memorised as many clues as he could as to the identities of Soviet moles in the West, and had enough information to make himself valuable to the CIA and MI6. Among his allegations was that there was a 'Ring of Five' who had been recruited in the 1930s who, unusually, were 'interconscious' (they all knew of one another's existence), or so he maintained. Such was the fevered state of mind of many at the top of the CIA, there was disproportionate uncertainty as to Golitsin's bona fides. Was he a plant, designed to spread doubt in the West? Or was he sincere? The answer rather depended on the politics of the respondent. MI6's boss Dick White, for one, was very impressed.

Golitsin was a skilled storyteller, releasing information only gradually, which played into the sceptics' hands. In any event, Golitsin's presence helped to keep the pot boiling. Other defectors, reliable and otherwise, also offered their services to the West, and these were just the sorts of event that Philby would not initially be told about and which, once checked, could confront him. He needed to be as vigilant as ever, and even that might not be enough. He could be ambushed at any time.

Philby had long prepared for the day the truth came out. His Russian masters were experts in 'exfiltration' and would doubtless do all they could to avoid him falling irretrievably into enemy hands. He said later that around that time he was given a warning by the British that his time would be up soon, but nothing came of it. If he wanted to follow Burgess and Maclean to Moscow, he imagined he would be welcome there, of course, and the Soviet Union would love to trumpet the arrival of so senior a British spy. He was aware of what he had to do, should there be a sudden need to escape. But is that what he wanted? He had always disdained defectors motivated by material things, but Guy Burgess was so lacking in Western comforts and so miserable in Moscow that he had been indulging unrealistic thoughts of being allowed to return to the UK. Philby claimed later he did not feel the patriotism that others for some reason ascribed to him. He said, famously, 'To betray you must first belong. I never belonged', and he shared little of the unquestioned sense of, say, Nicholas Elliott that his tribe and its history was inherently to be admired, but did he really want to break off contact with his five children?

The Soviet Union was looking even less like the utopia its advocates had envisaged, even nearly a decade after Stalin's death. Mounting evidence of the casual butchery of Stalin's regime and the more recent crushing of dissent in Eastern Europe bore no resemblance to the exercise of people's power he had signed up for in the 1930s. Philby never admitted publicly to any such doubts, but he most certainly had them.

Similarly, he must have hoped there might be another way. A few years earlier he had tried to acquire an Indian and then a Pakistani passport, having been born in a part of India that later became Pakistan. Maybe he imagined a life out of the reach of the major powers in a neutral country? But that offered no guarantee of safety. If he tried that, each side would continue to fear him talking to the other, and public servants from both sides, let alone British bereaved, had plenty of reasons to wish him dead. And whatever his own prospects, if the British renewed their questioning he would certainly be asked about his co-conspirators. MI5 was desperate to know the extent of the penetration. Would his oft-proclaimed loyalty to friends be strong enough to resist? Would the British seek to turn him, to work secretly *against* the Russians? But in that case, would he be able to carry it off with the Russians? Why should they trust him in any but the most minor role? And if he stayed put and sought to brazen things out, assassins from either side might come for him in any case, to pre-empt possible betrayal. There was no safe answer.

A series of family problems afflicted Philby that summer. His eldest son John had ridden a motorbike while uninsured and hit an elderly lady, breaking her hip; he was required to pay compensation, at a time when money was already a struggle. His daughter Josephine (Jo), who had caught the eye of many a young man in Beirut and who he would liken to Natasha in *War and Peace*, was undergoing a difficult, on-off engagement.

One account of Philby's time in Beirut describes him trying to recruit a prominent Arab politician, telling him he could do useful work for MI6. Philby continued the courtship, eventually offering the man money. In fact, the man had already been signed up by MI6, which he hadn't admitted.

This was more than misfortune, concluded MI6's bosses. How had Philby, who was never well off, been able to offer money unless he was recruiting for the KGB? According to this version, a tail, arranged by the Lebanese authorities, was put on Philby, revealing that he was sending indecipherable late-night signals to an Armenian, seemingly a middleman between Philby and the Russians. The Armenian was put in prison for some weeks, flushing Philby out and forcing him – strictly against protocol – to meet his contact in the flesh, which apparently he did in a flat above an Armenian sweetshop. Yet – it was reported later – the Lebanese authorities decided not to act, deciding it was not in the country's interest to involve itself further in other nations' matters, so seemingly no substantive progress was made. This seems an implausible reason for not proceeding, given MI6's closeness to the Lebanese authorities, and Philby himself affected to be amused by the story, calling it 'twaddle'. But the rest of the story was written with sufficient conviction for it not to be dismissed simply because Philby asks us to. Nor should it be dismissed because a major source for the article is known to have been Miles Copeland. The author, an American journalist called Edward Sheehan, had other sources, too: he confirmed this to Said Aburish, admitting he believed he had been misled and that about 30 per cent of the article he had written was wrong.

Kim's drunkenness was part of who he was. On a trip to Tehran in the spring of 1962 he had shocked his host by urinating on a tiled floor. As ever, his morning-after charm did its work. A few months later, in September 1962, he and his son Harry, Eleanor and her daughter Annie went on a short sightseeing trip to Syria. Unexpectedly, Kim returned to Beirut a day ahead of the others. When Eleanor rejoined him, she found him in a crumpled state, hugely drunk, on the terrace. He said the reason was that Jackie, their pet fox who had recently been added to the family collection, had died after a fall from their fifth-floor terrace. Philby was inclined to give Jackie – whose sense of balance was excellent – drops of whisky with his chopped liver, but to think of the fox having had a boozy night in with Philby, ending with the pathos of drunkenly toppling over the side, would be to venture too far into satire. Philby suspected the caretaker, never happy at the idea of a fox living in their flat, or the cleaner, who simply didn't like the smell of the fox, had thrown the animal over the side. Inclined towards sentimentality in domestic matters – he was once left distraught by finding a mouse floundering in the lavatory bowl – he was inconsolable. Nicholas Elliott said that, and the death of St John, were the only occasions he had seen Philby 'display visible emotion'.

7

The judgement of Solomon

The most calamitous episode that befell Philby was something of which he became aware only later. He knew that the waters were rising, or likely to rise, around him, though he knew little of what was happening in London and Washington. Even silence, though, would have been unnerving. He claimed later that he had had a suggestive visit from a colleague from London some time that year. Had a breakthrough been made that would convict him? If not, he wanted to sweat things out. He had after all defied the odds when Burgess and Maclean had fled. Two of his chattiest sources, Nicholas Elliott and Bill Eveland, had gone, and if he still had fellow Soviet moles in MI5 or MI6, as some believe, they would have had difficulty contacting him undetected. Then, in August 1962, a conversation in Israel crystallised thinking in London, with the most devastating of results.

Kim's friend Flora Solomon was born in Pinsk, Belarus, in 1895. Her father was Grigori Benenson, a larger-than-life banker and philanderer – his face was badly scarred when a spurned lover threw acid in his face – with a capacity for making, losing and remaking fortunes. He became extremely wealthy in pre-revolutionary Russia, partly as a result of his purchase of an oil field in Baku, Azerbaijan, and ownership of goldfields, later expropriated. Narrowly escaping the Bolshevik uprising, the family fled in terror to London in 1917 where Flora, by contrast, enjoyed a pampered and socially active life. In 1919 she married Harold Solomon, from a stockbroking family, and had a son, Peter, born in 1921, who many years later founded Amnesty International. In 1923, while her husband was posted in Jerusalem, their English friends St John and Dora Philby came to dinner, accompanied by their eleven-year-old son Kim.

By the mid-1930s, her fortunes had changed markedly once more. Her husband Harold, who had been a British administrator in Jerusalem, had died and her father, now spending a lot of time in New York, where he had bought a skyscraper for cash, had lost much of his money. Flora now had to earn a living. Through a family friend, Simon Marks, she was offered a job with Marks & Spencer, where the cossetted woman who had once asked indignantly 'Do you mean I have to *work*?' proved herself extremely industrious.

A dozen or so years after their first meeting, Kim Philby returned from the political upheavals in Austria. Flora was to learn from Bella, her Viennese refugee housekeeper, that he had married a communist, Lizi. Flora, a warm, flamboyant and formidable figure, had lost a brother, Jacob, in a German concentration camp in the First World War. She admired the young Kim Philby's political passion, both being alarmed by the rise of fascism in Germany and a general sense that the rich were getting too rich at the expense of the poor. After Lizi and Kim became estranged, Flora introduced Kim to her assistant at Marks & Spencer, Aileen Furse. The pair soon became a couple, had children and married (in that order, which raised some eyebrows), Flora acting as a witness at the wedding. With the Nazi violence against Jews becoming ever more threatening as the 1930s drew on, Flora, perhaps remembering her own need to re-establish her roots twenty years earlier, threw herself into helping refugees less comfortably off than she had been.

Her indomitability also came to the fore in her workplace, where, aggrieved at the underpayment of staff, she complained to Simon Marks. 'It's firms like Marks & Spencer that give Jews a bad name,' she told him. As a result, she was put in charge of a staff welfare system that in later years was held up as a model of good practice. It might have been a blueprint for private enterprise's capacity for accommodating and adapting to demands from what might loosely be called the left. Her subsequent work on food distribution during the war, for which she was awarded an OBE, also left a mark on public policy. After the war she worked helping set up the Jewish state, and with Golda Meir in helping Jewish refugees assimilate.

Flora's vigorous public works were complemented by much private warmth, and her protectiveness towards her former employee Aileen was to prove enduring. She had long known of Aileen's sometimes tempestuous past, and in the early 1950s became an ever more supportive friend as the mother of five tried to cope with her husband's infidelity, his lack of a job, their shortage of money and the suspicion that he might be a traitor to his country. To Aileen, Flora's friendship could be counted on. It was Kim Philby's misfortune that he made the same assumption.

In July 1962 in an article marking the tenth anniversary of the Egyptian revolution ('Nasser's pride and glory'), Philby wrote of how the country had successfully been converted into a successful 'co-operative socialist democracy'. Nasser was to Egypt what Tito was to Yugoslavia and Nehru was to India, said the article. This was the sort of thing that showed a clear bias in favour of Israel's enemies, Flora believed.

The following month, she attended a meeting of the

Weizmann Institute of Science, run by her friend Meyer
Weisgal, in Rehovot, Israel. One generous benefactor to the
Institute was Victor Rothschild, a distinguished scientist and
a supporter of all things Israeli. As the pair were chatting,
Solomon expressed her exasperation at Philby's continued
employment as a journalist in Beirut. 'How is it the *Observer*
can use a man like Kim? Don't they know he's a communist?'
she told a startled Rothschild. 'You must do something!' She
told Rothschild that Philby had asked her before the war to join
him in his 'important work for peace'.

It was a conversation that ultimately brought the end of Kim
Philby's freedom.

Rothschild told her he would think about it. Rothschild
himself had been a student at Cambridge in the 1930s, and had
known several of those who opted to work secretly for Moscow,
but what Solomon told him broke new ground. When they were
back in London he called Solomon and set up a meeting with
Arthur Martin, MI5's chief Philby expert, at his flat. She also
met Dick White.

Initially she was reluctant to say too much, claiming she was
simply drawing on hints he had dropped her in the distant past,
but she came to realise how much her own experience with
Philby filled out the picture. According to Chapman Pincher,
Solomon reported that Philby had gone further than expressing
a vague hope about working for peace, saying she admitted: 'I
know he was working for the KGB' and that it had been on her
conscience for a long time. But she would not, she told Martin,
testify against him in court.

Solomon also told Martin that she wished she had come a lot
earlier, a sentiment echoed – with some vigour, one imagines –
by Dick White, head of MI6, when he was told of her claim.

Why had she waited so long? The question hung over the
entire story. There was something unsatisfactory about her

account. For one thing, she claimed she didn't know about Kim's ostensible dalliance with fascism before the war. She wrote: 'Only years later, after Kim's defection to Russia, did I learn with everybody else that he had a cover job with a pro-Nazi organisation, the Anglo-German Fellowship.' This suggests a convenient forgetfulness. The doughty defender of refugees was a friend of the family, knew he had previously been earnestly anti-Nazi and she saw his wife Aileen every day at work. It would be extraordinary for the faintest dalliance with Nazism (phoney or otherwise) on his part not to be known to her. More likely, it seems, was that she had known of the job and of his intention to mislead. If so, did she not wonder why? And what more had he told her he was up to? Maybe she was in some way, at least, helpful to what Kim was up to, and maybe this was why she refused to go into the witness box against him? If so, she evidently had a de facto immunity.

In 1951, when Burgess and Maclean fled to Moscow, Philby came under suspicion and had to leave MI6. Did it not occur to her at least to mention her knowledge of his earlier sympathies? After all, she held plenty of parties with powerful people at her smart house in Hornton Street, Kensington. There was no shortage of well-placed people she could have told. But far from it, it seems. After Burgess and Maclean fled, Anthony Blunt had the task of secretly going through Burgess's flat, removing items that might incriminate Burgess and his co-conspirators. One of the items he removed, it emerged later, was a letter from Philby to Burgess, telling him that if he ever found himself in serious trouble with the authorities and at risk of being exposed, there was someone he could turn to in confidence – Flora Solomon.

If it was friendship that held her back, that was understandable, but why then breach that loyalty by blowing the whistle on him after nearly four decades? She complained to Victor Rothschild about his biased reporting on Israel, but few shared that view. Kim's father had been pro-Arab, but he shared little intrinsic sympathy in that direction and his reporting was unremarkable. And even if we accept her view as sincere, which we probably should, this was not a proportionate response. She also said, some time after the mysterious January 1964 death of Tomás Harris, who she believed had been working for Moscow, that she remained reluctant to give evidence for fear of what the Russians might do to her, inviting a belief that she knew the sort of secrets the Russians might want to silence her for. Yet she claimed to know none.

Her role remains mysterious. Peter Wright, author of the controversial memoir *Spycatcher*, said he found Solomon 'a rather untrustworthy woman, who never told the truth about her relations with people like Philby in the 1930s'. He was responsible for covertly recording Solomon's interview with Arthur Martin and going over the tape back at MI5's Curzon Street headquarters. Solomon described how she had had lunch with Philby on one of his visits to London during the Spanish Civil War when he suggested that she work with him. She said she was too busy rescuing Jewish refugees to do so.

With his customary asperity, Wright suggested she was ambivalent towards Philby, part fond, part vengeful, because, he surmised, she was one of his spurned lovers. It is true she may well also have been embarrassed by her own affection for Philby. In the mid-1930s he would have been in his mid-twenties at the time, she early forties. Others saw Flora's fondness for him as maternal. She said: 'The Kim Philby I now got to know was not a talkative man; he had a gentle charm, never drinking to excess at my house, and mingled easily with my other friends.'

But even here the spy world had an ulterior explanation. Nicholas Elliott told David Cornwell, better known as John le Carré, about conversations he had had with the MI6 psychiatrist who had been trying to help Philby's second wife Aileen.

He concluded: 'Never mind all his philandering, never mind that Aileen, whom I knew pretty well, said Philby liked his sex and was pretty good at it. He was homosexual ...' The psychiatrist was of necessity imprecise, but Elliott reported: 'He advised me to look for a mother figure. Somewhere there will be a mother figure. It was this woman Solomon.'

There is pretty much no other suggestion of Philby having had homosexual tendencies after leaving school. He had had an upsetting experience when he was eight or nine, and had had fleeting experiences, not entirely passive, at Westminster. Goronwy Rees, a witness of varying reliability, claimed Philby had been buggered by Burgess at Cambridge, though there is no other evidence for this. It was briefly suggested that Philby had had a homosexual relationship with someone on the British embassy staff, but this was almost certainly an invented rumour, sour grapes. And a tale of Burgess and Philby in bed together in Washington has a positively non-sexual, Morecambe and Wise feel about it. Articles in the media soon after Philby's defection suggested there may have been a homosexual element to his political stance, and one writer claimed he might somehow be 'an unconscious homosexual' because he 'dramatised and over-sentimentalised' his relationship with Eleanor while at the same time betraying her. It must have come as a shock to many Britons, even in a year when homosexuality in the UK was coming to be better understood, to learn that a traitor might be heterosexual. If Philby did have homosexual leanings, they don't appear to explain very much.

Given Solomon's vigorous Zionism and her friendship with Chaim Weizmann and Golda Meir, it is tempting to look for an Israel-oriented explanation for her delay. Nicholas Elliott suggested many years later it might have had something to do with a man called John Teague, who had been a senior SIS representative in the Middle East. Elliott claimed: 'Philby had been working for John Teague, who was head of station in Jerusalem, and Teague was anti-Jewish and she was angry.' This raises the question of what Philby had been doing for Teague, whose alleged anti-Jewishness, if true, seems to have gone unnoticed by scholars of the area. But in any case, Teague's period of greatest activity had been during the war and then up to 1953, when he returned to London. Once again, such facts as there are invite further questions about Solomon's delay.

Arguably there were better reasons for her reluctance to shop her friend. Between 1951 and 1956, Aileen had become increasingly alarmed at her husband's estrangement from her, his affair with Constance Ashley-Jones and their financial misfortune. Overlying all this was her mounting concern that he might indeed have been the 'Third Man' which, if proved, would of course multiply her existing worries. It would hardly be fair to expect Flora to pull the plug on such stability as Aileen was enjoying. And after Aileen's death at the end of 1957, inflicting further distress on her friend's grieving children – when their father was happily back in paid employment at last – would have seemed positively cruel. Her close friend and successor at Marks & Spencer, Stuart Lisbona, godfather to one of the Philby children and a source of great support to Aileen, would almost certainly have lamented any further distress being inflicted on them.

But Flora was nonetheless shocked at how Philby had treated his loving, tormented wife, callously abandoning her with a houseful of children and swanning off to the sunshine.

Those who knew Flora best point to an aspect of her character that, while not explaining the timing of her denunciation of Philby, certainly lends weight to the ultimate reasons for it. At her funeral, some words she wrote in old age about enjoying the feeling of being useful were read out. She continued:

'Finally, I feel I must voice my gratitude to the country of my adoption. The British, it is frequently said, are an intolerant race, yet I have seen enough of this country and its people to know that being a foreigner is no obstacle to fulfilment here. My Russian accent has never proved a disadvantage. The British must surely rank as the most exasperating, illogical, hypocritical of peoples. But they have a generosity of mind too, and a humility, and a capacity for endurance which is necessary for true greatness.

'I don't expect my English grandchildren to endorse this declaration of love of country. The young appear to be embarrassed by patriotism. But then, my grandchildren were born here while for me the odyssey from Baku has been a long, winding trail. Given the chance, and fortified against life's hazards by my personal trinity – Russian soul, Jewish heart, British passport – I would do it all again, the same way.'

In other words, her frequent mention of this trinity was more than a soundbite to advertise her good manners. 'She was fiercely patriotic to Britain, forever grateful for offering her sanctuary,' says someone who knew her well. While sophisticated souls either took patriotism for granted or disdained its manifestation in flag-waving and jingoism, for Flora it was a gift that had effectively saved her family and that of many other refugees before the war. Being British brought with it a set of values to be prized, and it had given her enormous opportunities both to enjoy life and to exercise practical, needs-based politics.

After her husband proposed to her at the Cavalry Club in London, she wrote: 'Leaving the club an engaged woman, I noticed Dollman's painting of Captain Oates as he walked to death in the Antarctic blizzard to grant Scott and the others a chance to live. Oh, the bravery, the grandeur, the glory of the British! And I was to be one of them.'

It is fair to assume that Flora never made a direct comparison between Captain Oates and Kim Philby, living a drunken, scared life in Beirut with a too-trusting wife, but she knew enough to be aware that his successful rehabilitation as a journalist was hardly the stuff on which heroic self-denial is built. Least of all was it patriotic. It called for scrutiny, if nothing else.

Solomon wrote later in her own defence that she, too, had believed that Philby's communism had been abandoned long ago. 'I had not volunteered information as every public statement pointed to his innocence,' she said, and she was not alone in assuming it. 'I was too remote from official circles to be aware of surviving suspicions.' Nonetheless, she aimed a barb at others who were taken in, saying his guilt was an example of how 'clubmanship and the old school tie could protect their own'.

Solomon's testimony was not cast-iron proof, just as Golitsin's wasn't, and was open to the charge of her having an animus against Philby. But it was definitely progress. Wheels began to turn.

The strain of his double life had been amplified at every turn. 'He did not cut an impressive figure,' said Patrick Seale of Philby at this time, 'tentative, anxious to be liked, not wholly at ease, a slightly touching middle-aged gentleman washed up on the edge of Beirut life.' But for now, Philby knew nothing of Solomon's denunciation of him, and he continued to service his journalistic and intelligence masters as they required. His journalism leaned towards reflecting on the news, rather than breaking it and, while he had had time off for bereavements and family upheavals, he continued to convey a pride in his professionalism. He liked to file his copy on time, was always dutiful and charming to his translators and sought to cater uncomplainingly for his editors' wishes.

He strived to play the pro. In late September, the theocratic ruler of Yemen, Muhammad al-Badr, who had only recently taken over from his autocratic father, was overthrown by a revolution. Its leader, Abdullah al-Sallal, was declared first President of the Yemen Arab Republic. Here, at last, was evidence of the Nasserite 'Arab street' exercising a degree of autonomy against the peninsula's outdated rulers. In the words of Patrick Seale, it caused 'kings to tremble and radicals to rejoice'.

Kim was among the first journalists to visit the capital, Sanaa, and then to meet Prince Faisal of neighbouring Saudi Arabia (which supported the previous regime), in mid-October. He had witnessed the thrilling aftermath of a revolutionary moment in an essentially agrarian economy, and loved it. The theocrats had had their comeuppance at last. It was hardly the rising, under chimney-filled skies, of the blue-collar industrial lumpenproletariat against capitalist oppressors along Marxist-Leninist lines, with an alternative administration primed to take over, but Kim admired its defiance. 'The country certainly boasts more rifles than ballpoint pens,' he wrote. 'More than half the newly appointed cabinet ministers have no offices. They work where they happen to be, more often than not in shared bedrooms.' His influence may well be evident in an unsigned article in *The Economist* welcoming 'the end of a long sleep in Arabia': 'Until something is done about the lacework of British protected states that festoon the eastern and southern coasts of the Arabian peninsula, the Arab portrait of Britain is indelibly adorned with the horn and tails of an old-fashioned proconsul.'

A month later, possibly intoxicated on this occasion by the rebellion, he returned to Yemen. It was the only time in his career as a foreign correspondent, said Patrick Seale, that Philby had ever taken sides.

To some, the events around the turn of the year were a devilishly clever piece of management of an extremely awkward situation, a deft shepherding of events towards a desired outcome. It also looks like a masterclass in bungling, and of a peculiarly British sort. We may never know for certain which it was.

Flora Solomon's revelation to Victor Rothschild in August 1962 about how decades earlier Kim had wanted her to join him in 'work for peace' had enormous consequences. Whether it was in itself seen as adding a crucial last piece of the jigsaw, or whether it merely helped tip the scales, adding weight to the testimony of Golitsin and others, is unclear. But it would certainly have added to the odds of Philby being seen as guilty by his colleagues.

The drift that MI6 boss Dick White had overseen, despite his own convictions, could continue no longer. Now, he felt, he had enough evidence to accuse Philby of working for the Russians. Yet the government could not simply put him in handcuffs in his flat in Lebanon and march him back to London. He would be too canny to go anywhere where he was susceptible to British arrest. The publicity surrounding a trial would do enormous damage to Britain's already embarrassed security establishment. But the more radical step of arranging an unpleasant accident was also ruled out, although the Lebanese head of secret police Colonel Tewfik Jalbout later said that the offer of a local team had been available. So a plan was hatched to confront Philby.

MI5's Arthur Martin knew more about his case than anyone and would spot any Philby lies immediately. But Nicholas Elliott, on hearing that Martin had been chosen and feeling that Martin, a non-commissioned officer, would not impress Philby, said that he, a brigadier, ought to be the one to go. Dick White had done excellent work at MI5 and moved to run the sister organisation in 1956 after the Buster Crabb scandal, when news broke that a frogman examining the hull of a visiting Soviet ship (acting for MI6 in defiance of the Prime Minister's orders) had died. White had long been convinced of Philby's guilt, and agreed that Philby would respond best if treated like a gentleman, a move that might have been designed to enhance MI6's self-image of cavalier superiority over its more methodical counter-espionage colleagues. Elliott had most reason to feel betrayed by Philby's treachery. He was much the best placed to exert maximum moral pressure and appeal to Philby's sense of decency. If Philby owed anybody, it was Elliott, the man who had defended him and been his boss in Beirut. And Elliott, too, having been made a fool of but with a residual fondness for Philby, would be the person with most interest in making an accommodation with him work. Such an approach might also obscure the fact that with Solomon unwilling to give evidence in public, there would *still* be insufficient evidence to prove Philby's guilt in court.

The Prime Minister needed to be told of a matter of such national security, and the gentlemanly approach chimed with his own. The imperative would have been damage limitation and pragmatism, not least because, embarrassingly, as Foreign Secretary, he had cleared Philby and his posting to Beirut. His inclination was to manage and control the culprit. There was no need for public humiliations. As he said in another context: 'When my gamekeeper shoots a fox, he doesn't go and hang it up outside the master of foxhounds' drawing room. He buries it out of sight.' And where the MI5 attitude was conventional enough to believe that those guilty of the highest crime in the land should be brought to justice, the more recherché (and, of course, public-school) Elliott could be relied upon not to be too tediously literal about the law.

To twenty-first-century eyes, the attempt to reason with Philby looks like the establishment organising a cover-up to protect its own, but there are better arguments in its favour, and it may indeed have been the least bad option. In another context Professor Sir Michael Howard wrote a mandarinate defence of a cover-up: 'It must always be a matter of very fine judgment whether such an agent should be exposed and justice seen to be done, or whether his cover should be preserved so that he can be used by our own security authorities' by planting false information, milking him of what he knows about the other side, and so on. 'The determining consideration is likely to [be] that, not of abstract justice, but [of] perception of the national interest.' He warns against 'discarding him by handing him over to justice', adding that if this course is to be effective, 'nothing could be done to indicate that he had forfeited the confidence of any of his employers, however eminent'.

Elliott and his colleagues knew how potent communism's appeal had been in the 1930s, and if Philby could be persuaded to play ball, admit that his juvenile convictions were misplaced and identify others whose leftist idealism had got the better of them, he could help MI5 root out the remaining Soviet subversives in its midst. And with the shocking length of the Blake sentence, the knowledge of how miserable his friend Burgess was in Moscow and his domestic stability in Beirut concentrating his mind, Philby's compliance seemed a real possibility.

This was all to happen without telling the Americans, who had not only warned about and suffered from Philby's treachery, but who were now the senior party in the UK–US intelligence partnership. Had they been told, they might well have asked to listen in on the encounter, which might have told them more than they needed to know (or, more likely, might have caused embarrassment at further British shortcomings). Britain still sought to behave with autonomy, but there was sheepishness. Dick White told the Prime Minister: 'We cannot ignore the new information. We would be criticised by the Americans if we took no action. We need to discover what damage he caused.' This looks like an understatement. The British were keen both to mollify the Americans, reassuring them that the damage to US interests had been minimal, and to make sure the Americans were in no position to judge the facts for themselves.

It is a striking position for the country that likes to believe it taught the world transparency.

Who had conspired with Philby? Who had been the ring-leaders? Where were they now? Philby's radical politics had been adopted over a quarter of a century earlier. Surely, with the right opportunity, he would move on and explicitly reject his past? And the right opportunity, it was felt, was an offer of immunity from his old friend Nicholas in exchange for a full confession.

The chaps would sort it out, and with any luck Kim would go along with a version that minimised embarrassment with the Americans.

8

Christmas 1962 – what Eleanor saw

We may never know if Philby knew in the autumn of 1962 that London had decided his time was up. We do know that he was in a bad way and that he had for a long time been preparing an escape plan, but would it work? Where would he go? Would he stick to it? Would it be thwarted? Would the prospect of the arrest and interrogation of a man who knew so much about Soviet methods and personnel, not least in London, prompt the Russians to take matters out of his hands? Would the British strike, maybe by arresting him as soon as he crossed the threshold of the British embassy? Or perhaps such legal niceties would be ignored? Would he be kidnapped, or even killed? Or maybe, after all, they still lacked conclusive proof? These were life-or-death questions that tormented Kim night and day.

Eleanor did not have the faintest idea these thoughts were going through her husband's head. All she knew – which was bad enough – was that Kim was drinking far too much, and for no obvious reason. The following is a narrative of what she must have known and observed over the next few months.

Unusually, the couple did not go to London for Christmas, Kim telling the editor of the *Observer* he planned to visit the following summer. Eleanor knew Kim was constantly depressed, but he soldiered on with work, showing more pat professionalism than journalistic zeal. On 22 December he wrote a news story about the Yemen, the country that had fired him up so recently, that might be held up now to journalism students as an example of how to kill the reader's interest. It suggests a man whose mind is not entirely on his job, or one whose foreign editor had more than one eye on the Christmas shopping, and probably both. The numbing first sentence read: 'The Arab reaction to the American recognition of the Republican government of the Yemen has followed the lines expected.' A marmalade-dropper it was not.

Around this time, Nicholas Elliott turned up in Beirut, giving little notice. He had booked himself into obscure lodgings and didn't want it known that he was in town. This furtiveness was unlike him, thought Eleanor, but he could not resist booking a table at Le Temporel, one of Beirut's most celebrated restaurants. If he hoped he was hiding his light, at least it was a candle light, and at a corner table. He also invited a female former MI6 colleague to make a foursome. Eleanor was suspicious: 'Something was going on between them which was escaping me.'

When Kim went to the lavatory, Eleanor wanted to ask Elliott what her husband was worrying about, but she lost her nerve. At the key moment Elliott followed Philby to the bathroom. When they returned, the public-school banter was renewed, neither letting on what was really going on, and Eleanor understanding only that whatever she was meant to think, the occasion seemed bogus.

Kim was reluctant to take up Christmas's opportunities to celebrate. On the rare occasions he did say he would go out, he would generally decline at the last minute. On New Year's Eve, he and Eleanor, having put the children to bed, shared a bottle of champagne on their terrace, a scene of some pathos in party city.

The following day was Kim's fifty-first birthday, and very nearly his last. Eleanor, believing she could snap Kim out of his melancholia, insisted on arranging the couple's by now traditional party, a joint lunchtime celebration of birthday and New Year. On a crisp, sunny day, Kim roused himself and managed to enjoy the occasion. He sparkled, as he generally could, and he enjoyed showing fellow journalist Eric Downton the signed first editions of all his late father's books on Saudi Arabia. Guests came and went, most of them drifting away by 2.30 p.m., leaving their hosts only mildly mellow with drink and planning a restful afternoon and evening. They had, however, reckoned without the bearlike social embrace of Miles and Lorraine Copeland, who breezed in, demanding to be accompanied to another party elsewhere in town. The Copelands were good friends and it would have been churlish not to. They moved on, and enjoyed more friends, more food and more drink, staying far longer than they had intended.

They somehow made it home. Then, while getting ready for bed, Kim was washing alone in the bathroom when Eleanor heard a crash. She rushed to help, and found he had cracked his head against a radiator. In trying to stagger to his feet, he had crashed against it again. Two wounds were pumping out blood; the bathroom was awash with it. She got him to the bedroom and smothered his head with pillows, but the blood kept pouring. She managed to summon a doctor. He insisted that Kim go to hospital. Several times Kim got as far as the door, but then refused to go. 'It was as if, deep down ... some instinct prevented him leaving the security of the house,' wrote Eleanor. Eventually they managed to push him into the lift and then on to the American University Hospital, where he had twenty-four stitches in the two cuts. A doctor took Eleanor outside to tell her that if he'd had one more ounce of alcohol in his blood, he would not have lived. He refused to stay the night, Eleanor eventually taking a chastened Kim and his injuries, including two black eyes, home.

What effect this must have had on the children in the house can only be imagined. They were used to having to fend for themselves.

On this occasion, not for the first time, Kim was abashed, swearing he would give up drink for ever. Still, though, he would not confide in Eleanor, batting away questions as to what he was worried about. He could barely move for six or seven days.

Three or four days later, Mary Gold, Peter Lunn's secretary, phoned, asking Kim to come to the British embassy to meet her boss, Nicholas Elliott's replacement as MI6 head of station, who had distinguished himself by organising the tapping of the Russian telephone cables in Berlin and Vienna after the war. Eleanor said he couldn't possibly go. Gold tried to insist, but he hadn't even had his stitches out. Kim, too, reiterated that he simply wouldn't go.

He was back on the booze before long, drinking beer when whisky seemed to be taking him too close to the abyss. But it was a mere pause in the breakneck tilt towards self-destruction. He mostly stayed at home, occasionally going out to see a contact. Eleanor knew that people in the espionage business are required to keep their secrets and not talk shop with their partners, but whatever was going on was seriously damaging home life.

On another occasion around the same time, Elliott and Eleanor had to put a drunken Kim to bed. According to David Cornwell, Nicholas Elliott told him as they were putting the incapable Philby to bed: 'You know what this is about, don't you? ... He's a bloody Russian spy.' Eleanor clearly knew no such thing, and makes no mention of this in her book, continuing to express mystification, almost as if she either didn't believe Elliott or didn't think it could have anything to do with his current gloom. (It is possible Cornwell's memory is at fault, or that he didn't believe the story.)

Elliott then left Beirut to start his new job at the head of the Africa department. Eleanor knew that Kim and Elliott's replacement, Peter Lunn, were never particularly close. Maybe that was the cause of whatever was upsetting Kim. Or maybe there was a problem with his journalism and his income was under threat, no joke with children still at private schools. Kim thought he was putting a brave face on things, but he was concealing only the cause of his unhappiness. The fact of it was plain enough, and by now normality involved enormous amounts of alcohol. Eleanor, though wanting to discourage Kim and despairing at his unshakeable mood, was also habitually taking refuge in the bottle.

On Saturday 19 January 1963, Kim and Eleanor accepted an invitation to go and visit a friend, John Carswell, a lecturer at the American University of Beirut, whose house at Tabarja, north of Beirut, overlooked the sea. They arrived before lunch and Carswell poured them both a succession of 'sighters' to put them in the mood for lunch at a fish restaurant across the bay. Carswell was too polite to ask why Philby kept nipping into his bedroom, but by the time they left to eat, they had had plenty to drink. Later that day, after yet more alcohol at lunch, Carswell returned home and found an empty bottle of sherry in his bedroom. Philby had been surreptitiously swigging from it while his host chatted to Eleanor. Still Philby let nothing slip.

There was some respite from the gloom, though. The following day, Kim suggested lunch at Lucullus, *à deux*. It was a tender and lengthy meal, said Eleanor, and the couple enjoyed a romantic time, listening to music and sipping martinis in front of an open fire. Times had been difficult, clearly, and a cosy meal offered only slight balm, but it was better than nothing. Importantly, their passion for one another was very much alive.

The next day, 21 January, Kim and Eleanor had supper at the home of Eric Downton. They had had a couple of drinks before they arrived, and tucked into several whiskies before having sherry, red wine and champagne with the meal. After dinner they had brandy and coffee, and more whisky.

Kim would occasionally get up restlessly, go out onto the balcony and return to sit and smoke. It seems that the cumulative effect of this mysterious, distant behaviour was enervating Eleanor, who told him so with some vigour. In another account, Eleanor was very aggressive towards their hostess. In any event, Kim responded – according to Downton's wife – by hitting Eleanor on the side of the neck with the edge of his hand. She fell back stunned and then retired for a lie down in the guest room. Kim said he would rest on the sofa as the Downtons headed for their own room.

A little later, Kim, having made inroads into a bottle of whisky he had located, was to be heard rolling some soapstone Eskimo carvings across the floor, as if they were bowling balls. Ever the host, Downton found a deft way of discouraging this and sat down with him. He was clearly in a bad way, and mused on the Depression, Spain, China, Cambridge, the LSE, Africa, Yemen, Nasser and rural poverty in Egypt. When Eleanor reappeared, Kim thanked Eric for 'a great evening' and they went home in a cab. Another night of torment had ended, in the higher reaches of alcoholic oblivion, in earnest debate. Downton, no bleeding-heart liberal, was impressed by what was exercising Philby: 'As we talked it struck me that here was a man deeply concerned for the world's under-privileged peoples.'

Two nights later, on 23 January, Eleanor and Kim were invited out to supper again, this time with the Balfour-Pauls, the backbone of British embassy social life, at their second-floor flat in the Yenikomshian building in Ras Beirut. Glen was the First Secretary and an expert in the Arab world, and was as steady and unshowy as a rock. To Eleanor, he was an honourable man whom everybody liked and trusted. Journalists knew where they stood with him, and his wife Marnie was much admired by Eleanor for the way she contended with polio. Apart from the Lucullus meal, Kim had barely been out of the flat for days, but the Balfour-Pauls were fond friends and Kim and Eleanor were happy to accept their invitation.

That winter afternoon, Beirut was paying the price for its normally beguiling weather. Winter brings ferocious, clattering storms which can last for days, the wind and rain pouring in from the sea, often making the streets impassable. Philby sat on the balcony and contemplated the view, as he did so often. Late in the afternoon he picked up a raincoat and went out, off to meet another contact, evidently, saying he would be back at about six, in good time to change for dinner. A little later, the phone rang. Harry answered, then called out that his father was delayed, and would meet Eleanor at the Balfour-Pauls'.

Eleanor arrived for supper, explaining that Kim was filing copy and would be along shortly, although she seemed 'slightly concerned', according to someone who was there. After more than an hour, now rather more concerned, Eleanor suggested they go in to dinner. She phoned home, but he hadn't called there either. The appalling weather was the most obvious explanation. Perhaps he had been hit by a car, or stumbled on the broken waterfront into the sea. Other guests, no more aware than Eleanor how journalists' social lives can be disrupted, tried to reassure her, but she insisted on going home. 'Kim's never done anything like this to me before. He's always scrupulously on time.'

She struggled home through the rain on foot, checking when she arrived that he hadn't hidden a note of explanation, out of reach of the children, in one of their secret hiding places. It was not until after midnight that, increasingly desperate, she rang Peter Lunn, the local MI6 boss. He was out, but his wife took a message. Ten minutes later Lunn called, offering to come round. Eleanor wanted to call the police and ambulance services, but Lunn suggested waiting till the morning. He asked if anything was missing. Nothing was. After Lunn had gone home, she went through the flat, finding nothing she didn't expect except a new British passport. Unable to sleep, she sat on the terrace and turned over all the possibilities in her mind. Notwithstanding the recent heavy drinking, he had been as loving as always, though there was a restlessness in him. She thought back and remembered the death of Jackie, the fox cub, which had shattered Kim. But that was four months ago. Could that really have anything to do with this evening? Surely not. It must be something worse. These were the darkest of thoughts to be wrestling with as dawn approached on her wedding anniversary.

At 7 a.m., Peter Lunn called again, arranging for two Lebanese policemen to visit the flat and take a statement. She encouraged them to check the hospitals. It was quite possible Kim had had a drink and done something to aggravate the wounds to his head. A friend arrived that morning from the States and, unaware of her despair, called to suggest meeting. Rather than sit around worrying, she agreed to this, but the friend was accompanied by a journalist, who had got wind of Kim's non-appearance at dinner. As calmly as she could, Eleanor explained that he had been called away on a story for the *Observer*. Of course she hadn't a clue where he was, nor what to tell the children. No one had the faintest idea where he was. She fretted and smoked and drank. Nothing helped.

Soon back in town was Nicholas Elliott, who had only recently left Beirut. He was anxious to be put in the picture, and was entitled to assume he would be told as much as anyone, but again Eleanor had little to offer. The idea that Kim had been sent on a story set a number of hares running, some more plausible than others. Some noted sagely how the uprising in Yemen had fired him up, and that the continuing upheavals there must have called him away. Or maybe the paper had sent him to southern Sudan, where there had been an uprising, or to Kurdish rebel lines in northern Iraq? Or perhaps he was in Baghdad, where the instability was mounting?

One acquaintance, Olga Matthews, claimed that a friend of hers had seen Kim the previous evening with two men who purportedly looked like Russians, near the Patisserie Suisse off the Bab Iddris tramline. What could that have meant? So what if she had? It didn't explain where he was now. Eleanor's book suggests she had an open mind as to where he might have gone. Each possibility that was mooted seemed equally likely, or so the book implies. He was a man around whom mystery swirled, and any apparently credible explanation could turn out to be no more than gossip. It was almost as if he encouraged it, believed Miles Copeland. 'I think he had to have attention.' Copeland, who had better reasons than most for knowing what had happened to Kim, seems to have taken advantage of Eleanor's heightened credulousness at that point, speculating with apparent confidence but less accuracy, purportedly seeking to offer reassurance.

Kim's children were terrified, and didn't know what to believe. A few days after Philby disappeared, from England Jo, his eldest daughter, called Afif Aburish, then twenty-two, whose family was well connected in Beirut. Could he find out what had happened? He called the Deputy Director of Internal Security, Colonel Omar Nuweiri. 'I said, "Uncle Omar, what is going on? You remember Jo Philby? She says her father has disappeared." He replied, "Are you going to the St Georges at lunchtime? I'll see you there." Nothing more. When I got there, he was furious: He said "Who do you think you are, getting yourself involved in international espionage? Stay out of it. Don't get your nose into this!" He told me off, as a good friend of my father. But he was in the dark too.' It would have been thrilling, had it not been so alarming.

At the end of January, as if on a mercy mission, Sam Brewer – who had moved back to New York and was now covering the UN – arrived back in Beirut. He had been in Washington and turned up offering comfort and support, and, of course, asking the questions everyone was asking, which Eleanor couldn't answer. Annie was delighted to see her father again, but the uncertainty continued to shroud their lives.

In fact, Sam had multiple motives for reappearing in Beirut. One, no doubt, was a journalist's wish to know as much as could be known about goings-on in his former backyard. The fact that he had been in Washington when Kim disappeared would have enabled him to touch base with thinking at the CIA and the FBI. Given his own intelligence links, it would be remarkable if he was not also reporting back to the States. His interests, after all, were in line with the US government's, as they often had been. Another reason for going to Beirut was that he could: his newspaper was not publishing at that point, having joined other New York-based papers in support of the *International Herald Tribune* staff in their dispute with their owner, a strike that was to last four months. Sam had no pages to fill, so was free to do as he pleased, and Eleanor was relieved to see a comforting face.

Another figure anxious to sidle up to Eleanor and learn as much as he could was Peter Lunn. Often he would buy her lunch and conduct a slow, lengthy interrogation, but he went no further, and didn't let on much. The closest Nicholas Elliott came to telling Eleanor of his belief was when he said: 'You do realise your husband was not an ordinary man?' To a polite and unassuming woman, the use of the past tense and the knowingness with which it was said must have been chilling.

As tongues wagged, at last a letter for Eleanor arrived at the Normandy. It was a handwritten note from Kim, telling her not to worry, that he would be in touch soon, that everything was going to be all right, and that she should tell people he was off on a long tour of the area. He had failed to put a stamp on the letter, which had delayed its arrival. But on the face of it, here was a sign that at least he had not had some terrible accident.

The letter also contained instructions. She later found $300-worth of Lebanese bank notes, to pay the rent, hidden in an old copy of Richard Burton's *Arabian Nights*. Later she found more money and a gold bracelet. And, in a typically romantic move, a note explaining that he hoped she would have some material he had brought back from a trip to Aden made up into a garment: 'For the sari, my adored beloved.'

Eleanor had no reason to doubt it was Kim who sent it, but it proved nothing about his safety. In her book, Eleanor offers little detail as to her conversations with Nicholas Elliott, but it is fair to assume both had their suspicions as to where Kim might be. The idea that this most loving and gentlest of men could willingly deceive her and abandon her was hard to compute. She seems to have clung to the idea that he could not possibly have chosen to inflict such distress on her. So there was a perverse, paradoxical reassurance in the idea that he might have been kidnapped. But that, obviously, was no place to take comfort. 'I was in total disarray,' she wrote. 'Had Kim been kidnapped? Had he left voluntarily? Was he a free agent? Was he dead?'

Lennie Copeland, whose mother Lorraine sought to calm Eleanor in those anxious days, remembers a woman in torment. 'She was crying a lot, in disbelief, mourning the loss of her husband.'

'She was shattered,' remembers her brother Stewart.

She continued her sculpture classes at the American University of Beirut, as Kim had encouraged her to do in his letter, as far as her meagre ability to concentrate would allow, while trying to give Harry, Miranda and her own daughter Annie a sense that nothing was amiss. She wrote numerous letters to her husband, but had nowhere to send them. And then, about two weeks after the evening at the Balfour-Pauls', another letter arrived at the Normandy, on 8 February. Again it was in Kim's handwriting, to 'My darling beloved', and he asked to be forgiven for not having written sooner. Contrary to media speculation, he said he had 'no intention of "disappearing" from your life for many years yet'. The tone was upbeat and slightly larky, seemingly unaware of the total bewilderment and distress he had caused Eleanor. There was no explicit mention of the future, or even of where he was, but he signed off with his customary outpouring of affection: 'Do you remember the first cable I ever sent you: "Constant thoughts, deepest love." They are still with you, more constant and deeper than ever. Happiness, darling, from your Kim.'

A week later, a letter from Kim with a Syrian postmark arrived. It repeated expressions of love, but ended with a disingenuous 'by the way', the catchphrase of the weasel, when what followed was anything but incidental. 'By the way,' he writes, 'I would like my scoop to be really exclusive, so please don't let any of my colleagues know where this letter comes from. In fact there is no real point in them knowing anything at all about it, is there? All love again, K.'

As ever, Beirut buzzed with gossip about where Kim might be, and Whitehall was well aware of the speculation, but still his disappearance had not got into print.

An internal memo from the Foreign Office's Permanent Secretary reported that correspondents in Beirut were well aware of Philby's disappearance. 'However, by mutual consent in order apparently to protect his reputation and career as a newspaperman [they] are holding off from filing a story.' But they did not need to hold off for much longer.

On the morning of Saturday 2 March, Eleanor received another cable, this one from Cairo. 'Fondest love deepest thoughts happy anniversary, arrangements for reunion proceeding.' This, once again, was unmistakeably Kim. He was using exactly the words he had used in previous years when they were apart for the wedding anniversary. But this was five weeks late. It turned out the longhand version had been handed in the previous day at a Cairo post office, signed 'H. Philby', but not in Kim's handwriting. Evidently somebody had sat on the message for five weeks after Kim had arranged for it to be sent.

Partly out of gratitude for the press's forbearance, but partly out of relief at hearing that Kim was indeed alive and anxious to reassure her, she agreed to speak to a small number of journalists that day. This was a green light for the *Observer* to write a story headlined 'Journalist missing in Middle East', admitting that it hadn't been in touch with its Beirut correspondent for five weeks, and confirming that it had asked the Egyptian authorities, through the Foreign Office, to see if he could be found in Cairo. As far as the paper was concerned, Eleanor had confirmed the rumours.

In dealing with the media, she was immediately out of her depth. To her, the story should have been 'Journalist safe', whereas the story they wrote for a readership that knew nothing of what had gone before was 'Journalist missing'. So on the day of the *Observer*'s story, she denied it, telling one reporter that her husband had not vanished but gone off suddenly on a story assignment. She said she had told journalists there were three children in England who would be very concerned and that she had tried to stop the *Observer* using the story, but 'the telephone line to London was garbled and they could not have understood'. She also told the reporter: 'I shall join my husband when he is ready. I was worried when I had no letter for three weeks, but when I received his cable yesterday I knew everything was all right.'

She was asked by the press if he might have gone to Moscow. She replied: 'That is a ridiculous idea. He went to Cairo, the Yemen and Saudi Arabia, and wants to go to Sudan and Ethiopia. He is not behind the Iron Curtain – and he did not leave by submarine. Somebody has actually said that.'

Rather than quelling media interest, Eleanor's brief remarks multiplied it. One American journalist camped around the clock on the kerb outside her flat. Eventually she took pity and posed for a picture. Everyone wanted to know where Kim was. It defied belief that a couple so publicly and obviously in love could be separated in this way, for one to have no idea where the other had gone.

How curious that Eleanor should try to persuade Kim's newspaper that he had gone off to write a story when the newspaper itself would be the one most likely to commission such a story. Official sources locally, with little apparent reason to lie, said that there was no sign of Philby in any of the places she believed him to have been.

Suspicion, never far from the surface in Beirut, was in overdrive, and her remarks just didn't sound true. It was recalled that Donald Maclean's wife Melinda had appeared to be in the know when her husband had disappeared, and indeed later joined him in Moscow. Was that how these things worked? The less she engaged with the media, the more mysterious the story became, and when she did, her version didn't add up. And as time went on, the inconsistencies mounted. She claimed to have received no word from Kim for three weeks when it was known she had. Initially she said nothing was missing from their flat, but she changed that story later. One of the cables she had received had been sent purportedly from a Mr Philby at the Cosmopolitan Hotel, Cairo, but the hotel had not seen him there. Nor, it emerged, did the signature on the cable resemble Philby's. But had she told journalists a fuller, more candid version of events – that she had not the faintest idea where he was, or why he had left, which was the tragic truth, and not that far from what she did say – she would also not have been believed.

Her day-to-day life was monitored by all sorts of people, including British and American security officials and representatives of TV, radio and the newspapers. Some of these had sewn up the porter and the maid, both of whom were being given backhanders to report back on her slightest move. She took to her bed one day, which the world's media knew immediately. 'Naturally Mrs Philby has been upset by all this talk linking her husband with Burgess and Maclean,' explained a friend, Kaye Brennan. Lebanese police moved into the block opposite to spy on Eleanor. She would turn the lights out in order to spy back on them. This was both entertaining and alarming for the youngest two of Kim's children, Harry and Miranda, who were staying at the time. Occasionally Harry, thirteen, would ask if his father was all right. Sometimes, when the pressure got too great, she and the children would decamp to the house of friends.

Those close to Eleanor rallied round. But who were her true friends in this situation? Sam, his paper still not being published, wanted to help Eleanor, and suggested that maybe he could ease the pressure by taking Annie away from the mayhem and media speculation. Perhaps Annie would like to go skiing in Switzerland until things cooled down. Eleanor was hugely relieved. She had not been comfortable with the children witnessing Kim's recent decline, but she would miss her terribly at such a difficult time. Then again, having her off the scene and in safe hands while the mystery was resolved would free her up. But the Easter school break was still a couple of weeks away. She resolved to ask Annie's head teacher if her daughter could take the extra time off school to go away with her father. The strike seemed likely to end soon, and Sam would need to return before long. The school agreed.

This was Sam showing a capacity for cunning. He had promised Annie, then fourteen, a nice skiing trip. Whatever was really going on beneath the surface – and at this point Eleanor's ex-husband, through his well-placed intelligence friends, probably knew as much if not more than she did – Sam felt Eleanor was not a safe custodian of his daughter. 'Eleanor told me that Annie was told on the plane that there would be no skiing,' said Susan Griggs. 'She said Sam had tricked her into giving up her daughter.' For a woman in a state of such bewilderment at losing her husband, losing her daughter must have been a body blow.

Though she felt her friends were all decent people, some had professional obligations as well. This was yet another area of uncertainty. Journalist Clare Hollingworth, who had been at dinner that night with the Balfour-Pauls and may well have been briefed by Eleanor, was among the first to suggest in print that the letters Eleanor had received from Kim could have been written much earlier and posted recently by someone else. She cast doubt on the idea that a good-looking Englishman could simply disappear in the Middle East, also expressing scepticism that he might want to go to Moscow or could be of any use to the Russians, fully twelve years after leaving the Foreign Office. For all Hollingworth knew, he might be on some secret mission for the Saudi Arabian government or, tired of Beirut, 'rushed off to live with one of the tribes'.

The American ambassador was one who offered to have her to stay to keep the immediate media pressure off her, but it was generally the Copelands who provided the greatest support.

Lorraine was as kind as ever. Lennie Copeland recalls that after her initial tearfulness, Eleanor acquired more grip: 'She pretty much moved into our house at one point. After a while she seemed to come out of it and handle it. Suddenly she became stoic. She must have talked to my mother about her plans.'

Glen and Marnie Balfour-Paul were on hand, offering such advice as they could. And Nicholas Elliott, ever the gentleman, and now in a new post in central Africa, visited and did his best to comfort Eleanor. Myrtle Winter, always an empathetic and encouraging figure who Kim liked and admired, offered help. US ambassador Dwight Porter and his wife Adele, also a painter, another US diplomat Dick Parker and his wife Jean, and her ever-faithful friends the Fisteres were also full of support.

Then, fully ten weeks after Kim had vanished, a small, bedraggled man appeared at Eleanor's door early one morning. He gave her an envelope and hurried away. The envelope contained a three-page typewritten letter, in Kim's elegant style and full of detailed instructions, and $2000 in notes. She was now being invited into the world of real subterfuge. She was to go to the British Airways (BOAC) office and buy herself a return ticket to London, plus two one-way tickets for Harry and Miranda. The false trail laid, a day or two later she was to amend the tickets to ones that involved changing in Soviet-controlled Prague. She was then to write the date on a wall near their flat, and she would meet Kim in the Czechoslovakian capital. If there was a problem, she was to draw a large 'X' instead. Also, she should expect further notification from a very capable man who she should trust. As proof of his bona fides, this man would bring a book token that she had previously given Kim.

Eleanor was worried, and her sense that Kim must have been kidnapped mounted. At the very least, she knew Kim did not have the book token. He had lost it, and left its replacement behind. Could he really have forgotten that he had neither?

But there were bigger problems. Somehow, it emerged quite quickly, the British authorities had got wind of the Prague plan, but how, she wondered. Who of those close to her could not be trusted? It was dispiriting and undermining, in addition to what she was already facing.

Quite apart from that, Harry Philby had no passport, and had no established British identity, having been born in Washington and with three previous male generations born abroad. Harry, who had previously travelled on his father's documents, would never get beyond the first passport check, wherever they were planning to go, particularly as the Lebanese authorities had just charged his father in absentia with an illegal exit of the country. Kim, surprisingly, had forgotten that, too – another reason for doubting the contents of the letter.

Eleanor shared some of these concerns with Nicholas Elliott and other trusted embassy and consulate friends. She was assured that Harry would indeed be allowed to fly, but only if Eleanor flew direct with him to London. The only answer was to play it straight, agree to co-operate completely and, largely for the benefit of the children, head for England. In any case, the Prague plan smelled odd. How much autonomy did Kim have? Even if he was free to decide, what would happen once the three of them landed in Prague? Would they stay there? Or fly back again? Or go elsewhere behind the Iron Curtain? In truth, she had little choice. At three o'clock one morning, she sneaked out of the flat to write an 'X' on the wall.

A date was set for the end of the school term in late May. She told only her most trusted friends, but – for different reasons – not the maid or the children. If others needed to be told anything, she would simply say she was leaving for a few weeks, and she cleaned the house as if that was the plan. In fact, she knew this was almost certainly her time to move on. She was sorting out which pieces of furniture to keep and which she wanted sent on – though who knew where? Miles Copeland III, a muscular teenager, remembers being pressed into service. 'They had an apartment full of furniture,' he says. 'I had to clean out and empty it.' He even managed to hang onto one or two pieces himself, which he still owns.

And then, again early one morning, in a brief moment between the children going to school and the maid arriving, a Russian came to the door. This was Petukhov, the man who had initially renewed the contact with Kim, not that Eleanor knew that. He was nervous, and though lacking the book token, assured her that Kim was well, was dying to see her and that she should do as he suggested.

But it wasn't possible. She explained about Harry's passport and how she was leaving in a week, and that her new plan was now unchangeable. Besides which, the whole manouevre had been unworkable. She couldn't possibly go to the Czech Airlines office surreptitiously when she was under such surveillance. Had this not occurred to anybody? The man seemed desperate for her to go with him, there and then, offering as much money as she thought she needed. Despite being low on funds, she declined. Feeling sorry for Petukhov, she delayed for ten minutes after he left before calling Nicholas Elliott, as she had promised she would if the trusted Russian materialised.

Word of the approach got back to London, of course. Up until that point, the government had said as little as possible, not being sure where Philby was and deciding to 'play it long'. Eleanor was not privy to the thought processes in London, but she may well have inferred the official funk. One internal memo three weeks after Philby disappeared even has a whiff of HMG hiding under the blankets, suggesting that even if a link was made in the public mind with the Burgess and Maclean fiasco 'there seems no need, however, for the Foreign Office to accept any responsibility in this matter since it is now more than 11 years since his appointment with the Embassy in Washington was terminated'.

That position was clearly untenable, or soon would be. It was unlikely that Philby would now turn up in some 'ostentatiously innocent way that would make us look foolish', which seems to have been the overriding, if forlorn, concern. On 24 May, Sir Bernard Burrows, chairman of the Joint Intelligence Committee, wrote to the cabinet secretary, seeking to identify how best to handle the coming media storm. It could only be a matter of damage limitation. A man with strong Marxist leanings had been working as a Soviet mole at the highest level of British public life for over a decade, and – despite grave misgivings in MI5 and among US allies – had been cleared by the government just eight years earlier. Yet the immediate concern, in late May 1963, was how to handle his wife Eleanor, now distraught and unpredictable.

Burrows wrote an internal memo: '"C" [Sir Dick White, head of MI6] now had definite reason to suppose that Philby ... is behind the Iron Curtain and has been trying to persuade his wife to join him. [Eleanor] is said to be drinking heavily and is sometimes apt to be indiscreet, but "C" has now heard that she at last appears to be alive to the dangers of joining her husband behind the Iron Curtain and is now planning to bring the two Philby children to London.'

Whitehall regarded Eleanor as a loose cannon. 'The potential embarrassment to HMG is now if anything greater than before,' wrote Sir Bernard, 'and the chance of involuntary publicity through the indiscretion of Mrs Philby and on the occasion of her arrival in the United Kingdom somewhat greater.' Whitehall's most senior people were being told Eleanor had been 'drinking heavily and is not being very discreet'. 'The fact that she has had letters from her husband from Russia may come out and perhaps the fact [DELETED] visited her husband shortly before his disappearance. Philby may also have told her that he confessed to [DELETED].' As we have seen, she may also have been told by Elliott that Philby had confessed. Any mention along these lines – of a confession, or that Elliott had visited, yet Philby had got away – was fraught and reeked of bungling. The official line could easily be made to look ridiculous. (Some accounts say that Philby had asked Elliott to break the news to Eleanor when they had had their encounter in January.)

Media interest was still mounting, but little help was being offered by the government. On the morning of 30 May 1963, the British Prime Minister Harold Macmillan, his Foreign Secretary the Earl of Home (later Sir Alec Douglas-Home), Sir Dick White, head of MI6, and three senior officials met to discuss how little the government could get away with saying. Whitehall was holding its breath in the hope that Mrs Philby would not be 'indiscreet'.

Meanwhile, a bogus medical certificate was being magicked up that the following day would allow Eleanor and the two children to be driven directly onto the runway at Beirut airport. The journalists waiting for her in London were given the slip and an official car arranged by Nicholas Elliott took Eleanor to stay with Kim's sister Patricia in Chiswick.

A dose of bursitis in her foot made Eleanor immobile for the next few days, perhaps just as well given the press pursuit of her. Eventually she emerged with a stick for a trip with Patricia to nearby Kew Gardens, where they hired a wheelchair and enjoyed some respite from the cameras and the demands of national security. It was to be a brief break. Once properly back on her feet, she was off to lunch with the Elliotts. There Nicholas, in the most gentlemanly of ways, set out more firmly than he had previously that he and his colleagues believed Kim was an active communist agent and that she should on no account try to join him in Moscow. Apart from anything else, he said, once there, she would find the Russians extremely reluctant to let her leave. In short, if she went to Moscow, she might never see Annie again. She and her daughter had become pawns.

For most people in the West, Soviet aggression over Cuba the previous autumn had been responsible for taking the world to the brink of nuclear war. The USSR had shown itself to be autocratic, militaristic, highly secretive, ideologically driven and illiberal. How could anyone work secretly to advance its cause, and how could any red-blooded, freedom-loving American fall for the kind of rat who did? 'Most people, particularly her US friends, would never imagine her going to Moscow, given the feelings about Russia and the Cold War at the time,' says Alice Brinton. 'That would have been a further betrayal and it might have invited further suspicions about her. I do remember people saying "how could she not have known? How could he have been so clever in keeping all that from her?"' But it was her future, not theirs.

In London Eleanor made frantic efforts to reach Flora Solomon. She may have heard that it was Flora's evidence that had provoked Kim's disappearance and wanted to know more, but even after pestering Stuart Lisbona, who had worked with Aileen at Marks & Spencer and had succeeded Flora when she left, she was unable to make contact.

Like it or not, it was looking more and more as if Kim had gone to Moscow. Why else was he continuing to be in touch, but so elliptically, and without explaining himself? He must be under orders. Nicholas had tried to bring Eleanor round to this view, adding as much detail of demonic Soviet behaviour as he dared, but without success. 'I put the fear of God into her,' he later said. She continued to doubt that Kim could simply choose to abandon her like that, and that if he was in Russian hands, he must have been kidnapped and made to do so. If that was the case, she wanted to know more. Maybe, Elliott suggested, Eleanor should meet his boss, Sir Dick White. There and then, Elliott picked up the phone. Within minutes White had joined them.

The pair were left in the Elliotts' drawing room, with coffee and a bottle of brandy. 'We have definitely known for the last seven years that Kim has been working for the Russians without pay,' he said, chancing his luck, knowing they knew no such thing for sure.* The embellished version did the trick. Eleanor was in tears. 'Much against my will I had to begin to think along the same lines,' she wrote. Four and a half months after Kim had vanished, when all the other possibilities had been eliminated, she had run out of alternatives.

Following a further story in *Newsweek*, on 1 July the Lord Privy Seal Edward Heath announced in the House of Commons that Kim Philby was indeed the 'Third Man' whose treachery had allowed Donald Maclean and Guy Burgess to escape, and that it was now assumed Philby was behind the Iron Curtain. Seeking to rescue any credit it could from the mess, the government pointed out that it had never closed the file on Philby, and that it now had new information. It also sought to reassure the public once more that since 1951 he had had no access to official information, and had been living outside British jurisdiction. Further, he had stopped working for the Russians in 1946, and his help to Maclean was an isolated gesture, born of friendship. A civil servant, presumably still learning his trade, suggested in a briefing note that the government should admit that 'prior to 1946 grave damage was undoubtedly done to the

---

* When Philby learned of White's claim to Eleanor, he was very disturbed, evidently believing it to be true. It undermined his belief that the most salient activity was him watching the British. If White's claim was true, they had been watching him, and more than likely feeding him false information to pass to Moscow. But of course it wasn't true.

national interest'. Unsurprisingly it was deleted from the final 'lines to take' briefing. This was no time for needless candour.

Lest Eleanor be in any doubt, four weeks later she woke and turned on the radio. The Soviet state newspaper *Isvestia* had said Kim Philby had applied for and been granted political asylum, said the BBC news. 'My last hope that he might still be secretly working for the British had to be abandoned,' she wrote. 'Now I had to believe he was a Russian agent. But I still wondered whether Kim was in Moscow of his own free will.'

She was not letting go of her faith in him.

9

London comes calling

The previous chapter described roughly how the first nightmarish months of 1963 appeared to Eleanor. Her adored husband had been depressed and drunker than usual. He then vanished, and she was not allowed to know why. For a long time all she knew was that something calamitous was unfolding. What was it?

Around the turn of the year, Nicholas Elliott arrived in Beirut. Eleanor and Kim and Nicholas and a colleague had had what in normal times would have been an agreeable meal at Le Temporel. But beneath the surface, as she suspected, was turmoil.

After Philby's dramatic fall in his bathroom, he had stayed at home for several days. During that time, he received the call asking him to come to the British embassy for a meeting with Peter Lunn. With his head bandaged, he had a good excuse, but that call signalled something. A foreign embassy is considered foreign soil, so an invitation to the British embassy might well have been an attempt to lure him somewhere he could be arrested. The minute the call came through, he knew the balloon had gone up, Eleanor was told by Kim later in Moscow. Three days later, Nicholas Elliott arrived in Beirut. Elliott's encounters with Philby have been reconstructed many times, but essential questions remain unanswered.

A few days after the aborted meeting, Lunn invited Philby to another one at a flat belonging to an embassy colleague. In the event, Philby arrived at the flat to find Elliott himself. He told Philby that the game was up, at which Philby did his best to protest his innocence once again. Elliott told him there was now proof of his guilt, without saying what it was, and Philby not asking. 'I once looked up to you,' said Elliott. 'My God how I despise you now.' Elliott told the man he had defended for so long that his life would be made a misery if he failed to acquiesce. Banks would turn him away. His passport would not be renewed. His jobs would come to an end. But in exchange for a full confession and the names of his fellow conspirators, he would be offered immunity from prosecution, in which case the world need never know. 'I'm offering you a lifeline, Kim,' Elliott told him, giving him twenty-four hours to think about it.

The following day, they met again for two hours. The fact that Philby turned up at all was a good sign for Elliott. It suggested, rightly or wrongly, that he had not been conferring with the Russians, who would probably have told him not to attend a second meeting, and quite possibly forced him not to. Philby admitted to having been recruited in the 1930s, but denied doing anything for the Russians in recent years apart from alerting Maclean to his imminent arrest, enabling him and, it turned out, Burgess to escape. At some point, Philby handed over two typewritten pages about his early contacts. A number of other names were discussed, but inconclusively.

Kim asked if Elliott would join him and Eleanor for dinner that evening. For him not to do so would set her worrying. In the event, when Elliott turned up at their flat later, Kim was incapably drunk and had to be put to bed. Elliott and Eleanor spent the evening chatting.

The following day, the pair managed their meal together, at lunchtime, with Eleanor and Elliott's colleague. When Kim went to the lavatory, Elliott followed him moments later. While there, Philby handed over a second two-page document, before the pair returned to the table for more inconsequential chit-chat. The following day, the pair met yet again. At some point in their meetings, other names were mentioned. Elliott asked whether Anthony Blunt was one of his fellow conspirators. No, he said. But instead of looking at Blunt, said Philby, MI6 should consider his colleague Tim Milne, his school friend since the age of thirteen and former deputy in MI6.*

The full import of what had happened needed to be worked on and checks run, but MI6 had their confession. Philby had accepted. Elliott went back to London in triumph, in preparation for flying to the Congo as part of his new job. Back in London, Dick White, who had been convinced of Philby's guilt for over a decade, was delighted. The traitor had been broken. White's feeling was: '[Philby] could have rejected the offer of immunity. Then I would imagine he would skip the country. But since he has accepted, he'll stay and co-operate.' As Elliott basked in his success, he speculated that Philby would probably stay in Beirut for the rest of his life. Either that or commit suicide, much as he was attached to his wife and children.

On 18 January, MI5's Sir Roger Hollis, delighted at the long-delayed but most welcome scalp, wrote to FBI director J. Edgar Hoover, who had been one of the USA's chief pursuers and whose challenge of Philby had made Macmillan's statement in defence of Philby in 1956 necessary. Hollis told Hoover

---

* It is not clear quite what Philby was suggesting by raising Milne's name. The identifying of him may have been less potent than it at first appeared. Milne wrote later what an MI5 officer had told him: 'Kim apparently said that he had mentioned me (among others) to the Russians as someone they might find it worth approaching. However, he went on to say that they had turned the idea down. Kim did not suggest, according to what I was told, that I had any knowledge of all this.'

excitedly that Philby's statement was essentially true. 'We have no evidence pointing to a continuation of his activities ... after 1946, save in the isolated instance of Maclean [and that therefore] damage to United States interest will have been confined to the period of the Second World War.' Following Elliott's coup, the job of topping and tailing could happily be left to others at some unspecified point in the future.

In fact, Philby's confession, seen by his MI6 colleagues as total submission, was anything but. He had lied about Blunt. His friend had indeed been recruited in the 1930s and had been under suspicion since Burgess and Maclean had vanished twelve years earlier. Philby had also, at worst, directed suspicion towards his entirely innocent friend and colleague Tim Milne and at best raised a complete irrelevance. The names he gave were either wrong or of people, guilty or not, who had died.

At some point after his initial conversation with Elliott, Philby contacted his controller Petukhov, telling him that he was due to be interviewed again. This was always likely to have only one outcome. No more interrogations – it was time for action. Moscow was terrified of the damage Philby could do to their interests if Philby changed sides and MI6 got him back to London. He was told he would be welcome in Moscow. It was time to move.

One weekday around that time, he was sitting in the Normandy, embarrassingly drunk. A London-based British businessman, Gordon Williams, who worked in aeronautics, walked in. The barman, Anwar Lamel, knew Williams, a frequent guest at the hotel, well. Lamel asked him if he would mind speaking to Philby, who Williams didn't know. An all but incapable Philby was making a nuisance of himself with the other guests. Lamel himself, by this point, had given up trying to placate Philby, but he knew the congenial Williams would handle the situation as well as anybody could. As it happens,

Williams worked for the Hunting Group of defence companies and, out of a sense of patriotic duty, used to report anything he picked up on his foreign trips to his 'collector' in London, a Mr de Laszlo of MI6, who was particularly interested in the arms capabilities of Saudi Arabia. Williams was to deny any such arrangement if ever challenged about it.

The ever-friendly Williams, not realising the sensitivity of Philby's predicament, was by nature inquisitive and chatted freely, innocently asking who he was, what he did and so on, by chance mentioning Shemlan, the language school where George Blake had been studying. This curiosity had a sobering effect on Philby. Was he being set up in some way? He became suspicious and edged away, tottering off into the night soon afterwards. Anwar the barman's objective had been achieved.

Kim's anxiety was reaching ever greater heights, not that Eleanor knew why. One of the few people to see him in those days was Patrick Seale, his *Observer* colleague. Seale recalled: 'He was weeping quite substantially. I have never seen a grown man weep as much as he. He was clearly frightened. I thought it was just drunkenness. I only understood later that he was under tremendous pressure and was worried that the Russians wouldn't save him in time.'

On the afternoon of 23 January, Philby left the flat, had a couple of drinks at the St Georges and called home, telling Harry he had been held up and would be arriving late at the Balfour-Pauls'. Recalling the day nearly twenty-five years later, he said: 'I knew exactly how to handle it. God knows I had rehearsed it often enough. Just a little stalling, just a little drinking to show nothing was afoot, just a little time to make assurances along the escape route doubly sure. Then, at a given signal, away and gone! ... I had friends as well as enemies in Beirut.'

Whether it was as smooth as Philby claimed is unclear.

He was given false papers, long kept in a safe, and a seaman's clothes, as arranged by the KGB's Vasili Dozhdalev, then in Moscow. 'The Russians were shocked to hear that Elliott had confronted Philby, and they were worried that if Philby went to the dinner that night, he could well be kidnapped, which is just what they would have done in that situation,' says Tom Bower. One well-connected former resident of Beirut still believes that that was indeed the intention – that Philby would be whisked away as he entered the building's exterior lift, next stop London. This seems unlikely. In any event, for all intents and purposes, by this stage the matter was in Russian hands.

The accepted narrative is that his Soviet contacts transported him to Beirut's quayside and onto the *Dolmatova*, a Russian freighter.* From there, sooner than scheduled, the ship eased out of the harbour, its priceless propaganda asset settled on board with a bottle of brandy. The longed-for confession that MI5 had sought was nothing like sufficient for the job. It was now worthless. Philby's departure made it so.

Peter Lunn, having informed the ambassador Moore Crosthwaite late the night of the dinner party that Philby had vanished, visited Eleanor and managed to familiarise himself with the contents of the Philbys' safe. Unknown to her, with the help of the Lebanese authorities, MI6 discovered that the bank notes had been issued to a Soviet diplomat. For MI6 at least, no further proof was needed, although this was kept secret for the time being.

Nearly six decades later, two questions present themselves. Both call for conjecture, and neither can be finally answered now, but some useful strands can be pulled together. The first

---

* For many years it seemed he might have gone overland through Syria. In 1994 two books from well-placed Russian sources asserted that he had taken the freighter from Beirut to Odessa on the Black Sea: Oleg Kalugin, *Spymaster*, p. 134; Genrikh Borovik, *The Philby Files*, pp. 348–50.

question is whether the eventual outcome – Philby fleeing to Moscow – was what the British authorities wanted all along, as has been suggested. Was there a conspiracy to encourage him to defect?

Had Philby been arrested, he would have had to be brought back to London to face a humiliating trial beyond the control of the security forces. But Philby might have doubted the sincerity of the immunity offer, or that such a deal would remain secret. And would Philby really reveal the names of all his fellow traitors? In which case, was allowing his flit to Moscow part of a plan to avoid embarrassment (and subsequent remarks by Elliott and others an attempt to obscure that fact), or was it cock-up, a case of MI6 resting on its laurels after a confession of sorts had been secured, enabling Philby to do the ungentlemanly thing and vanish when no one was looking?

The idea that it was planned to usher Philby towards the door has a number of adherents, mindful of the desire to minimise embarrassment to the British government after the Buster Crabb scandal, the trial of George Blake and the imprisoning of another Soviet spy, John Vassall. And this was the age when there was little public expectation of transparency on MI5 or MI6. The media knew not to get too close to anything really potent, even if it could. It wasn't until well over four years later that journalist Phillip Knightley was told, over a drunken dinner, that, to his amazement, 'the man running our secret operations against the Russians was a Russian agent himself'. In such a deferential age, it is understandable if a decision not to prosecute might be attractive.

The case for conspiracy rests largely on circumstantial evidence, but there is new evidence in its favour. A Briton working in the hotel and catering business in Beirut at the time was an aspiring hotelier called Simon Elliot. He made good friends with his near namesake (but no relation) Nicholas, and later lived near him in England. He was also on friendly terms with Kim Philby and Miles Copeland, who would frequently meet for a drink at his hotel, the Sands of Lebanon. (The pair rarely drank together at the St Georges, seemingly because they didn't want to be seen together.)

Interviewed recently for this book, Simon Elliot reported: 'I had an incredibly happy friendship with Nicholas. I was so fond of him. He knew he could talk to me in complete confidence, and I am quite certain he wouldn't have been spinning me a line. He had no need. I had a very long lunch with him at White's in London in the late 1960s, and he talked about Kim. We talked about whether Kim was encouraged to go. I remember utterly clearly Nicholas telling me that Philby said: "Well, what happens now?" Nicholas told me he had said to Philby: "You've got twenty-four hours' head start." I remember that with absolute certainty. It's not my imagination. He said, "We couldn't bring him back, there would have been a trial and the CIA would have been furious. We couldn't leave him in Beirut as he was a loose cannon. The only option was to push him."' If Nicholas Elliott had been spinning his friend a line, it would have been more productive to have disseminated it more widely, and to rather less discreet friends, than he appears to have done.

Alan Hare, an officer for MI6, said assassination was something the British were not equipped to do in Lebanon and in any case the political risks were too great. He claimed the most important thing was to confirm Philby's guilt, to help establish where the damage had been done. That, he said, was more important than bringing him to justice, and, as his usefulness was at an end, he was allowed to flee.

Another adherent to this view was Dutch-born George Blake, whose undercover work for the Russians landed him with a forty-two-year prison sentence in 1961. He was to escape, ending up in Moscow. Blake thinks Nicholas Elliott's message was straightforward: 'Don't come back to England.'

'It was probably because I was of foreign origin,' said Blake. 'I could more easily be made an example of. They also did not want another spy scandal. They were members of the Establishment and I was not.' Philby, too, expressed himself perplexed by the ease with which he was able to escape, and wondered if he had been encouraged to go. It certainly gave the Russians plenty to think about. Philby later wrote to Nicholas Elliott, suggesting his 'fade' (defection) might have been encouraged and saying he hoped they might meet in Helsinki or Berlin (a suggestion vetoed by Dick White). Philby also told Phillip Knightley the British wanted him out of the way to minimise further embarrassing disclosures when the Americans got their hands on him.

Such talk, on the British side, may be damage limitation, and the evidence for cock-up is strong, too. The British were guilty of calamitous wishful thinking. They believed that Philby was no longer in touch with the Russians, and in effect had nowhere to go. They believed if Elliott could persuade Philby to come clean, the game would have changed entirely, and could be taken at a leisurely pace. White's biographer Tom Bower sheds much light on this story: 'Dick liked the idea of Philby staying in Beirut and giving a detailed confession over a long period and then deciding what to do. There was no appetite for a prosecution.' Elliott himself said: 'He fooled me though. I thought he wanted to stay where he was.' Bower also quotes Peter Lunn: 'White didn't even think about [Philby going to Moscow].' 'It didn't arise,' admitted White. 'I thought Philby would come back for a final session.' The rage and frustration in Peter Wright's assertion that 'Roger [Hollis] and Dick [White] had not taken into account that Philby might defect' did not need to be spelled out.

Years later, perhaps inevitably over dinner at White's, former CIA operative Ted Shackley had the impression that Elliott was both chuffed at having secured Philby's confession but conscious of criticism that he had let him get away, in part by leaving Beirut after less than a week, before concluding matters with Philby. In Shackley's clinical phrase 'perseverance apparently took a holiday'. 'We misread his state of mind,' Elliott told Shackley, who said Elliott bore this guilty burden with great dignity. To MI5, Elliott's failure to bring Philby home was all the vindication they needed: he of all people should not have been given the job, which in any case should have gone to the professional spycatchers – in MI5.

Senior staffers in MI6 never fully understood something as unBritish as the ideological commitment that Philby had espoused. For a people, and in particular a public-school elite, so sceptical of the power of ideas – in this case the potency of Marxism – and so rooted in pragmatism, it just didn't make sense. They had assumed that kind old Kim would always be redeemable, that a love of cricket, England and family had been enough to make him renounce that silly communism business.

So, in language they would find familiar, they took their eye off the ball. The confession, they assumed, was the hard part, and everything else would fall into place. For them, there was no decent way of him coming back from that, but decency had little to do with it at that moment. Within a few days, the confession was as worthless as if Philby had stood at the rail of the *Dolmatova* and shouted, 'I'm Moscow-bound!' through a megaphone at the lunchtime drinkers on the St Georges terrace. The confession – whether he planned it as such or not – enabled him to fix up his lift with the Russians. The British ended up with the least useful of trophies. The case for reopening the Philby case had been to assess how much damage he and his friends had done – and who exactly they were – which they singularly failed to do. 'That was the point of it all,' said Nicholas Elliott, for whom the Philby defection caused devastating embarrassment. Elliott had come a long way on amiability and public-school polish, but to Hugh Trevor-Roper he was 'a poop – a typical member of the old-boy network', and to others he had insufficient experience of street-level intelligence work. It is not hard to imagine Philby at that moment enjoying his own typically cold-blooded assessment of his friend: 'I like Nick, he's just not very bright.'

Frank Wisner, son of one of the CIA staff with most reason to be aggrieved at Philby's escape, remembers his father reflecting on the affair. 'We exchanged intelligence with our British friends and they didn't listen and take us seriously. My father said it was a bad British habit to protect their old boys and that Philby had been favoured.' Just as the British had missed the first opportunity to question Maclean in 1951 – to the frustration of the Americans – by agreeing to another meeting the British gave Philby the time he needed to alert the Russians. 'Instead of taking more aggressive action there was a nice conversation which tipped him off ... He said that the style of the British was to treat each other with kid gloves ... to speak to him and have a follow-up conversation and see where we go next with this. That's all.'

His view is shared by MI5's Arthur Martin, the original choice to face Philby. When Elliott first returned to London with Philby's two-page document under his arm, Martin, whose idea it had been to offer Philby immunity, examined it. There were some useful admissions of guilt over his recruitment in the 1930s and Konstantin Volkov, but essentially Elliott, never a specialist interrogator, had been conned.

Listening to the tape, Martin 'pounded his knees in frustration' as Philby 'reeled off a string of ludicrous claims', his colleague Peter Wright recorded. 'We should have sent a team out there, and grilled him while we had the chance ...' According to Nigel West, Philby was to be confronted with his lies. It never happened. 'By the time Elliott was sent back to Beirut to confront Philby ten days later, he had disappeared.'

If there was a conspiracy to let Philby go, it seems Peter Lunn was not in on it. Several years later, he was reliably said to be 'still spitting tacks' at Nicholas Elliott's assertion that Lunn need not worry about Philby – that matter had been settled.

Wisner's choice of words reflects the benign Anglophilia of his father's generation of American diplomats, but, stripping away the courtesy, the gist is that the British blundered calamitously, not only in failing to identify the traitor in their midst for at least twelve years after the Americans first raised the alarm but also in failing to prevent him escaping. Remarkably, with hindsight, the British would have preferred not to know. 'What a shame we reopened it all, just trouble,' said White.

There is a further charge of sleepiness to be laid against the British. According to two very credible versions, Elliott also did not tell Philby unambiguously the terms of the immunity deal on the table, cleared by the Attorney General, speaking only of how a voluntary written statement 'might stand Kim in good stead' especially if he helped clear matters up in London. Maybe Elliott was not in a position to offer a concrete deal, either because he had not been told it was cut and dried and had been legally cleared, or because MI6's plan at that stage was still imprecise and they intended to play it by ear. In either case, if MI6 wanted Philby to return to London and do a deal, given the pressure Philby was under and the variables he needed to consider, the failure to make explicit the offer is an astonishing failure of communication. (One early version had Elliott saying, 'well, who knows, difficult as it is, something might be salvaged of your career'.) If the best that was on offer was really a vague, high-handed promise to look understandingly on his future, few people would be tempted in that position, let alone a man being asked to turn his back on thirty years of ideological commitment. Perhaps unsurprisingly, subsequent accounts, from both Philby's and the British side, claim the offer was firmer than in initial tellings. Yet Andrew Boyle had spoken to both White and Elliott in preparing his book, which referred to 'making no false promises' and Philby having to 'take his medicine'. Though his book was far from flawless, Boyle is unlikely to have invented such details.

If the Americans were angry before January 1963, they would have been furious afterwards, although there are few publicly available manifestations of this. For one thing, James Angleton told Verne Newton in 1986 that the British had broken their word to the Americans: 'I had an agreement with [MI6] that Philby would never be interrogated on foreign soil.' It has been reported that Philby was told by a Soviet contact that an American hitman had arrived in Beirut with the express intention of murdering him and disposing of his body in Beirut harbour. Philby, it seems, had become particularly aware of being followed, and received reports of a mysterious American asking questions about him in the bars he frequented.

What is certain is that the Americans were assiduously trying to catch him out, and at least two of his St Georges confrères believe that American pressure of some sort helped persuade him to head for Moscow. However explicit and threatening the American pressure, two related things are quite possible. One is that the Russians could well have told him they understood the CIA was trying to kill him, in an attempt to scare him into going to Moscow. The other is that an assassination by the Americans – with no British connivance – might have suited both nations. One advocate (after the event) of either kidnapping or murdering Philby in 1962 was David Cornwell. In a letter MI6 boss Dick White criticised the novelist's radical suggestion some years later: 'But the corpses of already famous 3rd men are more easily disposed of in novels than among the

Br. Diplomats & Home office officials. Moreover in terms of legal evidence it could still quite easily have been said that the wrong man had been disposed of. Who in our democracy accepts responsibilities of this kind?'

Talk of assassination may be taking us into the land of fable, in this instance at least. More convincing is an account written in the 1980s by academic, author and former diplomat with excellent CIA connections Robin Winks. According to Winks, Angleton had two agents, unknown to one another, watching him. 'Angleton wanted Philby returned in physical custody through the station chief in Beirut, his Yale classmate Ed Applewhite, and interrogated by someone Philby did not know.' This plan was thwarted by Philby's disappearance. Michael Holzman, biographer of Angleton and author of a book on his relationship with Philby, believes Robin Winks was told by Angleton himself 'that he wished to have Philby detained in Beirut'. Angleton would have had few qualms about the legality of effectively arresting Philby on foreign soil – the Lebanese government not being well placed to prevent it – and, once Philby's guilt was proven, the junior-partner British would be more worried about the political embarrassment than legal nicety. In any event, Philby's disappearance scuppered any such plan, adding to Angleton's fury.

There is a further oddity about the month before Philby disappeared, which may have a bearing on the 'cock-up or conspiracy' question. Nicholas Elliott, it is commonly asserted, arrived in Beirut on 10 January 1963, staying low-key for a few days and setting off a chain of events that traumatised Britain's spy bosses for years. Yet in her book, one of the most authoritative sources on the chronology, Eleanor reports Elliott's sudden but uncharacteristically low-key arrival in Beirut as having been *in December*, rather than January. Further, she remembers the meal at Le Temporel as being shortly before Christmas. The claim as to the timing is echoed in at least three other books, one co-authored by Eleanor's ghost writer Patrick Seale and Maureen McConville, who, writing ten years later – by which time any error could have been corrected – repeated that Elliott arrived just before Christmas (and that he had 'perhaps half a dozen meetings' with Philby) and that the two men 'agreed to resume' their conversation in the New Year. The claim is repeated in Page, Leitch and Knightley's biography, which reports on a visit by MI6 'at the end of 1962'. And the third iteration comes from no less a stickler for detail than Philby's former colleague Hugh Trevor-Roper, writing with the encouragement of MI6 boss Dick White, in early 1968. ('In 1962, in Beirut, he was faced with the evidence.')

Could they all have been mistaken? It seems unlikely, although Elliott did protest to one writer, insisting his trip had been after Christmas. But Eleanor, by way of emphasis, told Patrick Seale that Kim and his Russian friends had fully four weeks in which to organise the escape. There was mystification at how the British allowed things to drift on, at their lack of action. The discrepancy is curious. Did Elliott make two trips? Could he have made an earlier, similarly secret visit in December in order to play on Philby's putative sense of obligation to his friend, to have a feel for how an eventual confrontation might go, or might be steered? If so, the first encounter might have been a dry run, with the second, with the tape recorder running, providing legal cover and something to pacify the Americans, having something of the presentational about it. Equally, it may be an error of no significance.

The British were highly embarrassed, of course, by the Philby affair, and anxious to minimise the damage he was perceived to have done. Specifically, they wanted it to be accepted that Philby had ceased to spy for the Russians since 1949, when he had gone to work in the United States. The date is significant because it reassures the Americans (see Roger Hollis's letter, above) that they were in for no more surprises as regards their own secrets.* But by wanting to tell the Americans that he had been inactive for so long, they also made their job that much harder. By omission, they were in effect flagging up to Philby their ignorance of what he had been doing more recently. There was no compelling new evidence of recent activity for the Russians, Philby was able to conclude – and he knew better than most what was in the archives – and he could simply play for time. Philby confirms he may have given the impression of being tempted by the British offer. He told Genrikh Borovik: 'I do not rule out the possibility that [Nicholas Elliott] was certain he had planted doubts in me and made me think about the arguments he had used. My goal was to win time, if only a few days, and to do nothing that would push them into decisive action.'

Is there any room for synthesis between cock-up and conspiracy? On the face of it, either Philby was being urged towards the exit, or the British wanted an immunity deal in return for the names of the last communists from the 1930s. It looks as if something unforeseen knocked the immunity plan off course. Tom Bower, who spoke to White, Elliott and Lunn at great length about the affair, believes the British wanted Philby to come clean, which would enable them then to make a decision about leaving Philby in Beirut (without alerting the Russians) or suggesting he come back to London. But Philby – who according to Elliott was surprised at being confronted and tempted

---

* Philby told Genrikh Borovik that it was Elliott who proposed the 1949 cut-off, which presumably would have suited the British desire to reassure the Americans and keep them away from the investigation, whereas Dick White's version has Philby claiming to have had no contact after reforms by the Attlee government in 1949 – just the moment of his move to Washington, when he would have been of most use to the USSR. Neither version as to who suggested 1949 is convincing, although it had advantages for both sides.

to accept the immunity offer – felt obliged to tell the Russians. 'The Russians were terrified by the prospect of the damage Philby might do back in London if he turned against them,' says Tom Bower, who interviewed Vasili Dozhdalev, who devised Philby's escape, in Moscow. 'So he was told very forcibly that for his own and the USSR's benefit, he had to leave urgently.' There was little to discuss.

Was Philby really tempted? It is impossible to know, but the fact that the names he offered were useless suggests he was playing for time, at very least. At what point did Elliott and his MI6 colleagues realise that Philby was not keeping his side of the deal? Elliott had encrypted Philby's confession and sent it straight to Dick White in London. Arthur Martin, listening a matter of days or maybe weeks later (admittedly after Philby had disappeared), readily dismissed the contrasting claims about Milne and Blunt. Elliott said years later that being told *everything* about the damage done by Philby was 'paramount' if he was to be given immunity. Is it possible MI6 realised they were bogus rather quicker – and, as we shall see, there is reason to think in Blunt's case they did – and saw no point in persisting?

It is conceivable at least, says Nicholas Elliott's son Mark, who shares a widespread scepticism about his father's suitability for the job in the first place: 'It was a huge mistake for my father to be the person to go and confront Kim. He was so emotionally involved in the whole thing. I don't know how much clarity he had. There may well have been a plan and obviously it was in a lot of people's interest for Kim to hop it. I suspect it is true. The last thing they wanted was for Kim to come back ... They could have done a deal, and offered him one, but if he was not going to accept it – or he was not going to play straight – I think they wanted him out of the way.' Mark Elliott says his father wrote a full account, but the authorities will not release it.

Enter a knight

Was Philby tipped off in advance that the game was up? The question is of more than esoteric interest, because the encounter with Elliott aggravated official paranoia that Moscow's penetration had gone much further than had been supposed. Far from Philby telling all and helping MI5 and MI6 mop up the last remaining traitors, he succeeded in multiplying the uncertainty that Soviet defector Anatoly Golitsin had recently been engendering.

When Philby arrived for his meeting, his first words to Elliott were: 'I rather thought it would be you.' What did Philby mean by this? Was he really expecting Elliott, whose presence in Beirut was a secret? Or was this a very Philbyesque piece of mischief-making designed to unsettle his old friend?

Nicholas Elliott later claimed it was 'nonsense' that Philby had been tipped off, and that he 'wasn't ready at all'. It was simply that Lunn (or his office) had made the initial appointment, and Philby had been unaware Elliott was in town. Further, Elliott says his adversary was 'shaken' and decided to accept the immunity offer in return for helping with the assessment of the damage done by the traitors. It is hard to avoid the sense throughout that Philby – who once said truth was no more than a 'technical advantage' – was the more sharp-witted of the two. Tim Milne said later that 'Philby ran rings around Elliott'.

In any event, those who listened to the recording of Elliott's eventual confrontation with Philby, while allowing for Philby's compulsive game-playing, were perplexed. Peter Wright of MI5 wrote: 'There was no doubt in anyone's mind, listening to the tape, that Philby arrived at the safe house well prepared for Elliott's confrontation. Elliott told him there was new evidence ... [and Philby] never once asked what the new evidence was.' For a man who had denied and denied for years, Philby's lack of curiosity was remarkable. He knew there had been countless suspicions but no hard evidence. Suddenly, over a quarter of a century after his recruitment, there was, he was told, yet he expressed no interest in it. Further, MI5's experts who saw the pieces of paper that Philby handed over said they looked as if they had been more carefully and skilfully put together than could have been managed in just a day or so. That suggested there had been a tip-off.

If Philby's response was intended to unsettle, it succeeded. A generation of intelligence officers had the fear hanging over them that Philby might have been given advance warning.* Dick White of MI6, no wild conspiracy theorist, was initially persuaded that questions should be asked of MI5 boss Roger Hollis and his deputy Graham Mitchell, although he doubted it of both of them.† An industry looking for the 'Fourth Man', the 'Fifth Man' and so on sprung into life. He cleared Hollis quickly, although for some others the claim was not laid to rest for several decades and still has its adherents.‡

---

* Tom Bower said the remark fuelled a 'ferocious hunt within MI5 for the next decade'. Anthony Cave Brown said the search lasted a quarter of a century.

† For a full discussion of White's dealings with Arthur Martin of MI5 on the possibility of Philby having been tipped off, see Nigel West, *At Her Majesty's Secret Service*, pp. 81–2.

‡ Chapman Pincher and Nigel West agree that Elliott originally believed Philby had

The case against Mitchell was not quite so quickly dismissed, which allowed wild hares to run free. Another possible traitor was said to be the brilliant Victor Rothschild, university friend of Blunt and Burgess, who went to great lengths in the 1980s, contributing substantially to books by Chapman Pincher and Peter Wright, to ensure history gave him a clean bill of health. The sense that Rothschild must have known about his communist friends, at very least, is hard to shake, yet he remained a close friend of Dick White and was helpful in trying to identify and catch them.* There was a growing awareness that communism had made far greater inroads into the British establishment than was comfortably admitted, and other possible culprits came and went in the rogues' gallery, but the question of Philby's possible accomplice before his flight to Moscow was never answered.

The evidence that there was a tip-off is circumstantial. Had there been one, it might be argued, Philby would have been better prepared, or could have simply fled before Elliott reached him (although that might have alerted the British to a leak and incriminated whoever gave the tip-off). But he knew the British were unlikely to kidnap or kill him, and could only arrest him on British soil, so he could afford to hear them out and reflect on any offer. Indeed, he claimed later he had been warned by someone in British intelligence that the net was closing, and there was indeed something of a dialogue with him (whether he was sincere or not) in the belief that he would never take refuge in Moscow. But until there was hard evidence, he was safe.

---

been tipped off. Pincher, *Too Secret Too Long*, p. 378, and West and Tsarev (eds), *TRIPLEX*, p. 81. Much later Elliott wrote that he had learned that Philby had only told his Russian controllers of his confession after the event, citing this as proof that Philby could not have been tipped off by a traitor from MI5 or MI6. Yet it remains perfectly possible, if that traitor and Philby agreed not to alert the Russians to his imminent questioning, and if the confession was in order to play for time. Elliott, *With My Little Eye*, p. 97.

* Victor Rothschild remains an object of suspicion to some. See Roland Perry, *Last of the Cold War Spies*.

Did he know of Solomon's evidence, or Golitsin's, and that neither was sufficient to seal his fate? Or maybe they did have something conclusive? He couldn't know for sure. But if there was no tip-off, or even an intimation that things were coming to a head, his mood in late 1962 needs to be accounted for. He was in an appalling state, his wife at her wits' end to understand. The curious message he sent his former MI6 colleague Desmond Bristow also calls for an explanation. In December 1962 Bristow and his wife Betty received a card. The message read: 'Have a Happy Christmas and a Happy New Year. May not see you for a while. Love Kim.' 'It was his way of telling me he was the Third Man,' Bristow believed.

There was another possible straw in the wind. Philby loved animals, couldn't bear to see them in distress and was forever adding to the family's collection of birds, fish and various quadrupeds. After the mysterious death of their pet fox in the late summer of 1962, for Christmas the Copelands gave the Philbys a puppy, a bit like an Alsatian, to compensate for the loss of the fox. The children adored the dog but Eleanor said Kim was very much opposed to accepting it. Was this because he knew that the happy life in Beirut would soon be broken up?*

If there was a tip-off, who gave it? It has conventionally been believed by some that Yuri Modin had a hand in Philby's disappearance. While later searching for the source of the presumed alert, Peter Wright was shown CIA records that revealed that Modin had visited Beirut in September 1962, just after Flora Solomon had unburdened herself to Victor Rothschild. Others noted that at about that time Philby had returned unexpectedly,

---

* Philby later denied he had had advance warning, saying: 'There was no tip-off. There was no need for one ... I had been preparing for twelve years for this.' (Knightley, p. 217). The largest pinches of salt are required in any mention of Soviet operational matters, and particularly this one.

a day early, from a holiday with Eleanor and the children in Jordan, after which he had been depressed and prone to heavier than usual drinking (although this has generally been attributed to the death of the fox). Yet how could Modin have known about Solomon having revealed Philby's communist past? Nobody has explained this, other than with recourse to now discredited theories.* In fact, seemingly Modin never met Philby in Beirut, something he confirmed when I met him in 2001.† He said: 'I know your intelligence people think that I have been there ... I have been at that time in Beirut but I had no contact with Philby.' This, presumably, was the September visit identified by the CIA. In any event, KGB protocols make it unlikely for someone other than his recognised handler to be given such a task.

Someone with a real interest in alerting Philby to a coming confrontation was Sir Anthony Blunt. He had been an infatuated friend of Guy Burgess at Cambridge, and under Burgess's influence had signed up to work secretly for the Soviet cause. Following the tip-off from Philby, Blunt had come up with Burgess and Maclean's means of escape in 1951, and shared with many of his Cambridge contemporaries a sense that personal friendship superseded other loyalties. Unlike Philby, Blunt had done as much as he could to extricate himself from his obligations to Moscow, particularly after 1951. His faith in communism was long dead and – unusually for someone in his position – the USSR had few expectations of him. He had been allowed to leave with relatively few strings attached.

Yuri Modin, his then contact in London, said Blunt was not 'a Communist through and through ... even though he

---

* Modin would have known that the Soviet defector Golitsin was talking to the British, but there was doubt as to whether Golitsin knew enough to identify Philby specifically.

† Or arguably anywhere else, although there is some doubt about this, before 1963.

shared certain Marxist opinions'. According to Modin, Blunt felt that unlike the days of the Renaissance when rich patrons would encourage art, in the twentieth century, when the bourgeois state 'does nothing to develop it', only a totalitarian state could assume the patron's role. Blunt said later that Marx had provided an 'extremely interesting and fruitful' approach to art history, but then he 'gradually realised it was a gross over-simplification'. For politics more widely, while the analysis was useful, it was no guide to future action. Modin said his bosses in Moscow 'were quite sure that Blunt was not a communist at all. No doubt about that. They knew that, I knew that, and always said that. All the same, I was asked by my chiefs to make him more conformist towards communist thinking. When I tried it, Blunt was resisting everything I said. I [was] not in a position to influence him. I'm not clever enough to do that ... he was stronger than me, I understood that. Blunt was not a communist, he hadn't any idea of communism. He was very critical of Marx.'

It is one thing to reconsider youthful political adherences, but Blunt's enthusiasms involved secretly working to advance the interests of a hostile foreign power and people being killed as a result, and were less easily jettisoned. He was by now one of Britain's most accomplished art historians, and was Surveyor of the Queen's Pictures, as well as director of the Courtauld Institute. In short, he was living in terror of his guilty past being exposed. Also, Blunt feared being made by his Soviet bosses to go to Russia, which was 'totally abhorrent' to him.

How would Philby react if he was offered immunity by the British? Blunt knew that Philby was committed in his politics, but also that he adored his wife and children. Much as he found Russia's approach to politics admirable, Philby had evinced little desire to live there. Would he be willing to do a deal that would mean naming names, possibly including Blunt's? Could Philby possibly do a deal and *not* confirm Blunt's guilt, knowing that Blunt had long been the object of suspicion, at very least? A conversation with Philby along those lines would in itself be a good reason for Blunt to approach him. He would have wanted to know Philby's state of mind.

If Blunt indeed knew of the plan to challenge Philby, he would have been in a quandary. Setting aside his own interests for a moment, Blunt would at least have wanted to help Philby prepare. Philby could then either vanish, or stonewall, or confess, or take some other sort of evasive action. But a further question, of practicality and politics, arose. How was Philby to be informed? Philby's phone calls were almost certainly being monitored. To write to him – risky for the same reason – would also have wasted valuable time.

The simplest answer would be for Blunt to alert the Russians in London to pass the message on to Philby. But Blunt knew that if he alerted his Soviet masters, Philby's next move would almost certainly be decided for him in Moscow, and for the worse. The Russians would be entirely unsentimental about security risks, as they had been with Guy Burgess. The idea of Philby falling into the hands of British security professionals armed with compelling evidence of his guilt would have horrified them. He might accept immunity and blow their secrets, including the names of Soviet officers and agents, quite apart from Blunt. He might be turned, to work in British interests. How could they know if he had been? To pre-empt any such risk, if Philby didn't comply with Soviet plans, he might well be considered dispensable, and become the victim of a nasty, Moscow-inspired accident, and that would be that.

For his own and Philby's benefit, Blunt could not sit on his hands and watch his friend be ambushed by his British inquisitors, but alerting the Russians was no solution either. If Blunt aspired to act out of friendship, he could not condemn

Philby to a life of misery in Moscow if his friend would prefer otherwise. Maybe a formalised immunity deal that encompassed both men's guilt – if achievable – would have suited them both. But he couldn't be sure of Philby's state of mind. He had to let Philby choose, as far as was possible. And for Philby to be able to make a free choice, Blunt could not tell the Russians.

It is unclear how recently the pair had been able to speak freely (probably at least a year), nor how familiar Blunt was with Philby's thinking. As we will see, they had had a very public encounter, apparently by chance, around Easter the previous year at a British embassy party in Beirut, and Yuri Modin said they had been able to meet previously when Philby came to London. President Khrushchev had sought to move the USSR forward in the post-Stalin era, but given the bolstering of autocratic regimes in Eastern Europe since the war and the 1956 invasion of Hungary, it would be surprising if Philby was entirely happy at how the Soviet dream was turning out. Peter Wright wrote later: 'Blunt admired Philby, but there was a part of him that was frightened by his utter conviction, his ruthlessly one-dimensional view of life.'

But if Blunt's political faith had vanished, he still had faith in friendship. Brian Sewell says: 'Once the war had come to an end he wanted nothing to do with any of it. He may have been pulled in two different directions. Anthony, I am sure, was driven by friendship more than anything else once the war was over ... I think the relationship with Philby was much less clear [than with Burgess] ... I don't know what sense of obligation he had to Philby.' Either way, even if only for reasons of self-preservation, he needed to take the initiative. Inaction carried many risks, too.

Did Blunt fear that Philby would betray him if he was confronted and/or brought back to London? Peter Wright said Philby 'needed Blunt desperately' after 1951, to keep him informed of the case against him, but maybe that moment had passed. Sewell says: 'It may be that Anthony knew Philby well enough to make the assumption that if by betraying others [Philby] might save himself, he might well do it. I don't know. Anthony might have thought [Philby] a man without scruples, unlike Anthony [himself]. Anthony probably knew him better than anyone else. That might well have been his belief. I don't know. If I had been Anthony and some friend in MI5 or MI6 had tipped me off that Philby might be arrested and brought back, what I might calculate is that if he is offered immunity for sacrificing others, well, Burgess has gone, Maclean has gone ... I'm the one in the front line. [Blunt's visit to Beirut] may have been a last flicker of loyalty to someone who had been in the same game, on the same side, or it may have been entirely self-seeking, or it may have been a bit of both.'

If we accept for the moment that Blunt visited Beirut during the relevant months, is it not possible that the Russians, having somehow got wind of the renewed threat to Philby (possibly even from Blunt), were responsible for sending him there? It is possible, but unlikely, for three reasons. The first is that, while obviously the Russians knew of the Golitsin defection, it is unlikely they knew of the new claim by Flora Solomon and the threat to Philby. Who would have told them?

Second, Blunt would probably have refused any such request, had he known that the Russians could have got word to Philby just as easily. Yuri Modin spoke with some admiration of Blunt's insistence on maintaining as much independence from Moscow as possible (another reason for doubting Blunt would have told Moscow of the plan to confront Philby). 'For instance in 1938, at the start of the second world war, he volunteered and went into the British army [without asking us]. He was absolutely independent. He was helping us but at the same time he did not allow us to influence his own ideas about what communism is or what capitalism is.' After the war, and particularly after Burgess went to Moscow in 1951, that defiance was stronger than ever.

And third, they had no need to send Blunt on so risky a mission. Assuming they could trust their communications, they could simply notify Petukhov or someone else on the ground in Beirut, who could have passed on a message to Philby. That way, a trusted Russian would have those important conversations with Philby, rather than Blunt, a British friend whose faith in communism had evaporated. In short, if Blunt did go to Beirut to tip off Philby, it is likely he did so without Russian connivance or knowledge.

Blunt may have had the motive, but did he have the means? Clearly he did, because we know that he was in Beirut just a few weeks before Philby disappeared. The British embassy's press officer, Alan Munro, recalls being hurriedly invited by Sir Moore Crosthwaite to a drink at the British embassy to meet the distinguished Surveyor of the Queen's Pictures. Munro recalls it being some time after he married his wife Grania in late September 1962. The 'sudden' drink was attended by just a handful of those who could be summoned at short notice. This chimes with Sewell's belief that the visit was an impromptu one, Blunt presumably having realised he needed to get there before Philby's inquisitor. Sewell also believed the visit took place during the Christmas holidays (possibly even very early in January) in order not to alert his Courtauld colleagues and students to his absence. Glen Balfour-Paul, also on the staff of the Beirut embassy, confirmed Blunt's presence in Beirut in December 1962, and records that Blunt told his host he was in Lebanon because, he said, he 'wanted to search the northern end of the Lebanese mountains for a rare frog orchid, and in due course he told the Ambassador he had found one'. This is an extraordinary notion, given that Blunt had no particular interest in flora and fauna.*

One can only speculate as to why Blunt made this claim. It invites speculation as to whether the term 'orchid' is a euphemism for something, or it may have been so obviously and intentionally bogus as to invite speculation about another motivation. It was understood well enough that Moore Crosthwaite was homosexual, however much he sought to obscure the matter. It was assumed, too, that Anthony Blunt, his guest and sexual confidant of half a century, was also homosexual, and sophisticated souls in the embassy might have discreetly assured themselves that this in some way was the 'real' explanation for the visit. Of course, neither could 'come out' for fear of losing his job. So an unlikely tale such as a search for a midwinter orchid might have served as obvious cover to discreetly steer the gossips towards the two men's shared secret. If (*if*) that was the real reason, a cover story would be not just understandable but essential. If this surmise is true, it is quite possible that nobody, anywhere, except Philby knew what Blunt was really doing.

Some weeks before Blunt's visit to Beirut, he had been in Ireland visiting the estate of the Cochrane family at Woodbrook, Bray, County Wicklow. The family are owners of painted panels by the eighteenth-century Florentine painter Francesco Zuccarelli. Blunt visited the Cochranes, who he had long known (his brother Wilfrid having taught Desmond Cochrane, the 3rd baronet, art at Eton), bringing pictures of the cartoons of the originals, to advise on restoration of the panels. Blunt knew the Cochranes well enough to be aware of their connection by marriage with Beirut. Sir Desmond Cochrane's son Alfred, then living there, said 'it would have

---

* Journalist George Carey consulted a senior orchid expert at Kew, who said Blunt's claim was highly unlikely to be true. Curiously, orchids were a passion of the CIA's James Angleton.

been extraordinary for Blunt to have visited Beirut without visiting the family' (the Sursocks/Cochranes). Paradoxically, the fact that he didn't visit should not be cited as evidence that he wasn't in the city, merely that he wanted to keep the lowest of profiles.

Brian Sewell believed Blunt may have interrupted a trip to southern Italy in order to visit Lebanon to see his friend. Blunt was preparing a book on Baroque architecture which took him to Sicily. He could have taken a connecting flight from Catania or Palermo to Fiumicino airport in Rome. In 1962, Alitalia was indeed running direct flights to Beirut. Could Blunt have been on one of those? Alas, the paperwork no longer exists.*

This conjecture doesn't begin to match the standards of the professional historian, and the lack of available documentation makes reaching those an unlikely prospect. If we accept that Blunt was in Beirut, though, it seems almost inconceivable that he did not see Philby.

But a key question remains. If Blunt had urgent news for Philby, how did he acquire it? It can reasonably be assumed that only a handful of people knew of the plan to question Philby. They included the Prime Minister and his most senior aides, the Attorney General, the Foreign Office's Permanent Under Secretary, Sir Dick White and Nicholas Elliott (both MI6), Sir Roger Hollis, Peter Wright, Graham Mitchell and Arthur Martin (all MI5), Victor Rothschild and the cabinet secretary.

For this reason and others, the loyalty of most of them has been questioned at one stage or another, and Hollis and

---

* On a later trip, Blunt spent three weeks in Sicily with a photographer, Tim Benton, now professor of art history at the Open University, whose father Kenneth, incidentally, was in MI6. Benton recalls starting at 6 a.m. for long mornings of intense study of Sicilian churches, followed by a litre of wine at lunch. He remembers the maestro doing nothing suspicious – this was after his confession – other than the time, as if in a Greene or le Carré novel, when Blunt told what Benton thought 'an obvious lie', claiming 'I need to visit my tailor in Cefalù.'

Rothschild still have their snipers, but no compelling evidence has been found. It seems unlikely that any of them would have connived in assisting Philby's preparations.

But could some clue about the evidence against Philby have been let slip inadvertently? It is unlikely, when such vital issues were at stake, but anything is possible, and again conjecture takes a hand. Blunt belonged to a set of people for whom discretion was second nature. Among most of them, it was taken for granted that he should be trusted.

As we have seen, it was Victor Rothschild to whom Flora Solomon complained about Philby's long-term loyalty. Rothschild had also been at Cambridge with Blunt and Guy Burgess, and some even suspected him of Soviet leanings. But he was considered to understand the mindset of the sophisticated young men who had idealistically decided the best way to fight fascism was to sign up with the Soviet Union. In truth, though, at that time Rothschild was somewhat out of his depth on that score.

Rothschild was similarly trusting of Blunt, and often confided in him. Whether Rothschild did so on this occasion and told him of the Flora Solomon breakthrough on Philby is unknowable. It seems unlikely, on balance. If we accept Rothschild's bona fides, knowing of the suspicions about Blunt, he would have risked as little as possible. Rothschild's biographer, the late Kenneth Rose, thought it would have been thoroughly out of character for the 'cagey' Victor to say a word to anyone who didn't need to know. Apart, that is, from his wife.

During the war, Tess Rothschild was called Tess Mayor, who with Anthony Blunt and her friend Patricia Rawdon-Smith had rented the Bentinck Street flat owned by Victor Rothschild (at that time Tess's boss in MI5). Nervous and self-effacing, Tess, a beautiful, diffident, thespian figure, was someone of whom her fellow undergraduates spoke with awe, and she and her best friend, the politically driven and sexually adventurous Rawdon-Smith, made a formidable duo. Rawdon-Smith was the first woman with whom Anthony Blunt tried heterosexual sex.

Politically left-leaning and artistically inclined, Mayor spoke later in life of her relief that no one ever asked her to join the Communist Party.* During the war she worked with Rothschild for MI5 and kept a fairly open house in Bentinck Street, on occasions having to put an incapably drunken Blunt to bed. According to one account, she became the second (and last) woman with whom Blunt went to bed.† Tess's brother Freddie owned an art gallery in central London, later known as the Cork Street Gallery, and was friendly with Kim Philby.

In any event, Blunt and Tess were extremely close – Peter Wright said she understood Blunt's 'vulnerable side' – and closer than Blunt was to her husband Victor. She was by nature trusting, and saw no reason to doubt Blunt. Kenneth Rose put it like this: 'Her friendship with Blunt was not primarily political; it more resembled the uncritical attachment of a lover. In his company she found intellectual solace from a preoccupied and sometimes censorious husband, a shared world of art and ideas, a gentler understanding. As her sister-in-law Miriam put it, "Anthony was a sort of girlfriend".'

In 1964, having been interviewed around a dozen times by MI5 since 1951, Anthony Blunt admitted to MI5 that he, too, had been a Soviet agent, and agreed an immunity deal in return for him telling all he knew about his co-conspirators. The deal was agreed with the Americans, on condition that Blunt never set foot again in the USA. Having been told of Blunt's

---

* In November 1951 Tess Rothschild had helped Guy Liddell of MI5 to identify possible Soviet sympathisers.

† After her death, when the libel laws no longer applied, Tom Bower wrote that Peter Wright had been told that she and Blunt had slept together.

treachery, Victor Rothschild said he couldn't bring himself to tell his wife, asking Peter Wright to do it for him. It is a heart-breaking episode. After a long build-up, when Tess Rothschild asked if something was wrong, Wright told her: 'It's Anthony [. . .] he has confessed at last.'

"'What to? You are not saying he was a spy?"

"'Yes I am Tess."

'For a second she raised her hand to her mouth as if in pain; then she let it slip gently onto her lap. . . . Tess did not cry; she just went terribly pale, and sat hunched up and frozen, her eyes staring at me as she listened. Like Victor, she was a person for whom loyalty in friendship was of surpassing importance; to have it betrayed shook her, as it had him, to the core. "All those years," she whispered, "and I never suspected a thing."'

That moment must have been one of shattering betrayal in which an image of a brilliant, decent friend was trounced. It must have started a process of a thousand memories coming back to her, of small moments when she had taken Blunt into her confidence and he betrayed that trust. It was a devastating blow. It was probably, too, the start of her recalling individual episodes damaging to the security of a state she and her husband had done so much to enhance while working for MI5.*

Miranda Carter interviewed Tess Rothschild for her biography of Blunt. She said: 'It seemed to me that the revelation that he had been a Soviet spy was so painful to her she had excised a whole range of memories about him from her mind. She just couldn't process it and she couldn't understand it. His exposure was incredibly traumatic for her, I think she was really, really upset on a deep, personal level.'

Carter believes it is quite possible in the course of chatting that what Flora Solomon had said to Victor Rothschild came

---

* For a very different interpretation of these events, see Perry, *The Fifth Man* and *Last of the Cold War Spies*.

up. 'It wouldn't have occurred to her that Blunt was not trust-worthy or that what she said might be used by Blunt. They had all been in MI5/MI6 during the war, so they had this shared world where they were used to talking about secret things together. She had lived in the same house as Blunt and Burgess during the war, so if Philby came up as a subject, she might well have said "have you heard this interesting thing . . .?" It's perfectly possible.'

Tess Rothschild was horrified, even if to the handful in MI5 who had studied the matter closely Blunt's loyalty to the Crown had been questionable for years. Yet it is far harder to convict a spy than is commonly supposed. Unless he or she is actually caught in the act, it is extremely difficult to find clinching evidence – that does not compromise intelligence sources – that cannot be explained away by an imaginative lawyer. The lack of such evidence dogged the British authorities, particularly in the case of both Philby and Blunt.

After Guy Burgess fled to Moscow in 1951, suspicion fell on his friends. Few people were closer to him than Anthony Blunt, who an internal inquiry had found to have been a communist while at Cambridge. But Blunt was a benefi-ciary of naiveté among his former colleagues. Over lunch after Burgess's disappearance, Blunt convinced MI5's Guy Liddell – who had recruited him – that he had been 'inter-ested in the Marxian interpretation of history and artistry but had never believed in the way in which the Russians applied it'. Blunt confirmed that before the war he had engaged in anti-fascist activities with Burgess, but claimed he thought Burgess was acting on behalf of the British government. His Cambridge contemporary Goronwy Rees began making unprovable assertions about him, but in helping MI5 search Guy Burgess's flat after he and Maclean disappeared, Blunt had seemed the model of a patriot. Liddell concluded: 'I feel certain Anthony was never a conscious collaborator with Burgess in any [Comintern] activities.' George (G. K.) Young of MI6 said later that Blunt 'talked as a Marxist but [was] really an innocent. He was Guy's victim. He was more like the American leftists around Eleanor Roosevelt than a hard-boiled Communist.' Young believed Blunt was a broken man after the Burgess and Maclean affair.

After Blunt's confession in 1964, much was made of the many occasions he was questioned by MI5 between 1951 and 1964, but more than one writer has suggested these sessions were fairly gentle. Author Douglas Sutherland, who spoke to a number of employees in the late 1950s and early 1960s and was prevented by libel and a concern for national security from naming Blunt in 1962, wrote: 'Nor can I believe that frequent interrogations of Blunt, if really vigorously carried out, would have failed to break him.'

In the late 1950s Sutherland, whose book about Burgess and Maclean was published in early 1963, tried to alert the authorities to his belief that Blunt had been involved in their 1951 escape. He concluded that not only were they unsurprised, they knew already. 'Nobody in MI5 or MI6, many of whom I knew personally, asked me to tell them what I knew or how I came by the knowledge.' They must have had their own reasons for not arresting him, Sutherland concluded.

In the 1950s, Sutherland believed, 'MI5 knew everything they wanted to know', and that 'a decision was then taken to brush it under the carpet . . . By 1964, however, so many people knew of his involvement . . . that the authorities decided it was necessary to give him (and themselves) active protection.' It seems that a kind of corporate disbelief in 1951 was replaced by an all-too-knowing acknowledgement, in the very tightest of security circles at least, that the lack of hard evidence against Blunt, his assumed harmlessness, by that stage, to national security and his past and present usefulness to the royal family put him beyond prosecution.

Not only was he Surveyor of the Queen's Pictures, and any 'Moscow mole in the Palace' publicity would have caused embarrassment to a monarch who only acceded to the throne in 1952, but he had also visited Germany at the end of the war on behalf of the royal family. It remains unclear precisely and entirely what he was doing, and excitable stories sprung up about compromising documents revealing pre-war Nazi sympathy among Britain's royals, and that Blunt, knowing the royals' 'guilty secret' had a hold on them which made him unsackable. It is an enormously seductive story, but the details remain scant. In any event, to those who knew of the faith the Palace had placed in him, there would have been no shortage of reasons to hope the story would go away.* So that everyone was covered, the Queen's Private Secretary Sir Alan 'Tommy' Lascelles was informed that Blunt's communist past had been raised in official circles, before being dismissed as insignificant. The then Queen had already been alarmed by an intimation that Blunt might be an agnostic or even an atheist, so Lascelles felt his back was covered on the even more far-fetched notion of him being a communist. He was relieved to be told the gossip (and of its untruth) before she was, in case he needed to put her mind at rest.

Far from being put on the rack as a result of his close friendship with Guy Burgess, for those close to the matter, Blunt acquired a curious 'could well be guilty but untouchable' status.† He had taken on an enhanced role as a kind of consultant,

---

* According to Peter Wright, Sir Michael Adeane, the Queen's Private Secretary, mentioned to MI5 'an assignment he undertook on behalf of the Palace – a visit to Germany at the end of the war'. If Blunt mentioned this, said Adeane, 'please do not pursue this matter. Strictly speaking, it is not relevant to considerations of national security.'

† John Banville wrote a book called *The Untouchable* about him.

ostensibly helping Dick White and others look for traitors. Blunt and the very cultured White had been in MI5 together during the war and were on good terms, often discussing art and literature over lunch in the canteen and even spending one Christmas together. Tom Bower says: 'Blunt was regarded as an ally, and his help was sought to explain the relationships, especially with Philby.' This arrangement was nothing as crass as a conventional establishment cover-up. Had compelling evidence existed and had there been a belief that he would under no circumstances admit guilt or help identify others, Blunt would almost certainly have been prosecuted. But in the absence of a smoking gun, the man who had had the unwise friendship with Guy Burgess had a curious half-in, half-out status.

Not that this limbo was a comfortable state of affairs for Blunt. In 1956, he took a taxi home from a party with his old friend Rosamond Lehmann. In the cab, he burst out crying and sobbed: 'I'm very, very sorry, Rosamond. Can you ever forgive me?' When she asked what for, he just shook his head. Much later she realised Blunt had been on the edge of breakdown as a consequence of his constant proximity to being exposed.

After his appearance at a press conference in February 1956, Guy Burgess tried to pretend he was enjoying life in Moscow, but it was wholly unconvincing. He began to talk of returning to London, an outlandish idea given his disappearance of 1951, but even in his case there was no legal certainty of his guilt. In July 1958, his friend Blunt was contacted by MI5. He was told that if Guy Burgess returned to London from Moscow, Blunt, his former flatmate, would be expected to be a witness for the prosecution. Blunt wrote to Burgess: 'You would be arrested on landing – that is certain – and put on trial ... the whole story would be raked up again, many of your friends would certainly be called as witnesses, and mud would be slung in all directions.' As we shall see, Blunt's warning may have concentrated his own mind more than has been hitherto understood.

In the first edition of Andrew Boyle's *The Climate of Treason*, the book which led to the public revelation in 1979 of Blunt's role as a Soviet agent, he reported that 'Maurice', his pseudonym for Blunt, had come forward some time between February 1956 and 1958 to 'confess all he knew about the past link between himself and his fellow conspirators'. We now know that in reality Blunt's immunity deal was in fact agreed in 1964, as confirmed fifteen years after the event by Margaret Thatcher. In subsequent editions of the book, Boyle changed the text to conform with the correct date, and it is tempting to move on and skate over a journalist's error. He got the date wrong, but the important thing was that he had flushed out the 'Fourth Man'.

But there is a specificity about the original version that would not have happened by accident from as accomplished a journalist as Boyle. It should make us pause.

In the original version of Boyle's path-breaking book, he reported that no bargains were struck in advance, but that 'he received in the utmost secrecy the equivalent of a Royal pardon for turning Queen's evidence and contritely unfolding his own secondary but guilty role'. In fact the 1964 confession was agreed in advance, and legally sealed by Henry Brooke, the Conservative Home Secretary and the Attorney General, Sir John Hobson.

He also said that 'Maurice' (Blunt) 'had owned up, *quite of his own accord*' (author's italics) and shed light on the previous twenty-five years, so that 'leniency [for Blunt] doubtless seemed the sensible and proper course'. Yet we know that Blunt's formal confession came in 1964 only after it had become pretty well unavoidable.

The third error was the date. But is it possible that the 1964 deal only formalised what had gone before, as Douglas

Sutherland suggested? Boyle would not have simply picked a date out of the air, and the range of dates he originally suggested (February 1956 to February 1958) was plausible, and chimes with Rosamond Lehmann's story about his struggle to cope with the pressure. A story in *Private Eye* shortly before Mrs Thatcher's late seventies announcement said he had confessed in 1957.* He suggested Blunt may have confessed to pre-empt the possibility of Guy Burgess returning to London from Moscow, which, on and off, he had been threatening to do, but that had happened mostly in the years 1956–60. Burgess had died in 1963, so if Blunt was seeking to have a bearing on Burgess's movements, that must have been in 1963 or earlier, possibly much earlier.

One of the chief sources for Boyle's book was Sir Dick White himself, along with Nicholas Elliott and James Angleton. In great secrecy in early April 1979 White was sent the book for fact-checking before it was published. It contained a number of errors which went uncorrected before publication, but he did make 'a limited number of comments', and effectively confirmed Blunt's guilt. Boyle would surely have expected him to correct so significant an error as the timing of Blunt's confession – whether it was before or after Burgess's death, and so on – but he didn't. Boyle's son Ed believes Blunt's guilt had been well known but unprovable and that his father's initial version was correct, although he 'may not have appreciated the significance of his story at the time'.

The significance is tantalising. White shared the Prime Minister's reluctance to invite further scorn and embarrassment on MI5 and MI6 by having a public trial, and certainly not one he was not confident of winning.

The philosopher Stuart Hampshire believed Blunt confided

---

* Richard Ingrams, *Private Eye* editor at the time, has confirmed that Boyle, a friend, would have been the source.

in one or two friends in the security world about his treachery. 'I believe people knew, and knew because he told them, and then said "OK, let it run, and we'll see what else the Russians ask you to do. You needn't tell anyone else."' Hampshire agreed that would have been 'perfectly normal procedure', concluding that 'the only person who knows is Dick White and he's dead'. In fact Blunt had minimal contact with the Russians at that stage, but such dealings as there were could still have been of use.

By the late 1950s, Dick White realised he had underestimated the strength of the homosexual/leftist fraternity and was sure Blunt was guilty. Blunt's curious security limbo, bizarrely continuing as Surveyor of the Queen's Pictures, must have grated enormously with White. Though now in charge of MI6 and no longer responsible for catching subversives at home, he would still have wanted to leverage the situation to his advantage.

It is not hard to imagine White finding a form of words that left Blunt, with whom he had worked closely in the war, in no doubt that his guilt was obvious. Equally Blunt may have seen little point in protesting if his freedom and reputation were not threatened. By this time he had long lost any enthusiasm for Soviet politics and done all he could to sever contact with Moscow. It is possible, too, that the British authorities were more serious about prosecuting Burgess if he returned to London than has previously been understood. For that to succeed, Blunt would have to be their key witness. Similarly, if Burgess was seeking to return and to be given immunity, Blunt's role would have had to emerge from a full confession. No wonder Blunt accepted MI5's suggestion that he write to Burgess in Moscow, warning that his friends would be called upon to give evidence against him if he came back to London. The letter seemed to do the trick. Burgess did not return, and public embarrassment for both Blunt and the British authorities was avoided.

This, of course, is conjecture, but it is quite possible that Blunt – in owning up 'quite of his own accord' and/or to prevent a massively embarrassing trial – said if he could help White he would, while withholding from him anything truly useful about, for example, Philby.

Dick White admitted to being on 'embarrassing ground' in the context of Blunt. He told two authors he 'wasn't startled when I heard' about Blunt's eventual confession to MI5 in 1964 following an admission of espionage by his Cambridge friend Michael Straight.

If there was an arrangement, spoken or unspoken, between the two, Blunt almost certainly got the better of it. He was indeed effectively untouchable. Whatever Blunt had admitted before 1964, it was limited, and White had to be happy with whatever he could get from him. Had Blunt really set friendship aside and been both contrite and committed to helping the British authorities, he would have provided the evidence – even if only his own verbal evidence – necessary to convict Philby. But he didn't. His regret was for his own error of judgement – 'the biggest mistake of [his] life' – in signing up with the Soviet Union.

Whether he had quietly and explicitly confessed to White or not, he would have wanted to take advantage of his good relationship with him. 'From his unlikely vantage point in the Courtauld Institute, Blunt monitored developments inside MI5 and did his best to protect the interests of Philby, Burgess and Maclean,' wrote Nigel West and Oleg Tsarev. If hard evidence against his friend reached him – maybe via Flora Solomon and Tess Rothschild, or elsewhere – he would help his friend by flying to Beirut.

If this hypothesis is correct, Blunt's duplicity towards White personally – pretending to be helpful but in fact merely keeping White at arm's length from the provable truth about him and Philby – may also explain why in later life White displayed an uncharacteristic rancour towards Blunt: 'I have to say that Blunt was the man I most resented in that group. I think he went further than any of them in getting us to accept him ... He betrayed us all. He was a very nice and civilised man and I enjoyed talking to him. You cannot imagine how it feels to be betrayed by someone you have worked side by side with unless you have been through it yourself.'

This is not to say that White would not have welcomed further evidence that convicted Blunt, but while this was not forthcoming, he would have tried to make the best of it, possibly not even sharing it with anyone else, and conceivably not with MI5. It looks very much as if Nicholas Elliott was not in on it, although this would not be surprising. Dick White would have felt it was a 'need to know' issue, and he was on occasions frustrated at Elliott's shortcomings. He may well have restricted what Elliott knew and, on the other hand, indulged in a little invention. He told Elliott before the Beirut visit that there was now conclusive proof against Philby, from a new KGB source. This was highly doubtful. A 'Top Secret and Personal' Whitehall memo six weeks later acknowledged that, notwithstanding everything Golitsin, Solomon and others had said, apart from Philby's confession 'the case against him is legally very thin'. Nonetheless, White wanted to ensure Elliott spoke to Philby with conviction and would not fall for his wiles, so the senior man exaggerated the strength of their hand.

It might be assumed that so many years later, revealing documents would have come to light to confirm or deny the idea that Blunt tipped off Philby. But why would they? If it happened, almost nobody knew about it, and nobody who did know wanted it known more widely. The British and Russian authorities would have been unaware. Tom Bower reports that the Russians were shocked to hear that Elliott had confronted Philby, but that is to be expected. (If Philby had been tipped off and wanted to see what the British offered, he had no reason to alert the Russians in advance. Like Blunt, he would have known that would have been likely to accelerate his exit from Beirut, rather than allow him to make an informed decision on his future.) The only person who might have put two and two together as to what Blunt was up to was Sir Moore Crosthwaite. But at that point he knew nothing of Blunt's Soviet sympathies.

To Russia? For love?

In London in the summer of 1963, without both her daughter and her husband, Eleanor needed to take stock. Where would she go? Staying in the UK was an option, as the wife of a British citizen, and she had friends there. But her daughter was in the United States with Sam, while her own heart was still with Kim. She loved him, and wanted to understand. She knew that spies could only tell their spouses the barest minimum, but the lack of an explanation for so long was beyond reason – and so unlike her husband. A man of his solicitousness and sensibilities could have left her in the dark for so long only in truly exceptional circumstances. But maybe he had chosen this fate. In that case, she admitted later, it occurred to her that she was 'the victim of a monstrous and prolonged confidence trick'.

But if, as she suspected, he had been forced to go to Moscow, it would have consequences for her if she was to visit him there. The Elliotts, ever a source of support but always in accord with the interests of the British state, were extremely fond of Eleanor and in constant touch. Nicholas, who may have believed that Philby had gone under duress, had been tasked with keeping an eye on her.* One obligation was a human one to a woman –

---

* Philby suggested to his Russian controllers that that is what Elliott believed.

a civilian, as it were – who had been misled as spectacularly as he had himself. She was a victim. Another was to his own reputation and that of MI6. At worst, he had bungled the interrogation of the traitor and left Beirut, allowing Philby to walk clean away from the gentlemen's deal and escape to Moscow. At best he was incompetent, having defended a man who many of his peers in the intelligence community believed should have been stopped years earlier.

Elliott, for all his assured, patrician manner, was anxious, badgering Eleanor tirelessly. He knew that she had known nothing of Kim's spying for the Russians, and like many believed that his desertion of her would probably bring the end of their marriage. But she should be in no doubt, Elliott said, that if she went to Moscow she would never return, and that meant she would never see Annie again. Elliott knew the government of the Soviet Union was an autocratic, highly secretive monolith, and may well have known that Guy Burgess had been tricked by a false promise of being allowed to leave, so he would have used that to help persuade Eleanor. Moscow's claims to offering personal freedom for its citizens were a sham. Did she really want to sign up with a regime like that, as her husband had done so idealistically and misguidedly nearly thirty years earlier?

To pre-empt her being tempted, Elliott asked constantly if Kim had been in touch. He knew how persuasive his former friend could be. For Eleanor's part, Elliott's insistence that banal politics should override the love of her life was not a message she wanted to hear. She had been open with Elliott up to that point, and liked and trusted him, but who could be sure, with Kim's presence in Moscow now established, whether she could continue to be? She aspired to making her own decision, but was confused, and didn't know whose advice to trust.

In understanding that Nicholas Elliott's loyalties might not coincide with hers for ever, she came to reassess the friendship of others, too. Lorraine Copeland was a steady, unswerving figure, but as we have seen, Eleanor must have been torn. An issue remained unresolved in her mind, and maybe one of those close to her had sold her short on their friendship.

When Kim had been in touch with her some weeks after his disappearance, proposing they meet in Prague, she had been initially tempted by the idea of buying a ticket for London as a decoy and switching planes at the last minute, as Kim proposed. He wanted her to write the date they were to meet in Prague on a wall near their flat, and he would be there. In her book, she explained that the idea was not feasible because of Harry's lack of a passport, and the British consulate insisted he could only travel if he flew to London. She says she confided in Nicholas Elliott, and that he, unknown to her and out of devilry, wrote a spurious date on the wall, resulting in Kim spending three fruitless days waiting in Prague airport.

This is only part of the story. Eleanor confided in one of her friends that she planned to give the British the slip by switching planes, and somehow the plan reached MI6. Somebody had put loyalty to country ahead of loyalty to her. By performing a patriotic duty, that person scotched Eleanor's plan to switch planes. She had to fly directly to London.

Beirut was awash with spies, so it could have been a number of people close to her. The Copelands? The Fisteres? The sociable, viola-playing American Kaye Brennan, who had helped fend off journalists on Eleanor's behalf, and whose day job was working for the CIA? Probably none of these. It seems most likely that that person was Myrtle Winter. The colour and variety in her civilian life should not obscure the important intelligence work she did during her remarkable service in the war. In Bermuda, Myrtle worked for – and may have had a relationship with – Peter Wilson of MI6 (who she referred to as '*mon grand ami*'), and it was under him that she came to interrogate a number of Germans taken captive in the Atlantic. Wilson, a year ahead of Peter Lunn at Eton (and four ahead of Nicholas Elliott), had worked for Kim Philby in Section V of MI6. He later became chairman of Sotheby's and came under suspicion himself of being a Soviet agent.

Myrtle's capabilities and discretion were extremely useful to MI6 in Beirut. She shared a flat there, and later in London, with the extremely upright, Miss Moneypennyish June Lockett. Lockett, discreet, quiet but with a great and often unsuspected wit, worked for the head of UNRWA, another organisation assumed by Beirutis to have good relations with the intelligence services. Myrtle – described by her stepson as 'fiercely British' – had to choose whether to help her friend Eleanor find some sort of resolution to her tortured life, or to prevent her doing so and help the British minimise the damage of its biggest ever spy embarrassment. Evidently she chose the latter.

Nor did Eleanor yet know the basics. How had Kim got to Moscow? Was he happy there? How could a man so home-oriented not miss his wife and children?

At that point, the likeliest explanation, surely, was that he had gone under duress. In which case, should she go, to try to offer support? Or maybe Nicholas Elliott was right – if she went, she might never return or see Annie again. Or could her husband have gone of his own free will? In which case, with what expectation for their relationship?

Eleanor was not the only one made to feel a fool. While a few antagonists in spy circles had been confident Philby was a traitor, they couldn't predict the upshot of his exposure. But the rest of the intelligence world reeled at the news of Philby's defection, for the fact of both his disloyalty to the West and his evasion of Western scrutiny. The details, though, were unclear. It was by now assumed he had tipped off Burgess and Maclean, which answered the 'Third Man' mystery, but it was to be some years before the seriousness of his penetration of Whitehall became apparent to the public, the media being batted away with assurances about his lack of access to official papers for well over a decade. Few knew that he had headed the department responsible for prevention of Soviet subversion, and almost all who knew him had admired and liked him. Of his resignation after Burgess and Maclean disappeared, Tim Milne wrote: 'There were very few people in the service who inspired so much trust and respect as Kim, and so much affection among those who had worked closely with him. It seemed impossible that he had done anything other than act a little unwisely.' Glen Balfour-Paul said Philby was 'a close friend, infinitely entertaining and indeed helpful'. He told a friend he regarded him 'like a brother'. Even one of his most noted foes, Hugh Trevor-Roper, writing in 1957, said his company was 'as attractive as ever, his conversation as disengaged, and yet as enjoyable'.

At first few condemned him outright, and the instinct, initially, was disbelief. Alice Brinton's father, a Beirut-based businessman, and mother saw a lot of the Philbys. Although just nine years old at the time, she remembers the sense of unreality. 'I remember the aftermath, the stunning sense of incomprehension. All the adults just said "we just can't believe it." It seemed so out of character. They had befriended this man, and it was taken for granted that the USSR was bad and evil, so latterly, when it looked as if he might have gone there, there came to be a sense of anger at the betrayal.'

Now those people had a truly shocking reality to face. Among those most stunned was Miles Copeland, Kim's drinking and boating partner, whose families had spent so many happy hours enjoying the beauty of Lebanon together. 'The only time I ever saw my father smoke was when he learned Philby had defected,' remembers Lennie Copeland. 'He was standing there looking out over the verandah, and he quickly hid it from me, and said

"Never smoke".' Copeland wrote of his disbelief a decade later. He said he 'wouldn't believe it until he surfaced in Moscow and sent us all postcards. Believe me, it was a terrible shock.'

Pragmatic as ever, Copeland had been happy to take the CIA's entertainment budget, but he didn't believe in Philby's guilt, nor did he believe, in the unlikely event of Philby having spied for the Russians, that by that stage it merited quite as much effort as London's subsequent molehunt suggested. A degree of familial damage limitation may be in evidence here. 'I guess my father thought, if you're out to pasture as a spy in Beirut, how bad can it be?' said Miles Copeland III. '"OK, I'll go along with it," he thought, and he got into the spirit of it and they were friends. I know my father actually liked Philby and I also assume he must have been aware that whatever Philby was up to in Beirut could not be that important in the big picture. Certainly not as important as he had once been. Beirut after all was not the centre of the world and was only a bit player in the East–West game. In reality, as long as the West controlled the oil it did not really matter if a country was on the Russian or US/Western side.' There may be something in this; for all the money being spent on unseating governments, a certain degree of instability was taken as read in Western diplomatic thinking.

At one time Miles Copeland thought of calling his memoirs 'The Man Who Couldn't Hate'. His son Stewart says he didn't harbour grudges and gave a shrug at the world's surprises: 'My father used to say "diphtheria makes you ill, that's what it does." You take things for what they are. I don't think he was angry with Kim.' His mother Lorraine, protective of her friend Eleanor, was less philosophical.

Friendship with the Philbys must have brought complications to the Copelands' relationship. Whatever his other obligations, Miles was quintessentially a CIA man. Lorraine was as steady a friend as anyone could want, and, in her time in Beirut, Eleanor was in ever-growing need of personal loyalty. As she tried to work out what was driving Kim into ever-greater despondency, and later where he had gone, and then to decide whether she could or should join him, the presence of a loyal confidante – free from the power plays of the secret world – would have been invaluable. The man she loved had vanished without explanation. Her ex-husband Sam, she told friends, had tricked her into letting her daughter go to the States. If she really wanted to join Kim in Moscow, for example, giving the USSR a massive public relations fillip, a cool head with her interests at heart and possibly an accomplice willing to help her evade the West's clutches was what she needed.

Lorraine continued to be a good friend, generally from afar, but her loyalties must have been stretched. The interests of her friend Eleanor and, on the other hand, the interests of her husband, the CIA and the West as a whole were not necessarily the same. Eleanor wanted autonomy, and that might diverge from what MI6 and the CIA might like to happen. What Eleanor may well not have known is that Lorraine had her own intelligence background, having served with some distinction during the war, helping sabotage French railways during the German occupation, though mostly from London. She knew the importance of 'needing to know' and discretion. Did she know that her husband's friendship with the Philbys was being subsidised from Langley? It isn't clear. Miles dedicated one of his books to Lorraine, thanking her for 'overlooking' and 'forgiving'. 'There was a myth about my mother,' says Lorraine's daughter Lennie, '... that she didn't know anything about my father spying on Philby, but it turned out years later she also had been an agent for the British Special Operations Executive, which we never knew previously. She knew my father was CIA and she must have known what he was doing. It is impossible that she couldn't have figured out that he was keeping an eye on

him, although she maintained to her dying day that she didn't.'
The Copelands agree their parents were unconcerned by 'phony
moral issues'. In any case, while Eleanor's preferences and the
West's coincided, there were none. Maybe that was changing,
but first things first.

Eleanor was desperate to see her daughter Annie and tried to
persuade Sam to let her fly to London, thinking Annie might
enjoy seeing the two youngest Philby children. Sam, concerned
that she might take Annie to Moscow, would not agree, but
offered to pay for Eleanor to visit New York. She arrived early
in August. Initially she stayed in Greenwich Village, but soon
moved on to a relation's house in Long Island, where Annie
joined her. Still she wanted to understand what Kim had done,
and why. How else could she decide what her future was to be?

Long Island offered some slight balm, and being with Annie
was a godsend, but it was inevitably brief. She had many big
decisions to make, and still needed to have surgery on a muscle
that had been damaged years earlier after childbirth, an operation she originally planned to have performed in Beirut. Where
could she have it done? Where would she be living? Could she
take Annie with her? Would Kim come back to the West? As
she considered her future amid New York's vacationing beau
monde, a thousand permutations made her world as uncertain as ever.

And then, as if out of a clear Long Island sky, a letter arrived
from Kim, forwarded by one of Kim's sisters from London. It
was the first of several within a few days of one another. He
sounded in good health and expressed the strong hope that she
would join him in Moscow. Anticipating her concerns (and
doubtless mindful of what the British authorities were probably
telling her), he was insistent that if she didn't like it, she could
simply leave. Here was the enticement that had so worried
Nicholas Elliott, at that point 4000 miles away in London. Kim

wanted her to end her US holiday, go back to London, collect some money from the Soviet embassy, buy some warm clothes for the coming Moscow winter and leave the travel details to the Russian embassy.

Most importantly, Kim let Eleanor have a PO Box number in Moscow, where she could write to him, although she assumed her letters would be opened by security officials at least twice before they reached him. Eleanor's initial letters are inaccessible, but in them she poured out her feelings, including, unsurprisingly, her frustrations at all she had recently endured, and telling him of the birth of his first grandson. Philby replied very promptly, saying how delighted he was to hear from her after so long. He had begun to wonder how far pressure from friends and events was affecting her, and also indicated that there was a great deal that he could not tell her. During this period, he wrote to her frequently, expressing his hope that she was well and desperate for news. Most notable are his expressions of concern at her failure to reciprocate. There is an almost childlike neediness about his pleading with her for news.

Kim did not discourage Eleanor's anger towards Sam, saying he was bound to be unhelpful and that Annie should ignore her father's threats that she might never see her mother again. The Russians had treated him not merely well but with extreme generosity and, lest Western accounts of Russian technology were worrying her, assured her he had been supplied with the last word in fridges, washing machines, vacuum cleaners, floor-polishers, radios and a television.

He discussed how she might travel to Russia, and how best to dodge the press, whose behaviour he thought contemptible. Perhaps sensing her emotional exhaustion, he reassured her how rewarding she would find the end of the road, Moscow. He encouraged her to cancel her operation and have it done by world-class doctors in Moscow. A few days later, on her fiftieth birthday, he cabled her again, wishing her happy birthday and hoping they might spend the next half-century together.

The old softy had done it again. This was what Eleanor wanted to hear. She decided she would join him in Moscow, and flew to London on 17 September, staying at a new address the press was unaware of. Only Patricia Philby, Kim's sister and her trusted friend, knew of her plan.

On 25 September she went to the Russian consulate in Bayswater. She had been expected for some days, and was told she should leave two days later, sooner than she had imagined. She was given £500 – equivalent to around £10,000 today – to spend, not least on warm clothes. She crossed Hyde Park and at Harrods bought a coat, sweaters, tights, boots and a turban and gloves for her and Kim, plus two dozen handkerchiefs, before crossing the road to Montpelier Square for an appointment with the MI6 doctor, Dr Bott. There she calmly asked if she might postpone her operation by a week.

On the 27th she took a taxi to London airport and was met by a large, nervous-looking Russian who took her bags and ticket and led her to a bar. 'Seeing it was only 11.00am, I sensibly decided on a Guinness,' she wrote. The Russian was similarly moderate. She waited nervously in a dark corner, hoping not to be noticed while enjoying a marginally less sensible second Guinness. Shortly before one o'clock, she and the Russian walked across the tarmac to the Aeroflot flight, with no checks to be endured, into an empty first-class cabin.

As she landed in Moscow, night was falling. She walked down the steps wearing dark glasses, a turban and a camel hair coat. She saw three men in long, heavy coats, all wearing hats. She heard a familiar voice calling her name. It was Kim, in a dark blue felt hat, looking tired and thin. They hugged, and a driver and another young Russian called Sergei ushered them into a big, black official car waiting on the tarmac. She recalled later: 'All my fears in the plane, the piled-up tensions of months of uncertainty, the real horror of discovering that my husband was not the man I thought he was – all this was blotted out in the sheer pleasure of seeing him again.' As they sped away, she burst into tears. When they reached Kim's flat in a grey tower block in Sokol, fifteen minutes from the centre of Moscow, Sergei joined them for a brief glass of champagne before slipping away. At last she was alone with the man for whom she had left behind everything she believed in.

Kim was ecstatic to see Eleanor. He, conveyed around Moscow by Sergei, had gone to great trouble to equip the flat, from the most basic of fittings, in a way he hoped she would approve of. In Beirut, Eleanor had turned her artful eye to the furnishings, giving it a Middle Eastern style much admired by their friends, and, though in Moscow she said he had done a marvellous job in the circumstances, it was not quite marvellous enough. She would be taking control once more, and some of the furniture would have to go, however much time Kim had spent finding it. (She realised later she must have hurt his feelings somewhat.) There was no double bed, only two singles: the Russian way, she was told. The kitchen was better. Kim had acquired a washing machine from Czechoslovakia, a vacuum cleaner from Romania, a floor waxer from Yugoslavia and a Russian fridge.

To cap it all, he had bought a golden canary and a pair of budgerigars, a nod to their shared love of animals. Sadly, though, a fox would have been a bridge too far in Moscow, and there had been insufficient room for a piano, which Eleanor would have liked.

Philby's friend Guy Burgess had died six weeks earlier, and Burgess had left him several thousand books and the blue hat Kim had worn at the airport. Burgess had never felt at ease in Russia, to the discomfort of the Soviet authorities. There had even been talk of him returning to London, mostly put about by Burgess's friends. His mother was extremely ill, but it would have suited neither side in the great Cold War power game. Kim is reported to have said at the time: 'Burgess wanted to see me before he died, he wanted to tell me something important. And he was told that I was not in Moscow. Why are they so cruel?'

Twelve years earlier, Kim had been furious that Burgess, his Cambridge friend and house guest in Washington, had defied his advice not to accompany Maclean to Moscow in 1951, thereby casting huge suspicion on him. Burgess had been duped by a promise from Nikolai Korovin, the *rezident* in London, that if he accompanied Maclean for part of his journey to Moscow, he would be free to return. Philby's anger had passed and the friendship from Cambridge days endured.

But the Russian authorities decided Kim and Burgess should not meet. Mikhail Liubimov, an Anglophile former KGB officer, explained why the decision was taken, and is bemused by what he saw as the unworldly idea that they should meet. There was no upside in it for the KGB. 'Was the KGB a sort of charity?' he asked. 'Burgess was in a very bad state with his drinking. Philby had just arrived. The KGB was not interested in such a meeting, therefore both were told a lie. Burgess was told that Philby was very busy, Philby was told that Burgess was in a bad way. It's a normal thing that we do, or did, that any secret service does. They might have shared information. Something unexpected might have happened, and it was not necessary. They started from the assumption that it's better [they don't meet].' This sort of unsentimental practicality had been the bread and butter of Kim's daily life. To Eleanor, it was a world apart, and one Kim was not inclined to inflict on his wife. She didn't need to know.

Yet it seems that Philby defied his bosses and they did meet. After Burgess died, Philby wrote to Burgess's mother Evelyn

Bassett. In some respects his letter showed more kindness than candour. He told her that Guy had been happy in Moscow, and had many friends there. He also said he had visited Guy in hospital shortly before his death. The idea that they met is supported by Sergei Kondrashev, who supervised Burgess in Moscow. It was later claimed by Russian officials that Philby never knew how ill Burgess was until it was too late. In the unlikely event of that being true, it would have been no accident.

In their first few weeks in Moscow together, Kim and Eleanor caught up on the traumatic events of previous months. It was like old times, she recorded. They renewed their closeness like giddy teenagers.

That was Kim the man. But Kim the spy had a Soviet monolith looking over his shoulder, and rarely if at all did he share with Eleanor the operational details of his own experiences. For example, he claimed – truthfully or otherwise – that it had taken him some months to reach Moscow, and that he had had to do a lot of walking. He never told her why. There was speculation that he might have gone overland through Syria and Turkey, into Armenia or Georgia. Like Burgess and Maclean, Kim underwent scrutiny and debriefing, probably in a provincial town, for some months before being allowed to take up civilian life in Moscow. It is generally accepted now that he left on the *Dolmatova* for Odessa, although the uncertainty lasted for decades.

In their excitement at seeing one another, they never confronted some basic issues. Eleanor wrote later: 'He never once said to me "I've landed you in a situation you perhaps did not anticipate when you married me." He never seemed to think that any justification was necessary, and I in turn never asked him why he had not told me the truth.' Further, all those weeks of her trying to find comfort in the sporadic contact he made after he first left Beirut was never given any justification. To the modern ear, this is extraordinary. To Eleanor, it would have been improper to ask too much. Hers not to reason why.

Conversely, the KGB wanted to know everything about her dealings with the British and American authorities, and set Kim to work on squeezing every detail out of her. While Eleanor spoke of human and logistical difficulties, Kim demanded names of those who had spoken to her. She told him how the British had also been curious to know who she had met, and talked about Petukhov, the Russian who had come to her door in Beirut in May trying to persuade her to leave. She cheerfully mentioned that she had helped the British identify him. Kim knew this meant that his friend's career was over. A spy whose cover is blown needs to get out of town, if not out of the service.

A week or so after she arrived in Moscow, Eleanor was invited with Kim to meet the Macleans. Thanks in large part to Kim, Donald had been able to flee Britain twelve years earlier. He, too, had an American wife, Melinda, who had joined him in the Soviet Union with their three children. This would be Eleanor's first encounter with anyone other than Kim, Sergei and their housekeeper Zena – with whom Eleanor did not get on – since she arrived. If Kim was sugar-coating his experiences, this would surely become apparent at dinner.

The Macleans were extremely friendly to Eleanor, but were anxious for news of the West and couldn't disguise the fact that life as a family in Moscow was not without its challenges. Donald Maclean's relationship with Philby was the subject of much conjecture by MI5. How well had they known one another at Cambridge? Barely at all, Philby had stated. Others claimed to know better, and cited Kim's evasiveness on the subject as evidence of his untrustworthiness. In fact, Kim had drawn up a list of possible recruits for Moscow, with Maclean at the top and Burgess at the bottom.

Apart from their work for the USSR, they had little in common, Maclean being more obviously academic and less articulate and polished than Philby. However, for lack of more entertaining company, Kim and Eleanor would join the Macleans two or three times a week to play bridge and celebrate how they had outwitted the flat-footed British authorities. Eleanor felt more pity than empathy for Melinda, whom she regarded as being in a loveless marriage and in a country she had little taste for.

Late in November 1963, lying in hospital following her much delayed operation, she witnessed a commotion, but only when Kim arrived in the afternoon did she learn what had happened. America's vigorous young President John F. Kennedy had been assassinated in a motorcade in Dallas, Texas. Notwithstanding the Cuban missile crisis of the year before, when the US and USSR came close to launching a nuclear war, Kennedy embodied a youthful optimism that allowed many to hope for a more peaceful future, no small thing to a country that lost over sixteen million people in the Second World War. Tears were shed openly as staff and patients offered Eleanor commiserations. 'Whatever the political cynicism of the Russian leaders, the Russian people are profoundly attached to peace ... Kim, who talked a great deal about American politics, was profoundly moved and depressed by the tragedy.'

Eleanor's operation was not a success, quite apart from being conducted in part without anaesthetic, and she needed lengthy recuperation. Kim had also been ill, and the couple decided to visit the southern city of Baku, in what is now Azerbaijan, on the Caspian Sea. Because of Kim's enhanced status as a friend of the Soviet government, they were spared hours of queuing and had the luxury of a train compartment to themselves.

But subsequently, without the smooth attentions of Sergei

and exposed by their rudimentary Russian, life as 'ordinary' Soviet tourists was very ordinary indeed.

It was hardly the high life. Eleanor, though she had reset her sights, found herself growing frustrated. In Beirut, everything had been available at the right price, and copiously. In the USSR, too often the answer was '*Niet*', a grapefruit a reason for celebration. She had got used to food queues and shortages, but for their romantic rest and recreation trip her expectations had crept up and been disappointed. Kim was generally smiling and equable towards the frustrations. Such was the price of progress, he felt, but her standards were not Soviet ones, and she couldn't resist saying so. On the sleeper train back to Moscow, Kim lost his temper with her, for the first time in their married life, over some bureaucratic mishap. He gave up his berth to a young mother with a child and spent the night in the corridor, Eleanor sobbing as the train rumbled back to Moscow.

12

The independent traveller

Back in the capital in early January 1964, things returned to an even keel. Eleanor had once again recalibrated her expectations, determined to make her new life with the man she loved work for both of them. We are reliant on Eleanor's own account (in her book) of her time in Russia, and there is no reason to doubt it. She reported that Moscow's shortcomings were becoming less frustrating for being familiar, and she continued with the work of making the flat feel like home. Kim and Eleanor found a routine of contentedly shopping for food together, going to the post office and dropping in at the bar of GUM, the luxury store opposite the Kremlin, for a reviving glass of dry champagne (rather than the pricier, sweet variety the Russians preferred). Eleanor in particular wanted to immerse herself in Russian culture, visiting churches, concert halls and galleries. At home, she was in charge of juggling with the inflexibilities of the Soviet labour force and brightening up the overheated flat.

But the icy Russian winter took its toll on both of them. Kim had pneumonia, from which he had occasionally suffered in the past, and developed eczema, which badly affected his hands. They remained deeply in love, though the differences between them emerged more and more in confronting everyday life. Eleanor had lived abroad for most of her adult life, and had enjoyed embracing each country she had lived in. They had had a honeymoon in Italy, and in the biting Muscovite winter Kim would talk of the holidays they would take there, once they too had had a revolution. But she found Russia impenetrable, because of the cold, the shortages, the security concerns and a language that offered little assistance. What had started as an exciting, challenging facet of the picking up again of a love affair was becoming a cloud hanging over it, and she had not the faintest interest in communism. Kim's life, on the other hand, was an investment in an ideal. He had a huge emotional interest in its viability. He wanted to believe, and retained a sentimental, patrician empathy with the Russian people whose interests he had sought to serve. Eleanor would refer to him being in a 'tovarich mood', such as when he insisted on giving the workmen they had hired a slug of vodka before they started hanging pictures in the flat. The workmen were happy, even if their handiwork missed many of the targets set by Eleanor.

She continued to see no reason why their relationship shouldn't work, but she was also missing her daughter. Annie, too, was missing her mother, and was coming to believe the scare stories – that she might never see her mother again – might be true. Eleanor had been told she could visit the States whenever she liked, and knew that, having been given this most unusual privilege, she should take advantage of it. Besides, her passport was due to run out in October 1964, and if she allowed it to expire, as Melinda Maclean had, it would be hard to renew. So, with the worst of Moscow's winter over, she gave herself a treat to look forward to, promising Annie she would meet her on 30 June in New York. It was this prospect that sustained her as she battled with Russia's privations.

Increasingly Kim's eczema would prevent him from going out, so she had to shop alone, without his smiling facility for making himself understood in basic Russian. Braving the cold was an ordeal in itself, and the Harrods camel hair coat she had bought hopelessly inadequate. Nor were the Russian fur coats to her liking. Increasingly she suffered a loss of confidence. The consolations of having installed her own decor (castor bean plants and all) and observing the mating habits of the couple's budgerigars were scarcely going to keep her entertained, and she missed having a piano. While to the outside world she might have been a bit-part player, the wife of a diplomat, and showed him a dutiful devotion, she was a great deal more than just a housewife. Yet she was by this time short of confidence and at a loss to know how to achieve any sort of fulfilment.

The same concern had struck Kim's Russian masters. She continued to struggle with the language, and was showing few signs of enjoying the Soviet dream. It was not part of the plan that she would want to visit the US so soon, surely. What could they do to help? Eleanor had long had an enthusiasm for old Russian lacquer boxes, first made in the time of Peter the Great. But the making of these boxes was dying out as a skill, and they were now being made only in two small villages outside Moscow. She also had very much enjoyed visiting a number of Russian churches where restoration of them and their icons was taking place. She wanted to learn more, to build on her study of fresco technique thirty years earlier and if possible to assist in this work. Given the contribution Kim had made to the Soviet Union, it was hardly an outlandish suggestion, but the officials said her Russian needed to be better. Learning the language was, of course, desirable, but not in this instance necessary – an irrelevance, she felt. Even a student of Diego Rivera was not able to surmount the system.*

To help things along, she and Kim signed up to study Russian together, but her husband's facility for languages only

---

* Although Rivera himself, once lauded in the Soviet Union, fell foul of Stalin and was asked to leave in 1928.

highlighted her own shortcomings. Just when she should have been growing her own wings, her dependence on Kim was greater than ever. And just when she needed Kim's support – and he sought to provide it – she sensed a previously unnoticed weakness in him.

For the first time, Eleanor came to detect what she called 'a sea of sadness which lay beneath the surface of his life'. It was not that he ever criticised the Soviet way of life, but after nearly thirty years of subterfuge and living on his nerves in the cause of a brighter tomorrow, that tomorrow was disappointing him.

As Eleanor's June trip to the States approached, Kim sought ever more diplomatic ways of testing the strength of her desire to go, though he never tried to dissuade her. A promise was a promise, and she was entitled to hold the Russians to it, however much it might not have suited them. The Russians, always watchful, were not convinced about Eleanor. She might be an American spy, although her artless dealings with the espionage world suggest she would not have been a very good one. But even if she wasn't, Eleanor might say unguarded things once she had arrived. In fact, given that ingenuousness, that seemed quite likely. She might mention something trivial – like Kim's Russian name, or their address – which she hadn't realised was a state secret. Kim started muttering about difficulties she might face once in New York, which she didn't understand and dismissed. They told Kim she should not be allowed to go. Things came to a head a few days before Eleanor was due to depart. Kim told the Russians there would be no stopping her. She would go straight to the US embassy in Moscow if they tried. So off she flew.

But by insisting on it, she appeared ungrateful. To her, she was merely enacting the agreement that took her to Moscow in the first place, but to others it looked as if the rules did not apply to her. To Kim, anxious to show the party his appreciation of his large salary and the special concessions that had been made to make the couple feel at home, this was an embarrassment. Nonetheless, he knew how much he would miss her, and wrote a stream of loving letters, detailing in enormous detail the developments on the budgerigar front, his culinary accomplishments, his trips to the opera and his views on John le Carré's 'basically implausible' novel *The Spy Who Came in from the Cold*.

In travelling to the US, Eleanor was taking a stand to sustain two facets of her existence her hosts wanted her to forget: seeing her New York-based daughter and retaining her American citizenship. So her arrival on 30 June can only have been a grave disappointment. For one thing, to her surprise, Annie, then fifteen, was not there to meet her. And as she arrived, her name was paged. She reported to the information desk, where she was presented with an envelope. It contained a letter from the United States Immigration and Naturalization Service, informing her that in view of her marriage to H. A. R. Philby and her activities which were against the interests of the US government, her passport was being confiscated. Having been warned that she might never be allowed to leave the USSR, it was now looking as if her stay in her own country was going to be a long one.

But at least she had arrived. She wanted to see her daughter, and planned to take her to California to visit old friends. Sam, increasingly protective of Annie, was reluctant to agree. Besides which, their daughter was in limbo. Legally speaking, Eleanor had custody, but in fact Annie had been living in New York with Sam. This was not a sustainable state of affairs.

Eleanor took the opportunity to catch up with friends. Among them were the Copelands. 'The Man Who Couldn't Hate' remained his usual non-judgemental self, expressing no hostility to Kim. By this time he had opened an office of his

Kim Philby telling the world's press in 1955 he is not the 'Third Man', a performance
described years later by Dame Judi Dench as 'a complete lesson in acting'

St John Philby with
his sons Kim, Khalid
and Faris

Philby was heartbroken
when he came home from
holiday to find the fox had
met an early end

1453

A FOX THAT CAME TO STAY
Written and Illustrated by H. A. R. PHILBY

JACKIE, A FOX CUB REARED BY THE AUTHOR IN HIS BEIRUT FLAT. At three weeks of age and (right) three months

A FEW days before Easter, some friends offered us a baby fox, or rather vixen. They had bought her from a bedouin in the Jordan Valley for a few shillings and were trying to find her a good home. We viewed the offer with some suspicion, but one sight of the creature banished our doubts. She was hopelessly endearing. Because of her beauty and elegance (and also because of some doubt at that early age whether she was really a fox or a jackal), we called her Jackie.

When our friends bought the animal, she was a few days old: a tiny ball covered with baby fuzz, eyes hardly open, and in pretty bad shape. They bottle-fed her, and gradually weaned her on raw liver. We first saw her at the age of about four weeks. She was staying at a hotel that was formerly the residence of Gertrude Bell, Colonel Lawrence and other celebrities but is now sadly out of fashion because of the growth of ultra-modern hotels all over Beirut. She was already looking pronouncedly foxy, with a long snout ending in a polished black nose, huge ears and a gracefully curving brush. She was friendly and playful, flopping after us and chewing our shoes.

The next day she was in residence on our terrace, which is about 15 feet square. Because the nights were cold at that time, and because we felt that she might feel lonely at first, we put her to sleep in a cage in our bedroom. Her behaviour was perfect. Not a sound all night, except when we overslept. Then, at about 9 a.m., she would whimper slightly, suggesting that it was time we got up. When the warm weather set in, she was installed permanently, day and night, on the terrace.

For just over two months Jackie has been learning how to live with human beings, just as we have been learning how to live with a fox. The results from our viewpoint (and, I

Food is no problem. Milk; eggs, raw or hard-boiled; rice, raw liver; cooked scraps; veal-and-ham pie, ice cream: she eats them all and flourishes. Her staple is ordinary branded dog-food and dog biscuits. She has discovered whisky, by leaping on to the bar, breaking a bottle and lapping up the contents. She also likes sucking the stem of a pipe.

Another delightful characteristic is her friendliness towards strangers. As soon as a visitor comes in, her ears go back, her brush waves in abundantly extravagant sweeps, and she tap-dances in the wildest excitement. At

DIARIES FOR 1963

The new *Country Life Diary* (COUNTRY LIFE 25s.), is available bound in ivory or maroon leather, and contains 56 outstanding photographs mainly of country scenes in colour and black-and-white. Each week takes up a full quarto page, and dates of interest to the countryman are given, such as the starts of the important race meetings of the year and the openings of the shooting seasons. An introductory section includes a list of useful addresses such as those of the Kennel Club, the National Rose Society and the Animal Health Trust, two pages of sporting seasons, licences and records, a guide to the National Parks and nature reserves and a list of grants and loans available to landowners and farmers.

More specialised and smaller are the *Amateur Gardening Diary* (Collingridge), the *Homes and Gardens Diary* and the *Dog Owner's Diary* (COUNTRY LIFE) at 8s. 6d. each. The *Amateur Gardening Diary*, compiled by A. G. L. Hellyer, contains nearly 50 pages of tables, addresses and bibliography useful to the gardener, and each week has a paragraph of gardening advice suitable

the end of each performance, we find a small puddle somewhere. She seems to be particularly fond of children—and they of her.

Although born to the torrid temperatures of the Jordan Valley, she feels the heat even here. Most of the day she spends curled up under the couch, asleep, coming out only to eat or to greet arrivals. But as the sun goes down she wakes up, and the early hours of night are hours of wild play. Her toys are the usual ones for dogs and cats—balls, cotton reels, newspapers rolled up and tied with string. She tosses them away and bounds after them, from chair to table and table to chair, in a series of unbelievable leaps that carry her round the terrace with the speed of light.

Her agility, though admirable and spectacular in itself, has its drawbacks. Our terrace is bounded by a parapet about two feet high, and when she first took a flying leap at it, our hearts froze. But we need not have worried. She took a good look at two Arabs playing tric-trac on the pavement two storeys below, and an even longer one at a black-and-white hen who lives on a neighbouring roof. Then she dropped lightly down on the right side.

I have since recalled the passage in Mrs Joy Adamson's book, when she describes her fright when her famous lioness, Elsa, leapt to the edge of a precipitous crag. Mrs Adamson's comment that animals have no fear of heights has given us much comfort. Jackie now canters round the top of the parapet in carefree fashion, doing horrible damage to our geraniums and periwinkles, but remaining unscathed herself.

Another disadvantage of her agility and speed lies in the sphere of discipline. Like any puppy, she commits crimes, though perhaps

St. J. Philby
Dies Aged 75

From H. A. R. Philby

BEIRUT, October 1

ST. JOHN PHILBY, greatest of Arabian explorers, died suddenly, aged 75, in Beirut yesterday.

He was on the way to his home in Riyadh from the Orientalists' Congress in Moscow.

Philby's connection with Arab lands began 45 years ago on his secondment to Mesopotamia from the Indian Civil Service during World War I.

After succeeding Colonel T. E. Lawrence as the chief British representative in Transjordan, he resigned from Government service in protest against British Palestine policy. From then on he devoted his astonishing powers of concentration to the study of the Arabian peninsula.

Standard Oil

His literary output, formidable in quantity, has become almost legendary for thoroughness and accuracy.

His greatest contribution to Arabia was probably that to which he paid least notice—the negotiation of the East Arabian concession on behalf of the Standard Oil Company of California, a transaction which brought in its wake changes of which Philby himself heartily disapproved.

Alone among King Abdul Aziz's friends, he refused to compromise with modern convenience, and his old mud house in Riyadh was one of the very few remaining vestiges of Wahhabi puritanism.

St. John Philby was buried in Beirut yesterday according to Muslim rites. Mr. H. A. R. Philby is his only son.

Kim Philby prided himself on his
professionalism as a journalist. Here he
reports on his father's death

The CIA's Jim Angleton, Philby's companion for boozy lunches in Washington in 1950–1, who never really recovered after he learned the truth

Victor Rothschild, another brilliant Cambridge graduate from the 1930s whose wartime heroics and postwar public service for the British state did not prevent some accusing him of being a Soviet agent

Tess Rothschild, aesthete, Cambridge graduate, counter intelligence officer and later magistrate and penal reformer, and the wife of Victor. She had complete trust in Anthony Blunt and regarded him as 'a sort of girlfriend'

Eleanor Philby in London, mid 1960s

Eleanor and her ghost writer Patrick Seale around the time of the *Observer*'s
serialisation of their book

Kim and Melinda outside Moscow

From left: Kim, Rufina, Nishia Philby and her husband John, Kim's eldest son, in Moscow

Harold Macmillan, British prime minister from 1957 to 1963, who gave a green light to Philby being employed in Beirut. The patrician Macmillan believed spy scandals, like shot foxes, should be buried 'out of sight'

Peter Wilson, a wartime colleague of Kim Philby and Myrtle Winter who later became chairman of Sotheby's

Sir Dick White, head of first MI5 and then, after 1956, of MI6, who was convinced Philby was working for Moscow

The Queen and Sir Anthony Blunt. She is said to have admired his expertise and his humour

Brian Sewell, art critic and friend of Anthony Blunt who helped the former Surveyor of the Queen's Pictures after his exposure as a Russian spy

Kim Philby in the USSR, the loneliness of his struggle supposedly at an end

new company in New York, at the Rockefeller Center, where he was specialising in attempts to bring automation to the field of education in the developing world. Ever the Anglophile, he and Lorraine were thinking of moving to London, where he also had an office, but was reluctant to put his mastiff into quarantine for six months. And he had news from London. He had seen Nicholas Elliott, who seemingly had come close to being sacked following the confrontation with Kim in Beirut. Was that really true? If so, that would suggest there was no truth in the idea that Philby had been encouraged to slip away. But maybe that was why Copeland had been told that – to encourage the idea that Philby's escape had been unintended. Without hard evidence, the arguments could go on for ever.*

In the US, Eleanor had to endure a grilling by a couple of FBI agents. The damage Philby might have done in 1949 to 1951 during his spell in the US was still of interest. Did she know anything about his activities in Washington? She said she had never met him before he got to Beirut, so knew nothing. After a few cursory questions about their life together in Moscow, she was free to go.

The stay in New York afforded Eleanor an opportunity to contemplate what she had left behind. Relations with her first husband Sam were not good, and documents from Moscow report the divorcees as having had 'two frightful scenes'. Eleanor found him morose, almost friendless as a result and also in real danger of losing his job as the *New York Times*'s UN correspondent.

Now approaching his mid-fifties, Brewer was liked and admired by his journalist colleagues, but he had lost the hunger and vigour of his early career. His edge had gone. Albert L. Hennig, a CIA contact who kept in touch to see if Sam knew

---

* In the event, Elliott went on to be MI6's head of Western Europe.

anything about Eleanor's intentions, reported that Sam 'was in poor shape most of the time, useless owing to the amount of drink he took on'.

Harrison Salisbury, author of a book on the *New York Times*, cites Brewer's curiously flat, unjournalistic way of reacting to news stories for someone so long committed to journalism, and perceives a drag on Brewer's allegiance. Having examined Brewer's private news memoranda, Salisbury concludes that he 'never during his years on the *Times* achieved the level of work which Cy Sulzberger had expected ... a critic could not but wonder whether he was totally independent and objective as a correspondent'.

But the other reason, more convincing and upon which, sadly, there is more agreement, was that Brewer became stale and over-reliant on a handful of friends in government. Whereas in his hungry, early days he had been assiduous in following every lead, now he knew enough influential people to take his cue from them – at the expense of his critical judgement.

The UN job that he was now performing was a job for tired racehorses if ever there was one. Bill Eveland had written how useful Brewer could be in his earliest days in Beirut if he wanted to plant thoughts and stories. While this is an occupational hazard in an established journalist, and journalists are, or should be, forever weighing up the extent to which they are being used by their sources, Brewer acquired a reputation for such acquiescence, often to Eveland's advantage.

Said Aburish recalls Bill Eveland's cheery wave when he used to arrive at the St Georges and how the two of them 'exchanged furtive smiles which implicitly acknowledged Sam's sad reliance on Bill for what he wrote. No longer a great foreign correspondent, Sam had been reduced to a has-been mouthpiece for the CIA ... The *New York Times* and the CIA huddled over Gibsons and whisky-and-soda to organise what the world was going to hear the following day, a doctored version of the US government's point of view. In the words of a thrusting young journalist at the time, NBC's Tom Streithorst, it was "a sad day for journalism".'

What Eleanor may not have known – she doesn't mention it in her book – is that back in 1951, a matter of hours after the British authorities realised Guy Burgess and Donald Maclean had fled to Moscow, the CIA had tried to hire her husband. Cy Sulzberger received a visit at his office at the *New York Times* from Arthur Corning Clark of the CIA. Clark didn't mention the British traitors, whose absence was known to only a handful of people at that stage, but he asked Sulzberger if he would be willing to release Sam Pope Brewer. Claiming not to have spoken to Brewer beforehand, he said that for the next three years Brewer would be paid $10,000 plus $2000 as an overseas allowance, after which he would return to the newspaper. Sulzberger discussed the matter with his colleagues and turned it down. It was too compromising to the *New York Times*'s independence. The matter was barely discussed subsequently and only came to light decades later.

Whether or not that was the end of the story must remain a matter of speculation, but Harrison Salisbury, a towering figure in the *New York Times*'s post-war history, is in no doubt that the CIA wanted Brewer to help find the evidence that Philby, who he had known since the Spanish Civil War, had been working with the fugitives. In the end, Brewer did prove Philby's unreliability, but only in marital matters.

As for Brewer's intelligence links more generally, Harrison Salisbury is in little doubt: 'There is no real evidence that Sam did sever his connections. In fact he probably maintained them until the end of his life.' Salisbury concluded that 'a potentially first-class journalist had tailed off to second rank because he tried to serve two masters'. Given his wartime closeness to official sources, the fact of the CIA's attempt to hire him in 1951, his amenability to being steered by helpful officials and of course a cuckold's assumed animus, it would be extremely surprising if Brewer was not at least a little helpful to the CIA in its surveillance of Philby. Had Sam, like Miles Copeland, also been compensated financially by the CIA for the alcohol Kim Philby had drunk under his roof? Was he filing reports on the man who cuckolded him? We may never know, nor how much of this Eleanor was aware of. In her book, Sam's links with officialdom are not mentioned.

As the issue of Annie's custody threatened to drag on, Sam took the initiative. For the avoidance of further doubt, on Thursday 16 July he filed a suit in the State Supreme Court seeking legal custody for himself. There was, said the citation, 'a strong possibility that the defendant's present husband was a spy for the Soviet Union' and that the girl might be taken there by her mother. Once there, it was claimed, 'she would be indoctrinated with Communist principles and anti-American theories'. Philby complained to Eleanor that Sam was 'behaving like a hysterical old woman, but that is normal form with him and might have been foreseen'. Annie, quite old enough to understand at least the basics of the legal wrangle, worried that if she stayed in the States and her mother went to Moscow, she would be separated from her for ever. Kim, on the other hand, told Eleanor that it would hardly be fair to make Annie continue her schooling in Moscow and encouraged Eleanor to relinquish custody. This she did, but still Sam would still not agree to the California holiday. So the following day, using a false name, Eleanor ducked out of mounting media interest by booking herself and Annie onto a flight to the west coast. This gave rise to stories reporting that Annie was missing, presumably in the company of her communist-loving mother, although Eleanor's lack of a passport would have prevented them going very far, let alone, say, to Cuba. Kim in Moscow, desperate for news, egged Eleanor on with various disobliging remarks about her former husband. One of the papers ran a story saying that Eleanor was planning to take Annie to Moscow, which enraged Kim, who suggested Eleanor sue for libel. In the event, according to press reports at the time (seemingly the result of a briefing in New York), Eleanor called Sam from California to confirm Annie was well. Days later, the court issued an injunction preventing Annie from leaving New York and awarded Sam sole custody. Eleanor was not there to contest the award. She was on holiday with her daughter at the time. Feelings were running high.

Having resolved, or at least managed, one legal issue, Eleanor then had another to confront – her passport. But this was an election year, and Lyndon Baines Johnson (LBJ), striving to emulate the charismatic John F. Kennedy, assassinated a few months earlier, could afford to show no concessions to communism. The Republican challenger, it had been confirmed some weeks earlier, was Barry Goldwater, a right-winger who would have loved nothing better than to portray the renewal of commie-loving Eleanor's passport as a case of LBJ being soft on communism. Yet rejecting her application would have been unfair, so the issue was to be ducked, parked until after the election in November.

It was to be a long wait. Kim continued to send loving letters, going into ever more detail about the veal *à la moutarde* he had been planning for the Macleans, the opera he had been to and expressing disappointment at Eleanor's delayed return. For a man often dismissed as cold-blooded and ruthless, he reveals a most affectionate, sentimental side of his personality in his letters, including complaining mildly about Eleanor's failure to send enough letters in return. As summer turns to autumn, he writes of the football match that Sergei is to take him to, and of his feelings at the unseating of Soviet President

Khrushchev. He reveals his hopes for the opening up of life in the USSR. The party, he writes, should explain where he had gone wrong, while praising him for liberalising Soviet life and promoting the policy of peaceful coexistence. 'One has got to remember,' he says, 'that Communism first succeeded in Russia, and must for some time bear a specifically Russian imprint, including the centuries-old tradition of secrecy in government. Even a major revolution cannot wipe out that tradition in a generation . . .'

At around the same time, Philby applauds the defeat of Barry Goldwater, approvingly reporting a taxi driver telling him it showed that the people wanted peace. Elsewhere he shows an optimism and idealism that might surprise his ideological foes. LBJ, he says, is 'a politician of genius, and possibly (let us hope) a real statesman as well'. At the Bolshoi, for *La Traviata* that evening, he plans 'a caviar sandwich and a glass of champagne in honour of LBJ'.

The election done, the wheels of the new administration started moving and Eleanor's prospects of joining her husband for such evenings soared. She was to be allowed a new passport, allowing her to travel anywhere apart from those countries all Americans were prevented from visiting, e.g. Albania and Cuba. The cost was around $2500, which set Eleanor thinking that a lawyer might be able to claim some of the money back from the State Department, on the grounds of wrongful action and for compensation.

After nearly five months away, seeing Kim again was long overdue. But there was a price to pay. Annie was distraught at her going, and doubly so for the fact that she would not be able to return for a year at least. She had been away from Moscow for too long, and had to bed herself in again with Kim and the Soviet authorities. She flew back to Moscow on 28 November, pausing en route at Copenhagen airport to buy the couple of bottles of whisky which Kim had been badgering her for, having sent ahead two large packages crammed with ball-point pens, rubber bands, staplers, paperclips, a garlic crusher, Sellotape and other items too trivial to impede Moscow's march of progress.

Things had changed when Eleanor returned. Where she knew that relations had been tricky when she had left, she could put that down partly to the very fact of her going. Now, right from the start, Kim seemed more settled, if not comfortably so, and the distance between them had widened. It was Sergei who greeted her off the plane, as Kim waited in the car. As they were driven home, Eleanor chattering happily with news of New York, Kim gestured to her to stop, fearing Sergei's eavesdropping. The much-vaunted two bottles of whisky were produced, but even they were the cause of friction. Sergei wanted to know where Eleanor had bought them. Was it possible someone had poisoned them? Eleanor found the idea that the CIA might try to kill him in this way laughable. Kim, as if making some sort of statement, opened one of them and drank it as fast as he could.

In her absence, Kim's Russian had improved. It was never very good, and, as might be expected of the son of a British colonial administrator of the time, he generally spoke to his handlers in English, but it was always going to be better than Eleanor's. The Russian teacher had been dispensed with and now Eleanor was alone with her Linguaphone records.

Kim now had an office to go to, where he was working on what turned out to be an unreliable book in collaboration with Gordon Lonsdale, aka Konon Molody, a UK-based Russian spy recently swapped for a British spy, so she saw less of him during the day than previously. Increasingly he would come home incapable from his editorial sessions with Molody, if that is what they were. Where previously he had been an assiduous celebrator of anniversaries and buyer of presents, now his imagination was rarely stirred. The spur had gone.

Initially Eleanor put his worry down to problems at work, maybe to a sense that he was not being appreciated by his masters, but that couldn't be all it was. He affected to feel as warm as ever towards her, and strove to be kind and solicitous. His language was endearing, even syrupy. Behind all that, though, he was closing down. His health was not good, but there was something more. It wasn't that he wanted to be cruel or distant. On the contrary. Selfishly, scaredly, he ducked addressing the problem. Confident that Eleanor would always have a drop with him, drink was once again a ready refuge, a short cut to insensibility and a land where on a good day problems weren't allowed to intrude. Ominously, she was reminded of Kim's distant, drink-filled gloom from his last few weeks in Beirut. There was a big problem, and once more she was not privy to it.

The Macleans, to whom Eleanor found herself warming, for lack of much alternative, were also having a difficult time. Kim told Eleanor he had had a major argument with Donald after he claimed that Kim might still be working for the British, and Melinda was finding her husband more and more difficult. She weepily confided in Eleanor about Donald, telling her angrily that she was rearranging their flat so that she wouldn't have to share a room with him, beside which Eleanor's own problems seemed puny. Nonetheless, she felt a bond had been formed by the episode and she began speaking more trustingly to Melinda, fishing for reassurance that Kim still loved her. Melinda replied: 'He did, until a while ago.'

Whatever she meant by this, it was not good news. Kim had known the Macleans longer than she had, and Melinda was well placed to confirm she wasn't imagining the distance between them. Eleanor hoped a trip to Leningrad for the pair of them – to celebrate both Christmas and their wedding anniversary – might help bridge the gap. Kim seemed happy to go along with it, as long as there was plenty to drink. He spent the preceding three days drunk, and then had a boozy lunch and a party at the station, insisting on his friends seeing them off. While away, he was distant and impatient. One remark, when the pair were sitting at lunch, was particularly telling, both of his irritation at Eleanor's failure to assimilate and join his heroic proletarian struggle and of the simple fact that, in her words, 'his courtesy was gone'. He said simply: 'Why do you always look so damned smart?'

Maybe there was nothing specific to be read into the fact that Kim's kindness was directed so much towards others these days. Increasingly he seemed concerned by Melinda's difficulties, and she reciprocated by inviting Kim and Eleanor to stay for the St Patrick's Day weekend in the snow at their dacha outside Moscow. There, as ever, much alcohol was consumed, and Kim had a fall, badly damaging his wrist. Again, drink was the medicine, and now Eleanor was getting angry. Even alcohol couldn't hide the fact, diagnosed back in Moscow, that the wrist was broken. He was in a pitiful state. After a week trapped in a sweltering flat to escape the extreme cold outside, Eleanor had had enough and demanded to know what was going on.

Kim could dissemble no longer. He told her that Melinda was desperately miserable. Donald was impotent and he felt a need to make her happy.

It was the admission she feared, and his gall was breathtaking: 'I don't want you to leave. Of course you can stay on. You know I'm very fond of you and Melinda understands my very special feeling for you.'

Eleanor facetiously asked if he wanted her to be 'the assistant housekeeper in charge of birds', but otherwise her anger and upset were held in check. She later wrote that she should have reacted violently and confronted matters head on. It just seemed such a mistake, an aberration born only of her having to stay in the US so long, during which time Melinda and her friends had made Kim as small-minded as they were. She knew there were problems, but asked herself if perhaps she had been a victim of politics. Had the Russians told Kim to end it? (It was a recurring concern: she once speculated inconclusively that maybe Kim had been instructed to marry an American, to help advance his access in the States.) In the end she decided simply that kind old Kim had fallen for some age-old womanly wiles. Her fury was directed more at Melinda than at Kim.

Which is perhaps why she was so forbearing of Kim's 'you can stay on' remark. Eleanor does not make much of it in her book, but he was serious. Just as his father had done nine years earlier, when Kim had been so scandalised, he was proposing that he and the two women should live as a threesome under one roof. A friend of Eleanor's from the time reports: 'He was absolutely serious. Having begged Eleanor to join him in Moscow, he now wanted her to stay with him while he also took up with Melinda Maclean.' It was a stunning slap in the face. Perhaps more remarkably still, she tried it, for about a fortnight, but it was never going to work. He now had a new favourite. At one point he gave Melinda a book with the inscription: 'An orgasm a day keeps the doctor away.' Arnold Deutsch's priapic alumnus had overcome any squeamishness about loyally respecting his friend Donald's marriage, let alone his own. For Eleanor, it could hardly have been more dispiriting.

On top of Kim's damaged wrist, he now began to suffer from serious chest pains, and was diagnosed with tuberculosis and pneumonia. His life was in danger. Naturally Eleanor visited him in hospital, supplying newspapers and other reading matter, but all the time Melinda was visiting, too, at different times. Still he spoke most romantically to her, not wanting to hurt her feelings. Here was the sweetness of nature, the gentleness, and the complete lack of contrition or shame – or seemingly even acknowledgement – about his responsibility for what Eleanor had gone through for their love.

These embers were never going to take light again, she decided. Enough was enough. She told him she might go back to her roots and live in Ireland, which he thought an excellent idea. There being no extradition between the UK and the Irish Republic at that time, he hoped he could come and visit. He gave her his most prized possession, his Westminster School scarf, and a farewell letter, calling her the best friend he would ever have. She read it endlessly.

If we assume Kim's offer to Eleanor to allow her to remain living with him and Melinda was sincere, we can probably dismiss a notion floated by Anthony Cave Brown. This was that the KGB had decided 'Philby must get rid of Eleanor if he wished to work' because she had become an 'operational embarrassment'. Kim's relationship with Melinda, said Cave Brown, was 'part of a stratagem by which Kim rid himself of Eleanor', cooked up in order to force her out. But the fact that Kim and Melinda had a relationship, and that Eleanor left, is in itself not proof of such a plan, attractive though it is to lovers of intrigue. Nor does he provide any other evidence, or any hint of there being any unidentifiable sources for such a plan. What happened may not have been determined by design.

As Eleanor left for the airport on 18 May 1965, she asked one of Kim's colleagues to give him a letter she had written. It said that if he ever reconsidered, she would come back, but he needed to understand how manipulative Melinda had been. She could not live in the same city as her.

13

'Swinging' London, 1965–8

Back in London, the marriage over, Eleanor struggled to make sense of things. She stayed with a variety of concerned friends – the Copelands, Susan Griggs, the Porters, the Izzards in Tunbridge Wells (where she had 'endless chats, downloading a sense of betrayal') – but there could be little balm for a trust so comprehensively shattered. Alcohol, which had long played an increasing part in her life, came to the fore. She was, by this time, by any definition, an alcoholic. As ever, she could not be sure who to trust. Lorraine Copeland would always be her friend, she felt. She was less confident about Miles.

Susan Griggs remembers receiving calls from out of the blue from Miles Copeland, also in London. 'Ah! Eleanor's here, we must see each other again,' he would say, opportunistically thought Susan, who felt Eleanor needed protecting. 'Whatever I said was sufficiently frosty for him not to ever call me back again. Eleanor considered them close friends, so she told Miles everything she knew and he was feeding it all straight back to the CIA. It made me think "what a snake". He didn't tell her things that he knew but he told them all the things that she told him. That's how they knew to meet her when she got back to meet Annie. He was a CIA man. So he was doing what his job entailed, but she wasn't well served by her supposed "friend".'

Myrtle Winter, still working with MI6, would also exhibit an unwonted interest in Eleanor's movements, often sending letters to Susan Griggs's parents. 'She knew they had been close to Eleanor,' says Griggs. 'She was obviously collecting information. This wasn't just chat, it wasn't just "if I come to London I'll have a place to stay". She was collecting information. And it was always "Have you heard from Eleanor? Who have you been talking to?"'

Griggs believes that Philby had always been destined for Moscow, sooner or later, but Eleanor's incomprehension at Kim's devotion to the Soviet cause never left her. 'I don't think he was tempted by anything the West ever offered,' said Griggs, who had her to stay in London, trying to console her. 'Every night of the week, she'd get so drunk, she'd say, repeatedly: "I challenged him ... I asked him if it ever came to a really, really life-and-death choice between me and the children on the one hand and the Party on the other, who would win. She said he looked at her in disbelief and just said 'the Party, of course'." That was the dealbreaker, of course ... that and Melinda moving in.' Eleanor said she could live with playing second fiddle to the Communist Party, but not to Melinda. Patrick Seale believed the problem was wider. 'The relationship collapsed not because of Mrs Maclean, but simply because Eleanor's independent spirit could not comply with the heavy constrictions of Moscow life', he wrote.

The British newspapers, desperate for something verifiable to report, were thrown a bone that summer, reporting that Philby had made an official application to divorce Eleanor, on the grounds of her desertion – her refusal to share his life in Moscow, although even that is in some doubt. How much had Eleanor really meant to Kim? Was he essentially the 'copper-bottomed bastard' that MI6's John Sackur had described, who knew nothing of loyalty and love, least of all to women, who moved on when he got bored? A handful of marriages and a number of affairs would encourage that view. Certainly he was unfaithful to Lizi, Aileen and Eleanor. Yet, this being the enigmatic Philby, it has also been claimed that he was truly unfaithful, in the fullest sense, to none of them – that he was a serial monogamist, and that his extra-marital relationships took place only once the marriages were over, even if not in law. Typically, though, it was generally he who did the deciding.

Peter Wright said Philby had 'an Arabian attitude to women', living his life 'from bed to bed'. John le Carré, who thought Philby 'spiteful, vain and murderous', saw little to admire. He believed Philby treated women as his secret audience: 'He used them like he used society: he performed, danced, phantasized with them, begged their approbation, used them as a response for his histrionic talents, as a consolation for a manhood haunted by his father's ghost. When they came too close he punished them or pushed them away.'

Yet so many of the most perceptive, acute people thought of him otherwise. Though well read, he never made those less so feel stupid or inferior. He treated children as equals and had a way of imparting knowledge that was more sharing than didactic. He had an affinity with women, who often found him sweet-natured and huggable. Even Elizabeth Elliott, whose husband had more reason than most to hate Philby, spoke late in her life with remarkable affection about him. Designer Thea Porter remarked how he 'had scholarly tastes and liked imparting information to women, taking them by the arm and seating them beside him at parties'. And up to middle age he seems to have explored and exploited the opportunities that presented.

As a spy, he had to be cold-blooded. As a lover, he could be anything but. Molly Izzard believed that in the 1930s he had tried to commit suicide over his relationship with Frances Doble. One day she noticed a scar across his wrist and asked what it was. He said it was something he was not very proud of and dated back to his time in Spain, but wouldn't elaborate. When Eleanor asked the same question, she wasn't even told that much, and was told not to ask again.

But Eleanor was special to him. One diplomatic wife, on meeting Kim and his 'new woman', found her 'not the kind of sexy attraction you would expect to attract Philby'. His love letters to her are extraordinarily affectionate and sentimental, not that that makes them insincere. He and Eleanor were regarded as the happiest couple in Beirut, two individuals obviously, totally, charmingly at ease in one another's company. Lennie Copeland suggested that maybe it was the tangles and conflicts in his own head that made him fall for someone as politically guileless as Eleanor. She represented the straightforwardness and simplicity that were so far from a mind haunted by the countless contradictory untruths he had spun. (That may also have something to do with his love of animals.) Eleanor didn't chivvy him and didn't try to change him – he had enough on his plate – something for which he would express gratitude in his most heartfelt letters to her. She would gaze at him admiringly at parties, and when he misbehaved – bottom-pinching and so on – she would sometimes tick him off, but would also chide others for doing so, explaining that he meant no harm. It was 'just Kim'.

His stutter was another part of his winning persona. A CIA colleague wrote: 'his efforts to overcome an attack were so monumental and so dogged that sympathy and admiration were aroused in equal measure.' A former professional colleague who cannot be named said: 'He hated his stutter. It was a burden for him – a terrible mental and physical handicap, a hurdle he knew he always had to get over, particularly with new and official contacts. With people he knew well he hardly stuttered at all.' Nor did he tend to stutter when speaking a foreign language.

His MI6 colleague Desmond Bristow says Philby would attempt to buy time when, under pressure, he needed to work out what was safe to say, given the number of lies he had told, often snapping his fingers to bring the hiatus to an end. That is not to say it was entirely bogus, merely that it offered opportunities. Others, wishing to be kind, would help him, completing a word he was struggling with. But Eleanor's attitude to the stutter is revealing of their relationship. He stuttered less with her, often when relaxedly reciting poetry quietly at home. And in the company of others, she never presumed to complete his words, simply pretending there was no problem.

Latterly in Beirut, as drink and fear got to him, he aged prematurely, and would rely on her more and more, becoming panicky if he didn't know where she was. 'The Philbys were a devoted couple. They never quarrelled: on the contrary, they seemed almost helplessly dependent on each other. Whenever Kim was distressed or melancholic, he seemed to cling to Eleanor like a very frightened small boy,' wrote Edward Sheehan, the well-connected American journalist who specialised in the Middle East. This element of his partner as a carer became much more pronounced as he aged further in Moscow with his last wife, Rufina. They went out little, and he contented himself with domesticity.

Genrikh Borovik, the closest Russian writer to Philby, speculated as to how much Eleanor was an invention of his mind and how much there was a real attraction to 'a simple open woman "without complexes" who loved him deeply and with whom he could forget his loneliness'. But Borovik was sure of one thing: 'He was deeply sincere in his feelings for her. During our conversations in Moscow, he always stopped talking about her as soon as Rufina entered the room or came on to the terrace where we were talking.' He would not discuss his relationship with Eleanor as he did those with Lizi and Aileen.

The old sentimentalist regarded her as the best friend he would ever have. But she didn't fit the plan. She didn't buy the Soviet dream as he did. Moscow hadn't grown on her, and she didn't much mind who knew it. She still adored her husband but, tiresomely, she would have a mind of her own. She felt imprisoned in a suspicious country and had a much-loved teenage daughter needing to see her in America. For Kim, that was an insurmountable embarrassment.

As a father, Kim gave outsiders the impression of being besotted with his children. He would buy them presents and loved playing with them. It is perhaps intrusive – and tempting fate – to delve into this matter when four of his children are still alive. He seems to have enjoyed his children most when they were truly children, and as they grew and his worries and his alcoholic intake increased, his distractions from them became all the greater.

Nicholas Elliott, whose memoir tries to avoid being vindictive towards Philby, talks of missed birthdays and children coming some way down the social priority scale. One of those involved in the care of the children after Aileen died told a friend that Kim had not been firm enough or concerned enough about his children, citing John Philby having left school without his A levels and abandoning art school. John also went on to have difficulties with the law for what might charitably be called high jinks as a young man. A loving and admiring son, he visited his father in Moscow frequently and travelled extensively with him in the Soviet Union, but his father never explained the political choices he had made. He worked successfully as a joiner near King's Cross in London and married three times. His daughter Charlotte is a thriving writer of thrillers in London. He died in 2009.

Friends from Beirut continued to help Eleanor in London, allowing her to sleep on their sofa or in their spare room for the odd week. But not everyone was pleased that she had come to

London. To some she was stigmatised by trying to make a life with a traitor. The popular press had no time for sophistry and offered little sympathy. Most of those who had been close to her helped her, knowing not to breathe a word to journalists.

But Eleanor was bruised and bewildered, high and dry, having lost custody of her daughter and now being uncertain where to live. Some of Sam's relations in the States were unforgiving, chuckling at how they had heard she hadn't liked the cold in Moscow and was heading home. But some others who might have been expected to feel animosity were sympathetic. Josephine Philby said later: 'I don't really blame her for not liking it, and I think she was absolutely horrified by what Dad had done, and I don't think she had any clue, otherwise she would have coped with it better.'

Eleanor decided, as she had mentioned to Kim, that she would move to Ireland, whence her ancestors had come, and in the summer of 1965, after a spell in a hotel, she took a ground-floor flat in Sandycove, a suburb of Dublin, with her much-treasured Siamese cat. She had enough money to go and live there, painting and allowing the emotional tornado to subside. She continued to visit London, but for the eighteen months from mid-1965 she based herself away from it all.

The flat was overlooked by the celebrated Martello tower, scene of the beginning of James Joyce's *Ulysses*, and had a long, thin garden that ran down to the sea. Sandycove, agreeable but less smart than it has since become, attracted an arty crowd and few people – least of all the press – were aware that the friendly American lady was the former wife of one of Britain's most notorious spies. 'She was quite an exotic figure, I remember. Tall, slightly Katherine Hepburn-y, always open for a chat,' remembers the author Iain Sinclair, who was studying English and Fine Art at Trinity College, Dublin, and who lived in the ground-floor flat next door.

There was no garden partition between the houses and, as a student, Sinclair was grateful to be invited in to watch American films on her television, much prized in those days, and she seemed pleased to have thoughtful company. 'We had things in common we could talk about – film, art, books. She was convivial and had a dry sense of humour. But we never discussed Beirut at length. I didn't want to probe. She very much gave the impression of being in hiding. She was happy talking to these arty students because there was no comeback and no one was making anything of it. She seemed pretty solitary and melancholy but she was happy to have us in her flat, sharing a few drinks.'

Long-distance relations with Kim remained civil, even amicable, and Eleanor saw a bit of his eldest son John, who shared her artistic and creative leanings. Kim had made gently disapproving remarks about Eleanor's growing liking for the Beatles, which he had light-heartedly said he thought hinted at her acquiring alarming capitalist tendencies. So it was double-edged that she should send him – with considered piquancy – one of her favourites, 'Help!', released as a single in July 1965.

Kim was having to move house because, as his Soviet masters explained, Eleanor knew his address and British or American intelligence might use the knowledge to his disadvantage – possibly to murder him, they believed. He continued to express concern for Eleanor's welfare, and would send friendly notes saying how he hoped that Annie's athlete's foot had cleared up, for example. But his musical tastes – like much else – were not to be changed easily. A few weeks later, on 10 August 1965, the traitor's OBE was annulled. He played the curmudgeon, wishing that he had got in first by returning it in protest at the Beatles being awarded the MBE two months earlier.

Eleanor was the beneficiary of some money left her by an aunt, but was without a reliable source of income. The legacy of her marriage to Kim – the damage to her self-esteem and to her sense of trust – was compounded by an urgent need for money. On that score, certainly, Kim was in her debt. Kim's sister Pat had mentioned that Eleanor's first-hand experience would be of considerable value to the newspapers, and maybe she should tell her story. This affronted Eleanor's sense of propriety, and not simply because she was having ever worse dealings with the journalists charged with following her. She did mention the idea to Kim, though, who, rather than opposing the idea outright advised against it, gently and probably disingenuously warning her of the inevitable loss of privacy that selling her story would involve.

If that was not the answer, what did Kim propose? He had been sending her occasional cheques, drawn, humiliatingly, on Melinda's account, but Eleanor decided to bring in a legal firm to help secure a lasting agreement for more regular payments. Kim acknowledged that cheques arriving in dribs and drabs was not satisfactory and promised to find a better arrangement.

Calling in reinforcements seems not to have helped. Kim wrote a wounded letter to Eleanor about her decision to bring in legal help and asked her to name an annual figure she thought she needed. He said he thought there was no need for them to divorce unless Eleanor was planning to marry again.

She seems to have wanted to hasten things along, and mentioned to Kim that she had been made a huge offer by a publisher to tell her story. Kim applied the charm, telling her it was entirely her choice, but reassured her that there was no need for her to accept any such offer, and that he would sort things out very shortly. In the event, although there was interest from André Deutsch and others, the publisher's enormous offer did not materialise. Neither was Kim able to stump up the capital sum he had been hoping to produce, but he did promise to pay £150 a month (now worth around £3000) into her account.

He pointed out that his salary in Beirut had been around £4000 a year (in today's money, approaching £80,000), which he said had paid for himself, Eleanor, two children in Beirut and three in the UK. It is hard to know how far the contributions by Aileen, Tomás Harris, Nicholas Elliott and Philby's former mother-in-law Mrs Alleyne (and other family members, financially and in kind) had gone in meeting school fees, repayment of a book advance from André Deutsch and subsistence, but it was stretching things for Philby to claim that less than £4000 covered the family's costs.

That would be enough to keep Eleanor ticking over while she considered her options. She admitted to feeling 'desperately in need of friends', but very few wished to see her. She understood why, given Kim's politics, but that didn't cure the loneliness. And in any case, she couldn't be sure who her real friends were. How much were the friendly ones keeping tabs on her? Miles Copeland, as we have seen, always seemed to be more inquisitive than friendship required, which may explain why Eleanor's daughter cut one of the Copeland children dead when they bumped into one another at college in the States. She was very fond of Nicholas Elliott's wife Elizabeth, whose discretion must have been sorely tested when in 1963 her husband had been trying to infer Eleanor's intentions. As she considered joining Kim in Moscow two years earlier, Eleanor had been still trusting enough to ask Elizabeth: 'What would *you* do if the man you loved went behind the Iron Curtain?' Elizabeth admitted reluctantly she would follow him to Moscow.

'My mother stayed friends with her and was very fond of her,' remembers Mark Elliott. 'The sense I got was that Eleanor felt bitter that my father had given her bad advice when he warned her that if she went to Moscow she would never be allowed to leave.'

When in London, she mixed with a smart, arty set, and

resumed a friendship with the designer Thea Porter and other former Beirut residents. This was a London that was beginning to swing.

Unsurprisingly she continued to drink heavily. 'She was very drawn and thin, a total alcoholic, but in a very different way from Kim,' says Mark Elliott. 'When he got drunk he was a total extrovert but Eleanor was just a quiet drinker. She wasn't an outgoing person.' Iain Sinclair remembers her 'not as a falling-down drunk, but just quietly well oiled'.

Eleanor had pretty much escaped the reporters. In the tranquillity of Ireland, though, she was the subject of another sort of hounding. She received a letter from the Inland Revenue in London, saying that she owed tax on money she received in the UK. She pointed out that she had been living abroad, as would have been well known to the British authorities, but this cut no ice, and a large bill needed to be paid. London seemed to be making it clear that though her friends were for the most part loyal and understanding, she was to receive no special treatment from the British state.

She had kept in touch with Patrick Seale, Thea Porter's brother, and Kim's immediate successor as the *Observer*'s correspondent in Beirut, who was now mostly in London. The *Observer* had begun publishing books, but was generally paying the market rate to outsiders. It was Seale who suggested that the paper's journalists could produce their own words, and that Eleanor, who he knew had a story to tell and needed to make some money, should write one, with his collaboration. In the autumn of 1966, unannounced, he was given a year's sabbatical to write Eleanor's story.

Seale was ideally placed. Born in Belfast, he was the son of Reine Attal, a midwife of Tunisian-Italian origin, and Morris Seale, an Arabist and biblical scholar. Shortly after his birth in 1930 his family moved to Syria, where for twenty years they ran the Irish Presbyterian mission. Seale was a man of notable intelligence. He spent three years at Balliol College, Oxford, and did military service on the Suez Canal. He said later he had been turned down for a full-time career in the army when his commanding officer told him that antisemitism would prevent him reaching the high rank he merited. Until then, Seale had no idea that both his parents were Jewish converts, nor that his father's real name had been Segal. He knew the Middle East well, had been Philby's deputy on the *Observer* and possessed plenty of emotional intelligence.

The book he wrote with Eleanor was intended not as a score-settler but a gracious portrait of a love affair with a man whose mind, she discovered too late, was elsewhere. One of the reasons for writing it, she explained when the plan was launched, was to come to an understanding of how she could have had a marriage that – she said without irony – had been 'perfect in every way' even though her husband 'shut me out of a whole side of his personality'.

With her tax bill in mind, she decided to move once more, though hardly to a cheap part of London, taking a flat in Thurloe Place, opposite the Victoria & Albert Museum in South Kensington, and began collaborating with Seale, who was just across the river in Worfield Street, Battersea, in earnest. Money, she admitted, was the main reason for writing the book. 'I felt it about time, since Kim could not give me any security.'

The *Observer* (circulation 800,000 copies) intended to serialise the book in late 1968, but its chief competitor, the *Sunday Times* (circulation 1.5 million), was never going to ignore the biggest spy story for decades, even if initially the *Observer* thought it had the field to itself. Quite when the *Sunday Times* started on its own book is unclear, but certainly a paragraph in the *Daily Express* in April 1967 about the Seale book induced a terror of being scooped. The *Sunday Times* put a large team on the case, confident of beating the *Observer*'s intended publication date of the summer of 1968. This prompted Eleanor's book to be brought forward by months, triggering a race in the dark, with each side claiming to have made remarkable progress and being nearly ready to publish. Much subterfuge followed, and when Seale interviewed Philby's son John (signed up by the *Sunday Times*, and busy taking pictures of his father in Moscow on its behalf) and realised how far advanced its efforts were, the urgency was stepped up yet further. The game of bluff was complicated in late September by a D-notice, by which the government threatened to prevent publication of the most damaging revelations. It seemed the *Sunday Times* was closest to the finishing line and planning to publish imminently, so the *Observer* decided to begin its expose on Sunday 1 October 1967, Seale and his co-reporter Maureen McConville working through the night to complete it. As it turned out, the *Sunday Times* had been planning its revelations for the following week, and when the first editions of the *Observer* came in, its rivals hastily threw together its own best effort. As planned, the first chunk of Eleanor's book appeared a week after its initial news stories.

High horses were mounted in the following weeks as the newspapers were accused of rewarding traitors, after Philby was reported to have had dealings with the *Sunday Times* over the use of some of his pictures. The paper insisted it had not paid him, had kept the Foreign Office informed and had no wish to undermine British security, merely to expose the extent to which Philby had done so.

At one point it was felt that any advance Eleanor received for the book might be frittered away. When she asked to be paid, a protective friend explained that it might be better if she tried to cope without it for the moment. After all, she would only spend it on drink. In a rebuttal worthy of W. C. Fields, she demanded: 'And what, pray, do you think I want to spend it on?'

There was something fitting about the book being destined for the *Observer*. Not only had it been the paper for which Kim had worked, but its proprietor David Astor took a particular interest in politics and was untroubled by the overlaps between the worlds of journalism and spying. Whether he knew about Philby's duties for HMG was never clear, although G. K. Young of MI6 was pretty sure he did.* When it became public that Philby had turned up in Moscow, somebody from the Foreign Office rushed over to the *Observer*'s office to say 'very sorry we didn't warn you', as the *Sunday Times* gleefully reported. But it was hardly a paper of *ingénus*. Remarkably, the 'fifth' of the Cambridge Five, John Cairncross, had been employed by the *Observer* in Rome some years earlier. Another senior journalist, Mark Frankland, had left MI6 (to the extent that anyone ever truly does, as he suggested) to become a journalist. And John de St Jorre, who covered the war in Biafra for the paper, was another former MI6 officer. The paper's links with spookery became something of a joke. One reporter, Colin Smith, was anxious for promotion but asked his bosses if there was any point in him applying as he had never worked for MI6.

Eleanor's book, called *The Spy I Loved*, was remarkable, revealing for the first time Philby's intensely affectionate and sentimental side through his letters. They made compelling, if prurient, reading, and helped explain to the wider public what she had seen in the man so triumphantly savaged in the newspapers.

Seale is the most thoughtful and fluent of writers, but the national mood, or at least the face manifested in newspapers, was not receptive. The reviews, perhaps understandably, focused on Philby, reviewers never failing to signal, gloatingly, what a blackguard he was. 'What a neat Stendhalian irony there is,'

---

* According to Philby, Elliott said he had told Astor, but Astor denied this.

said *The Times*, 'in the spectacle of this 50-year-old revolutionary drinking himself quietly into a stupor and champagne
during an evening of bridge and Scrabble with the Macleans!'

The *New Statesman* called it 'intimate, painful and even ...
shame-making'. Rebecca West, whose previous writings on
treason would have given the reader little hope of a surprise
opinion, was insistent on flagging her disdain in the *Sunday
Telegraph*. She called *The Spy I Loved* a 'pathetic ... sad little
book which is deplorable from many points of view' and its
subject 'the nastiest little rat who ever spied in the Balkans'. His
letters, from which Eleanor quotes freely, 'are banal and even
idiotic', and part of one of them, curiously, 'would hardly have
made a school magazine'. Beyond the eternal questions about
loyalty, the vulgar abuse is of a high calibre, admittedly, but it
remains essentially abuse. 'In every line of this pathetic volume
there is apparent a conviction that she and Philby and the group
to which they belong are somehow in the right: that they have
a commanding status which nothing can destroy. Drunkenness
for them is not drunkenness. It is annulled by their worth.'
Norman Shrapnel in the *Guardian* called it a 'rather touching
little memoir'. Malcolm Muggeridge, Philby's former colleague,
called it 'an artless and moving picture', but is most exercised
not by Philby's treachery but his resort to cliché in a love letter
in response to Eleanor's reserved disposition. 'Still waters run
deep!' he splutters in outrage.

Over fifty years later, it is easy to forget how exceptional
this flurry of activity in the public space was. Try as journalists
might, they had been able to discover little, the authorities in
neither Britain nor the USSR having much reason to tell the
whole truth. At the time of the serialisation of Eleanor's book,
another newspaper, keen to join in with the Philbiana, reported
excitedly that Philby and Melinda Maclean had got married.
The story looked like an unconvincing attempt to show that

the *Mirror*, too, could break stories about Philby. Purportedly the story had been confirmed by one of his children, her father having been divorced from Eleanor the previous year. Josephine was quoted as saying: 'Melinda would never live in sin. She is just not that kind of person.' Eleanor reported: 'I can't help being a little unhappy at the news that Kim has "remarried", if only because I was not aware of being divorced.' In fact the story was not true. The Philby children's continuing desire to keep the press at arm's length is understandable.

The thin but nevertheless revealing content of a rather more authoritative item in *The Times* the following month is suggestive of how little the press and radio had to go on. The headline was simply 'Philby seen in public'. The journalist had rushed to his typewriter late the previous evening after seeing Philby, accompanied by Melinda Maclean, at a concert given by the Moscow State Philharmonic, featuring the great cellist Mstislav Rostropovich. As Philby left the auditorium, the journalist approached him. Having initially pretended not to speak English, Philby conceded, smiled and said he had nothing to say. The report said he 'looked as though [his clothes] were the ones in which he defected', a rumpled dark suit, beige sweater and red tie. He was 'reported to be living in a modern apartment house on the edge of Moscow', but otherwise 'nothing is known of his present activities'.

Given the thin pickings on which the media was trying to feed, it should be no surprise that there was an appetite for Philby's direct collaboration in a variety of projects. He was planning his own book, but this would be written under Soviet control and therefore treated with scepticism in the West. But the interest was definitely there. David Frost wanted to conduct an interview for London Weekend Television, and the BBC was also keen. Meanwhile, Denis Greenhill, head of Britain's Foreign Office, armed with both carrots and sticks, scurried

round warning senior media executives that any thought of
lending respectability to Philby's doings, let alone paying him,
would be greatly frowned upon by the government and quite
possibly illegal. Philby, on the other hand, wanted money to
pass on to his children. At one point he told the *Sunday Times*,
which was showing interest in publishing his memoir, that he
would 'not give a story to a capitalist newspaper unless they paid
handsomely for it'.

One vehicle that would purportedly pay handsomely would
be a feature film about Philby's life, or so Miles Copeland, ever
in search of money-making ventures and its moving spirit, told
him. In November 1967 Copeland wrote a friendly note to
Philby telling him how much interest there was in his memoirs, saying that in any such film he was sure Philby 'wouldn't
want to make your old personal friends look any worse than
they already look'. The film would be 'anti-bureaucracy', but
'would allow individual bureaucrats to show up as honorable
enough human beings. The Philby image we have in mind
would be neither good nor bad in any narrow moral sense,
but a great historical figure of considerable complication.'
Such flattery, and offers of 'one hell of a lot' of money, was
Copeland at his most 'pragmatic'. He offered to collaborate
'with Soviet interests' or even a Soviet production company
'although it would probably lack the touch required to make
a movie for a wide Western audience . . . Once you hear all we
have in mind, I feel certain you will be interested, even excited
at this unique opportunity.'

It was also Copeland at his most ingratiating. Michael King
of the *Daily Mirror*, son of proprietor Cecil King, reported
on an off-the-record conversation Copeland had had with a
Mirror reporter about the film. This was a different Copeland.
He said: 'Philby is a vain man, and is mostly interested in what
posterity thinks of him. We can call him a knave and a crook

and he won't mind but he could never bear to be called weak, incompetent or a failure in anything . . . I would want Philby to be filmed accurately – and cut down to size.' Copeland claimed the damage done by Philby had been exaggerated, and acknowledged that his main concern for the film was libel, which is why he needed Philby's blessing. Copeland was for ever coming up with money-making schemes, and this was to be no small venture. He planned for it to star Trevor Howard as Philby and Ann Todd as Eleanor. It would be directed by David Lean, no less, Todd's former husband. He planned to pay Philby, though his children, not him, would benefit. Besides, 'the Treasury would stop the payment to Russia'.

The scheme never got off the ground, and in hindsight seems naïve in the extreme. Just as the Soviet authorities prevented Philby talking to Western news outlets by insisting on Soviet journalists asking the questions, so other objections were put in the way of the film.

As Copeland's conversation with the reporter widened, he turned to Philby's now ex-wife, whose book was being serialised. 'Eleanor is as naïve as Patrick Seale makes her out,' he said. 'When Philby vanished we told her all sorts of stories to put her mind at rest and the more fantastic they were the more easily she accepted them.'

This was the sort of friend – engaging but inconstant, implicit with the sinuousness of the espionage world – that she had had enough of in Beirut and did not need in London. She and Susan Griggs, an infinitely better friend, met every Thursday for a meal, taking turns to cook, and possibly arranging a cultural trip, even if only across the road to the V&A. Sometimes Patrick Seale would join them. She travelled, and spent some weeks in Tunisia, a sign perhaps of her indecision about the future. Meanwhile Eleanor's daughter Annie, to whom she had had access both in the States and on visits to London, had turned eighteen and was to continue her education on America's east coast. Once again, with London's welcome wearing thin – at this point tax laws were limiting the amount of time she was allowed to spend in the UK without incurring further costs – and with concerns about her health – both her alcoholic intake and other nagging worries – increasing, a move seemed in order. Her friends, including Patrick Seale and others from Beirut, continued to offer what help they could. They felt sorry for her, and she seemed broken.

Early in 1968 she and Patrick Seale travelled to the States to promote her book. Given her mistrust of the popular media, it was never likely to be a roaring success. She objected to the crass questioning of some TV presenters and on occasion refused to appear. One said: 'I have never had such a rough time since I interviewed Eleanor Roosevelt!' 'I'm in good company then,' replied Eleanor. Nonetheless, returning to the land of her birth, and of her daughter, offered some promise of relief.

Eleanor visited Amsterdam, a city she had never known well, and in the spring of 1968 she set sail for the States. In the meantime, Sam had married an Argentine-born friend of them both. Eleanor decided to return to the west coast, settling on her own in a comfortable house north of San Francisco. There, at last, a woman who had made the mistake of falling in love had some chance of escaping her role as an object of pity, a betrayed fool, a traitor's dupe. With the help of her book advance, she bought a house not far from the sea, and she moved in in the summer. Her relationship with Annie – though she was destined to be studying on the east coast – was what she had hoped it would be. Some sort of loving, trusting normality had been restored. This was somewhere to put her feet up.

One day, just a few months later, her neighbours, after knocking persistently on the door to no response, forced their way in. A malignancy in her throat had caught up with her.

She had died soon after returning home, passing away on 14 November 1968, and was cremated nearby soon afterwards.

Susan Griggs says Eleanor not only had the harshest of deals from the whole affair, but has not been well served by subsequent writing. As an unshowy person, she was easily overlooked and naturally, having married one of the most notorious spies of the century, she was by comparison a bit-part player. To some she was merely 'pleasant, loyal and long-suffering', as one member of the British embassy staff put it. 'The easy thing to say about Eleanor was that she was the betrayed wife,' says Griggs. 'But she was a lot more than that. She really was. Eleanor was slender. She was not beautiful but her face was very alive. She had a great smile, and she was funny. She was soft-spoken, wry and had a real brain in her head. She wouldn't make the obvious joke about, say, a politician but she would make the kind of aside that made everybody, laughing, go: "*Yes!*" in recognition.'

It was a courage and strength of belief in love that had made her follow Kim to Moscow. Where those who knew her less well saw her as a bit-part victim, as collateral damage, a casualty of one of the Cold War's most intriguing figures, others were impressed by her desire to make the relationship work. Alice Brinton was one who admired her decision to go to Moscow. 'It couldn't have been easy for her as she knew she would shock friends and family (particularly among the Americans) by doing so,' says Brinton. 'So any admiration for her at the time was muted, but in hindsight one sees the devotion and/or love for her husband.'

There was an almost uncomprehending, obdurate defiance in her decency. 'Armour plated in innocence', she survived her unwitting marriage to a Soviet spy 'with personality triumphantly intact', said Patrick Seale.

Nicholas Elliott also applauded that spirit. He, too, hadn't been able to believe in anything other than Kim's goodness until it was too late. He knew what his former friend could be like, and admired her insistent belief in him. Even twenty-five years later, when he wrote his memoirs, he believed Eleanor 'would probably not have regretted the difficult and brave decision to join him in Moscow and try to make a new life together'. And who is to say that, had she not had to stay in the States for so long in 1964, she might not have been vindicated?

14

Brian and Anthony

While Eleanor had been trying to sort out her life and finances in London and elsewhere, the wheels of the spy world had continued to turn, though well away from the public's gaze. The 1963 revelation of Kim Philby's treacherous burrowing at the establishment's heart renewed the question of how many more idealists with little time for conventional patriotism had been politically moulded by the 1930s' 'climate of treason', in Andrew Boyle's memorable phrase? Confronting Philby should have provided the answer, but it did no such thing. Philby was the 'Third Man', but there was still no knowing how many others there might be.

As MI5 weighed up the ramifications of Philby's unmasking, events moved swiftly. An associate of Philby, Blunt and Burgess, artist and art dealer Tomás Harris, who, sixty years on, remains enigmatic, was due to be questioned by MI5 following further evidence from Flora Solomon, whose assertions about Philby had been so spectacularly vindicated. She had said Philby and Harris 'were so close as to give me an intuitive feeling that Harris was more than a friend'. Neither man was actively homosexual, so her meaning was clear. Harris had paid back the advance on a book Philby never wrote, helped pay Kim's children's school fees, arranged for Melinda

Maclean's travel to Moscow, and many suspected that at the very least he knew more secrets than was good for him. One day in January 1964 he was driving along a road that he knew well in Mallorca in broad daylight. His car crashed and he was killed. His death has never been satisfactorily explained.

Within fifteen months of Philby going to Moscow, another three Soviet agents had been formally confirmed as such – though secretly – by the British authorities. In the case of none of them was it a big surprise, and a case can be made that at least two of them had previously given a partial confession. John Cairncross, then living in Cleveland, Ohio, admitted that he had spied for the Russians. He was warned not to return to the UK, and in 1964 moved to Rome. Before he was twenty-one, Michael Straight, an England-educated American student at Trinity College, Cambridge, had been recruited, somewhat reluctantly, by Anthony Blunt. The impressionable Straight felt ambivalent at being asked by Blunt in 1937 to leave friends and family and return to the USA to perform Moscow's work, and Blunt later said he had always feared Straight would turn him in. After several false starts, in 1963 Straight eventually did so, to the FBI, leaving Blunt, later confronted again by MI5, little room for manoeuvre.* Clearly

---

* The paradoxes surrounding Straight's confession are multiple. The accepted version is that his own radical politics had long moved on and he needed to come clean about his past in order to take up a prestigious public job in the arts offered by President Kennedy. Yet not only did he turn the job down – making his FBI vetting unnecessary - he told his mother at the time he barely considered it. He wrote to her on 6 June 1963: 'I was called back to the White House on Tuesday, for lunch with Arthur Schlesinger and Augie Hecksher. I was asked, to my astonishment, to take Hecksher's post, setting policy for the arts. I thought about it for one day, and realized that it would be a mistake.'

He expressed loyalty to Blunt, yet he shopped him, offering to testify against him in court (though an official document said Straight's evidence could not be used for Blunt's prosecution – see West, *Cold War Spymaster*, p. 227), while also claiming he didn't realise that Blunt's and Burgess's guilt was unproven. He says there was no prior collusion, or mention of immunity, between him and Blunt,

and undeniably he was guilty, and now – however much MI6's boss Dick White may have suspected or known of the secret – MI5 knew it. Blunt was offered immunity from prosecution. Was there much point in pretending any longer? Kim Philby was in Moscow. Guy Burgess had died a few months earlier. Blunt's own belief in communism, such as it was, was in the past, and he had done his best – with marked success – to save his friends from the British courts. This was the end of that particular road.

In any event, Blunt confessed and accepted the legally sanctioned immunity deal that he was offered. Even the Prime Minister was not told, and life went on as before. Blunt went back to his Poussins and the Palace, hampered only by the continued probing of his MI5 interrogators seeking further miscreants. Years later Blunt claimed, not entirely convincingly, that 'a certain event' had freed him to confess. He never spelt out what it was. More likely is that, in this new climate not so much of treason but of immunity, the 'certain event' had been the culmination of several events.

In the late 1960s and 1970s, while Kim Philby was reconciling himself to life in the USSR, Anthony Blunt, who had rejected all attempts to lure him to Moscow, continued to excel as an art historian, writing books on Poussin, Picasso and Sicilian Baroque, his secret past as a Russian agent unknown to all but a handful. As Arnold Deutsch had

---

who, on the face of Straight's account in his 1983 book, was in danger of receiving a prison sentence comparable to that of George Blake. Blunt was, he said, grateful to him for lifting a weight from his shoulders. The publicly available version remains incomplete, at best.

Roland Perry, in *Last of the Cold War Spies*, questions Straight's claim to have renounced his loyalty to Moscow. For another interpretation of events, see www.coldspur.com/category/espionageintelligence/.

Blunt's biographer Miranda Carter says Blunt and Straight had little in common by 1963/4. She also says that Blunt disputed Straight's subsequent account. John Costello, in *Mask of Treachery*, reports Straight's denial of any collusion with Blunt in 1963/4.

predicted nearly thirty years earlier, he was never likely to give up his career for the sake of 'our work'.

One of the few who was let in on the secret was Brian Sewell, who had been one of Blunt's students at the Courtauld and became a close friend and confidant. Some regard Sewell as having been Blunt's star pupil, others as having been his lover. In either case, Blunt took Sewell into his confidence, or, rather, he asked a friend to. In the late 1960s, Blunt asked Sewell to take a picture to Andrew Gow, friend, executor of A. E. Housman and artistic guide to Blunt in his early years at Trinity College, Cambridge. After a look at the picture, the dry-as-dust Gow began talking to Sewell in highly confidential terms, revealing that Blunt had been a Soviet agent but had been given immunity from prosecution. It is unclear why Sewell needed to be given this information, but he was in no doubt that Blunt had asked Gow to tell the former pupil about his dark secret. A dozen or so years later, in 1979, following his exposure as having spied for the Russians, Blunt underwent days of intense media pressure, with photographers and report- ers swarming around the block of flats in central London where he lived while friends offered shelter from the storm. He answered few questions, and when he did, a haughty air and unwillingness to display contrition played into the hands of his many opponents in the press. Sewell, then working at Christie's was relied upon to shield Blunt from press queries. Though some of Blunt's friends became mildly competitive in the context of others being close to Blunt and claim Sewell's importance has been exaggerated, when Blunt went away to escape the press hounds it was Sewell's job to affect to be helpful but give little away. He also had a hand in encouraging former students to make public statements in support of Blunt's work at the Courtauld against those who felt the traitor should pay the due price.*

After leaving Christie's, Sewell became the art critic for the *Evening Standard* in 1984. As a mere reporter of gossip with the Londoner's Diary in the late 1980s, I found him terrifying and not very likeable. He struck me as elitist – for all the wrong reasons – intolerant, misogynistic and intellectually completely intimidating, and he seemed to positively enjoy *not* trying to dispel such impressions.

After several years of seeing how wrong I had been in almost all respects, in the late 1990s I plucked up the courage to ask him if he would ever talk to me about Sir Anthony Blunt, which I had assumed would be taboo. I had been told a number of outlandish tales about Blunt, and, if I trod carefully, imagined Brian would be well placed to confirm or deny, but it was a very long shot that he might say yes. To my surprise, he agreed to have lunch, at which he said what he knew, and didn't claim to know more than he did. But clearly he knew a lot.

Most of all, it was obvious he had been terribly close to Blunt, and we talked about him frequently. Brian wanted a decent book contract to write a 'big' book about Michelangelo, the greatest of artists, he felt, but his agent had long been trying to persuade him to write an autobiography. Aspects of the activities of the Cambridge Five continued to fascinate me, and in the early 2000s we agreed that he would talk to me with a view to my writing something in the future. 'I am cynical enough to know why people want me to write an autobiography,' he told me. 'The chapter on Blunt would be the one everyone would read.' He didn't want to 'tell all' about Blunt in a public

---

* London's great and the good indulged in protracted debates as to whether his mistakes should be left in the past or be paid for. See David Cannadine, *A Question of Retribution?*

forum, but he said he was happy 'to give you what information I can.' As it happened, after he discovered the identity of his father – the composer Peter Warlock – he did succumb to the temptation of writing a memoir, but he stuck to his intention of omitting the key story about Blunt.

He had been infatuated with his former teacher. I suggested that this rather mirrored the way Blunt himself had been infatuated with Guy Burgess, and he agreed. 'I adored him,' said Sewell. 'I think I saw things in Anthony that other people didn't see in him.' One day over lunch I asked him if they had been lovers and he howled with laughter, as if the very idea was absurd, though clearly he knew that was the commonly held belief. He said something about how he couldn't imagine him and Anthony in bed together – the sort of thing I, as a straight man, couldn't possibly understand, he said. What bound them together was a love of art above all.

Sewell was adamant that Blunt's dabbling in politics, a tragic blight on his career, was one he deeply regretted. During the war, Blunt provided the Russians with approximately 1800 official documents, but that, Sewell believed, was purely in the interests of fighting fascism. There was no residual belief in communism or loyalty for the Soviet Union. 'Once the war had come to an end he wanted nothing to do with any of it. He may have been pulled in two different directions. Anthony I am sure was driven by friendship more than anything else once the war was over. If saving Burgess's bacon meant dropping material somewhere, then OK, but that is not the same as supplying information.'

In this instance, Sewell, though the least credulous of people, seems to have been attaching too much importance to what sounds like Blunt's version of events. At the end of the war, Blunt persuaded a colleague to compile a list of all MI5's agents in diplomatic premises in London, which he then passed on to his Russian controller. He continued in this vein, though seemingly in decreasing quantities, until about 1951, so any idea that Blunt made a clean break with the Soviet Union after the war is not correct. For one thing, as Sewell suggests, he felt loyalty to his fellow conspirator friends and would continue to help ensure their safety. For example, in 1950 he acted as a go-between for Burgess, who was about to leave for the United States, in passing on to Yuri Modin details of secret talks to be held in Washington, and other documents. But other examples have emerged which do not easily qualify as 'saving Burgess's bacon', in Sewell's term.* In February 1951, for example, he identified the person charged with penetrating the new East German intelligence organisation. Did Burgess really have no other means of passing on documents? Blunt may have believed that to be the case. Nonetheless at his 1979 press conference, this exchange took place:

Q: 'What did you do for the Russians between 1945 and 1951?'
A: 'Nothing.'
Q: 'Absolutely nothing?'
A: 'No.'

Further, Blunt, by that time working chiefly on art history, claimed he was 'in no position to give [the Russians] anything of interest . . . they realised I was no longer interesting'. Yet, if only acting as a messenger for Burgess, he provided plenty. Spy writer Nigel West wrote after the telling Russian documents were revealed: 'Undoubtedly the damage inflicted by Philby, Burgess and Blunt can only be described as colossal, and on a much greater scale than has ever been publicly admitted.'

---

* He had a close call when he was stopped on the street in 1949 carrying a bundle of documents.

This is not to deny that Blunt was keen to get out. As his biographer Miranda Carter says, 'He was worn out and bored by it, found it horribly stressful and just wanted to get back to the thing he really minded about – art history.' And as the years passed, Sewell says, the enormity of his wrong choice became clearer and clearer to the essentially non-political Blunt.

Sewell remembered thinking how Blunt's statement, drafted by cabinet secretary Sir Robert Armstrong, read out to TV cameras in the office of *The Times*, had failed to communicate Blunt's true feelings.

'If Anthony had written it himself there would have been an element of contrition. He genuinely regretted being wrong. I remember Anthony saying, long before 1979, that he had increasing doubts about communism during the war, and at the end of the war he learned so much of what had happened in Russia under Stalin that he was completely repelled by it. Maybe up to May 1945, with the Cossack problem, he learned so much so quickly and it was so appalling that that was the end of it. My impression has always been that he learned something in 1945 and that this completely cut the communism out of him. Nothing came in instead. He vowed at that point never to have any politics. There was an element of contrition ... "How could I have been such a fool? How could I have been so duped?"'

We talked at some length about claims in Miranda Carter's biography that Blunt found Sewell's advocacy on his behalf in 1979 excessive, as if Sewell was too keen to thrust himself into the limelight, and that friends had been asked to help distance him. Sewell was, after all, something of a showman, and latterly a controversialist. For someone so shy, he enjoyed giving a performance. He was mystified, and tried, genuinely I think, to understand. Why, if that was the case, did Blunt choose to do so much with him? 'Frankly I didn't believe it. I did feel anger sufficiently energetically to want to find out [but] it's a dead episode, and there is nothing I can do. All I know is that I am absolutely confident that it is not true.'

Brian recalled a day in 1983 when he went to Blunt's flat to talk about Poussin landscape drawings. They circled copies of images on the floor, discussing their merits, the sequence in which they had been executed and so on. 'I spent the whole enormously pleasurable day there. The following morning Anthony was dead. It seems to me inconceivable he would have used me as a sounding board for a whole day if he'd wanted me off his back.'

Clearly Blunt admired Sewell's eye as an art historian, but was disinclined to say so. A mutual friend told Sewell years later that Blunt had called Sewell his 'most wide-ranging student' and that he was wasted at Christie's, and should have been in academe. Blunt, it seems, was extremely generous with his time to his students, but not demonstrative.

As Blunt grew older and more frail and in need of protection from the media, Sewell (with two eminent former colleagues) increasingly took on the role of carer. He feared Blunt might decide he had had enough. Sewell wrote to a confidant at the time: 'I am fearful for him. Unlike ordinary mortals whose levels of response are either single or interwoven, Anthony has an ice-cold strand to his nature that is separate from his functions as an art-historian and an affectionate and lively human being. His affairs are in order, his work as an historian largely complete, he has discarded the promised book on his espionage role, and there is no reason why he should not make himself comfortable with a bottle of whisky and an overdose. I have seen him through his cancer and cataract operations, and I know how rationally he can balance the quality of life against the effort of living it.'

Sewell says that had the 1979 exposure not happened, Blunt and his partner John Gaskin would have parted company. 'John had started behaving like a not quite discarded mistress – always complaining – and Anthony was at his wits' end ... He didn't know how to break with him. John would never have gone to the press about Blunt, but Anthony was bored out of his mind by someone with whom he had nothing in common. Whatever sex was there had gone. John became just disagreeable, unpleasant, the humour had evaporated. He hadn't a good word to say for anybody.' Sewell says Blunt was almost never disloyal about friends, but Gaskin had become so exasperating that he took Sewell into his confidence. 'Anthony poured out a good deal about John, but about nobody else.' He recalls Blunt's frustration that Gaskin would find consolation – sometimes obsessively – in nothing more challenging than kitchen chores. 'If I ever hear him slicing carrots again, I'll kill him,' confided Blunt on one occasion.

Sewell, who also found Gaskin's muscular charm had worn off in later life, did the lion's share of taking Blunt to hospital, feeling rather than being told of Blunt's appreciation. 'There was no hugging, except when he was so frail and needed to be,' said Sewell. 'He must have cared for me in some sense. It wasn't John Gaskin who took him to various hospitals. He could have got anybody to do it.'

The Queen had long known of Blunt's guilt and gone along with covering up the presence of a 'Traitor in the Palace', in order to prevent the Russians knowing he had been rumbled, and the few who needed to know had kept the matter under wraps for fifteen years. The Queen Mother, whose own politics in earlier years has been the subject of speculation, had been seen at the opera with him, a Kremlinesque sign for those alive to it that he was still a *persona grata*.

Blunt was heartened to receive a supportive letter from Prince

Charles, who had evidently not been in on the secret until Mrs Thatcher's announcement. 'Anthony was on the verge of tears as he read the letter,' remembered Brian Sewell, who said the letter was supportive, sympathetic and regretful. 'Anthony had a catch in the voice,' said Sewell. He was similarly moved when the staff of the local Italian restaurant applauded him after Sewell persuaded him to go out for a meal following a deluge of denigration in the media.

Alan Bennett's play *A Question of Attribution* contains a scene in which the Queen walks in on Blunt supervising the hanging of one of the Queen's pictures. The Queen engages brightly in conversation with her ill-at-ease employee, while Colin, Blunt's young assistant, hides under a banquette in embarrassment. Sewell told me that a very similar episode happened to him with Blunt at Buckingham Palace, and he speculated that Bennett might have got wind of the story through mutual friends and used it in the play. I asked Sewell why he had never mentioned his suspicion before. Evidently stung by previous criticism, he said he hadn't wanted to be accused of muscling in. In fact, it was pure invention on Bennett's part.

On 8 November 1981 the *Sunday Times* ran a story under the headline 'Blunt's secret visit to Philby in Beirut'. The story claimed that Blunt made a visit 'under the cover of a British Council-sponsored trip'. For those in the market for conspiracy theories, this was perfect. Blunt had indeed gone to Beirut with the British Council but, the paper suggested, the real reason was to see Philby. In response to the story, Blunt replied, admitting that in 1961 the two had indeed met during that visit, but 'my meeting with Philby was entirely due to chance and occurred at a party at the British Embassy'. He suggested that was the last time he saw Philby, making out that the trip was innocuous and of no significance. The *Sunday Times* said it was standing by its story, but the claim now looked hollow. Blunt's trip had not been secret at all – it was all above board and public. He had given two lectures, appeared on national television and given a recorded interview to Radio Liban. It was about as far from secret as could be.

At the age of twenty-two, Susan Schlaefle (then Susan Nicholas) spent Easter 1961 with her uncle Moore Crosthwaite at the British embassy. Her stay coincided with a visit of around a fortnight that Blunt made with John Gaskin. Schlaefle remembers Blunt as 'lofty, with his nose in the air'. 'I was just "Moore's niece"', she remembers. 'He had no interest in me being there and hardly addressed a word to me beyond "good morning". John Gaskin was nice and affable but he was not. Blunt would have had plenty of opportunity for seeing Philby if he wanted to. He was very busy on British Council business, and did [TV and radio etc.], but that aside his time was his own. Blunt was away all day. What he did all day, God only knows. He just disappeared. Whether he was fraternising with Philby or not, I don't know. I had no idea, and I don't suppose anyone else did. So I spent a lot of time, just passing the time of day with Gaskin.' Whatever Blunt got up to in any spare moments on that trip in 1961 – and surely it would be surprising if they had not arranged some sort of rendezvous, aside from the 'chance' meeting at the embassy – the *Sunday Times*'s account, that he had gone secretly to see Philby, was deflated.

But what Blunt knew, and the *Sunday Times* never discovered, was that Blunt made a second visit to Beirut. The first one, at Easter 1961, was well publicised, in Beirut at least. The second one, in December 1962, just a few weeks before Philby disappeared, was the significant one. It was arranged at short notice, spurring his welcoming host Moore Crosthwaite to arrange an impromptu drink at the embassy (which Blunt, wanting to keep a low profile, would presumably have preferred not to have taken place). It was during that occasion that Blunt made his claim about looking for an orchid.

In 1979, for one person in particular, the picture had become sickeningly clear as a result of Blunt's exposure by Mrs Thatcher. After retiring in 1966, Sir Moore Crosthwaite returned to England and renewed his friendship with Blunt and others, buying a large house in Clapham, south London, which he shared with Dick Spaulding, an uncomplicated, muscular and saintly American. Crosthwaite went to enormous lengths to help his siblings' offspring, including financially, playing the role of benign uncle to a tee. Brian Sewell remembers Blunt, though a few months Moore's junior, taking an elder brother role in Moore's company. 'Moore was an endearing but silly old fuddy duddy. Watching Anthony with Moore was interesting. Anthony was always incredibly patient with him, very good and sweet.'

But suddenly things started falling into place. Moore Crosthwaite, an irreproachable patriot who had known nothing of Blunt's pre-war Soviet sympathies and had assumed his friend had no enthusiasms beyond the artistic, tumbled to what Blunt had been up to. He concluded that the real reason for Blunt's surprise visit in Beirut in December 1962 (i.e. the second visit) was not to see him or to look for an orchid but to see Philby. His anger was volcanic, and he never spoke to Blunt again. Sewell recalled being summoned to meet Crosthwaite in central London.

'Moore felt betrayed. He didn't want to be seen talking to me. He was terrified.' Crosthwaite had asked to see Sewell in order that Blunt should be in no doubt of his feelings. 'Moore was really hysterically angry. He felt that he and everything he had done during his life had been put at risk by Anthony's visit and that he had not been told the true reason for the visit. That deceit was unforgivable. He was almost in tears with anger and disappointment.'

The encounter took on a tragi-comic air. 'I had to meet him in Harrods to be told this, in the book department, so we wouldn't be noticed and [to be] quite certain it couldn't be bugged. And in the hustle and bustle of Harrods at that time of year one was unlikely to be overheard ... you wouldn't have someone listening in with an ear trumpet. And that was the extent of the meeting. There was nothing else to discuss.'

Crosthwaite had been interviewed about Blunt, his continental cycling partner of the late 1920s, in Sweden when he was ambassador there in the mid-1960s. It is not known how much he mentioned of Blunt in Beirut. He may have chosen not to add to the case against Blunt because he doubted the claims could be true. (He did not know that by then Blunt had made his secret confession to the authorities.) This may explain why he was now, in the Harrods book department, quite so concerned about eavesdroppers. Sewell said Crosthwaite was interviewed again in late 1979 or early 1980, but he didn't know how much the former ambassador revealed.

Susan Schlaefle confirms that the second visit in late 1962 hugely upset her uncle when, years later, he realised the real reason for the visit was to see Philby. She says Blunt behaved in 'the most incredibly disloyal way'. 'Moore was absolutely devastated,' she said. 'You'd feel you'd been completely used and trampled on. He was disgusted and upset ... He was extremely bitter about it and about how he had been taken advantage of.'

After the public exposure of Blunt in 1979, he spoke little. But those who spoke for him were keen to emphasise that his enthusiasm for the Soviet Union had died long before, and that after the war his role had been essentially non-existent. This was as true as the Russians would allow it to be, but he had not severed contact entirely – because at the very least he still felt an obligation to his 'friends', those who had made the same decision he had made in secretly signing up with

Stalin. He failed to mention his role as a go-between in the six years after the war, and that this continuing loyalty to friends meant he had helped Burgess and Maclean to escape in 1951, and that he had helped the Russians bale out an impecunious Philby in the early 1950s. To that list, surely, can be added that he colluded with Philby before he was confronted by the British in the winter of 1962/3.

How did Blunt prevent the story of his travels gaining currency after the *Sunday Times* story in 1981? In short, I suggested to Brian Sewell, in his letter responding to the paper, Blunt lied. He misled the reporters. Not exactly, said Sewell. 'This is Anthony dissembling ... he knows they've got hold of the wrong visit, so he's safe.' In 1981 Blunt could confidently answer questions about the first visit, which wasn't secret at all.

Sewell says Blunt was 'furious' with Mrs Thatcher for making public his immunity deal, but in 1981 he remained as keen as the British authorities to play down the extent of his activities. The revelation that he had made a second, secret visit to Beirut at just the moment his friend Philby was about to be confronted would have been very incriminating. It would have been an invitation to the press to ask further questions and would have wrecked the narrative, convenient for both Blunt and the government, that he had done 'absolutely nothing'. By contrast, as Sewell pointed out, there was no great controversy about Blunt going to Beirut with the British Council in 1961. 'Whatever MI5 and MI6 knew about Kim Philby in 1961 wouldn't have been dangerous enough to prevent [Blunt] visiting the embassy in Beirut. But a couple of years later was a very different kettle of fish.'

Sewell said: 'I think he would have perceived considerable menace if he'd admitted he tipped [off Philby] ... at that particular juncture. If that had got out, it would simply have thrown ... he must have decided it was worth the risk of lying, but in fact it wasn't a lie, it was dissembling . . . The visit that he is writing about is one that is out in the open. The visit we are talking about is one that he made covertly. They were talking about a visit of which everybody knew [in 1961], the British Council knew, lots of academics in Beirut [knew] . . . and so he could deny that there was anything in it.'

Blunt had faced a considerable risk with his Beirut venture. He and Philby were both extremely adept at shaking off anyone following them, but Blunt was under suspicion by MI5 (or at very least on its radar) and being seen with Philby – at a time when Philby's guilt or innocence was the hottest of topics and he might well have been being watched, in a city where spies were thick on the ground – would have been hugely incriminating. It might also have risked the Russians becoming involved. They had long tried to persuade Blunt to defect to Moscow, and he had been resolute in refusing, but they were not above kidnapping their own agents in order to keep them out of harm's way. Although there was self-interest in him travelling to Beirut, he was also being loyal to his friend in the face of danger.

Even if there was a tip-off, Philby didn't flee immediately, but waited to see what Elliott had to offer.

Sewell suggested that 'Anthony may have been frustrated at Philby's staying put'. I have no idea if Sewell was in reality saying that he knew this for sure and was wanting to steer me towards this truth while remaining loyal to Blunt, or whether he really didn't know. In any case, by waiting, Philby imposed a need on himself to play for time – in this case, to confess, which was to be implicit in his eventual departure in any case. As part of his playing for time, Philby denied Blunt's guilt, both verbally and in his two-page document. He may never have had any intention of doing otherwise, but Blunt's visit may well have bolstered that loyalty. Whether Blunt trusted Philby or not, there was no doubt in Sewell's mind that Blunt went to Beirut to alert him. Their common experience, at very least, remained a bond.

In his play *An Englishman Abroad*, Alan Bennett has Guy Burgess in Moscow countering a common misconception – that because he and Maclean had fled England together they must have been close friends. The invented Burgess speech runs: 'Maclean is not my friend, no ducky, oh no. He's so unfunny, no jokes at all. He's the last person one would have chosen, had one had the choice. Here we are in this terrible tandem together. Debenham & Freebody, Crosse & Blackwell, Auden and Isherwood, Burgess and Maclean.'

Conversely, Blunt and Philby had not been obvious friends. Philby felt something of an inferiority complex about Blunt, according to MI6's Desmond Bristow, and early in their association the great aesthete found Philby's 'need to charm' irksome. Their most common bond was their 1930s idealism when they had both fallen in with Edith Tudor-Hart, who Blunt later described as 'the grandmother of us all'. But in later life, as two survivors and two apologists for Guy Burgess, they came to be much closer than has been commonly supposed.* The book by Barrie Penrose and Simon Freeman contains a telling quote from Brian Sewell just a few years after Blunt's death in 1983: 'Anthony was capable of long-term affection and to his dying day spoke of Kim Philby with great affection ... the affection that Anthony had for Kim seemed to me at least as strong as any he expressed for Guy Burgess.'

Either could have betrayed the other to the British authorities, yet both held firm.

Certainly Philby shared the fury at the Thatcher decision to unmask Blunt. While the tabloids went for the kill,

---

* Hugh Trevor-Roper called Burgess an '*homme fatal* whom no one knew with impunity'.

1500 miles away Kim was angry with Mrs Thatcher on his friend's behalf. 'He got immunity, and she violated it. This is unprecedented for the British – they keep their word,' said Rufina Philby, voicing her late husband's feelings recently, and recalling his appreciation of class nuance. 'Kim worried about Blunt. Especially after Thatcher's performance ... He said she was a bourgeois, not a lady.' In fact, before making the announcement Thatcher had confirmed that the deal did not include a commitment to confidentiality, though this did not prevent her being accused of ratting on the spirit of the arrangement.

Some weeks after Thatcher's 1979 announcement, a package arrived at Philby's flat in Moscow, anonymously. It contained no message. Nor did it need one. Philby recalled: 'When I opened it I found a fine engraving of a column in Rome, that of the Emperor Marcus Aurelius Antoninus, the Antony who had done battle against the Germans ... It was so like Blunt to have done something like that.' Philby kept it on his wall 'to remind me of the battles we fought against the Germans'. He thought if he acknowledged it, even in a private letter (that would be likely to be opened), he would embarrass Blunt, so he never did. Philby's reaction to being confronted by Elliott, whether influenced by Blunt or not, encouraged neurosis and a thirty-year molehunt among the British authorities. The mischievous Philby, if not Blunt, would have been delighted.

There remains one final possibility. That having at least acknowledged a degree of guilt in the mid-1950s, Blunt was helping Dick White more than has ever been admitted (though short of incriminating Philby). Is it possible that White – believing that Blunt was now acting as a patriot – asked Blunt to travel to Beirut during the Christmas break to try to persuade Philby to confess? That Blunt, a figure trusted by both sides, was being used – as he had been a few years earlier when Guy Burgess was considering returning to Britain – to convey London's thinking? Such a possibility does not mean that Blunt had admitted he knew of Philby's guilt – he could merely have been acting as a messenger – but White had been long convinced Philby was guilty and maybe he hoped Blunt would be a convincing advocate for the benefits of confession. If White believed that on balance Blunt had been helpful to MI6's cause and he believed a Philby confession could do the same thing, who better to act as its salesman than Anthony Blunt himself? If Blunt travelled to Beirut to see Philby at White's instigation, that would be another reason for him to keep his visit low-profile. Yet for Blunt to go to Beirut and not see his friend Sir Moore Crosthwaite would have appeared extremely odd, hence, possibly, the semi-private visit and the need for the claim about looking for an orchid.

Could it be that Nick Elliott was not the first emissary who MI6 hoped might persuade Philby to tell all? If so, Nicholas Elliott seemed to know nothing about any previous visit by Blunt, or indeed of official knowledge of Blunt's guilt. He told Andrew Boyle later that as he travelled to Beirut to confront Philby he thought to himself: 'If that scoundrel Blunt only knew where I was going, he'd sit up in his bed, sweating.'

White's later conversations gave little encouragement to the idea that Blunt was travelling on his behalf, and the trip itself was known to only a handful of people until recently. There is no conclusive evidence either that Blunt was White's emissary or, conversely, that Blunt's visit was conducted with the intention of tipping off Philby, just as there are no solid grounds for many Philby-inspired theories. Tom Bower believes that out of the three MI6 people he spoke to who were chiefly concerned with the challenging of Philby – White, Elliott and Peter Lunn – White was the only one who seemed to be holding anything back. Blunt's second Beirut visit and his refusal to acknowledge it remain unexplained.

15

Unspent convictions

Where did it all go wrong? The reason the marriage was doomed is that Eleanor and almost everyone else underestimated Kim's attachment to the ideals of his early adulthood. Most of those who regarded themselves as friends assumed that his enthusiasm for the left and communism was just a youthful fling. Certainly most of his compatriot acquaintances were taken in by the pretence he began in the mid-1930s. What they didn't realise was that in his own hierarchy of priorities, even for this loving husband and father, politics trumped everything.

Stalin once said that implementing communism in Britain would be like putting a saddle on a cow. The implicit utilitarian liberalism of the British mindset – the loathing of rigid ideology, articulated by George Orwell's writing – made an attachment to doctrine and dogma faintly ridiculous, and was certainly not the sort of thing most public-school chaps had much time for. But Kim was ripe for the plucking when he signed up with Moscow. He had a social conscience, loathed his parents' boss-class friends (any idealism they had having been corrupted out of them by money), had seen how the social democratic left vacillated and shrank when it was needed most, despised the failure to confront fascism and equated any moderation of the principles of his youth with selling out, just as the Labour Party had done. And he contributed his own gifts – including a monstrous talent for deceit – to the struggle. The path was set early.

Where many in the West would have endorsed the diagnosis, they would not have endorsed his prescription – the abandonment of openly espoused liberal democratic politics by going undercover. And if they once did admire the means and admired the Soviet 'experiment' of the 1930s, the revelation of Stalin's purges, the show trials against the Trotskyists of 1936–8, the restrictions on personal freedom and the widespread poverty opened the eyes of most of them.

His friends also took it for granted that Philby's politics were the same as theirs. Ideologies and politicians come and go, but twentieth-century government was essentially about muddling through and making the best of whatever the circumstances. If democracy came under threat, then all means possible should be used to protect it, but everyone knew that moderate old Britain knew better than to have much truck with autocrats and extremists. Indeed, *theory* itself was generally thought pretty rum. It occurred to almost nobody that easy, genial Kim might still be fighting the political struggles of the 1930s, shooting for the same utopia that so many had abandoned.

He never moved on. Hugh Trevor-Roper remembers meeting who he thought was a kindred spirit but realised Philby's mind was fossilised. 'He was I believed an intellectual and yet he never seemed willing to discuss any intellectual subject. How one longed, in those drab, mechanical days, to escape from routine work and routine postures and to discuss ideas! And yet Philby, who seemed so intellectual, so sophisticated in his outlook, who was so different from most of our colleagues, and whose casual, convivial conversation I found so congenial, never allowed himself to be engaged. In the end I sometimes wondered whether he was really an intellectual after all.' ... Like the sixteenth-century Jesuits 'the subtlety of their minds does not entirely evaporate, but it is withdrawn from the world of ideas. It is exercised only at surface-level, on trivialities, outside the area of real thought. At the heart, in the mind, on all real topics, it is closed for ever: frozen, sterilised, sealed up.'

Cambridge contemporaries would confirm that Philby decided early on his enthusiasms. Among playwrights, he admired Ibsen, but his preferred novelists were Russian – Turgenev and Dostoyevsky whose work he read repeatedly, as if there was no point in reading anything else. Along with the communism, he became a Russophile as young man.

In his foreword to *My Silent War*, Graham Greene wrote of Philby's 'chilling certainty in the correctness of his judgement, the logical fanaticism of a man who, having once found a faith, is not going to lose it because of the injustices or cruelties inflicted by erring human instruments'.

Philby, of course, would contest Trevor-Roper's 'death of the mind' thesis. His adherence to the course he had set himself in the 1930s can be explained as follows. He had three options, he said. One was to give up politics entirely, but it was 'politics alone that give [his tastes and enthusiasms] meaning and coherence'. Second, he could switch politics, but he saw the politics of the Baldwin–Chamberlain era as not mere folly but 'evil'. In a counter to the charge of conceit, he says he didn't fancy being a querulous, Muggeridge-style outcast, 'railing at the movement that had let *me* down, at the God that had failed *me*' (his italics). Or he could 'stick it out, confident in the faith that the principles of the revolution would outlive the aberration of individuals, however enormous'. He quotes an exchange in a Graham Greene novel. '"The poor, right or wrong," she scoffed. "It's no worse – Is it? – than my country, right or wrong. You choose your side once and for all – of course, it may be the wrong side. Only history can tell that."' Later he says, notwithstanding political quarrels with friends and the appalling events of his lifetime, he is confident history would vindicate him. From his Moscow window he sees 'the solid foundations of the future I glimpsed at Cambridge'.

This high-minded account should be read with an awareness of how Stalin's Soviet Union treated those who turned their back on it. Plenty of people have speculated that Philby could have chosen to opt out – maybe in 1939 or in 1944, or 1955/6 – but breaking with the Russians would have brought a considerable cost. Did he know so much that they would have wanted to silence him? It is impossible to know, but there are few if any signs that he ever wanted to sever his ties, however autocratic the Stalin regime or how many people he was sending to their deaths.

But the most spectacular underestimation of Philby's commitment was by the Russians themselves. It was there that the key to his tragic tale lies. When he left Beirut for Moscow, in a sense he felt he was going home. A friend reported that he once told Eleanor (in Moscow) that he had always dreamed of going to Moscow and been frightened that he would never make it. He had served in the field, and had survived as an agent for a remarkably long time. The time for the furtive double life was over. Now, with the help and grateful support of the Soviet government, with a sigh of accomplishment and relief he could reveal himself and his driving beliefs to the world, and – still just fifty-one – he could help build a better world. But few believe that his subsequent twenty-five years in Moscow provided the reflective vindication and contentment he had hoped for.

Philby's opponents, many still fighting the first Cold War, are inclined to gloat over the Soviet Union's economic problems and Philby's personal circumstances in a small Moscow flat, where he drank too much and wistfully pored over English newspapers and the cricket scores, while living in hope of the arrival of chutney, mustard, marmalade, kippers and decent whisky.

Philby insisted that the deprivations he suffered in Moscow were insignificant, and that he had no regrets about the choices he had made. The new Jerusalem he wanted to help build was going to take longer than a couple of decades. But Mikhail Liubimov confirms a widespread impression in the West that he was thoroughly unhappy. He felt, said Liubimov, 'a complete disillusionment from Soviet reality'. 'He saw all the defects, the people who are afraid of everything. That had nothing to do with any Communism or Marxism which he had a perception of.'

Philby had been politically weaned on the heroic fight against fascism and a brighter future based on an optimistic aspiration for the improvability of human nature. Murray Sayle said he was a Marxist only in a tribal sense. 'The more I saw of Kim, indeed, the less he looked like New Soviet Man and the more he came over as a stubborn, old-fashioned English eccentric, sticking to rusty guns and be damned to the lot of you.' His associates say he was never very engaged by philosophy. Beyond his anti-fascism, he had imbibed plentifully from a kind of romantic, meliorism-related optimism pegged hopefully to a Marxist analysis of capitalism. The killing of millions in the Stalin purges had had no place in that.

Just as wars change those who fight them indelibly – though there must be some mitigation when there is a sense of shared purpose with one's peers – so the espionage business had left a huge mark on Philby in his comparatively friendless mission.

His former KGB colleague Mikhail Bogdanov talks of Philby's 'good hardening up' process in the mid-1930s when he was required to jettison his left-wing friends and feign support for fascism. It was the start of nearly three decades when he suffered, tricked his friends, kept his wife Aileen and children in the dark, lived in fear of slipping up and being exposed and imprisoned, all for the sake of his dream. He was required to deceive on an encyclopaedic scale, which, however adept at it, would shake the equanimity of anyone.

Christopher Andrew says, 'Philby had an extraordinary personality change over twenty or thirty years, and for very obvious reason. Doing bad things and having good people killed, even for the best intentions, actually changes your personality – and ought to change your personality. It's a punishment for doing bad things.' His stammer helps Philby appear unthreatening, apparently not a controlling individual. 'So here is one of the British traitors' most controlling personalities – as he subsequently becomes – with extraordinary personal charm and a speech impediment.' He thus finds his métier. 'This modest individual becomes extraordinarily pleased with himself.'

Hugh Trevor-Roper had Philby in mind when he wrote: 'Ideological conversion is a form of intellectual cautery: the intensity of the experience burns out a part of the mind so that it can never be restored. So the culture, the urbanity, the sophistication of such men may remain untouched elsewhere; but where the faith is involved they are moral and mental automata. The sixteenth-century Jesuit, ex-humanist and new machiavel, poet and assassin, equivocator and saint, has his successors in a new age of ideological strife.'

But the truth, which Kim was reluctant to admit to Eleanor, was that the Russians did not trust him. He had displayed the submissiveness coefficient that Borovik had alluded to, but the object of his devotion remained aloof and at one remove. In that context, his relationship with Eleanor was doomed.

The fact of not being trusted is surely the greatest, most truly ironic of his tragedies, compounding an already less than competent handling of him by the Kremlin's agents. Had Philby had his way, it ought to have been possible to assert 'Moscow couldn't believe its luck', but often it simply *didn't* believe its luck. On and off, and led by Elena Modrzhinskaya, it believed the bonanza of documents he and others provided was too good to be true.

Espionage was central to Philby's essence. According to Peter Wright, he could never understand the importance of art in Anthony Blunt's life. Blunt himself told Wright: 'Kim and I had different outlooks on life. He only ever had one ambition – to be a spy. I had other things in mine.' To help in achieving that goal, Philby had a zealot's faith, he was ideologically fired up by the fight against fascism, he helped recruit a network of like-minded subversives, nightly he risked his career by removing highly sensitive, invaluably revealing documents from Whitehall, he was uninterested in money, he alienated many who loved him, but still Moscow suspected him.

Not only did it mistrust him, but years after the doubts should have been stilled, its behaviour towards the new arrival, initially at least, in reality verged on the contemptuous. He was 'tossed aside', admitted Oleg Kalugin. Efforts were made to show appreciation of Kim. Individually, the Russians who sought to make Eleanor feel welcome were kind, but they were under instructions. In fact, she never really saw the bigger picture – that in those early years the authorities felt his usefulness had been exhausted.

Ultimately a burned-out spy is a useless spy. Boris Volodarsky, the academic expert on extramural KGB murders, says foreign spies were regarded as dispensable. Just as he doubts Aileen Philby would have been one of its victims – 'The KGB couldn't have cared less about Aileen' – they obviously didn't care much about Philby, he says. 'For them generally, foreign agents for the KGB are trash, expendable staff. They only care about their own officers working undercover, especially illegals. If you study the life of almost every Western traitor in the Soviet Union after his defection, you'll agree.'

The signs were there from the morning he arrived in the

Soviet Union. An official put his hand on Philby's shoulder and said: 'There is a rule in our service: as soon as counterintelligence takes an interest in you, this is the beginning of the end. We know that British counterintelligence became interested in you in 1951. And now it's 1963 . . .' This was the truth, key parts of which had been obscured – at best – from him up till then. In the previous days, while preparing his escape from Lebanon, he was tricked. 'He was told he would be in Lubyanka,' said Liubimov. Others imagined he was to be made a KGB general, or put in charge of the KGB's work in Britain. But none of this was true. He was designated a mere agent, rather than an officer, of the KGB, an important distinction. He was not to work in the Lubyanka after all. He only visited the building twice in twenty-five years, and then for trivial matters. Nor would he be involved in policy, nor given an office of any description, initially at least. Instead, he was constantly observed.

'Any normal man who'd accomplished the feats Philby had would [expect to] get his own study, his own telephone, a desk. It never happened. Nothing happened. He became a sort of a little beggar somewhere in a little apartment. It was three rooms but very small . . . The KGB told him they were afraid the British MI6 was going to try to assassinate him, so he had to have guards all the time, close surveillance,' Liubimov said.

Philby called his first few months in the Soviet Union 'the most idiotic period' of his life. He had already told the Russians all he knew, but was required to repeat himself. He was, he said, like a boiling kettle, so bubblingly full was he of good intentions as to the contribution he wanted to make. These hopes for involvement in policy were understandable, but even Mikhail Liubimov was surprised at his expecting it from the start. Here was the ingenuousness that the young Lennie Copeland saw. 'How naïve, especially coming from a professional intelligence officer,' wrote Liubimov, who didn't meet Philby until 1975 but discussed his early years in Moscow at length. Would any country in the world allow defectors immediate access to its agents' files? 'Philby could not grasp that he was no longer a valued agent, but a problem, especially given the KGB's obsession with secrecy.'

Where SIS was embarrassed, the KGB failed to exploit its victory. How could it be sure he wasn't a plant, part of a devilish British plot? Whether he was or not, how could they be sure he wouldn't give an unguarded interview or, even worse, simply return to London? Far from coming home to a rapturous welcome after all that sacrifice, here he was, pathetically looking for signs of approval from his masters. 'I was full of information that I was keen to hand over, I wrote countless memos, until I realised that no one wanted them, no one even read them,' he said. It was a disappointment shared by his fellow moles Guy Burgess, Donald Maclean and George Blake, none of whom were given jobs befitting of their talents and sacrifices for the Soviet cause. 'Blake in particular was amazed he wasn't given a proper job,' said Tom Bower, who got to know Blake in Moscow in the 1990s. 'None of them could believe they weren't trusted.'

Anthony Blunt understood how much Philby needed approbation from above. Ten years earlier, in London, the Russians wanted Blunt to hand over cash to the unemployed Philby, then extremely hard up. Blunt told Yuri Modin: 'Meet him yourself. He needs that. Maybe more than the money.' 'The KGB was too stupid and impotent to make use of him,' Liubimov told Ron Rosenbaum. 'This destroyed him. This ruined his life ... he wanted to be a hero of this country,' Liubimov says. 'But they did everything to prevent him from this.'

So desperate was he that, when a cab failed to arrive for him, he half jokingly asked if he could be put in charge of the local taxi service – he would know how to make the system more efficient. Despite obviously craving a role and more than a cursory acknowledgement of his past service and appreciating his privileges – travelling to Cuba, Bulgaria (for the food) and Czechoslovakia, tickets to the Bolshoi – he never gave any reason to think he might rock the boat. He was exemplary in obeying official diktats about personal behaviour and discretion.

But a big reason why his commitment was doubted was Eleanor. Clearly he was in love with her and wanted her to be happy. Yet she was not buying into the dream, merely tolerating her husband's devotion to it, as if it was a favourite piece of ugly furniture that he refused to throw out. She insisted on travelling abroad to see Annie, which sent tremors of paranoia around the Lubyanka, which was already wary of her husband. What was she up to? Who was she seeing? What was she bringing back?

She was devoted to Kim. Why else would she be there? But by remaining so independent, so impervious to the spirit-numbing effect of Soviet rule, so unsettled and, simply, so *American*, she didn't fit the script. 'It was very hard for an American lady to live in Moscow in those times,' says Mikhail Bogdanov. 'It was like day and night, two completely different civilisations. I remember the very, very poor quality of life. You cannot compare Moscow now and then. You had to queue for bread and tomatoes. There were shortages of everything. For her it was very difficult to get used to this, as it was for him. That is why he started to drink again.'

Where Kim wanted to ingratiate himself with the Kremlin and continued to nourish futile hopes of being allowed to help build the Soviet Union's brighter tomorrow, Eleanor was looking the other way. Why are the shops so poor? Why is it so cold? Why won't they let me restore church frescoes? Eleanor wanted to straddle two hemispheres and hang on to both her husband and her daughter, but in the end she couldn't, the choice taken out of her hands by Kim's affair with Melinda Maclean. She felt Melinda had seduced her blameless husband, but ultimately she still found his ideological commitment baffling. He believed with his politics he was taking a stand for humanity, for the improvability of the lot of the oppressed and for fairness. To her, that had nothing to do with decency and love.

Amateur psychologists adduced Cambridge in the 1930s as an explanation for Philby's otherwise unaccountable behaviour. They also pointed to his father. The record of middle-class Englishmen in the first half of the twentieth century as standard-bearers for female emancipation was poor and the assumptions of St John Philby – colonial adventurer, explorer and savant of the Arab world – complied entirely with those standards. He was also on occasions a fierce father. Kim was born left-handed but made to use his right for writing. He was circumcised at nine months and found the experience as distressing as most little boys do. The letter St John wrote to his (St John's) mother at the time is telling: 'It is a good thing to have had it done – I hope he will not be such a wet little boy in future. Really he is a perfectly sweet child and I do hope he is going to develop an intellect as I hope he will do all that I would have liked to do myself.' Kim may never have seen the 'wet little boy' letter, but the wording reflects a strikingly demanding tone even allowing for the attitudes of the time. Further, St John loading up his expectations on his son's shoulders, which Eleanor believed he longed to live up to, must have compounded a natural diffidence in his son, who told Nicholas Elliott that he blamed his father for his stutter.

At the age of seven Kim was told he was expected to win a scholarship to Westminster and Cambridge. This he later managed, though he had wanted to go to Oxford. Westminster, which generally he enjoyed, also brought what must have been distressing experiences – with homosexuality and confirmation into the Church of England. He told a friend he had had a near-breakdown after being made to take confirmation, at odds with his own and his father's atheism.

He learned from his father not to be frightened of having strong opinions. The certainty that gave him allied itself at an early stage to a child's natural priggishness. Kim said himself that he had sympathy for the underdog and the oppressed from the earliest age. He reacted against his grandmother saying 'don't play with those children Kim, they're dirty and you'll catch something'. He later called himself 'a godless little anti-imperialist by the age of 8', having asked why Jesus cured only one leper when he could have cured them all, and complaining about 'Christ's conjuring trick' at the wedding in Cana.

But the echoes of his father's life in Kim's career are clear. St John never truly lived down his departure from the colonial civil service. The sense of certainty about his choices is also evident in his son, though Kim's ego was better concealed than his father's – a lesson learned from him, perhaps. St John fell under the spell of Ibn Saud and dedicated himself wholeheartedly to the Saudi cause and the unification of the Arabian Peninsula, rather as Kim did to communism.

A feeling common in Beirut was that Philby's lack of loyalty to Britain had come from his father, but then so did his lack of conventional beliefs of any sort. He was brought up with few of the handrails – love of country, class, church, profession, locality – that, for better or worse, customarily guided public-school boys through life. Resenting his father, he had to find his own bearings. He also lacked the sort of moral cut-out that usually prevents the squeamish middle classes from scandalising their peers in matters big and small, though he was more skilled at mitigation. Where St John the wicketkeeper would cheat at cricket or report a pilot for flying too close to Mecca or plot to damage British oil interests or endorse fascism, Kim would father children out of wedlock, pinch women's bottoms and rat on those who thought he was a friend – and all with something he did inherit, St John's sense of unassailability.

The writer Mel Trotter spoke to several people who knew both men. He wrote: 'Maybe Kim recognised in himself the same belligerence as his father but he had the ability to conceal it with charm and discretion. He was different from Harry, who disliked anyone who didn't agree with him. Charm was a quality that helped deceive friends, enemies and wives. It brought satisfaction to the talented spy but not happiness.'

His ideological commitment and flair for mendacity produce a mix that would bring discomfort to the decent. How could he live with himself, misleading, let alone hurting and killing so many people? We cannot know how indifferent he was. In some other respects he showed an admirable warmth and sensitivity, yet the eye was always cold-bloodedly on the political, which trumped all else.

It is tempting to see Philby as exceptional, and where his treachery was concerned he was indeed one of few. But, as MI6 authority Stephen Dorril says, 'Philby is not unique among MI6 officers in seemingly having what appear to be two personalities. What seem like negative traits could be positives for an intelligence officer. It may be a bonus to have the ability to switch from one to another – from the secretive, reserved and largely unreadable persona to the gregarious, very charming soul of the party intelligence operative.

'There is a neglected psychological idea – doubling – which may explain this behaviour. In drama two actors may play on stage at the same time two aspects of the same person. The technique has been used to understand how the Nazi doctors in Germany were able to be on the one hand model citizens, loving fathers and caring doctors whilst at the same time undertaking some of the most horrendous acts of inhumanity ever inflicted on a person. They were "doubling". It may be more common than we care to acknowledge.'

In concealing his true political loyalty, he left a trail among those with good reason to regard themselves as friends. After he arrived in Moscow in 1963, Philby wrote to a left-wing Palestinian friend, Walid Khalidy, with whom he had been accustomed to having long, detailed conversations about radicalism in the Arab world, the best way forward for the refugees and so on. He sent Khalidy, an academic who had appreciated Philby's words of support for the Arab cause, a letter expressing regret at his need for a swift exit, recalling fondly the chats long into the night that they used to have and saying 'I wish we could have spoken the truth to each other.' Khalidy was furious, remembers a friend. 'But that's exactly what I thought we were doing,' said Khalidy. He was amazed that Kim couldn't see a problem, simply expecting acceptance.*

Tim Milne was perhaps the man with most reason to feel cheated. He had behaved as a true friend to Philby on countless occasions and tolerated his generally drink- or women-related excesses, yet his colleague turned out not to be who he had assumed. He said later he did not regret knowing Philby, who had enriched his world, for all the difficulties he had caused him. 'I do not feel bitterness toward him, only sadness,' he wrote, but he never made contact with Philby again. Milne barely spoke to his family about the betrayal, and his daughter

---

* Hugh Trevor-Roper points to how the 'blindly egocentric' Philby clearly values the respect of his former friends, but seems quite unaware of having lost it. 'In his memoirs he regularly assures his old colleagues of his continuing "affection and respect" for them. For his old chief, Sir Stewart Menzies, he expresses "enduring affection". He protests that he does not wish to "embarrass" any of them. He seems to assume that if he spares them embarrassment, they will return his respect. He expresses regret for having had to lie to Menzies' successor, "the honest Sinclair," but hopes that Sinclair "now realises that, in lying to him, I was standing as firmly on principle as he ever did." And in his Preface he solicits sympathy from those whom his revelations may embarrass by explaining that "I too have suffered personal inconvenience through my connexion with secret service."'

recalls arriving at his home to see him gazing balefully at a bonfire. On this, she believed, he had thrown any papers that tied the pair together, his way of trying to move on. 'If the personal picture of [Philby] I have presented is friendlier than several others that have appeared, well, that is how I saw him,' wrote Milne.

As Ben Macintyre recounts in his book about their relationship, Nicholas Elliott was also mightily misled for years, although Elliott's public-school polish and phlegm concealed his fury later in life. In one of Elliott's books, though, he struggles to hide his bitterness in describing Philby's neglect of his children. He loved them 'after his fashion', said Elliott, but was uninhibited about getting drunk in front of them, and on one occasion risked Harry's life after knocking him into the sea during a picnic. Elliott chides Philby for his lack of involvement with his children's education and talks of a lack of warmth.

Mark Elliott is in no doubt as to the damage the affair did his father. 'Both Nicholas and Kim were incredibly complex characters, and both in their public and private lives were capable of remarkable betrayal. They were very close friends.'

The simple fact of the duplicity required by his profession and his friendship with Philby compounded an underlying insecurity. 'I found my father did some pretty bad stuff, not on the level of Philby,' says Elliott Jnr. 'Whether he had a conscience about it, I don't know, but he believed in the British cause. My father had a difficult time with his father. Claude epitomised the great and the good. He was not a religious man but he never told a lie. He was as straight as they come, and had very good instincts about people ... He didn't have that hurt, wounded quality that was very deep inside my father ... I think [my grandfather] had some severe questions about my father's moral positions in his job.

'My father used to take me to dinner at White's. It was bit

of an ordeal for me. ... There was an old buffer there who said: "Oh Nicholas Elliott ... not the man your father was." I wanted to punch the guy, but my father just didn't react. That was something he always had to live down. My father was a deeply sensitive, easily hurt person. He just wouldn't show it ... he was really bitter towards Kim, although you never saw that ... He could have been head of MI6. He was head of MI6 for Africa ... He didn't get a CMG. Everyone got a CMG, even Paul Paulson [Elliott's predecessor as SIS head of station in Beirut]. For my father that would have been important.'

The Americans in Beirut all seemed to have liked Philby, even if many back home didn't trust him. As G. K. Young put it: 'Philby was friendly with all the yanks in Beirut. A lot of them babbled. He was pretty good at getting them to talk.' (This may well have been precisely what Young hoped Philby would do in Beirut – get an idea of what the US was thinking and doing on the ground.) Of those in Lebanon, in a crowded field the person whose own career was most professionally damaged by Philby was Bill Eveland. Though more a professional acquaintance and useful contact than someone with a legitimate claim on friendship (even if he did lend Kim and Eleanor his flat in Rome for their honeymoon), Eveland used to drop his guard to a remarkable degree, notably with his friend and drinking partner Sam Brewer.

But Eveland was to pay a heavy price. The CIA operations that went wrong in the area – and there were said to be many – were blamed by the CIA on Eveland's indiscretion with Philby. (It may not be too big a leap to suppose that Philby's advance knowledge of the US Marines' 1958 invasion was down to Eveland, although some believe it came from MI6.) In 1959 Ed Applewhite had Eveland eased out of Beirut, via Washington, and into a job in Rome, having been deemed a security risk for passing secrets to Philby.

Eveland always denied the claims, and sought to be either charged or cleared, so that he could be given his pension. But his years in Lebanon haunted him. In November 1965 Eleanor Philby, interviewed by the CIA, reported with a characteristic lack of guile that 'all [Kim] had to do was to have one evening with Bill Eveland in Beirut and before it was over he would know of all his operations'. Eveland ran up a large hotel bill in Singapore, was gaoled for fraud and wrote a book revealing precisely the sort of details the CIA had accused him of revealing, few of which reflected his former employer in a good light. He died in poverty.

Sam Brewer, of course, was mightily misled by Philby, in more ways than one. Yet even he – for professional or other reasons – carried on dealing with Philby after Eleanor's change of allegiance. 'Like so many others, Brewer had fallen under Philby's spell,' said Harrison Salisbury. Brewer's employers, like Eveland's, tried to learn more about the sort of information Brewer might have passed on to Philby, but he was not disposed to talk. His record 'was not satisfactory to us and neither was his work', the paper concluded, and, in the end, decided to let him go.

The most famous employee of the CIA, James Angleton, Philby's frequent lunching partner in Washington, was another whose life was ruined by Philby. Angleton, brilliant and driven, never overcame the fact of being so comprehensively duped. One of his biographers, Tom Mangold, said: 'You cannot exaggerate how much Philby's betrayal of Angleton contributed to Angleton's paranoia and subsequent alcoholism and madness.' The concerns that Angleton voiced about the extent of Soviet penetration reverberated for years.

Esther Whitfield, Philby's loyal secretary in London, Turkey and Washington, had to leave MI6 in 1951 after Burgess and Maclean fled. She had lived in Philby's attic in Washington and

Burgess had hoped to marry her. She was personally blameless and knew nothing of her friends' Soviet links, but as someone who worked very closely and socialised with Burgess and Philby, no chances could be taken, and in the 1950s she was subject to particular interest from MI5. Before Guy Burgess died in 1963, he entrusted his will – of which the other beneficiaries were Burgess's Russian boyfriend Tolya, Blunt and Philby – to her. A sense of constantly being followed made her move to Rhodesia, where she lived with her brother for several years. She never repeated the professional achievements of her early years, moving to Alicante in Spain and eventually back to England. She died on 20 April 1989.

Philby's activities in the Ukraine, Albania, Turkey and Germany, when, directly or indirectly, he confounded so many of those who were struggling to assert national autonomy and liberal democracy, caused too many deaths for them to be counted reliably. It is true that in several instances the deaths would probably have taken place without Philby – he merely provided corroboration – but in time his allegiance became clear. Some, perhaps many, of those who died he knew personally. Yet this most sentimental, gentle man who suffered from the most human and banal of phobias (heights, apples, horses, the sight of blood) and who loathed seeing suffering dehumanised himself for his cause, taking on the role of remote, cold-blooded killer. Anthony Blunt was asked by his inquisitors about his feelings for those who died as a result of his treachery. 'There were no deaths,' said Blunt, almost as if he had forgotten. When reminded about an agent who was executed by the Russians after Blunt told the Kremlin he was feeding information to the British, he suggested that didn't count. 'He was a spy,' said Blunt. 'He knew the game; he knew the risks.'

Spies are paid to have hard hearts and not show weakness, but, inside himself, did he not feel a bit bad? When Kim and Eleanor were living in Moscow, Lorraine Copeland wrote to Eleanor with news, adding that she found it 'painful to think that during the years we all loved Kim and had him constantly in our homes, he was all the while laughing at us'. Kim was stung. He wrote at the bottom of Eleanor's reply: 'My dear Lorraine, I hope you never have to learn, as I have, that one lives one's life in several planes, and that when there is a conflict between the plane of one's ideals and that of one's friends it is, believe me, no laughing matter. Please accept, for whatever they are worth, my assurances that I will always have only the fondest thoughts for you and my other friends in Beirut.' It is a sentiment his friend Tim Milne found convincing: 'Friendship was always important to him. When he went to Moscow he gave up many things, but I should be surprised if he regretted any of his deprivations except that of his family and the people he knew best. He was sentimental and very loyal to friends, even Guy [Burgess], who he didn't really like.' It is true that Philby was furious at Burgess going to Moscow in 1951, winced at some of Burgess's other excesses and initially disliked his showiness, but the admiration for his brilliance remained. Graham Greene wrote that 'not the least admirable of Philby's human qualities [was] that for all those dangerous years he put up with Burgess, without nerve or humour failing him, or his affection'.

When politics and the personal come into conflict, he told Phillip Knightley, 'I have to put politics first. The conflict can be very painful. I don't like deceiving people, especially friends, and contrary to what others think, I feel very badly about it. But then decent soldiers feel badly about killing in wartime.' His friend Graham Greene sympathised, glossing over the fact of Philby's declaration of war being undisclosed: 'One cannot reasonably weep at the fate of the defecting spy Volkov, who was betraying his country for motives perhaps less idealist than Philby's.'

I asked Philby's KGB friend Mikhail Liubimov if he thought Philby had any regrets, either about his treachery or about the deaths he caused. He told me: 'He himself never considered himself to be a traitor ... he had to betray the people who fought against him ... I don't think he had any remorse ... it was a war ... the agents in Albania ... why? They were enemies.' This is not in any way to excuse Philby's behaviour, merely to observe that with the hardening of his heart, he paid an enormous price, much of it through his liver.

'The Albanians, Georgians, West Ukrainians, Armenians who were sent from Malta and betrayed by him ... they were the guys who chose to be on the path of war,' says Mikhail Bogdanov. 'They were not British. It was a war. Like any troop leader in war, he can be a teddy bear with his family but he has to kill and order his soldiers to kill the other side.

'On certain occasions he suffered, like with Tim Milne, Nicholas Elliott, maybe James Angleton, they had very good relations but the poor guy went crazy. Again he had a very hardening time in 1934 and '35 when he was asked to break all his communist connections and become pro-fascist. He suffered. It was very difficult for him just to throw away those friends at that time.' From the 1930s, in his mind he was only ever a warrior. He just never let his compatriots know until 1963.

Meanwhile, Kim's life after Eleanor in Moscow continued in its unsatisfactory way. The relationship with Melinda broke down, and she returned to Donald in 1968. Philby drank more heavily than ever and, little used by the KGB, towards the end of the 1960s slashed his wrists in a suicide attempt.

Earlier he had been afforded some sense of purpose by being allowed to write his memoirs, published in the West in 1968, which provoked much controversy as newspapers weighed up making a bid for serialisation as against the taint of association with a traitor. Most gave it a miss, discouraged by some vigorous below-the-surface lobbying by Whitehall, while feeding their readers' curiosity with brief reports of what was in them. Serialisation rights for the book were acquired by *Paris Match* magazine, prompting British mandarins to encourage the *Sunday Times* to write an obliging article asking 'Is there a French Philby?' Though clearly written under state control, his memoirs are generally regarded as offering enough truth to make them worth a sceptical reading. Philby and the KGB wanted the book serialised in an upmarket newspaper, which was precisely what Whitehall didn't want. For some time the *Sunday Times* was tempted, eventually deciding that running Philby's book might detract from the paper's own account of his life, written by the Insight team. The *Daily Express* stepped in to carry Philby's pleadings. Eleanor, accurately or otherwise, was quoted as saying Kim's *My Silent War* was long, dull and extensively rewritten by the KGB. She also believed it was for him 'just another way of needling the Americans'.

Kim's sense of mischief – and outright trouble-making – never left him, and some of his utterances from Moscow should be seen in that light. Others were more soundly based. As ever with a man for whom the word 'intriguing' might have been invented, the truth is evasive. One of his first missives from Moscow was to Nicholas Elliott: 'Dear Nick, I wonder if this letter will surprise you. Our last transactions were so strange that I cannot help thinking that perhaps you wanted me to do a fade' (i.e. to defect).* He suggested they meet in Finland, asking Elliott not to mention the idea to his wife or to Dick White.† He did both and didn't take the bait. Did Philby really believe MI6 had planned to push him towards doing a 'fade'? Did he

---

* Philby knew Elliott hated being called 'Nick' rather than Nicholas.

† Philby may have wanted one last opportunity to outwit his friend. Elliott said later, 'I mean, who the *hell* did he think I was, not telling them. The first person I'd tell was Elizabeth and, immediately after that, I'd tell Dick White [...] he wants to meet me because he's lonely. Well of course he's lonely. He shouldn't have gone.'

really want to express a degree of personal remorse at so comprehensively trampling on his friend's trust? A bit of both? It is impossible to know. But he seems to have remained on letter-writing terms with several of those from Beirut who wanted to keep up with him.

Contrary to the claim of some conspiracists, in Moscow Philby didn't meet his fellow mole George Blake until the spring of 1970. Initially they got on well. In July of that year the Blakes introduced him to Rufina Ivanovna, a Russian woman of Polish heritage twenty years his junior, originally as a possible companion for one of Philby's sons. Kim and Rufina hit it off, and the pattern of hurling himself into a relationship repeated itself, the pair marrying at the end of the year. Rufina said much later that she believed Philby had been trying to drink himself to death, but a new marriage raised his morale enormously.

By now living in a new, more central flat, off what was Gorky Street (now Tverskaya Street) and near Tryokhprudny Pereulok, he cut down on his drinking and found many more consolations in domesticity, although that would always take second place to his political aspirations. In that sphere, he continued to be isolated. For a long time the great master spy was not allowed to meet or lecture to KGB trainees, for fear that, with his impressive recall for faces, he might vanish back to London and reveal their identities to MI6. That was the biggest concern, confirmed the KGB's Mikhail Liubimov.

In addition to the contentedness he found with Rufina, the early 1970s brought an improvement in his standing with his Soviet hosts. Oleg Kalugin, at the suggestion of KGB chairman (and later President) Yuri Andropov, took responsibility, in short, for cheering Philby up. Andropov wanted more spies to defect to the USSR, and he wanted them to know how well they would be looked after. Though Philby had little interest in material possessions, he positively glowed at the improved furniture and fittings and the access to a special grocery store that Kalugin provided. He also sought his opinion on Western espionage. As a result the 1970s saw a considerable improvement in his mood. His sense of purpose increased and his drinking declined.

Miles Copeland lamented the damage Philby did to the West. 'What it comes to is that when you look at the whole period from 1944 to 1951, the entire Western intelligence effort, which was pretty big, was what you might call minus advantage. We'd have been better off doing nothing.'

Though unable to convince Moscow of his ultimate loyalty, he was at least able to advertise to the Russians his *dis*loyalty towards the country he had abandoned. David Cornwell said Philby's influence was ubiquitous and had haunted his entire career as an MI6 officer. 'The more one discovered about him the more evident it was that whatever one was doing in the past could have been compromised by Philby.' The Russians knew so much about Western security, he said, that if some disaster had not taken place 'it must not have happened by kind permission of the KGB'. Philby was happy to cause serious disruption, most notably in 1971 when he gave an interview to *Isvestia* and then to an Estonian magazine, *Kodumaa* (Homeland), published by the Soviet Committee for Cultural Relations with Compatriots Abroad.

In the latter interview, he identified specific MI6 activities in the Middle East, and named seventeen members of MI6 operating at the time in Lebanon. He accused these agents of being prepared to arrange a coup, of collusion with violent elements against 'unwanted activists' in the country and of organising propaganda operations across the region. 'Such operations have poisoned the atmosphere of the Near East for decades and are organised by [British intelligence] in almost all states.'

He also claimed that 'the most disquieting fact ... is that [British intelligence] has penetrated the means of English mass news media on a wide scale'. Unimpeachable documents, he said, show 'that the respectable BBC is capable at any time of broadcasting the basest disinformation prepared by [British Intelligence]'. He claimed that 'scores' of paid British agents were working with the staff of British newspapers, 'ready to fan the campaign of the cold war started by the Conservative government.'

When they discovered his treachery MI6 moved as many of its staff as possible to other areas. So shaken was the service by this breach that a relation of one of those who had to move was told not to collaborate with this book, half a century later. An organisation whose existence was only publicly admitted in 1994 and believes that revealing any secret is, in the words of one expert, 'bad for business', would have found the naming of individual agents damaging indeed. One of those named, David Spedding, a stalwart of anglophone amateur dramatics in Beirut, later became head of MI6.

This sense of a man with scores to settle was perhaps most evident when he denounced one particular former colleague. This journalist, he told Genrikh Borovik, 'enjoyed proving the amorality of my entire life'. Philby listed the man's charges against him. That he drank too much, he had too many wives, he was a hypocrite, a slob and a liar. But his man had failed to make public one key thing – that Philby had recruited him to work for MI6, probably in 1961 or 1962.

Philby explained how suitable this man, whom he called 'P', was. He was good at languages, knew the Middle East well and was anti-communist, so he recommended him to Nicholas Elliott, something of an expert in reeling in journalists to work for their country. 'P', clearly knowing of the allegations still hanging over Philby, said he wanted to be sure that anything he told the British would be passed on only to the British. Philby assured him that he would not be involved and that 'P' would deal only with another Brit. And so, the following day, 'P' met Nicholas Elliott and agreed to work for MI6, for money.

Philby revealed this some time between 1985 and 1988. Tantalisingly, he would not utter the name of the journalist, although he later held up a book the man had written and showed it to Borovik.

Those familiar with life in Beirut thought they knew, although the suggestion was something of a 'fun rumour'. This was none other than Patrick Seale, his colleague on the *Observer* and frequently his stand-in in Beirut and ghost writer of Eleanor's autobiography. Borovik writes that 'P' took Philby's place (at MI6), but did not stay long, and moved to England soon afterwards. 'I doubt that he worked at [MI6] for long,' said Philby. 'But undoubtedly, he remained a "friend" of the firm. [MI6] usually uses such "friends" over and over.'

It is known that Philby was extremely put out by Eleanor writing a book that contained so many of his love letters, and his anger at Seale for his complicity in the venture may be enough to explain Philby's attack on him. Whether there was substance to the mud that Philby threw or not, some of it stuck.

Seale, who enjoyed an illustrious career and wrote a number of successful books, was a journalist by nature. Those who knew him well admired his extensive contacts and – for a Westerner – his understanding of the Middle East, on which he wrote several books, though latterly his links to the brutal Assad regime in Syria led journalists at the *Observer* to believe his professional detachment had been irredeemably compromised. Philby's allegation raises the question of Seale's role as the writer of Eleanor's book. As we have seen, the trauma she suffered with the disappearance of her husband in January

1963 was compounded by the enormous interest in her. How could she not know her husband was working for the Russians? What would she do next? Would she go to Moscow? And in trying to regain a sense of equilibrium, she needed all the help she could get from her friends. Yet this most ingenuous and straightforward of people was ending up surrounded by spies, whether amateur or professional. Who were her friends? Her ex-husband Sam? Whatever his attitude to her, he was certainly also close to the US authorities. Nicholas Elliott and Elizabeth, the spy and his wife? She liked them very much, but their loyalty was to one another and the government that paid their bills. The Copelands? The same applied, and her compatriots in Washington were as keen as anyone to keep tabs on Eleanor. And so many other people in Beirut, 'friends' when it came to swimming in the Mediterranean, watercolouring in the hills and archaeological trips into the desert, had different calls on their loyalty. It was that sort of place.

Could Patrick Seale, a most intelligent and sensitive man who had showed such human sympathy and support for her, be a spy, too? Was his ghost-writing of her book part of MI6's surveillance of her? Was he telling a sanitised version of her story? An *Observer* colleague said that in later years: 'We were never quite sure where Patrick was coming from.' For lack of evidence to the contrary, we must assume that Eleanor never got to know of Philby's claim to Borovik, and it is quite possible it never came up between her and Philby (to the extent that they were in touch) while Seale was preparing the book. But had he been in the government's pay, she would presumably have liked to know that. Perhaps Philby's claim is untrue. Perhaps it is true, or had been true briefly, and she did know and didn't care.

Nearly fifty years after it was published, it may be tempting fate to say Eleanor's book bears no hint of being 'the establishment version'. Those who knew Seale saw him as essentially a story-driven writer, someone who wanted to break news and explain what was going on. His friends say it is quite conceivable that he might have provided Whitehall with, for example, a slightly more detailed, esoteric version of the news reports from, say, Syria, than he was sending to his many newspaper outlets.

Seeing himself as essentially a fact finder, he would have said there was no conflict between reporting on the truth for a newspaper-reading public and, secondarily, helping the British Foreign Office have a better understanding of what was happening on what was then loftily called 'the Arab street' or, specifically, inside the Syrian government. Such a role, he may well have reasoned – or even insisted – would be a long way from the more dangerous or morally tricky tasks sometimes expected of spies. He never clarified the position, his preferred conversation being more likely about France or the arts. An edition of a book by spy writer Morris Riley, alleging Seale had worked for MI6, was pulped at Seale's insistence, but that proves little. In the 1950s, after Seale decided against a career in the army, he applied to join the civil service and let it be known he would be interested in joining MI6. He attended an interview at a flat off Old Brompton Road in London. There was interest in his intelligence and knowledge of languages but, he told friends, he was told his background was 'not trustworthy enough'. That story, too, proves little.

In short, Philby's testimony continued to be unreliable. In 1981 in a speech to young East German recruits, Philby explained that his escape from Beirut had been made easier because Peter Lunn, taking over from Nicholas Elliott, had gone skiing at a key moment, enabling Philby to slip away. In one version of the story, Philby claimed Lunn had been away for four days before returning on the very day Philby disappeared. This is part of the slack and unprofessional caricature that Philby was wont to paint about his former colleagues. But he was gilding the lily. Security was certainly slacker than it should have been, and Lunn was an accomplished and frequent skier, often at the Les Cèdres resort nearby. But those close to the action swear he was in central Beirut on the day in question and in previous days. In any event, if Philby was being watched (and Eleanor said later she had no sense that he was), it is almost unthinkable that the immediate responsibility would have been the MI6 head of station's. As the journalist in him might have put it, 'Lunn went skiing' was a story too good to check.

Philby prided himself on his honour being intact. He had not sold out on the principles he had adopted in the 1930s, and therefore the faith remained – the world he had contributed to building would get better and better, including for Britain. Of his time in Austria in the 1930s, he said, 'I understood what side of the barricade my place was. I felt ceaselessly that my ideals and convictions, my sympathies and will, were on the side of those struggling for a better future for mankind. The heroic Russian people, building a new world, were the personification of these ideas.' In joining the Soviet intelligence service, he said, 'I thought at that time, and still think, that in my work I served my own British people.' Asked if he was happy, he replied: 'The greater part of my life is behind me and, looking back over the years, I believe I have not lived them in vain. Yes, I am happy.'

That was said to Murray Sayle in December 1967, with great conviction, despite his relationships with both Eleanor and Melinda having collapsed, his Soviet masters still impervious to his past sacrifices and refusing to give him any serious responsibilities. As Ron Rosenbaum points out, this was part of Philby's last great disinformation operation. He had publication of *My Silent War* still to come. Maybe that was giving him hope. But the Russian authorities wouldn't allow it to be published there for another twelve years.

Philby believed 'The evening of my life is golden,' and it is true he reached an accommodation with his lot. But in 1979 Kalugin stepped down. His successor, says Kalugin, 'didn't understand the enormous complexity of men like Philby ... living with the weight of betraying their countries and living in a strange land'. As a result, Philby, though living well and in relative freedom, 'never again enjoyed the support and friendship that I and my underlings had given him'. Kalugin kept up with him, and the pair appear to have spoken candidly. Philby would complain about the callousness of his new minders and about how illiberal the USSR was, even though he preferred the new president Andropov (who succeeded in 1982) to Brezhnev. He spoke sadly of Russia's provinces: 'He was disgusted by the squalor of life, the dirt, the shoddy upkeep of buildings, and the ubiquitous rudeness and boorish manners of the Soviet masses. He detested the increasing passivity of the people, the sense that no one, at any level, wanted to take responsibility for what was happening in the country.'

It was a return to frustration, though not as bad as the previous version. Nonetheless, call it pride or conviction, he went on believing and wanting to contribute. His brain, said Oleg Gordievsky (whose undercover work *against* the Soviet Union Philby came close to exposing) was as sharp as ever. His value in contributing to the KGB's folk memory was now more appreciated. He gave lectures to young recruits, among them one to Stasi agents in East Germany in which he insisted that no agent should ever succumb to interrogation ('never, ever confess ... Admit only what is harmless'), omitting to mention that he himself had done so, if only to buy time, although seemingly he never admitted even that to the Russians.* He continued to hanker for enlightenment between

---

* Christopher Andrew said in this context Philby had 'confessed a remarkable amount'. Nigel West reports that over twenty years after Philby's death, the KGB called off a conference with Philby's granddaughter Charlotte after it became clear that his admission to Nicholas Elliott of his guilt was to be discussed.

East and West, and even hoped he might be invited to play a role. The attitude that Desmond Bristow identified, speaking of the Philby of the late 1940s, lived on: 'Russia was not an enemy. As he saw it, Russia and the West would be able to get together and he tried to promote that, too soon. I don't think he felt a traitor to any country.'

For all the much-derided drunkenness, the self-image of moral seriousness was still alive. This was not a man who had given up – he retained a sense of moral arrogance. Nicholas Elliott called him intellectually arrogant and egocentric, but also gentle and incapable of malice.

And beneath the conceit and certainty, there was prickliness. The first time he met both Graham Greene and Ernest Hemingway he hadn't liked either. In *The Human Factor*, which has obvious echoes of Philby's story, Graham Greene writes of the lead character, whose convictions led him to defect to Moscow where he ekes out his life in a grubby, second-rate flat which he based on Eleanor's description of their Moscow flat. On the phone to his wife in London, Greene's character reassures her: 'Oh, everyone is very kind. They have given me a sort of job. They are grateful to me ...' On reading the manuscript before publication, Philby suggested Greene change it. He thought it misleading and melancholic, perhaps suggesting that the life the hero was leading was by now pathetic. Greene thanked his friend but said he felt he had conveyed the mood he wanted.

Similarly, Philby's devastatingly perceptive character judgements did not extend to himself. A reporter informed him that a Hollywood film was to be made of his life, telling Philby that he was to be played by British actor Michael York. 'But he's not a gentleman,' replied Philby.

Even if this was a joke, as Philby might have tried to pretend *post facto*, it is revealing. Though an expression from another age, the tag 'gentleman' is one bestowed by others. The first disqualification of being a gentleman, even sixty years ago, would be to claim 'I am a gentleman'. Here is a man with undiminished certainty in his own judgements, whose sense of his own moral probity remains bombproof. The mask of uncertainty had slipped. Here was one of those rare and long unsuspected glimpses, possibly of unBritishness, of 'not belonging', but certainly of conceit.

A far more appealing aspect of that self-depiction could be seen in the courteous way he behaved when out in public in Moscow. Rufina said he would always hold doors open, which often meant a long wait as a sea of people flowed through. 'He was often lost on the subway . . . I couldn't find him,' she remembered. This was not an affectation. Rufina recalled a sense of melancholy when he walked Moscow's streets. 'He did not consider his work in vain . . . But he was very worried when he saw the poor old people. Almost tearful. He would help countless old ladies across the road, or carry their bags. He would keep saying: "They won the war. Why are they so poor?"'

Gradually came evidence that he was coming to be more trusted by the Soviet authorities, of him being accepted for the long haul. Influential writers came to acknowledge that, though he had been awarded the Order of Lenin (after Blake, which he resented, regarding him as an upstart) and the Red Banner (in 1965) and the Order of Friendship of the Peoples in 1980, he had not been fully appreciated. His Russian biographer Dolgopolov wrote of his trawl through some of the archives in the late 1980s: 'I started to talk about his contribution to the victory over Nazi Germany. When I examined the materials carefully, I felt a sense of injustice. How could it be that he did so much but was not a Hero of the Soviet Union?'

He started to campaign quietly, but President Gorbachev seemed not to want to upset the British.

Then things were set in train, but he never lived to see it happen.

The rush to advertise disapproval of Philby is an understandable urge among Western writers, but there is little magnanimity on show from his ideological foes. Nicholas Elliott said crisply: 'The world is well rid of him.' Some indulge in straightforward abuse. His former colleague Hugh Trevor-Roper writes of 'esoteric and intense' Cambridge, with its 'introverted coteries' and the Apostles, an 'egregious secret society of self-perpetuating, self-admiring narcissi'. He called Blunt a 'sanctimonious Cambridge prig' – which of those three words were intended to carry most venom we cannot know – disdaining his 'thin, precise voice'. Oleg Gordievsky comes close to some sort of explanation, saying Philby was motivated by ideology, but 'what he did not admit was that he was also motivated by narcissism, inadequacy, his father's influence and a compulsion to deceive those around him'.

This 'compulsion to deceive' idea also appeals to Murray Sayle, who writes: 'Was what attracted him the nature of the job itself, the idea of having a secret self, inaccessible even to his friends, his wives and their former husbands and, as the agent of one intelligence agency inside another, a doubly secret self? Was it not so much the cause, the vision of a twenty-one-year-old, never re-examined during a busy spy's life, but the love of deceit and, by extension, of spying itself that kept him at his dead-letter drops and secret inks all those lonely years?' Rudyard Kipling has a curious echo of this. He wrote of the character after whom Philby was named that 'what he loved was the game for its own sake – the stealthy prowl through the dark gullies'.

David Cornwell talks of Philby's 'addiction to deceit'. 'What may have begun as an ideological commitment became a psychological dependency, then a craving. One side wasn't enough for him. He needed to play the world's game.'

One claim that Philby kept confined to a small circle concerns

Konstantin Volkov, whose attempt to defect to the West was thwarted by Philby. The customary belief is that Volkov was tortured and executed for his treachery. Shortly before he died, Philby made his remark about Volkov being 'a nasty piece of work' and how he had deserved everything that was coming to him. He would discuss the matter no further. Yet now, a new version of the story emerges. According to retired intelligence General Yury Kobaladze, Volkov was not executed, but was sent to prison. Interviewed for this book, Rufina Philby said: 'Kim and I had no secrets from each other. And when he was worried about something serious he of course shared it with me, so I remember it very well. The case of Volkov tormented him very much. He asked his curators: "What was Volkov's fate?" To this he was answered: "He is alive."' Rufina says this happened very early in his time in Moscow. 'He talked about it a lot over the years.'

Was Philby told the truth, when George Blake, in comparable circumstances, wasn't? Did he see any evidence to corroborate the extraordinary idea that Stalin's henchmen spared Volkov's life? Does Volkov have any living relatives? Did he say this so that he would not look bad in his wife's eyes? Why if, remarkably, he really believed it, did he not tell any of those who interviewed him late in life? Had Philby been told by the KGB not to admit to any soft-heartedness *pour décourager les autres*? Like so many things with Philby, it is a mystery, and one that he might have enjoyed others speculating on.

Eleanor wrote that Kim 'betrayed many people, me among them. But men are not always masters of their fate. Kim had the guts, or the weakness, to stand by a decision made thirty years ago, whatever the cost to those who loved him most, and to whom he too was deeply attached.' There was constancy, but to dogma. In Hugh Trevor-Roper's devastating phrase, 'this subtle, sophisticated man was an undeviating stalwart of the changing party line'. Philby's eldest daughter Jo, speaking for her family, had some sympathy for her stepmother Eleanor, so shocked at Philby's assertion that in his mind the Communist Party came before Eleanor. 'Probably he might have said that to all of us too,' she said. 'That's the way he thought.' Tellingly, Eleanor believed that his secret commitment brought a desperate need for stability, empathy and love to enable to him to function, and that he found it with her.

He died in 1988, having latterly restricted himself to two glasses of cognac a day, for fear that his wife Rufina might leave him if he allowed himself to drink any more. He was given a KGB funeral and his contribution praised. He was, though, 'brought to tears' by disappointment, said Rufina. He didn't live to see the Berlin Wall came down, in 1989, heralding the end of communist rule in Russia.

In London, over twenty years earlier, around the time of Eleanor's book's serialisation, David Astor, the editor of the *Observer*, suggested to Patrick Seale that it would be a friendly gesture for him to meet her. Seale arranged the encounter, and ushered her into Astor's office. She was emotional and disinclined to say very much, and Astor, full of sympathy, wanted to express respectful support without being overbearing. Very few words were spoken. At one point, Eleanor produced a small, crumpled piece of paper and showed it to Astor, who read it, handed it back wordlessly and hugged her to him. Seale took her downstairs and put her in a taxi. He sprinted back up and into his boss's office, demanding 'What does it say?'

Evidently Eleanor found some comfort from Philby's ultimate unreachability in a line from Chinese nationalist leader Chiang Kai Shek, who had led a ferocious fight against China's neighbours and against the influence of Soviet Russia. The note read simply: 'Japan is a disease of the skin; Communism is a disease of the heart.'

Postscript, January 2022

Many episodes in the Philby story remain cloudy, and after the first edition of this book went to press, a new one presented itself. As with so many others, the more one discovers, the murkier the story becomes.

I learned that Philby's defender Nicholas Elliott had a long-standing (possibly 15-year) extramarital affair with a Swedish woman. The relationship was brought to an end when Elliott's wife Elizabeth came across a letter from the lover while the Elliotts were in Beirut (1960-62). Elliott was to all appearances an upright, conventional figure, and the matter would have caused him embarrassment. The feelings of his Catholic wife, a dutiful, loyal and widely respected figure, can only be guessed at.

I was torn between thinking on the one hand that this was a private matter, irrelevant to this story and best left alone and, on the other, that it is relevant to Elliott's public service role, particularly where Philby is concerned. I resort to the muckraker's defence, I hope excusably and not too cheaply.

Is it possible Philby had a hold – implicit or otherwise – over his compromised friend? Elliott's son Mark believes the affair was known about by Elliott's bosses and hardly anyone else. It is not hard to imagine it being treated as "one of those things" and kept within a tight circle ("the boys") who saw it as personal, hardly fatal and at worst ill-advised. If infidelity was to happen, better a steady affair with a lover regarded as "safe" and discreet (assuming that is what she was, of which we can't be sure), than the risk of a losing a respected officer to some humiliating Soviet honey trap.

Whether Elliott would have pre-emptively informed his bosses is uncertain. Doing so might have threatened his career. Equally, he might have thought doing so made him invulnerable (beyond the presumed anguish at home).

In most circumstances Elliott's affair, given his friendship with a suspected Soviet agent, would have set alarm bells ringing. Assuming Philby also knew, it would have been a sensible precaution to accept that Moscow knew as well, or might one day be told, and would want to exploit a perceived susceptibility to blackmail. Yet we know that most of his close colleagues, at least, regarded Philby as a proven patriot. In MI6, the perception of risk barely existed. In MI5, they would have been fuming.

This was the era of John Vassall, blackmailed by the Russians over his homosexuality and subsequently gaoled, and of John Profumo, who resigned as a minister after lying over his relationship with a woman having an affair with a Soviet official. In some circumstances, Elliott's lapse – if something that lasted over a decade can be so described – would have meant the end of his career, or the end of his time at the sharp end of the espionage business. At the very least, it is an unflattering glimpse of the boys' world of two generations ago where the chaps play around and keep the women in the dark as far as possible.

Elliott is in no position to explain his position and, for different reasons, nor is MI6. But the affair is of a piece with the age of the soon-to-be-overtaken amateur. It is a disappointing coda to the career of a popular figure, and a saddening one to come across.

Notes

I. Beirut beckons

2　*denounced as 'sad' and 'pathetic':* Rebecca West, 'Another Philby exposure', *Sunday Telegraph*, 14 January 1968.

3　*'Mrs Blaine L. Kerns':* *Spokane Chronicle*, 16 December 1910.

5　*'carelessness could cause the loss':* Eleanor Kerns CV, submitted 1943, State Department file, National Archives and Records Administration, St Louis.

6　*considered her reports:* E. Kerns, State Department file.

6　*'promotion of ideas':* Eleanor Kerns CV, 1943.

7　*'The principal battleground of this war':* Quoted in Stacey Bredhoff, *Powers of Persuasion: Poster Art from World War II* (Washington DC: National Archives and Records Administration, 1994), introduction.

7　*'The truth sometimes seemed lost':* Winkler, pp. 4–5.

7　*'Most were passionate interventionists':* Ibid., p. 6.

7　*'A lovely girl':* Doris Virginia Metcalf, interviewed by Jewell Fenzi, from 8 July 1988, The Association for Diplomatic Studies and Training Foreign Affairs Oral History Project: Foreign Service Spouse Series. Available at https://adst.org/wp-content/uploads/2012/09/Metcalf-Doris-Virginia.pdf.

8　*the target of an extensive propaganda onslaught:* For a discussion of British propaganda efforts in Turkey, see Edward Corse, 'Keeping the Pot Boiling: British Propaganda in Neutral Turkey during the Second World War', 4 December 2018, https://blogs.kent.ac.uk/munitions-of-the-mind/2018/12/04/keeping-the-pot-boiling-british-propaganda-in-neutral-turkey-during-the-second-world-war/.

8　*Egemen Bezci . . . has written extensively:* Egemen B. Bezci, 'Turkey's intelligence diplomacy during the Second World War', *Journal of Intelligence History*, 15:2 (2016), 80–95.

8　*'They wrote material and submitted it':* Interview with Egemen Bezci.

8　*tantalisingly saying only:* E. Philby, pp. 36 and 65.

8　*'It is very unlikely that someone':* Interview with Egemen Bezci.

10   *'People coming in':* Scott Anderson and Hugo Lindgren, 'The Spies Fighting Communism During the Cold War', Intelligence Squared podcast.

11   *'tiny, pert, pretty':* Ralph Ingersoll, *Report on England: November, 1940* (New York: Simon & Schuster, 1940), p. 44.

12   *'not unlike an earthbound Spitfire':* Garry Campion, *The Good Fight: Battle of Britain Propaganda and The Few* (Basingstoke: Palgrave Macmillan, 2009), p. 301.

12   *'I made him swear':* Salisbury, p. 501.

14   *Eleanor told a friend:* Seale notes/private information.

16   *'The individual you feel certain':* Sacheverell Sitwell, *Arabesque and Honeycomb* (London: Robert Hale, 1957), p. 6.

16   *'Many Lebanese kept a gun':* Philp Mansel, *Levant: Splendour and Catastrophe on the Mediterranean* (London: John Murray, 2010) p. 311.

17   *'were convinced beyond all doubt':* Mary Ann Heiss, 'Introduction', H-Diplo Roundtable on *America's Great Game: The CIA's Secret Arabists and the Shaping of the Modern Middle East, H-Diplo Roundtable Review,* XV:40 (2014). Available at https://networks.h-net.org/node/28443/discussions/34057/h-diplo-roundtable-america%E2%80%99s-great-game-cia%E2%80%99s-secret-arabists-and

18   *It was, as we now know:* For a full examination of the aims and funding of the American Friends of the Middle East, see Wilford.

18   *'brought a dash of New World idealism':* Nigel Ashton, 'Review', in Ibid.

18   *'From those Elysian days':* Quoted in Grose, p. 162.

21   *'He was a dedicated journalist':* Interview with Afif Aburish.

21   *'She was always helping with Sam's paperwork':* Ibid.

2. When Kim – 'nothing like a former spy' – met Eleanor

24   *'This was an age before Vietnam':* Interview with Frank Wisner.

26   *But once more:* Interview with Afif Aburish.

27   *'the first Socialist':* St John Philby, *Arabian Days: An Autobiography* (London: R. Hale, 1948).

27   *'He made no pretence':* British Library, IOR/L/PS/12/15, f. 44r.

28   *'stupendous source of strategic power':* Mark Curtis, *The Ambiguities of World Power: British Foreign Policy Since 1945* (London: Zed Books, 1995), p. 21.

29   *The encounter between Eleanor and Kim:* This account of the meeting at the St Georges brings together several versions, from both those who were there and others.

29   *'quiet, polite':* Eveland, p. 259.

29   *'his loneliness':* E. Philby, pp. 28, 29.

30   *'his very being carried':* Aburish, p. 84.

31   *'We wanted in Egypt a leader':* Copeland (1989), p. 198.

32   *'a monster in Nasser':* Eveland, p. 170.

33   *These reached the Americans:* Pincher (1978), p. 90, and Pincher (2014), pp. 205–6.

34   *Sam asked Kim:* Downton, p. 326.

34   *She was variously described:* Eveland, pp. 258–9.

34 *'integrity, courage and humour'*: Elliott (1991), p. 187.

34 *'rangy, steady-drinking American'*: Beeston, p. 29.

35 *'She was very wry, funny'*: Interview with Susan Griggs.

35 *'So you're joining'*: Recounted by Celia Adams, interview with the author.

36 *'The fact that Burgess'*: Internal MI5 memo, quoted in West (2018), p. 214.

36 *'While in government service'*: Hansard, vol. 545, 7 November 1955.

37 *'He really could not'*: *Sunday Express*, 15 November 1970.

38 *'He was for her a master'*: *Observer*, 17 November 1968.

38 *'Once in a while'*: Interview with Afif Aburish.

39 *'thought of nothing but work'*: Eveland, p. 259.

40 *The children revelled*: E. Philby, p. 34.

40 *'not just sightseeing'*: Ibid., p. 30.

41 *Sam, entirely unaware*: Seale notes/private information.

41 *One husband discovered*: Ibid.

42 *One male official*: Munro, p. 37.

43 *Eleanor said later*: Seale notes/private information.

44 *'last chance appointment'*: Page, Leitch and Knightley, p. 275.

44 *'an unsocial animal'*: Interview with Stewart Copeland.

44 *'Like all the other women she knew'*: Interview with Susan Griggs.

45 *'intellectually curious and absolutely tireless'*: Interview with Andrew Garrard.

45 *'Everybody loved Kim'*: Interview with Lennie Copeland.

45 *'I remember the tinkling of glasses'*: Interview with Stewart Copeland.

46 *'Archaeology was a bond'*: Interview with Miles Copeland III.

47 *'it must be nearly 900 weeks'*: E. Philby, p. 35.

47 *'she was not at all a wise'*: Seale and McConville, p. 141.

47 *Neil Furse . . . felt that Aileen*: Ibid., p. 113.

48 *'[She] never really conquered'*: Ibid., p. 114.

49 *Nor, according to one report*: Cave Brown, p. 208.

50 *'Aileen committing suicide'*: Ibid., p. 465.

3. Beneath Kim's surface

53 *'I had already decided'*: Knightley, p. 33.

53* *claimed late in life*: Knightley, pp. 77–8, Andrew, p. 172.

54 *'What impressed and alarmed us'*: Milne, pp. 21–2.

54 *'The Nazis were not yet in power'*: Ibid., p. 22.

54 *'merely a reactionary means'*: Ibid., p. 35.

55 *'the most independent-minded person'*: Ibid., p. 36.

55 *'In Germany, unemployment was rife'*: Knightley, p. 34.

56 *He helped socialists*: Letter to Patrick Seale from Eric Gedye.

56 *'He behaved like a gentleman'*: Barbara Honigmann, *Ein Kapitel aus meinem Leben* (Munich: Hanser, 2004), p. 59.

57 *'an amazing conversation'*: Borovik, pp. 29–33.

58 *'[Philby] comes from a peculiar family'*: Costello and Tsarev, p. 146.

58 *'with unfeigned contempt and hatred'*: Borovik, p. 147.

58 *'I like [Philby] the most'*: Nikolai Dolgopolov, 'Kim Philby reports',

Rossiskaya Gazeta, 2 September 2020, https://cambridge5.ru/news/tpost/
fkneyr0s2z-kim-filbi-soobschaet.

59   *'strain of irresponsibility'*: K. Philby, p. 107.

59   *'An avowed communist'*: Quoted in Cave Brown, p. 245.

59   *'No one who did not go through'*: Cecil Day-Lewis, *The Buried Day* (London:
        Chatto & Windus, 1960), p. 211.

59   *'bourgeois career'*: Borovik, p. 29.

59   *'shutting off the world from the inner keep'*: Milne, p. 242.

61   *'Tommy was an amazingly generous fellow'*: Knightley, pp. 83–4.

62   *'schoolboy nonsense'*: Seale and McConville, p. 168.

63   *He let his bemusement show:* Borovik, p. 146.

63   *'a tactical necessity'*: Blunt press conference, *The Times*, 21 November 1979. A
        Phillbyesque sense of being vindicated by events, and even having foreseen
        the future, must have added to the sense the press conference that Blunt was
        unrepentant.

63*   *'continue on the true path'*: Maly, who seemingly anticipated his fate, told Philby
        to 'continue on the true path'. Maly was shot for purported disloyalty. His name
        was cleared in 1956. Sotheby's catalogue of Philby papers, July 1994.

64   *'submissiveness coefficient'*: Borovik, p. 147.

64   *'was due only to his persistence'*: Christopher Andrew, 'Moles, Defectors, and
        Deception: James Angleton and His Influence on US Counterintelligence',
        seminar at the Woodrow Wilson Center, 29 March 2012, https://www.
        wilsoncenter.org/event/moles-defectors-and-deceptions-james-angleton-and-
        his-influence-us-counterintelligence.

65   *'Philby was never in a position'*: Interview with Nigel West.

65   *'My father never met Hess'*: Rosenbaum.

65   *'contributing to Moscow's distrust'*: Quoted in Rosenbaum.

66   *The claim from Phillip Knightley:* See Knightley, p. 110.

66*   *'One of the reasons I acted as I did'*: See Sotheby's catalogue of Philby papers,
        July 1994.

67   *But spy writer Nigel West reports:* Nigel West, 'With Friends Like These',
        International Journal of Intelligence and CounterIntelligence, 27:4 (2014), pp.
        845–54.

67   *'not a single valuable British agent'*: Quoted in West and Tsarev, p. 161.

68   *'he doesn't bring pick-ups back'*: Carter, p. 263.

69   *'I know what you're doing'*: Knightley, pp. 77–8.

69   *'more closely than ever'*: Dolgopolov, 'Kim Philby reports'.

70   *Through a series of manoeuvres:* K. Philby, pp. 92–101.

70   *'The fox was not merely guarding'*: Macintyre (2015), p. 90.

70   *'a young Englishman'*: Quoted in Owen Bowcott, 'Stalin "picked Philby for plot
        to kill Franco"', *Guardian*, 14 November 2001.

70*   *remains the subject of some debate:* See West (2018), pp. 40–57.

71   *one of these agents was acting as the head:* Pincher (1984), p. 266. The question
        of what was meant by 'acting head of' or 'fulfilling the duties of' has been
        much discussed. The document is reproduced in full in the Nigel West,
        Historical Dictionary of British Intelligence (Lanham: Scarecrow Press, 2014).

71   *'something of the greatest importance'*: K. Philby, p. 119.

71   *'The only course'*: Ibid.

72   *'obvious relief'*: Ibid., p. 122.

72   *'Sorry, old man'*: Macintyre (2015), p. 99.

73   *'I thought he was just irresponsible'*: Harrison, p. 178.

73   *Volkov admitted planning:* Andrew and Gordievsky, p. 379, Andrew and Mitrokhin, p. 182.

73   *Eleanor asked Philby:* Seale notes/private information.

73   *'was "a nasty piece of work"'*: Knightley, p. 138.

73   *'a perceptible change'*: Milne, pp. 162–3.

74   *'sordid private life'*: West (2018), p. 201.

74   *'made a most pleasant impression'*: Malcolm Muggeridge, 'Refractions in the Character of Kim Philby', *Esquire* (September 1968).

75   *'Of a frightening thinness'*: 'Christopher Felix' (nom de plume), *Observer*, 15 October 1967.

75   *'I remember liking him definitely'*: Interview with Feyhan Sporel.

75   *'entirely corrupted'*: Trevor-Roper (1968), p. 87.

76   *'We knew in advance'*: Dorril, p. 212.

76   *'this dirty trick was used by Philby'*: Akhmedov, p. 193.

76   *'how [does] the Soviet intelligence'*: Ibid., pp. 191–7.

76   *'ratted'*: Erik de Mauny, 'The last time I saw Philby', *South China Morning Post*, 24 July 1994.

77   *'withdrawn from the world'*: Trevor-Roper (1968), p. 81.

77   *Burgess jumped into the sea:* Milne, pp. 171–2.

77   *Whitfield was widely admired:* Seale notes/private information.

77*   *The Whitfield-Burgess relationship:* See Purvis and Hulbert.

78   *she later admitted:* Milne, p. 171.

78   *Esther Whitfield said:* Seale notes/private information.

78   *'Among other things'*: Kalugin, p. 134.

79   *an academic debate continues:* See letters, *The Times*, 15 and 17 September 2020.

79   *'We didn't need Kim Philby'*: Interview with Mikhail Liubimov.

80   *He told Angleton:* Yossi Melman and Dan Raviv, *The Imperfect Spies: The History of Israeli Intelligence* (London: Sidgwick & Jackson, 1989), p. 82.

81   *Philby's final words:* K. Philby, p. 171.

81   *He was astonished:* Seale notes/private information.

81   *What transpired suggests:* Interview with Yuri Modin, who said he was against the plan: 'I thought more highly of British intelligence than my colleagues did . . . [Burgess] was thinking he would go to Paris and then return . . . But Korovin said no. You go to Moscow. [Burgess said:] 'How can I go to Moscow when I've got to return?' Everybody knew Burgess wouldn't want to stay because the atmosphere of Moscow didn't appeal. It was very difficult.'

81   *'took him out'*: Blunt press conference, *The Times*, 21 November 1979.

81   *'I have no doubt'*: Anthony Blunt, unpublished memoir, British Library, MS Add 88902/2, folio 51.

82   *'But I found in Prague'*: See Graham Greene, 'Our man in Moscow', *Observer*, 18 February 1968.

82   *'only just remembered'*: The National Archives (TNA): KV2/4115, MI5 commentary on serial 703. See also West (2018), pp. 146–8.

82   *'I'm no good to you now'*: Seale and McConville, p. 264.

82   *He had received a message:* Macintyre (2015), p. 161.

83   *'for all practical purposes'*: West (2018), p. 181.

83   *Just as he was fearing:* Borovik, p. 303.

83   *'For my part'*: TNA: FCO 158/28.

84   *'He was seedy'*: *Observer*, 15 October 1967.

84   *Philby had diverted McCargar:* Cave Brown, p. 447.

84   *'Several times during this period'*: K. Philby, p. 190.

85   *Blunt admitted many years later:* Blunt press conference, *The Times*, 21 November 1979. His words betray a conscious and risky insubordination rather than the casual choice of a man who had opted easily to sever his link with Moscow.

85   *'through the most ingenious of routes'*: K. Philby, p. 190.

85   *A colleague believes:* Milne, p. 188.

86*   *According to Modin:* Modin, p. 283.

87   *'To whom should a wife's'*: Borovik, pp. 310–12.

87   *'I know you're the Third Man!'*: Seale and McConville, p. 270.

87   *'That is why she tried to set fire'*: Seale and McConville, p. 273, interview with Feyhan Sporel.

87   *'I think to Russia'*: Borovik, p. 311.

88   *A call she made to the Foreign Office:* Knightley, p. 191.

88   *'Aileen's letter seems to me'*: Letter to Dora, 14 October 1955, Harry St John Philby Collection, St Antony's College, Oxford.

88   *'They went off to Newmarket'*: Interview with Simon Elliot.

88   *an internal memo to Patrick Dean:* TNA: FCO 158/28.

89   *Thanks to a statement:* Shubin, p. 186.

89   *'rock', 'truly breathtaking'*: Modin, pp. 284–5.

89   *'Here was a man'*: Stephanie Bunbury, 'I want to play a slug: Judi Dench on Red Joan and the rest', *Sydney Morning Herald*, 24 May 2019.

89   *'I have never been a communist'*: *The Times*, 9 November 1955.

89   *'It was thought'*: TNA: CAB 301/269.

90   *'cast iron promise'*: Roy Perrot, *Observer*, 7 July 1963.

90   *'What's the betting'*: Milne, p. 191.

4. Settling into the city of spies

92   *'it was safest'*: Letter to Noel Annan, quoted in Davenport-Hines and Sisman (eds), p. 397.

92   *It seems he went to the Foreign Secretary:* Seale notes, from an off-the-record conversation with White's friend Hugh Trevor-Roper. In Seale and McConville's book (p. 284), they make no mention of Macmillan's apparent complicity in the decision.

92   *Genrikh Borovik reports:* Borovik, p. 327.

94   *'Suddenly PR firms':* Interview with Afif Aburish.

94   *Said Aburish wrote:* Aburish, p. 19.

95   *'It is impossible':* Aburish, p. 191.

95   *John Slade-Baker:* Barr, p. 228.

95   *'had no need':* Interview with Susan Griggs.

96   *'how do you monitor':* Aburish, p. 192.

96   *'distasteful':* Ibid., p. 80.

97   *'Why the hell is':* Interview with Afif Aburish.

97   *'If you are in Lebanese security':* Aburish, p. 192.

98   *'His writing was clear':* Lewis, pp. 249–50.

99   *'The most striking thing':* Observer, 15 May 1988.

99   *Soon afterwards, she went to Sam:* Seale notes/private information.

100   *'for Annie's sake':* Eveland, p. 260.

100   *It seems he suspected Eleanor:* Seale notes/private information.

100   *'We shall take a house':* Seale and McConville, p. 292.

101   *'one of those Moslem elements':* New York Times, 11 June 1957.

102   *She had not visited him:* Seale notes/private information.

102   *'it always makes me feel mad':* Cave Brown, p. 468.

103   *'there would be about a dozen':* Letter to Dora, September 1956 file, Harry St
John Philby Collection, St Antony's College, Oxford.

103   *'sad account of neglect':* Cave Brown, p. 468.

103   *'My mother literally drank herself to death':* Knightley, p. 201. At one point
Philby told a friend his mother was 'quite happy on two bottles a day': Seale
and McConville, p. 281.

104   *'the luxuries of risking her neck':* Letter to Dora, 2 May 1957, Harry St John
Philby Collection, St Antony's College, Oxford.

104   *'obviously a very sick woman':* Knightley, p. 203.

104   *Clare Hollingworth spoke of Aileen:* Seale notes/private information.

105   *'He is convinced':* In Andrew, p. 433.

105   *Nicholas Elliott went to his grave:* Interview with Mark Elliott.

105   *'Characteristically':* Milne, p. 191.

106   *Melanie Learoyd took responsibility:* Seale notes/private information.

106   *'She can't even die in an uncomplicated way':* Cave Brown, p. 482.

106   *'I have wonderful news':* Beeston, p. 29.

107   *'dazed by the news':* E. Philby, p. 38.

108   *'A Middle East diplomat said today':* New York Times, 13 July 1958.

109   *'Clever wonderful you':* E. Philby, p. 39.

109   *'That sounds like the best possible solution':* Ibid.

109   *Ed Applewhite later asked him:* Cave Brown, p. 483, interview between Cave
Brown and Applewhite.

110*   *Dennis Spragg . . . believes:* Stewart, 'My Dad the Spy', Audible podcast.

111   *'find and groom a messiah':* Copeland (1989), p. 147. See Riley, pp. 83–5, for
example, on Philby's strong connections with Nasser's Egypt.

112   *'the only man who ever used the CIA for cover':* Aburish, p. 81.

112   *'We had a lot of family outings':* Interview with Stewart Copeland.

113 *'It was a different day'*: Interview with Frank Wisner.

114 *'The women would sunbathe'*: Interview with Stewart Copeland.

114 *'You'll never get anyone to believe you'*: Copeland (1989), p. 212.

114 *'We'd hold a buffet dinner'*: Ibid.

115 *'I didn't have the slightest suspicion'*: Copeland (1974), p. 188.

115 *would always duck*: 'The Spy Who Went into the Cold: Kim Philby, Soviet Super Spy', *Storyville*, BBC Four, 2013.

115 *'Kim ended up as a journalist'*: Interview with Miles Copeland III.

116 *'My mother . . . was a realist above all'*: Ibid.

116 *'You can always spot a spy'*: Interview with Lennie Copeland.

5. 1958 – some old friends resurface . . .

118 *'we feared the worst'*: Dwight D. Eisenhower, *The White House Years: Waging Peace, 1956–1961* (Garden City: Doubleday, 1965), p. 269.

119 *'the beginning of decades'*: Bruce Riedel, 'Beirut 1958: America's origin story in the Middle East', Order from Chaos, Brookings, 29 October 2019, https://www.brookings.edu/blog/order-from-chaos/2019/10/29/beirut-1958-americas-origin-story-in-the-middle-east/.

120 *'We reacted because we thought'*: Richard B. Parker, 'Lebanon: The US Can Make a Difference', in Kenneth J. Alnwick and Thomas Fabyanic (eds), *Warfare in Lebanon* (Washington DC: National Defense University, 1988), p. 35.

121 *he was furious:* Seale notes/private information.

122 *'cheap and colourful'*: E. Philby, p. 39.

122 *in truth she hated it:* Seale notes/private information.

122 *'He would sit out on his terrace'*: E. Philby, p. 39.

122 *'She wanted them to have'*: Interview with Afif Aburish.

122 *'Nobody ever worried'*: Interview with Stewart Copeland.

124 *invaluable source of intelligence:* See Nicholas Rankin, *Defending the Rock: How Gibraltar Defeated Hitler* (London: Faber & Faber, 2017).

125 *'The photographic archive'*: *The Times*, 16 June 2008. See also 'Some of the Palestinians – Restored', Movie Masterclass, 25 September 2018, http://moviemasterclass.com/some-of-the-palestinians-restored.

126 *'The Americans are crazy'*: Larsson, p. 113.

126 *'immensely tall and immensely handsome'*: Elizabeth Longford, quoted in J. Sutherland, p. 87.

127 *Crosthwaite also lodged with Stephen Spender:* J. Sutherland, p. 87.

127 *'Moore is a great social success'*: Letter to Isiah Berlin, September 1930, quoted in J. Sutherland, p. 113.

127 *'an appropriate adjective or verb'*: Munro, p. 33.

128 *'clutch of second-rate entertainers'*: Ibid.

128 *'Must you?'*: Ibid., p. 36.

128 *'like a man encased'*: J. Sutherland, p. 416.

129 *'stuffy'*: Ibid.

129 *'querulous, secretive, ashamed'*: Sewell, pp. 124–5.

130 *'a lovely boom town':* Martha Gellhorn, 'The Arabs of Palestine', *The Atlantic* (October 1961).

130 *Smart work by the embassy:* Munro, p. 38.

132 *'I have been waiting':* Borovik, p. 333.

132 *'Philby sent us excellent reports':* Interview with Yuri Modin, Cave Brown, p. 480, and K. Philby, p. 199.

132 *'It is likely':* Milne, p. 219.

133 *the happiest of her life:* E. Philby, p. 51.

133 *of whom Eleanor was terrified:* Seale notes/private information.

133 *'Everyone seemed to warm':* Interview with Miles Copeland III.

134 *The registrar . . . told Eleanor:* Seale notes/private information.

135 *'We all knew each other':* Interview with Alice Brinton.

135 *'I realised my parents':* Interview with Mark Elliott.

135 *'It was a drinking society':* Interview with Alice Brinton.

136 *'It was fun':* Interview with Frank Wisner.

137 *'much too sophisticated':* Cave Brown, p. 485.

137 *'This young man':* Interview with Frank Wisner.

137 *'[Kim] came across':* Bower, p. 292.

137 *'unconventional, secluded life':* E. Philby, p. 50.

138 *'It was a most agreeable reunion':* Bower, p. 292.

138 *'He was one of us':* Interview with Alan Munro.

138* *as did White:* Bower, p. 292.

140 *'There are good reasons':* Interview with Alfred Sursock Cochrane.

140 *'Philby swung round':* Larsson, p. 117.

141 *'5ft 9ins tall. Brown hair':* West and Tsarev (eds) (1998), p. 311.

143 *'The whole ceremony':* Diary entry for 30 September 1960, John Slade-Baker Collection, St Antony's College, Oxford.

143 *'I was perhaps the only member':* K. Philby, p. 132.

143 *'the slightest temptation:* Ibid., p. 131.

144 *'If you feel strongly enough':* Macintyre (2015), p. 228.

145 *But, she speculates:* E. Philby, p. 49.

145 *'would have been thunderstruck':* Knightley, p. 132.

146 *'Don't you think':* Elliott (1991), p. 184.

146 *'pound the officer's head':* Page, Leitch and Knightley, p. 279.

146 *One account has:* See Seale and McConville, p. 303, Knightley, p. 209.

146 *'bruised and scarred':* Seale and McConville, p. 303.

147 *'Kim and Eleanor were falling down':* Interview with Susan Griggs.

147 *'It wasn't a trick':* Knightley, p. 103.

6. What's wrong, darling?

148 *after the intestate Aileen's death:* Seale notes/private information.

149 *scattered ten $100 bills:* E. Philby, p. 52.

149 *'years of happiness in store':* E. Philby, p. 53.

150 *They were taken back to the party:* Seale notes/private information.

150 *His evident Zionist sympathies:* Munro, p. 38.

152 *'to recruit and run agents':* Pincher (2009), p. 471.

152 *'would be evaporated':* Interview with Dick Dyerson.

152 *'Dyerson's tale is fascinating':* Interview with Stephen Dorril.

153 *Prompted largely by idealism:* See Roger Hermiston, The Greatest Traitor: The Secret Lives of Agent George Blake (London: Aurum, 2013).

154 *'Kim was looking terrible':* Beeston, p. 34.

155 *'as loving and attentive', 'the easiest':* E. Philby, pp. 31–2.

155 *'Where's Eleanor?':* Seale and McConville, p. 304.

156 *'You know Moyra':* Beeston, p. 32.

156 *'the wall of Anglo-American caution':* Borovik, p. 336.

157 *'upset and surprised':* Ibid., p. 337.

157 *'Sometimes it was hard':* Ibid.

157 *'I did not understand right away':* Borovik, pp. 336–7.

158 *'Eleanor came to ask':* Larsson, p. 116.

159 *Deakin concluding that Philby:* Knightley, p. 209.

159 *Dick White, for one:* pp. 503–7.

160 *'To betray you must first belong':* Murray Sayle interview, Sunday Times, 17 December 1967.

161 *One account of Philby's time:* Edward R. F. Sheehan, 'The Rise and Fall of the Soviet agent', Saturday Evening Post, 15 February 1964.

162 *'twaddle':* K. Philby, p. 200.

162 *Sheehan confirmed this:* Aburish, p. 82.

162 *'display visible emotion':* Elliott (1991), p. 187.

7. The judgement of Solomon

165 *'It's firms like Marks & Spencer':* Andrew Seth and Geoffrey Randall, The Grocers: The Rise and Rise of the Supermarket Chains (London: Kogan Page, 1999).

165 *'co-operative socialist democracy':* Observer, 22 July 1962.

166 *'How is it the Observer':* Solomon and Litvinoff, p. 226.

166 *'important work for peace':* Ibid.

166 *When they were back in London:* Bower, p. 293.

166 *'I know he was working:* Chapman Pincher, speaking on 'The Spy Who Went into the Cold: Kim Philby, Soviet Super Spy', Storyville, BBC Four, 2013.

167 *'Only years later':* Solomon and Litvinoff, p. 165.

168 *'a rather untrustworthy woman':* Wright, p. 173.

168 *Wright suggested:* Ibid., pp. 172–3.

168 *'The Kim Philby I now got to know':* Solomon and Litvinoff, p. 165.

169 *'Never mind all his philandering':* John le Carré, 'Afterword', in Macintyre (2015), p. 291.

169 *almost certainly an invented rumour:* Balfour-Paul, p. 187.

169 *'an unconscious homosexual':* Robert Shields, 'Trying to understand Philby', Observer, 19 November 1967.

169 *'Philby had been working':* le Carré, 'Afterword', p. 291.

170 *'Finally, I feel I must voice':* Solomon and Litvinoff, p. 229.

171 *'Leaving the club'*: Ibid., p. 83.

172 *'I had not volunteered'*: Ibid., pp. 226 and 227.

172 *'He did not cut'*: *Observer*, 15 May 1988.

173 *'kings to tremble'*: Ibid.

173 *'The country certainly boasts'*: *Observer*, 28 October 1962.

173 *'Until something is done'*: *The Economist*, 20 October 1962.

175 *'It must always be a matter'*: Sir Michael Howard, letter to *The Times*, 21 November 1979.

176 *'We cannot ignore'*: Bower, p. 295.

8. Christmas 1962 – what Eleanor saw

179 *'Something was going on'*: E. Philby, p. 6.

180 *He sparkled:* Downton, p. 334.

180 *'It was as if'*: E. Philby, p. 8.

181 *'You know what this is about'*: John le Carré, afterword to Macintyre (2015), p. 293. See also *The Pigeon Tunnel*, p. 174, where he calls Elliott's account 'a fiction he has come to believe rather than the objective truth'.

183 *In another account:* Beeston, p. 31.

183 *'As we talked'*: Downton, pp. 334–5.

184 *After more than an hour:* Andrew Boyle conversation with Clare Hollingworth, Andrew Boyle Papers, Cambridge University Library.

184 *'Kim's never done anything'*: E. Philby, p. 3.

186 *'I think he had to have attention'*: TNA: CAB 301/678.

186 *'I said, "Uncle Omar'*: Interview with Afif Aburish.

187 *'You do realise your husband'*: E. Philby, p. 18.

188 *'For the sari'*: Quoted in Cave Brown, p. 522.

188 *'I was in total disarray'*: E. Philby, p. 12.

188 *'She was crying a lot'*: Interview with Lennie Copeland.

189 *'She was shattered'*: Interview with Stewart Copeland.

189 *'My darling beloved'*: E. Philby, p. 14.

189 *'By the way'*: Ibid., p. 15 Philby has another giveaway 'by the way' in a letter he writes to Nicholas Elliott much later in the story, when, again, he asks for discretion. Undated letter from Kim Philby to Nicholas Elliott, Cleveland Cram Collection, Georgetown University Library, Washington DC.

190 *'Fondest love'*: Quoted in Cave Brown, p. 524.

191 *'the telephone line was garbled'*: *Daily Express*, 4 March 1963.

191 *'That is a ridiculous idea'*: Ibid.

192 *'Naturally Mrs Philby'*: *Daily Herald*, 5 March 1963.

193 *'Eleanor told me'*: Interview with Susan Griggs.

193 *'rushed off to live'*: *Guardian*, 27 April 1963. Hollingworth was the first journalist to write an article suggesting that Philby might have defected to Moscow, but it never appeared in print. Guardian editor Alastair Hetherington told her to 'Be your age', telling her the piece would risk 'millions of pounds' worth of libel fees'. See Lewis, p. 249.

194 *'She pretty much'*: Interview with Lennie Copeland.

194 *full of detailed instructions:* E. Philby, p. 19.
195 *At three o'clock one morning:* Ibid., pp. 19–20.
196 *'They had an apartment':* Interview with Miles Copeland III.
196 *Feeling sorry for Petukhov:* E. Philby, p. 23.
196 *'there seems no need':* TNA: CAB 301/269.
197 *'"C" [Sir Dick White, head of MI6]':* Ibid.
197 *'The potential embarrassment':* Letter Bernard Burrows to Burke Trend, 24 May 1963, in ibid.
198 *Some accounts say:* Costello, p. 551.
199 *'Most people':* Interview with Alice Brinton.
199 *'I put the fear of God into her':* Elliott (1993), p. 94.
200 *'We have definitely known':* Bower, p. 306.
200 *'Much against my will':* E. Philby, p. 56.
200 *'prior to 1946 grave damage':* TNA: CAB 301/269.
200* *When Philby learned:* E. Philby, p. 77.
201 *'My last hope':* Ibid., p. 58.

9. London comes calling

202 *The minute the call:* Seale notes/private information.
203 *have been constructed many times:* This account draws from a number of writers, including Tom Bower, Andrew Boyle, Nicholas Elliott, Nigel West, Genrikh Borovik, Ben Macintyre, Christopher Andrew and Peter Wright.
203 *'I once looked up to you':* Boyle (1979), pp. 436–7.
203 *'I'm offering you a lifeline':* Bower, p. 298.
204 *'[Philby] could have rejected':* Bower, p. 300.
204 *or commit suicide:* Bower, p. 300.
204* *'Kim apparently said':* Milne, p. 249.
205 *'We have no evidence':* Andrew, p. 436.
206 *'He was weeping':* 'The Spy Who Went into the Cold: Kim Philby, Soviet Super Spy', *Storyville*, BBC Four, 2013.
206 *'I knew exactly':* Knightley, p. 216.
207 *He was given false papers:* Bower, p. 301.
207 *'The Russians were shocked':* Interview with Tom Bower.
207 *MI6 discovered that bank notes:* Bower, p. 303.
207* *two books from well-placed Russian sources:* Kalugin, p. 134 and Borovik, pp. 348–50.
208 *'the man running our secret operations':* Knightley, p. 8. The term mole, used in the context of espionage, appears to spring from the enthusiasm of spy author John le Carré for Kenneth Grahame's book *The Wind in the Willows*. A little bashfully, he admitted in an interview the reference 'may' have come from that. 'John le Carré', *Mark Lawson Talks To . . .*, BBC Four, 5 October 2008.
209 *'I had an incredibly happy friendship':* Interview with Simon Elliot, June 2020.
209 *'The only option was to push him':* Nicholas Elliott told his friend David Cornwell many years later: 'My dear boy, nobody wanted him back here.' Sisman (2015), p. 246.

209 *Alan Hare … said:* Seale notes/private information. Hare was speaking to a journalist just four years after Philby had fled, so for face-saving reasons he may well have been less than candid on MI6's behalf.

210 *'It was probably because':* Purvis and Hulbert, pp. 327–8.

210 *also told Phillip Knightley:* Knightley, pp. 215–16.

210 *'Dick liked the idea':* Interview with Tom Bower.

210 *'He fooled me though':* John le Carré, 'Afterword', in Macintyre (2015), p. 294.

210 *'White didn't even think about':* Bower, p. 129.

210 *'It didn't arise':* Ibid., p. 301.

210 *'Roger [Hollis] and Dick [White]':* Wright, p. 194.

211 *'perseverance apparently took':* Shackley, p. 31.

211 *'That was the point of it all':* Rosenbaum.

212 *'a poop':* Letter to Noel Annan, quoted in Davenport-Hines and Sisman (eds), p. 397.

212 *'I like Nick':* Seale and McConville, p. 296.

212 *'We exchanged intelligence':* Interview with Frank Wisner.

212 *some useful admissions of guilt:* West (2016), pp. 80–1.

212 *'pounded his knees':* Wright, p. 194.

213 *'By the time Elliott was sent back':* West (2016), pp. 80–1.

213 *'What a shame':* Bower, p. 304.

213 *two very credible versions:* Boyle (1979), p. 437 and Knightley, p. 259.

214 *'making no false promises':* Boyle (1979), p. 436.

214 *'I had an agreement':* Costello, p. 552.

214 *'But the corpses':* Dick White to Hugh Trevor-Roper, 14 January 1968, Dacre Papers 10/45, Christ Church Archives, Oxford.

215 *'Angleton wanted Philby returned':* Winks, p. 405.

215 *'that he wished':* Interview with Michael Holzman.

216 *'perhaps half a dozen':* Seale and McConville, pp. 308–9.

216 *'In 1962, in Beirut':* Trevor-Roper (2014), p. 96.

216 *did protest to one writer:* Letter to Andrew Boyle, Andrew Boyle Papers, Cambridge University Library.

216 *There was mystification:* Seale notes/private information.

217 *'I do not rule out the possibility':* Borovik, p. 32.

217* *Philby told … Dick White's version:* See Bower, p. 299 and Borovik, pp. 344–5.

218 *'The Russians were terrified':* Interview with Tom Bower.

218 *'paramount':* le Carré, p. 180.

218 *'It was a huge mistake':* Interview with Mark Elliott.

10. Enter a knight

219 *'shaken':* Rosenbaum.

220 *'Philby ran rings':* Milne, p. 254.

220 *'There was no doubt':* Wright, p. 170.

220* *'ferocious hunt':* Bower, p. 296; Cave Brown, p. 506.

222 *'It was his way of telling':* D. Bristow, p. 266.

222 *The children adored the dog:* Seale notes/private information.

222 *Peter Wright was shown CIA records:* Wright, p. 193.

223 *'a Communist through and through':* Modin, p. 85.

224 *'extremely interesting and fruitful':* Blunt press conference, *The Times*, 21 November 1979.

224 *'were quite sure that Blunt':* Interview with Yuri Modin.

224 *'totally abhorrent':* Blunt press conference. Not everything Blunt said on that occasion was true, but it can be said with confidence he hated the idea of going to Moscow.

226 *'Blunt admired Philby':* Wright, p. 229.

226 *'Once the war':* Interview with Brian Sewell.

227 *'needed Blunt desperately':* Wright, p. 229.

227 *'It may be that Anthony':* Interview with Brian Sewell.

227 *'For instance in 1938':* Interview with Yuri Modin.

228 *'wanted to search':* Balfour-Paul, p. 188.

229 *It was assumed, too:* Sewell, p. 140.

229 *'it would have been extraordinary':* Interview with Alfred Sursock Cochrane.

229* *George Carey consulted:* See 'The Spy Who Went into the Cold: Kim Philby, Soviet Super Spy', *Storyville*, BBC Four, 2013.

231 *thoroughly out of character:* Interview with Kenneth Rose.

232 *'vulnerable side':* Wright, p. 215.

232 *'Her friendship with Blunt':* Rose, p. 239.

232* *In November 1951:* West (2018), pp. 149–50.

232+ *Tom Bower wrote:* Tess Rothschild obituary, *Daily Mail*, 5 June 1996.

233 *'It's Anthony':* Wright, p. 216.

233 *'It seemed to me':* Interview with Miranda Carter.

234 *'interested in the Marxian interpretation':* TNA: KV4/473.

234 *'I feel certain':* West (2018), p. 122.

235 *he was questioned by MI5:* Penrose and Freeman, p. 365.

235 *'Nor can I believe':* D. Sutherland, p. 150.

235 *'Nobody in MI5':* Ibid., p. 144.

235 *'MI5 knew everything':* Ibid., p. 156.

236 *He was relieved to be told:* West (2018), and TNA: KV4/473.

236* *'an assignment he undertook':* Wright, p. 223.

237 *'Blunt was regarded':* Bower, pp. 131–2. Also Andrew, p. 439.

237 *'I'm very, very sorry':* Carter, p. 398. Lehmann's biographer Selina Hastings pinpoints the date 1956. See S. Hastings, pp. 293–4.

237 *He was told that if Guy Burgess:* H. Nicolson.

237 *'You would be arrested':* TNA: KV 2/4128 Serial 1204a: letter to BURGESS from BLUNT discouraging his return. In a cabinet meeting in February 1959, it was acknowledged that the legal evidence for prosecuting Burgess for espionage was very weak. Blunt may have been unaware of this advice.

239 *He suggested Blunt:* Penrose and Freeman, p.391-6

239 *White was sent the book:* Andrew Boyle Papers, Cambridge University Library. This did not prevent White from denouncing the book after its publication and encouraging his friend Hugh Trevor-Roper to do so in print.

239 *'a limited number of comments':* Bower, p. 377.

239 *'may not have appreciated'*: Interview with Ed Boyle.

240 *'I believe people knew'*: Carter, pp. 320–1.

240 *write to Burgess in Moscow:* TNA KV 2/4128 Serial 1204a: letter to BURGESS from BLUNT discouraging his return. Burgess may have been miffed by Blunt, who was every bit as guilty as Burgess, being used as a messenger by MI5. *Observer* journalist Mark Frankland interviewed Burgess in Moscow and said one moment he talked about Blunt 'with affection', but in the next breath would say something snide about Blunt and MI5 (Seale papers/private information). A letter from Burgess to his mother about his hope of being allowed a secret visit to London, that emerged from MI5 files in 2017, also suggests a degree of mistrust of Blunt. Dick White's friend Hugh Trevor-Roper, writing in 1979, accepts Boyle's chronology in assuming that Blunt confessed before 1963 (and makes no mention of Michael Straight). He says Blunt feared exposure by Burgess: 'I suspect it was this fear which prompted Blunt to make his confession – a confession which may in fact have been unnecessary, since Burgess then died in Moscow, having revealed nothing.' *The Secret World*, p. 165.

241 *'embarrassing ground'*: Bower, p. 375.

241 *'wasn't startled when I heard'*: Penrose and Freeman, p. 409.

241 *'biggest mistake of [his] life'*: Manuscript memoir of Anthony Blunt, British Library. The memoir was held back from public access for twenty-five years, as a condition of its donation. The manuscript was de-reserved on 23 July 2009.

241 *'From his unlikely vantage point'*: West and Tsarev (eds) (1998), p. 185.

242 *'I have to say that Blunt'*: Penrose and Freeman, p. 251.

242 *Dick White would have felt:* See Bower, p. 303.

242 *'the case against him'*: TNA: CAB 301/269.

11. To Russia? For love?

244 *'the victim of a monstrous'*: E. Philby, p. xiii.

244* *Philby suggested to his Russian controllers:* 'Escape to the USSR: Kim Philby's secret documents revealed', Russia Beyond the Headlines, 1 January 2012, https://www.rbth.com/articles/2012/01/01/escape_to_the_ussr_kim_philbys_ secret_documents_revealed_14133.html.

247 *'fiercely British'*: Interview with Davut Gurlé.

248 *'There were very few people'*: Milne, p. 178.

248 *'a close friend'*: Balfour-Paul, p. 183.

248 *'as attractive as ever'*: Trevor-Roper (2014), p. 295.

248 *'I remember the aftermath'*: Interview with Alice Brinton.

248 *'The only time I ever saw'*: Interview with Lennie Copeland.

249 *'wouldn't believe it'*: Copeland (1974), p. 188.

249 *'I guess my father thought'*: Interview with Miles Copeland III.

249 *'My father used to say'*: Interview with Stewart Copeland.

250 *'overlooking' and 'forgiving'*: Copeland (1989).

250 *'There was a myth'*: Interview with Lennie Copeland.

251 *offered to pay:* In recounting this, Eleanor makes one of the very few

complimentary mentions of Sam in the whole of her book. It was written a couple of years after the immediate anger at Sam's sleight of hand in taking Annie to the States had subsided.

252 *Philby replied very promptly:* E. Philby, p. 59.

252 *Kim did not discourage:* Seale notes/private information.

253 *'Seeing it was only 11.00am':* E. Philby, p. 67.

254 *'All my fears in the plane':* Ibid., p. 1.

255 *'Burgess wanted to see me':* Rufina Philby, interview with Nikolai Dolgopolov. Available at https://proffu.ru/en/agent-sssr-kim-f-kim-filbi-sovetskii-britanskii-shpion-esli-by-ty-znala-kak-ty.html.

255 *Burgess had been duped:* Conversation with Mikhail Liubimov. When I asked him how Burgess could have been so naïve as to believe the Russian's promise, Liubimov replied simply: 'He was an honest man.'

255 *'Was the KGB':* Ibid.

256 *supported by Sergei Konrashev:* Lownie, p. 320, and an account from the time, quoted in Purvis and Hulbert, loc. 8507.

256 *'He never once said':* E. Philby, p. 89.

258 *'Whatever the political cynicism':* Ibid., p. 88.

12. The independent traveller

261 *'tovarich mood':* E. Philby, p. 111.

263 *'a sea of sadness':* Ibid., p. 89.

265 *After a few cursory questions:* 'Escape to the USSR: Kim Philby's secret documents revealed', Russia Beyond the Headlines, 1 January 2012, https://www.rbth.com/articles/2012/01/01/escape_to_the_ussr_kim_philbys_secret_documents_revealed_14133.html.

265 *'two frightful scenes':* Ibid.

266 *'was in poor shape':* Cave Brown, p. 540.

266 *'never during his years':* Salisbury, p. 507.

266 *'exchanged furtive smiles':* Aburish, p. 17.

267 *'There is no real evidence':* Salisbury, p. 501.

268 *'behaving like a hysterical':* Cave Brown, p. 542.

269 *suggested Eleanor sue for libel:* Seale notes/private information.

270 *'One has got to remember':* E. Philby, p. 146.

270 *'a politician of genius':* Ibid., p. 149.

270 *The cost was around $2500:* Philby memo to KGB. 'Escape to the USSR'.

271 *Eleanor found the idea:* E. Philby, p. 155.

272 *Kim told Eleanor:* Ibid., p. 159.

272 *'He did, until a while ago':* Ibid., p. 163.

273 *'his courtesy was gone':* Ibid., p. 165.

273 *'I don't want you to leave':* Ibid., pp. 169–70.

274 *'He was absolutely serious':* Interview with Susan Griggs.

275 *She read it endlessly:* E. Philby, p. 174.

275 *'Philby must get rid':* Cave Brown, p. 535.

13. 'Swinging' London, 1965–8

276 *'endless chats'*: Interview with Sabrina Izzard.

276 *'Whatever I said'*: Interview with Susan Griggs.

276 *'She knew they had'*: Ibid.

277 *Eleanor said she could not live:* Seale notes/Private information.

277 *'The relationship collapsed:* Observer, 17 November 1968.

277 *'copper-bottomed bastard'*: Knightley, p. 8.

277 *'an Arabian attitude'*: Wright, p. 229.

277 *'spiteful, vain and murderous'*: John le Carré, 'Introduction', in Page, Leitch and Knightley, p. 23.

277 *'He used them like he used'*: Ibid., p. 14.

278 *'had scholarly tastes'*: Venetia Porter (ed.), *Thea Porter's Scrapbook* (London: Unicorn, 2019).

279 *He said it was something:* Seale notes/Private information.

279 *'his efforts to overcome'*: Anonymous CIA source, *Observer*, 15 October 1967.

279 *'The Philbys were a devoted couple'*: Edward Sheehan, *Sunday Telegraph*, 16 February 1964.

280 *'a simple open woman'*: Borovik, p. 329.

282 *'I don't really blame her'*: Josephine Philby, speaking on 'The Spy Who Went into the Cold: Kim Philby, Soviet Super Spy', *Storyville*, BBC Four, 2013.

282 *'She was quite an exotic figure'*: Interview with Iain Sinclair.

285 *He pointed out that his salary:* Seale notes/private information.

285 *'desperately in need of friends'*: Observer, 8 October 1967.

285 *'What would* you *do'*: E. Philby, p. 63.

285 *'My mother stayed friends'*: Interview with Mark Elliott.

286 *'She was very drawn'*: Ibid.

286 *'not as falling-down drunk'*: Interview with Iain Sinclair.

287 *'perfect in every way'*: E. Philby, p. xiii.

287 *'I felt it about time'*: Evening Post, 26 January 1968.

288 *'And what, pray'*: Interview with Susan Griggs.

289 *Whether he knew:* According to Philby, Elliott said he had told Astor, but Astor denied this. Knightley, p. 199.

289 *the Sunday Times gleefully reported:* 20 March 1988.

290 *'an artless and moving picture'*: Observer, 14 January 1968.

290 *another newspaper: Daily Mirror*, 3 October 1967.

291 *'I can't help being a little unhappy'*: Observer, 8 October 1967.

291 *'looked as though [his clothes]'*: The Times, 13 November 1967.

292 *'not give a story'*: TNA: CAB 301/678. Denis Greenhill to Burke Trend.

292 *'wouldn't want to make'*: TNA: CAB 301/677. Letter from Copeland to Philby.

292 *'Philby is a vain man'*: TNA: CAB 301/678, Copeland to *Daily Mirror*.

293 *'the Treasury would stop'*: TNA: CAB 301/678.

293 *'Eleanor is as naïve'*: Ibid.

294 *'I have never had'*: Patrick Seale, *Observer*, 17 November 1968.

295 *'The easy thing to say'*: Interview with Susan Griggs.

295 *'It couldn't have been easy'*: Interview with Alice Brinton.

295 'Armour plated in innocence': Patrick Seale, Observer, 17 November 1968.
296 'would probably not have regretted': Elliott (1991), p. 189.

14. Brian and Anthony

The evidence from Brian Sewell in this chapter comes from a series of interviews with Sewell by the author, mostly conducted at his house in Wimbledon in the late 2000s.

297 'were so close as to give me': Solomon and Litvinoff, 226.
298* 'I was called back': Private information. See also Straight, and 'Interview with Michael Straight', The Fred Fiske Show, 26 January 1983, transcript available at https://www.cia.gov/readingroom/docs/CIA-RDP88-01070R000100570002-1.pdf.
299 MI5 knew it: Straight, p. 325.
299 As Arnold Deutsch: West and Tsarev (eds) (1998), p. 133.
302 approximately 1800 official documents: See West and Tsarev (eds) (2009).
303 in 1950 he acted as a go-between: Madchen File No. 83792, vol. 2, 249, note from Paul, quoted in Purvis and Hulbert.
303 In February 1951: West and Tsarev (eds) (1998), pp. 178–9, 185–6.
303 Q: 'What did you do for the Russians': Blunt press conference, The Times, 21 November 1979.
303 'Undoubtedly the damage': West and Tsarev (eds) (1998), p. 186.
303* He had a close call: Carter, p. 333.
304 'He was worn out': Interview with Miranda Carter.
304 Blunt's statement: See Blunt's press conference, The Times, 21 November 1979.
307 it was pure invention: Correspondence with Alan Bennett.
307 gone to Beirut: GEN/360/8B
308 'lofty, with his nose in the air': Interview with Susan Schlaefle.
310 'the most incredibly disloyal way': Ibid.
313 'need to charm': Carter, p. 257.
313 'the grandmother of us all': See The Times, 21 August 2015.
313* 'homme fatal': Hugh Trevor-Roper (2014), p. 164.
314 'He got immunity': Rufina Philby, interview with Nikolai Dolgopolov. Available at https://proffu.ru/en/agent-sssr-kim-f-kim-filbi-sovetskii-britanskii-shpion-esli-by-ty-znala-kak-ty.html.
314 'When I opened it': Knightley, p. 241.
314 Is it possible that White: This is the view of spy writer Antony Percy, aka Coldspur. See http://www.coldspur.com/category/espionageintelligence/.
315 'If that scoundrel Blunt': Boyle (1980), p. 470.
315 Tom Bower believes: Interview with Tom Bower.

15. Unspent convictions

318 'He was I believed': Trevor-Roper (2014), p. 81.
319 He had three options: K. Philby, p. xxxi.

319   '"*The poor, right or wrong*"': Graham Greene, *The Confidential Agent* (1939; London: Vintage, 2002), pp. 67–71.

320   '*the solid foundations*': K. Philby, pp. xxxi–ii.

321   '*a complete disillusionment*': Rosenbaum.

321   '*The more I saw of Kim*': Murray Sayle, 'My Friend Kim', *Spectator*, 21 May 1988.

321   '*good hardening up*': Interview with Mikhail Bogdanov.

322   '*Philby had an extraordinary*': Christopher Andrew, 'Moles, Defectors, and Deception: James Angleton and His Influence on US Counterintelligence', seminar at the Woodrow Wilson Center, 29 March 2012, https://www. wilsoncenter.org/event/moles-defectors-and-deceptions-james-angleton-and-his-influence-us-counterintelligence.

322   '*Ideological conversion is a form*': Trevor-Roper (1968), p. 80.

322   *submissiveness coefficient*: Borovik, p. 147.

323   '*Kim and I had different outlooks*': Wright, p. 229.

323   '*tossed aside*': Kalugin, p. 135.

323   '*The KGB couldn't have cared less*': Interview with Boris Volodarsky.

324   '*There is a rule*': Rufina Philby, interview with Nikolai Dolgopolov. Available at https://proffu.ru/en/agent-sssr-kim-f-kim-filbi-sovetskii-britanskii-shpion-esli-by-ty-znala-kak-ty.html.

324   '*He told me*': Rosenbaum.

324   '*Any normal man*': Ibid.

324   '*How naïve*': Mikhail Liubimov, 'A Martyr to Dogma', in Philby, Liubimov and Peake, p. 280.

325   '*I was full of information*': Philby, Liubimov and Peake, p. 59.

325   '*Blake in particular*': Interview with Tom Bower.

325   '*Meet him yourself*': Borovik, p. 308.

325   '*The KGB was too stupid*': Rosenbaum.

326   '*It was very hard*': Interview with Mikhail Bogdanov.

327   '*It is a good thing*': Letter to May Philby, 26 October 1912, Harry St John Philby Collection, St Antony's College, Oxford.

327   *Eleanor believed he longed to live up to:* Seale notes/private information.

329   '*Maybe Kim recognised*': Mel Trotter, 'The King's Man: Like Father, Like Son? – Part IV', Aramco Expats, 25 June 2020, https://www.aramcoexpats. com/articles/the-king-s-man-like-father-like-son-part-iv/.

329   '*Philby is not unique*': Interview with Stephen Dorril.

330   '*I do not feel bitterness*': Milne, p. 246.

330* '*In his memoirs*': Hugh Trevor-Roper, 'The Ideal Husband', *New York Review of Books*, 9 May 1968.

331   '*after his fashion*': Elliott (1991), p. 187.

331   '*Both Nicholas and Kim*': Interview with Mark Elliott.

332   '*Philby was friendly*': Quoted in *Sunday Times*, 15 May 1988.

333   '*all [Kim] had to do*': Knightley, p. 211.

333   '*Like so many others*': Quoted in Cave Brown, p. 541.

333   '*You cannot exaggerate*': Interview with Tom Mangold.

335   '*painful to think*': Cave Brown, p. 488.

335 *'My dear Lorraine':* Ibid.

335 *'Friendship was always important':* Milne, p. 247.

335 *'not the least admirable':* Graham Greene, 'Our man in Moscow', *Observer*, 15 February 1968.

335 *'I have to put politics first':* Knightley, p. 254.

335 *'One cannot reasonably weep':* Greene, 'Our man in Moscow'.

336 *'He himself never considered':* Interview with Mikhail Liubimov.

336 *'The Albanians, Georgians':* Interview with Mikhail Bogdanov.

337 *'just another way of needling':* Daily Express, 12 March 1968. See also *Evening Post*, 26 January 1968.

337 *'Dear Nick':* Undated letter from Kim Philby to Nicholas Elliott, Cleveland Cram collection, Georgetown University Library, Washington DC.

337+ *'I mean, who the* hell *':* le Carré, p. 183.

338 *Rufina said much later: Philby's Choice*, RT Documentary, 30 June 2016, https://www.youtube.com/watch?v=P-SnKzglU7g.

339 *'What it comes to': Crossbow*, vol. 20 (1984), p. 22.

339 *'The more one discovered':* 'John le Carré', *Mark Lawson Talks To . . .*, BBC Four, 5 October 2008.

339 *'Such operation have poisoned': Kodumaa*, 41:677 (13 October 1971).

340 *'enjoyed probing the amorality':* Borovik, pp. 337–40.

341 *'I doubt that he worked':* Ibid.

344 *'I understood what side':* Translation of *Isvestia* article, *New York Times*, 19 December 1967.

344 *'The greater part':* Murray Sayle interview, *Sunday Times*, 17 December 1967.

345 *'The evening of my life is golden': Philby's Choice*, RT Documentary, 30 June 2016, https://www.youtube.com/watch?v=P-SnKzglU7g.

345 *'didn't understand':* Kalugin, p. 145.

345 *'He was disgusted':* Ibid.

345* *'extraordinary self-delusion':* Andrew, 'Moles, Defectors, and Deception'.

346 *'Russia was not an enemy':* Privately recorded tape made by Desmond Bristow in conversation with friends in the 1990s.

346 *based on Eleanor's description:* Graham Greene, 'Invention and Prediction', *Spectator*, 4 October 1980.

346 *'Oh, everyone is very kind':* Graham Greene, *The Human Factor* (London: The Bodley Head, 1979).

346 *Greene thanked his friend:* Rosenbaum.

346 *'But he's not a gentleman':* Ibid.

347 *'He was often lost':* 1TV news report, 6 January 2020, https://youtu.be/J_EhUFXyhjs.

347 *'He did not consider':* Rufina Philby, interview with Nikolai Dolgopolov.

347 *regarding him as an upstart:* Bower, p. 384.

347 *'I started to talk':* Nikolai Dolgopolov, 'The secret life of legendary spy', Russia Beyond the Headlines, 1 January 2012, https://www.rbth.com/arts/2012/01/01/the_secret_life_of_legendary_spy_14132.html.

348 *'The world is well rid of him':* Elliott (1991), p. 190.

348 *'esoteric and intense':* Trevor-Roper (2014).

348 *'what he did not admit'*: Macintyre (2019), p. 64.

348 *'Was what attracted him'*: Murray Sayle, 'My Friend Kim', *Spectator*, 21 May 1988.

348 *'what he loved was the game'*: Rudyard Kipling, *Kim* (London: Macmillan, 1901).

348 *'addiction to deceit'*: le Carré, p. 175.

349 *'a nasty piece of work'*: Knightley, p. 138.

349 *'betrayed many people'*: E. Philby, p. xiii.

349 *'this subtle, sophisticated man'*: Trevor-Roper (2014), p. 72.

350 *'Probably he might have said'*: Josephine Philby, speaking on 'The Spy Who Went into the Cold: Kim Philby, Soviet Super Spy', *Storyville*, BBC Four, 2013.

350 *'brought to tears'*: Tom Parfett and Richard Norton-Taylor, 'Spy Kim Philby died disillusioned with communism', *Guardian*, 31 March 2011.

350 *'Japan is a disease of the skin'*: Lewis, p. 250.

Bibliography

Many of the sources listed here will be familiar to those interested in the so-called Cambridge Five. Apart from those sources cited in the endnotes, much of the new material came from on the record or background conversations with those named in the acknowledgments, or with those who preferred not to be named. Thanks are due to Alexander Seale, who allowed me to have sight of some of his late father's notes drawn up in preparation of the book he ghost-wrote with Eleanor Philby.

Aburish, Said K., *The St George Hotel Bar: International Intrigue in Old Beirut: An Insider's Account* (London: Bloomsbury, 1989)

Akhmedov, Ismail, *In and Out of Stalin's GRU: A Tatar's Escape from Red Army Intelligence* (London: Arms and Armour, 1984)

Andrew, Christopher, *The Defence of the Realm: The Authorized History of MI5* (London: Penguin, 2010)

———————— and Dilks, David, *The Missing Dimension: Governments and Intelligence Communities in the Twentieth Century* (London: Macmillan, 1984)

———————— and Gordievsky, Oleg, *KGB: The Inside Story of its Foreign Operations from Lenin to Gorbachev* (London: Hodder & Stoughton, 1990, 1991)

———————— and Mitrokhin, Vasili, *The Mitrokhin Archive: The KGB in Europe and the West* (London: Allen Lane, 1999)

Balfour-Paul, Glencairn, *Bagpipes in Babylon: A Lifetime in the Arab World and Beyond* (London: I.B. Tauris, 2005)

Barr, James, *Lords of the Desert: Britain's Struggle with America to Dominate the Middle East* (London: Simon & Schuster, 2018)

Bassett, Richard, *Hitler's Spy Chief: The Wilhelm Canaris Mystery* (London: Cassell, 2006)

Beeston, Richard, *Looking for Trouble: The Life and Times of a Foreign Correspondent* (London: Brassey's, 1997)

Bennett, Alan, *An Englishman Abroad* in *Plays 2* (London: Faber & Faber, 1998)

Borovik, Genrikh, *The Philby Files: The Secret Life of Master Spy – KGB Archives Revealed* (London: Little, Brown, 1994)

Bower, Tom, *The Perfect English Spy: Sir Dick White and the Secret War, 1935–90* (London: Heinemann, 1995)

Boyle, Andrew, *Poor, Dear Brendan: The Quest for Brendan Bracken* (London: Hutchinson, 1974)

————————, *The Climate of Treason: Five who spied for Russia* (London: Hutchinson, 1979, revised 1980)

Bristow, Bill, *My Father the Spy: Deceptions of an MI6 Officer* (Ross-on-Wye: WBML, 2012)

Bristow, Derek, *A Game of Moles: Deceptions of an MI6 Officer* (London: Little, Brown, 1993)

Cannadine, David, *A Question of Retribution?: The British Academy and the Matter of Anthony Blunt* (Oxford: British Academy/ Oxford University Press, 2020)

Carter, Miranda, *Anthony Blunt: His Lives* (London: Macmillan, 2001)

Cave Brown, Anthony, *Treason in the Blood: H. St. John Philby, Kim Philby, and the Spy Case of the Century* (Boston: Little, Brown, 1994)

Connolly, Cyril, *The Missing Diplomats* (London: Queen Anne Press, 1952)

Copeland, Miles, *The Game of Nations: The Amorality of Power Politics* (London: Weidenfeld & Nicolson, 1969)

————————, *The Real Spy World* (London: Weidenfeld & Nicolson, 1974)

——————————, *The Game Player: Confessions of the CIA's Original Political Operative* (London: Aurum, 1989)

Corera, Gordon, *The Art of Betrayal: Life and Death in the British Secret Service* (London: Weidenfeld & Nicolson, 2011)

Costello, John, *Mask of Treachery: Spies, Lies and Betrayal* (London: Pan, 1989)

—————————— and Tsarev, Oleg, *Deadly Illusions* (New York: Crown, 1993)

Davenport-Hines, Richard, *Enemies Within: Communists, the Cambridge Spies and the Making of Modern Britain* (London: William Collins, 2018)

—————————— and Sisman, Adam (eds), *One Hundred Letters from Hugh Trevor-Roper* (Oxford: Oxford University Press, 2014)

Deacon, Richard (ed.), *Escape!* (London: BBC, 1980)

Dorril, Stephen, *MI6: Fifty Years of Special Operations* (London: Fourth Estate, 2000)

Downton, Eric, *Wars Without End: A Personal Adventure* (Toronto: Stoddart, 1987)

Driberg, Tom, *Guy Burgess: A Portrait with Background* (London: Weidenfeld & Nicolson, 1956)

——————————, *Ruling Passions* (London: Jonathan Cape, 1977)

Durschmied, Erik, *Don't Shoot the Yanqui: The Life of a War Cameraman* (London: Grafton, 1990)

Elliott, Nicholas, *Never Judge a Man by his Umbrella* (Norwich: Michael Russell, 1991)

——————————, *With My Little Eye: Observations along the Way* (Norwich: Michael Russell, 1993)

Evans, Harold, *Downing Street Diary: The Macmillan Years, 1957–1963* (London: Hodder & Stoughton, 1981)

Eveland, Wilbur Crane, *Ropes of Sand: America's Failure in the Middle East* (New York: W. W. Norton, 1980)

Grose, Peter, *Operation Rollback: America's Secret War Behind the Iron Curtain* (Boston: Houghton Mifflin, 2000)

Harrison, Edward, *The Young Kim Philby: Soviet Spy and British Intelligence Officer* (Exeter: University of Exeter Press, 2012)

Hastings, Max, *The Secret War: Spies, Codes and Guerrillas 1939–1945* (London: William Collins, 2015)

Hastings, Selina, *Rosamond Lehmann: A Life* (London: Chatto & Windus, 2002)

Holzman, Michael, *James Jesus Angleton, the CIA, and the Craft of Counterintelligence* (Amherst: University of Massachusetts Press, 2008)

——————————, *Kim and Jim: Philby and Angleton, Friends and Enemies in the Cold War* (London: Weidenfeld & Nicolson, 2021)

Ivanov, Sergey, 'The Moscow life of Kim Philby', *Pravda*, 31 January 2004

Jeffery, Keith, *MI6: The History of the Secret Intelligence service 1909–1949* (Bloomsbury: London, 2010)

Kalugin, Oleg with Montaigne, Fen, *Spymaster* (London: Smith Gryphon, 1994)

Knightley, Phillip, *Philby: The Life and Views of the KGB Masterspy* (London: André Deutsch, 1988)

Larsson, Theo, *Seven Passports for Palestine: Sixty Years in the Levant* (Pulborough: Longfield Publishing, 1995)

le Carré, John, *The Pigeon Tunnel: Stories from my Life* (London: Viking, 2016)

Lewis, Jeremy, *David Astor* (London: Jonathan Cape, 2016)

Lownie, Andrew, *Stalin's Englishman: The Lives of Guy Burgess* (London: Hodder & Stoughton, 2015)

Lunn, Bernard, *Biography of Peter Lunn* (published privately, 2018)

Lycett, Andrew, *Ian Fleming* (London: Weidenfeld & Nicolson, 1995)

Macintyre, Ben, *A Spy Among Friends: Philby and the Great Betrayal* (London: Bloomsbury, 2015)

——————————, *The Spy and the Traitor: The Great Espionage Story of the Cold War* (London: Penguin, 2019)

Mangold, Tom, *Cold Warrior: James Jesus Angleton, the CIA's Master Spy Hunter* (London: Simon & Schuster, 1991)

Milne, Tim, *Kim Philby: The Unknown Story of the KGB's Master Spy* (London: Biteback, 2014)

Modin, Yuri, *My Five Cambridge Friends* (London: Headline, 1995)

Muggeridge, Malcolm, *The Infernal Grove: Chronicles of Wasted Time: Number 2* (New York: William Morrow, 1974)

Munro, Alan, *Keep the Flag Flying: A Diplomatic Memoir* (London: Gilgamesh, 2012)

Newton, Verne W., *The Butcher's Embrace: The Philby Conspirators in Washington* (London: Macdonald, 1991)

Nicolson, Harold, *Diaries and Letters 1930–1964* (London: Penguin, 1984)

Nicolson, Nigel (ed.), *Vita and Harold: The Letters of Vita Sackville-West and Harold Nicolson, 1910–62* (1992; London: Weidenfeld & Nicolson, 2007)

Page, Bruce, Leitch, David and Knightley, Phillip, *Philby: The Spy who Betrayed a Generation* (London: Penguin, 1969)

Penrose, Barrie and Freeman, Simon, *Conspiracy of Silence: The Secret Life of Anthony Blunt* (London: Grafton, 1986)

Perry, Roland, *The Fifth Man* (London: Sidgwick & Jackson, 1994)

————————, *Last of the Cold War Spies: The Life of Michael Straight, the Only American in Britain's Cambridge Spy Ring* (Cambridge, MA: Da Capo, 2005)

Philby, Eleanor, *Kim Philby: The Spy I Loved* (London: Pan, 1968)

Philby, Kim Philby, *My Silent War* (London: MacGibbon & Kee, 1968; London: Arrow, 2003)

Philby, Rufina, Liubimov, Mikhail and Peake, Hayden, *The Private Life of Kim Philby: The Moscow Years* (London: St Ermin's, 1999)

Philipps, Roland, *A Spy Named Orphan: The Enigma of Donald Maclean* (London: The Bodley Head, 2018)

Pincher, Chapman, *Inside Story: A Documentary of the Pursuit of Power* (London: Sidgwick & Jackson, 1978)

————————, *Too Secret Too Long: The Great Betrayal of Britain's Crucial Secrets and the Cover-Up* (London: Sidgwick & Jackson, 1984)

————————, *Treachery: Betrayals, Blunders and Cover-Ups: Six Decades of Espionage against America and Great Britain* (New York: Random House, 2009)

————————, *Their Trade is Treachery: The Full, Unexpurgated*

Truth about the Russian Penetration of the World's Secret Defences (London: Biteback, 2014)

Purvis, Stewart and Hulbert, Jeff, *Guy Burgess: The Spy Who Knew Everyone* (London: Biteback, 2016)

Rees, Jenny, *Looking for Mr Nobody: The Secret Life of Goronwy Rees* (London: Phoenix, 1997)

Riley, Morris, *Philby: The Hidden Years* (London: Janus, 1999)

Rose, Kenneth, *Elusive Rothschild: The Life of Victor, Third Baron* (London: Weidenfeld & Nicolson, 2003)

Rosenbaum, Ron, 'Kim Philby and the Age of Paranoia', *New York Times Magazine*, 10 July 1994

Rowse, A. L., *All Souls in My Time* (London: Gerald Duckworth, 1993)

Salisbury, Harrison, *Without Fear or Favor: The New York Times and its Times* (New York: Times Books, 1980)

Saunders, Frances Stonor, *Who Paid the Piper?: The CIA and the Cultural Cold War* (London: Granta, 1999)

Seale, Patrick and McConville, Maureen, *Philby: The Long Road to Moscow* (London: Hamish Hamilton, 1973)

Seaton, Jean, *Pinkoes and Traitors: The BBC and the Nation 1974–1987* (London: Profile, 2015)

Sewell, Brian, *Outsider II: Always Almost: Never Quite* (London: Quartet, 2012)

Shackley, Ted, with Finney, Richard A., *Spymaster: My Life in the CIA* (Dulles: Potomac Books, 2005)

Shubin, Vladimir, *The Hot 'Cold War': The USSR in Southern Africa* (London: Pluto, 2008)

Sisman, Adam, *Hugh Trevor-Roper: The Biography* (London: Weidenfeld & Nicolson, 2010)

——————————, *John le Carré: The Biography* (London: Bloomsbury, 2015)

Smith, Chris, *The Last Cambridge Spy: John Cairncross, Bletchley Codebreaker and Soviet Double Agent* (Stroud, The History Press, 2019)

Solomon, Flora and Litvinoff, Barnet, *Baku to Baker Street: The Memoirs of Flora Solomon* (London: Collins, 1984)

Steinacher, Gerald, *Humanitarians at War: The Red Cross in the Shadow of the Holocaust* (Oxford: Oxford University Press, 2017)

Straight, Michael, *After Long Silence* (London: Collins, 1983)

Sutherland, Douglas, *The Fourth Man: The Story of Blunt, Philby, Burgess and Maclean* (London: Arrow, 1980)

Sutherland, John, *Stephen Spender: A Literary Life* (London: Penguin, 2005)

Trevor-Roper, Hugh, *The Philby Affair: Espionage, Treason, and Secret Services* (London: William Kimber, 1968)

———————— (ed. Edward Harrison), *The Secret World: Behind the Curtain of British Intelligence in World War II and the Cold War* (London: I.B. Tauris, 2014)

Turk, Michele, *Blood, Sweat and Tears: An Oral History of the American Red Cross* (Robbinsville: E Street Press, 2006)

West, Nigel, *Venona: The Greatest Secret of the Cold War* (London: HarperCollins, 2000)

———————— (ed.), *The Guy Liddell Diaries: Volume I: 1939–1942* (London: Routledge, 2005)

———————— (ed.), *The Guy Liddell Diaries: Volume II: 1942–1945* (London: Routledge, 2005)

————————, *At Her Majesty's Secret Service: The Chiefs of Britain's Intelligence Service, MI6* (Barnsley: Frontline, 2016)

————————, *Cold War Spymaster: The Legacy of Guy Liddell, Deputy Director of MI5* (Barnsley: Frontline, 2018)

———————— and Tsarev, Oleg (eds), *The Crown Jewels: The British Secrets at the Heart of the KGB Archives* (London: HarperCollins, 1998)

————————, *TRIPLEX: Secrets from the Cambridge Spies* (New Haven: Yale University Press, 2009)

West, Rebecca, *The Meaning of Treason* (London: Macmillan, 1949)

White, Terence De Vere, *A Fretful Midge* (London: Routledge and Kegan Paul, 1957)

Wilford, Hugh, *America's Great Game: The CIA's Secret Arabists and the Shaping of the Modern Middle East* (New York: Basic Books, 2013)

Winkler, Allan M., *The Politics of Propaganda: The Office of War Information 1942–1945* (New Haven: Yale University Press, 1978)

Winks, Robin W., *Cloak & Gown: Scholars in the Secret War, 1939–61* (New York: William Morrow, 1987)

Wright, Peter with Greengrass, Paul, *Spycatcher: The Candid Autobiography of a Senior Intelligence Officer* (New York: Viking, 1987)

Acknowledgements

Far too many people helped in the writing of this book for me to thank adequately. I would have liked to thank the librarians and archivists of institutions in the USA, Beirut and Oxford, but Covid ensured they were untroubled by a visit from me. For her online help, though, Cara Moore Lebonick at the State Department's National Archives in St Louis is owed huge thanks.

Of former residents of Beirut, Susan Griggs gave me invaluable insights, links and support, without which the book would not have got off the ground. Her warmth and good cheer in the face of my half-baked questions was positively heroic. Afif Aburish, another former Beirut inhabitant, was as generous, patient and well informed as his late brother Said used to be during my days on the *Independent on Sunday*. Their brother Wagieh was similarly kind and full of helpful suggestions; Alan Munro was saintly in his forbearance at my request for telling details. Charlie Glass, a Beirut resident of some years after the events described here, was a fount of wisdom and connections and an invaluable source of insight, and Celia Adams filled in many gaps in my knowledge. Mark Elliott, son of Philby's colleague Nicholas, was wonderfully candid and unstinting about his years as a boy who spent his school holidays in Beirut and about his relationship with his father. He was also most generous in sharing some of his family pictures. John and Peggy Carswell were enormously helpful and painstaking – and accommodating – at their beautiful house in Andalucía. Sadly Peggy has since passed away. Mel Trotter, former pilot, writer and a frequent visitor, provided many telling details about life at the Normandy Hotel and the comings and goings of Philby father and son, plus much welcome encouragement during my long haul. Simon Elliot, friend of the late Nicholas Elliott, was also very helpful in depicting Beirut life in the early 1960s.

This book began its life when, some time in the late 1990s, I bashfully asked my colleague Brian Sewell, art critic of the *Evening Standard*, if he would ever talk to me about Anthony Blunt, his adored mentor from the Courtauld Institute, in whom I had long had an interest. There were aspects of the story that very much interested him (and, following our lunch, me). He did not wish to write about them himself, but he agreed to help me to do so. I had a demanding job on the paper at the time, but managed to squirrel away bits and pieces that were germane to what Sewell had told me. In the course of my moon-lighting, I spoke to Glen Balfour-Paul, a former First Secretary at the British embassy, who was able to confirm aspects of the story. I also managed to see Yuri Modin and Mikhail Liubimov in Moscow, and Rufina Philby, who died in the spring of 2021. Alfred Sursock Cochrane and Sylvana Sursock helped shed a good deal of light on Beirut life, much of it notwithstanding the sadness surrounding the death at ninety-eight of Yvonne, Lady Cochrane, as a result of Beirut's devastating explosion of August 2020. Neil Bratton, formerly of the American University of Beirut, was an always entertaining and well-informed source, and his daughter Siwan was outstandingly kind and supportive in helping me unearth some of Beirut's secrets. Susan Schlaefle and Henrietta Gordon were also extremely kind in sharing their impressions with me.

Special thanks are due to George Carey, who was generosity itself in helping my attempt to push forward an aspect of the story in which we were both interested and which he was the first to float publicly in his pathbreaking BBC film, *The Spy Who Went Into the Cold*. Steve Dorril was endlessly patient with my questions about the minutiae of MI6 operations. Undaunted, he made invaluable suggestions and improvements to the manuscript. Similarly, Nigel West was kind enough to read an early draft and painstakingly haul me out of a great many heffalump traps. Richard Frost, who edited Tim Milne's memoir about Philby so adroitly, came up with countless good ideas for lines to follow up and, after reading the text, with encouragement for my approach. Michael Young, Michael Holzman, Scott Anderson and Simon Kuper also read the book and were kind enough to point out errors and/or make helpful additions and other suggestions.

Any howlers and misinterpretations that remain are all my own work. The tireless Andrew Lownie, distinguished biographer of Guy Burgess and omniscient source on all spook matters, was ever obliging in his encouragement and inspiration, offering good ideas and an exceptional point of reference. My friend and agent Heather Holden-Brown was boundlessly supportive and full of good ideas. She and my friend Peter Kennealy both went way beyond the extra mile in reading the manuscript and assiduously picking up errors and rescuing the text.

This book would not have happened without James Gurbutt's willingness to take a chance on it, and his support during its writing in the dark hours of lockdown is hugely appreciated. Zoe Gullen is an exceptionally accomplished editor and a delight to work with, picking her way through the booby-traps I unwittingly laid across her path with humour and tact. Linda Silverman and Grace Vincent were deft in the face of my dafter ideas, and in improving the text, Richard Collins was as sharp-eyed as any writer could have hoped. I was very fortunate to work with all of them.

In the context of the above, the cold recitation below of the names of others who helped might appear more dutiful than grateful, which would be wholly wrong. I hope they know how much their help has been appreciated. In countless cases, only they could have provided it, even if some corroboration was available elsewhere. The same goes for those whose names do not need to appear below.

Elizabeth Alpren
Christopher Andrew
Mary Aylmer
Jamie Balfour-Paul
Jenny Balfour-Paul
James Barr
Richard Bassett
Sophie Batterbury
Brigid Batticombe
Gill Bennett
Tim Benton
Egemen Bezci
Fiona Beeston
Paul Bellsham
Fran Benenson
Gillian Bennett
Mikhail Bogdanov
Fiona Booth
Mark Booth
Tom Bower
Alice Brinton
Bill Bristow
Michael Broad

Jennifer Browne
Charlotte Brunskill
Jean and Tom Bryan
Margaret Bullard
Jamie Buxton
Frank Callanan
Jo Carlill
Miranda Carter
Scott Clift
Matthew Cobb
Ann Collet-White
Lennie Copeland
Miles Copeland III
Stewart Copeland
Edward Corse
Barbara Czyzewska
Malcolm Davidson
Nina Dodge
Adam Dyerson
Dick Dyerson
John de St Jorre
Beatie Edney
Natasha Fairweather

Andrew Franklin
James Fox
Linda Gamlin
Patrick Garrett
Derek Glashan
Maisie Glazebrook
Anthony Glees
Miles Goslett
Paul Greatbatch
Patsy Grigg
Davut Gurlé
Jemima Haddock
Bill Hale
Marshall Hall
Lucinda Hawksley
Roger Hermiston
Jenny Hill
Paul Hill
Philip Hook
Steve Hopgood
Peter Horsburgh
Chris Hough
Richard Ingrams

Sabrina Izzard
Nicola Jeal
Mark Jones
Walid Khalidy
Fady Khoury
Edwin La Fontaine
Stephen Langford
Adam Lines
Magnus Linklater
Laura Longrigg
Bernard Lunn
Tom Mangold
Andrew Martin
Simon Matthew
Philippa Mole
Jim Muir
Siobhana Mukhi
Matthew Norman
Simon O'Hagan
Hayden Peake

Tony Percy
Nigel Perrin
Charlotte Philby
Roland Phillips
Jim Piddock
Penny Pocock
Ellen Porter
Venetia Porter
Joan Porter MacIver
Stephen Pritchard
Donald Reeves
Kenneth Rose
Steve Rosenberg
Rosemary Sayigh
Alexander Seale
Orlando Seale
Yasmine Seale
Andrew Sinclair
Adam Sisman
Mick Smith

Gennady Sokolov
Dick Spaulding
Feyhan Sporel
Andrew Snodgrass
Sylvia Syms
Roger Tamraz
Jonathan Tarr
Stewart Tendler
Debbie Usher
Greg Whitmore
Hugh Wilford
Judith Wilmot
Keith Wilmot
Sheila Williams
Frank Wisner
Francis Yelin
Mark Young
Martin Westlake
Joan Wheeler-Bennett
Fehmi Zorlu

Huge thanks are due to my wife Emma and daughters Eleanor and Alice for putting up with my obsessive immersion in this book.

Index

Picture Credits